Shojo Beat

Godchild

Earl Cain Series 5

Vol. 2

Story & Art by Kaori Yuki

Contents

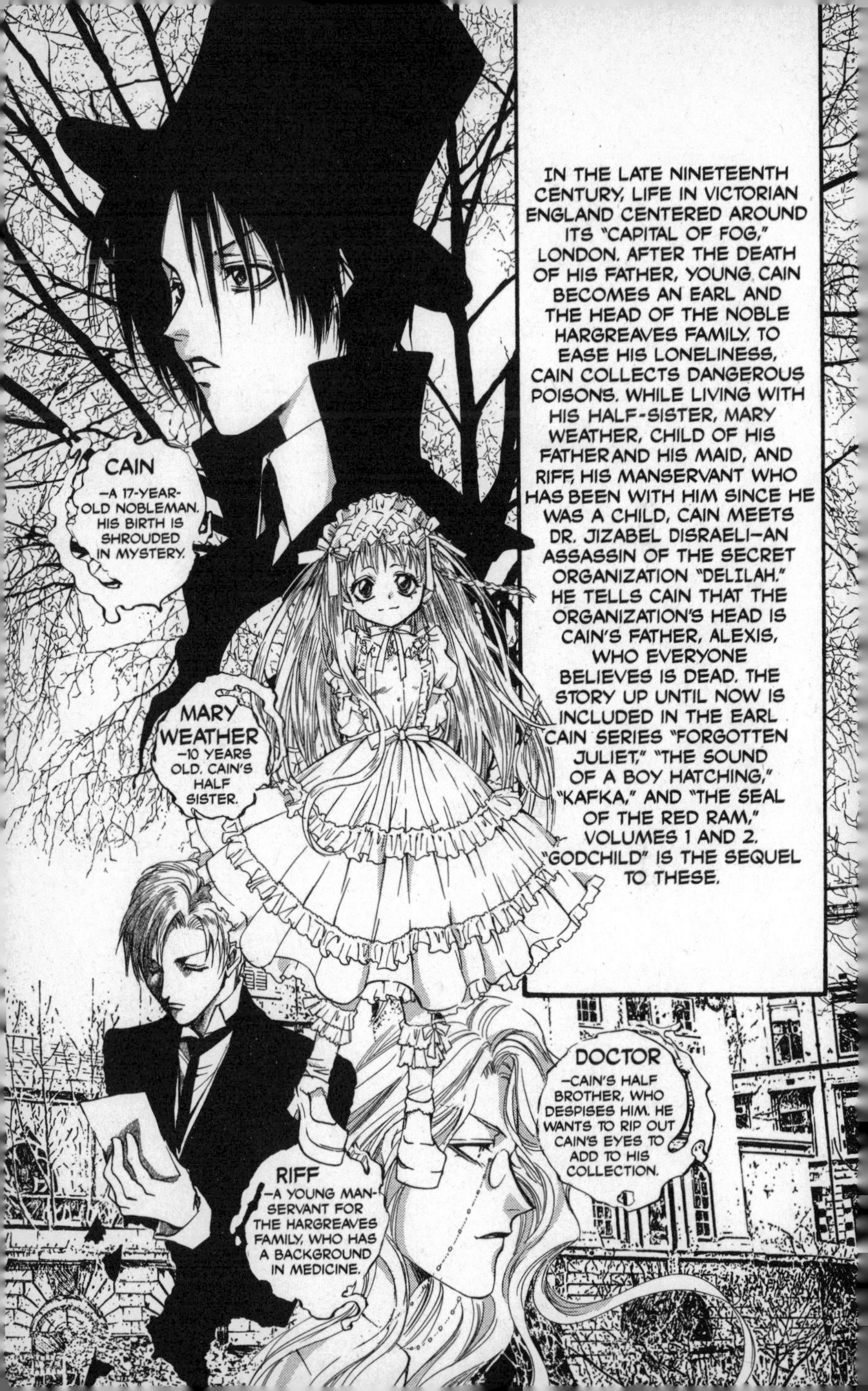
IN THE LATE NINETEENTH CENTURY, LIFE IN VICTORIAN ENGLAND CENTERED AROUND ITS "CAPITAL OF FOG," LONDON. AFTER THE DEATH OF HIS FATHER, YOUNG CAIN BECOMES AN EARL AND THE HEAD OF THE NOBLE HARGREAVES FAMILY. TO EASE HIS LONELINESS, CAIN COLLECTS DANGEROUS POISONS. WHILE LIVING WITH HIS HALF-SISTER, MARY WEATHER, CHILD OF HIS FATHERAND HIS MAID, AND RIFF, HIS MANSERVANT WHO HAS BEEN WITH HIM SINCE HE WAS A CHILD, CAIN MEETS DR. JIZABEL DISRAELI—AN ASSASSIN OF THE SECRET ORGANIZATION "DELILAH." HE TELLS CAIN THAT THE ORGANIZATION'S HEAD IS CAIN'S FATHER, ALEXIS, WHO EVERYONE BELIEVES IS DEAD. THE STORY UP UNTIL NOW IS INCLUDED IN THE EARL CAIN SERIES "FORGOTTEN JULIET," "THE SOUND OF A BOY HATCHING," "KAFKA," AND "THE SEAL OF THE RED RAM," VOLUMES 1 AND 2. "GODCHILD" IS THE SEQUEL TO THESE.
CAIN —A 17-YEAR-OLD NOBLEMAN. HIS BIRTH IS SHROUDED IN MYSTERY.
MARY WEATHER —10 YEARS OLD. CAIN'S HALF SISTER.
DOCTOR —CAIN'S HALF BROTHER, WHO DESPISES HIM. HE WANTS TO RIP OUT CAIN'S EYES TO ADD TO HIS COLLECTION.
RIFF —A YOUNG MAN-SERVANT FOR THE HARGREAVES FAMILY, WHO HAS A BACKGROUND IN MEDICINE.

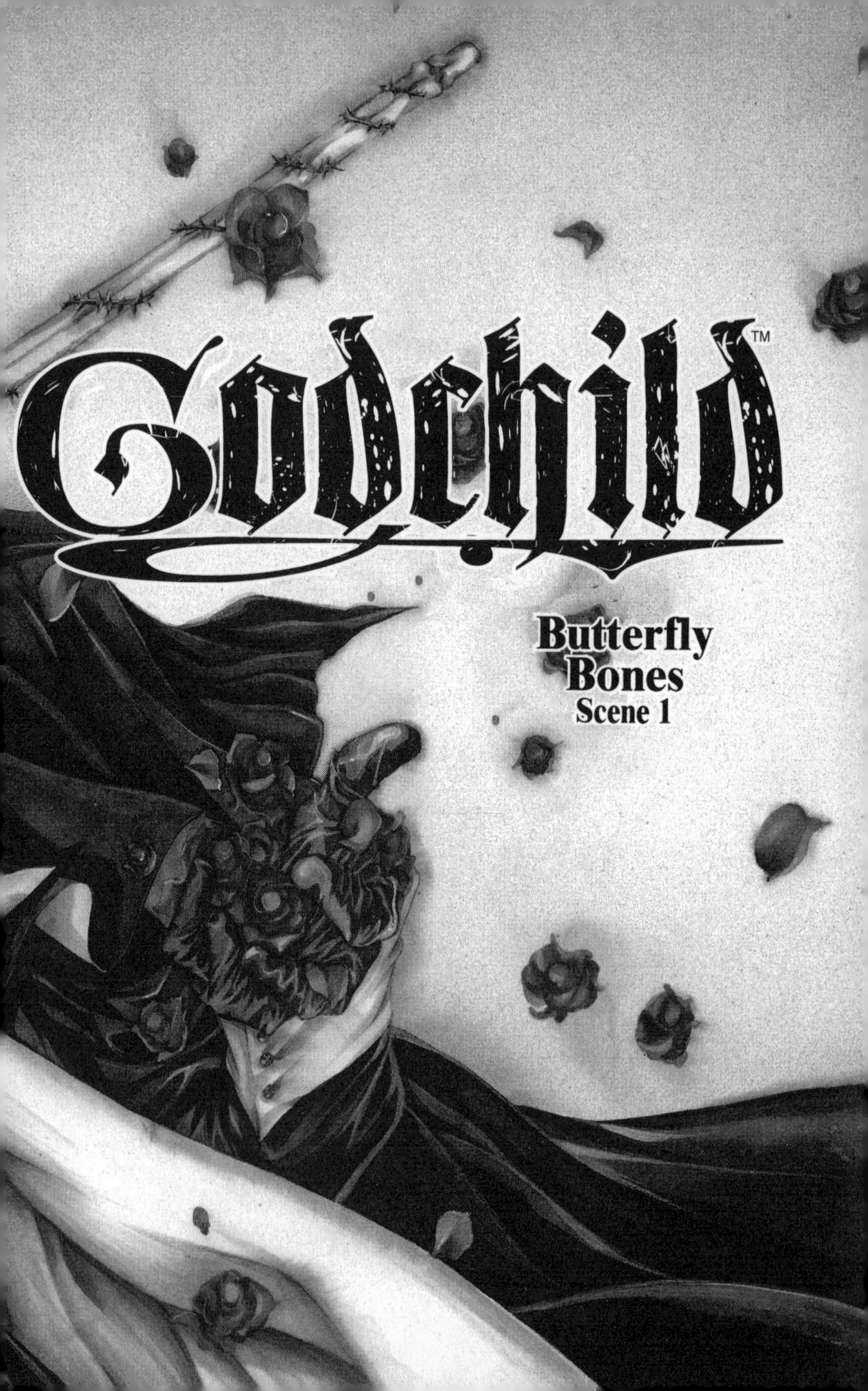
Godchild™
Butterfly Bones
Scene 1

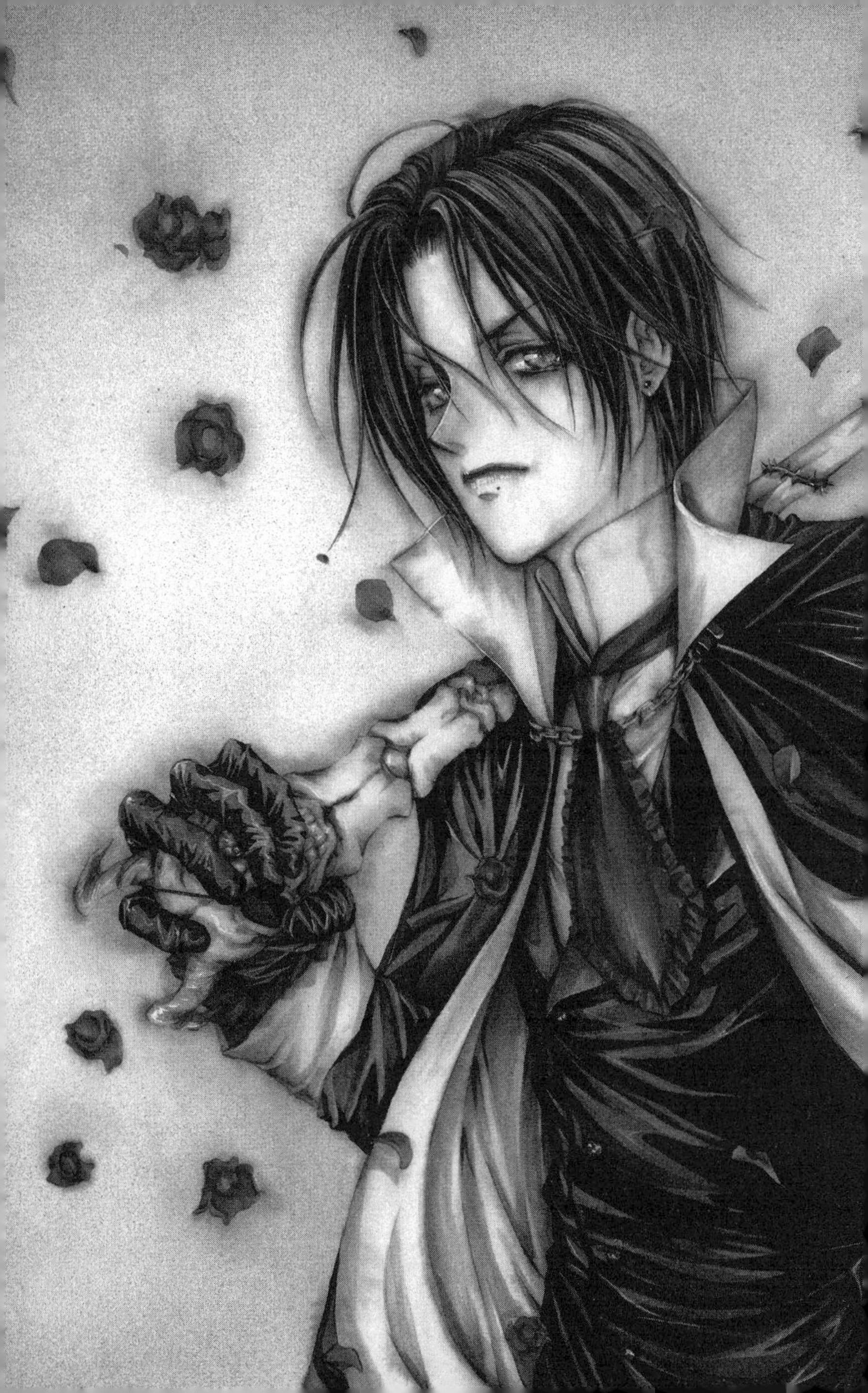

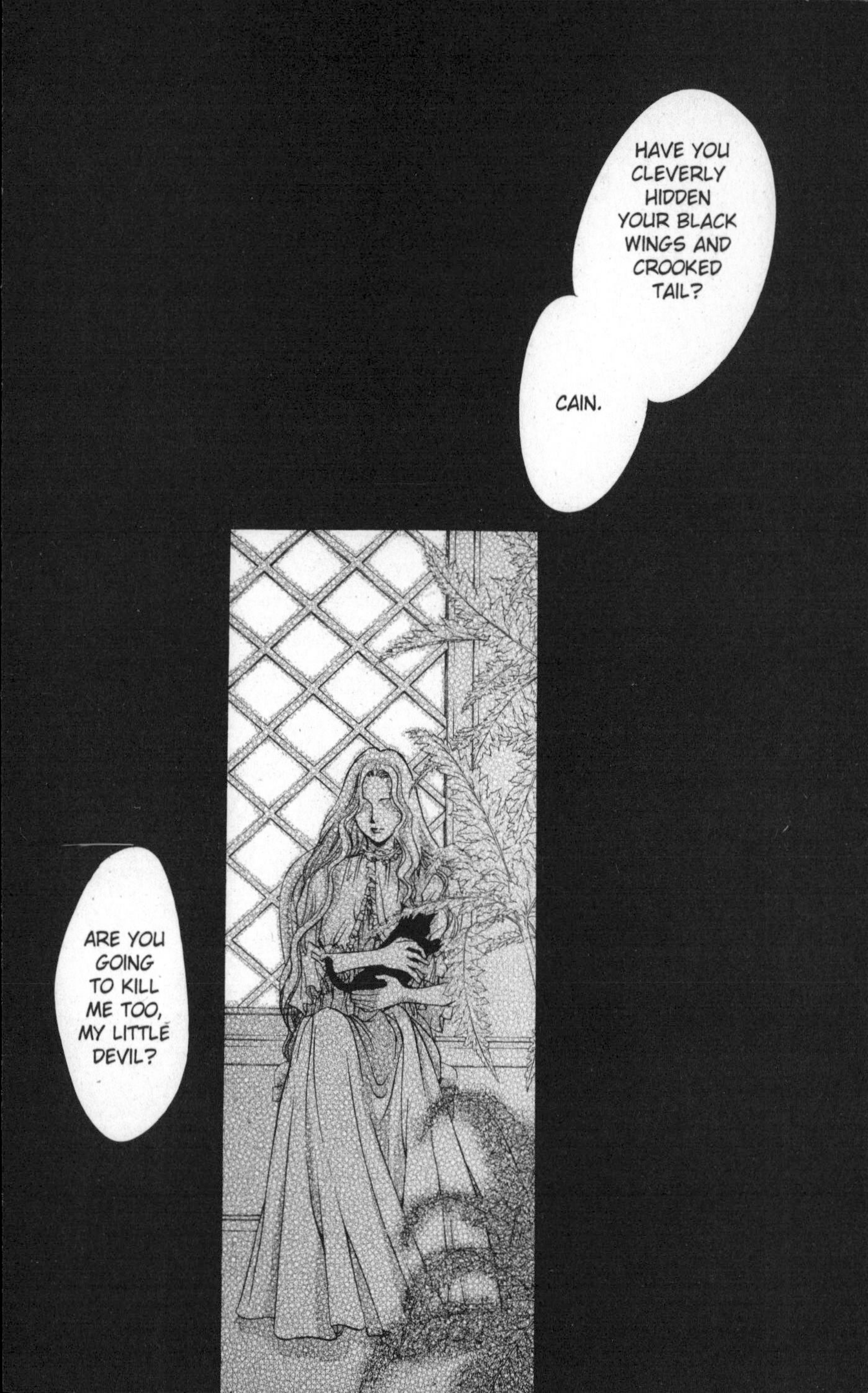
HAVE YOU CLEVERLY HIDDEN YOUR BLACK WINGS AND CROOKED TAIL?
CAIN.
ARE YOU GOING TO KILL ME TOO, MY LITTLE DEVIL?

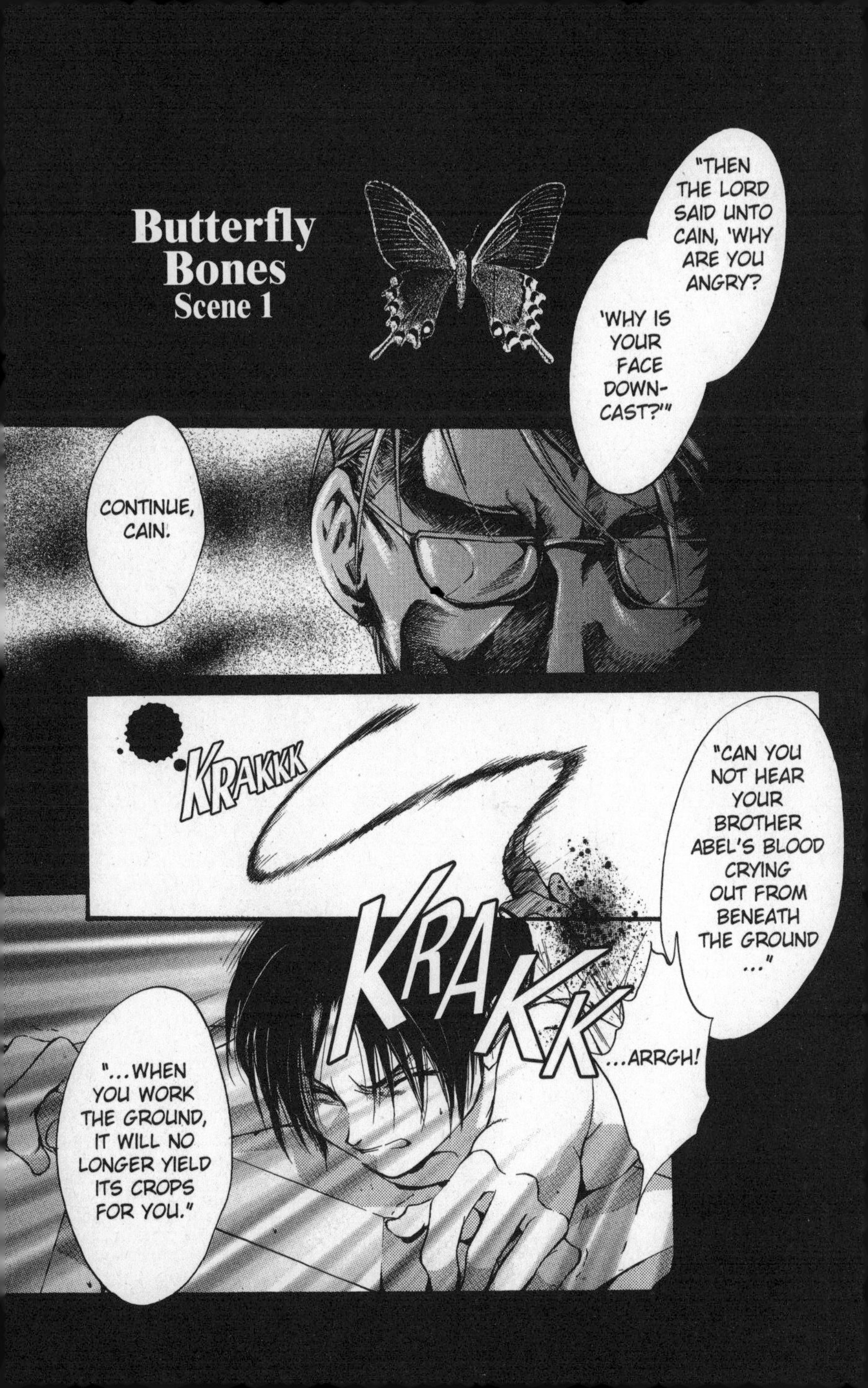
Butterfly Bones
Scene 1
"THEN THE LORD SAID UNTO CAIN, 'WHY ARE YOU ANGRY?
'WHY IS YOUR FACE DOWN-CAST?'"
CONTINUE, CAIN.
KRAKKK
"CAN YOU NOT HEAR YOUR BROTHER ABEL'S BLOOD CRYING OUT FROM BENEATH THE GROUND ..."
KRAKK
...ARRGH!
"...WHEN YOU WORK THE GROUND, IT WILL NO LONGER YIELD ITS CROPS FOR YOU."

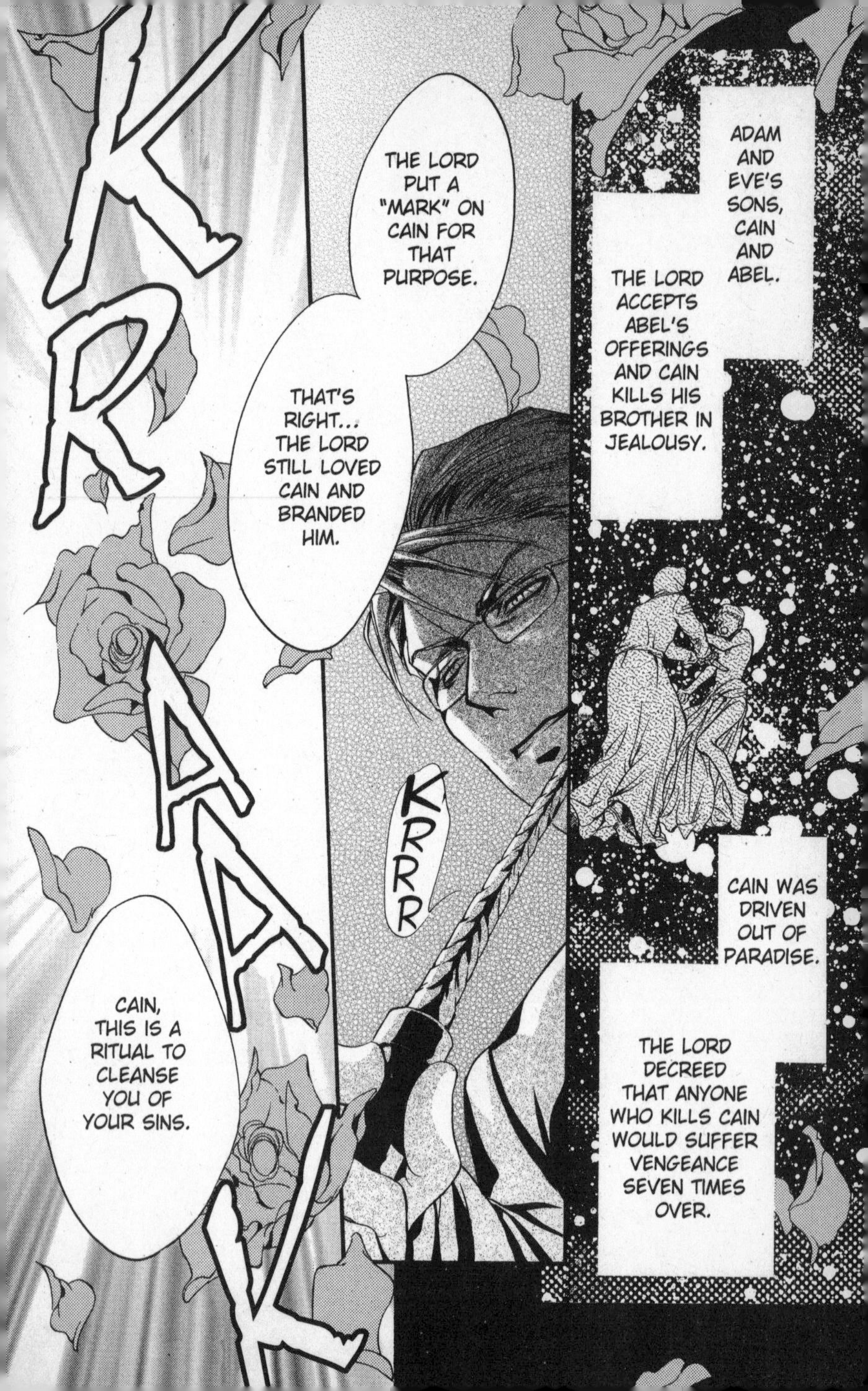
ADAM AND EVE'S SONS, CAIN AND ABEL.
THE LORD ACCEPTS ABEL'S OFFERINGS AND CAIN KILLS HIS BROTHER IN JEALOUSY.
CAIN WAS DRIVEN OUT OF PARADISE.
THE LORD DECREED THAT ANYONE WHO KILLS CAIN WOULD SUFFER VENGEANCE SEVEN TIMES OVER.
THE LORD PUT A "MARK" ON CAIN FOR THAT PURPOSE.
THAT'S RIGHT... THE LORD STILL LOVED CAIN AND BRANDED HIM.
KRRR
CAIN, THIS IS A RITUAL TO CLEANSE YOU OF YOUR SINS.
KRAAAK

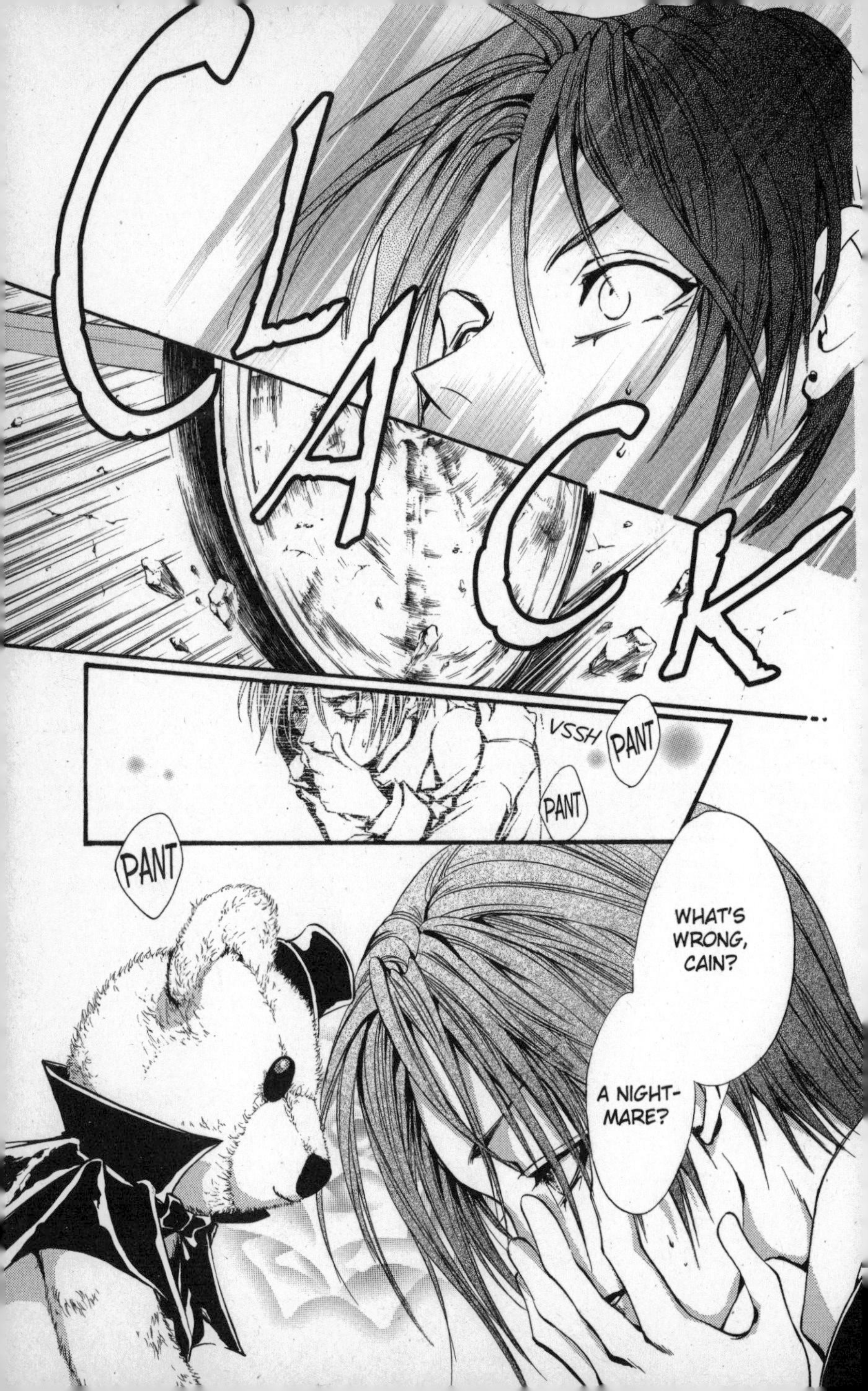
CLACK
VSSH
PANT
PANT
PANT
WHAT'S WRONG, CAIN?
A NIGHT-MARE?

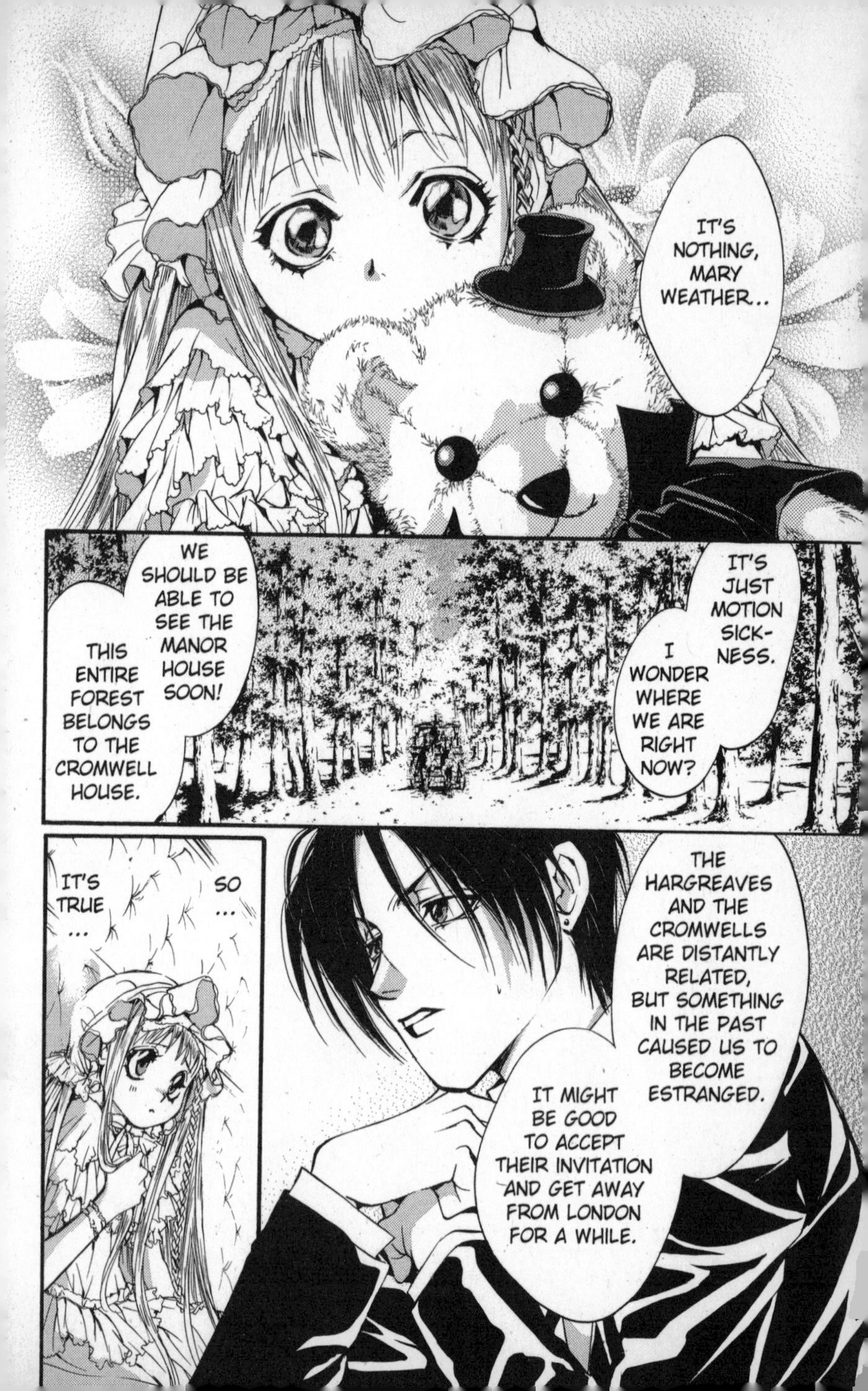
IT'S NOTHING, MARY WEATHER...
IT'S JUST MOTION SICK-NESS.
I WONDER WHERE WE ARE RIGHT NOW?
WE SHOULD BE ABLE TO SEE THE MANOR HOUSE SOON!
THIS ENTIRE FOREST BELONGS TO THE CROMWELL HOUSE.
THE HARGREAVES AND THE CROMWELLS ARE DISTANTLY RELATED, BUT SOMETHING IN THE PAST CAUSED US TO BECOME ESTRANGED.
IT MIGHT BE GOOD TO ACCEPT THEIR INVITATION AND GET AWAY FROM LONDON FOR A WHILE.
SO ...
IT'S TRUE ...

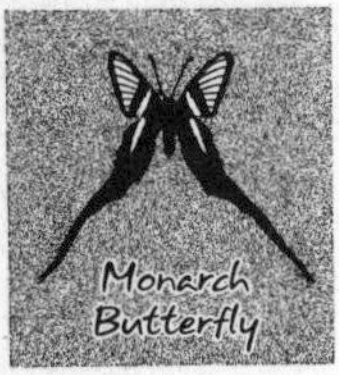
Monarch Butterfly

Butterfly Bones...

Apparently, there are six of these bones that run from near the eyes to the bone interior. Large wings and small wings. Shaped like a butterfly. I don't know too much about it, but I don't really like butterflies. The word "butterfly" may have come from a word that means "an insect that produces excrement resembling butter." I'm a little shocked. It has the word "butter" in it, so I thought that it might mean something tastier. (Like Alice's "Bread and Butterflies.") Surprisingly, the name sounds nicer in Japanese (ageha). Marie reminisces on this page because she met the doctor in a previous story called "Kafka." At first she only caught a glimpse of him through the doorway, so she didn't know what he really looked like, but if she had only known, she wouldn't have been kidnapped. Trivial stuff. Maybe no one will care about it.

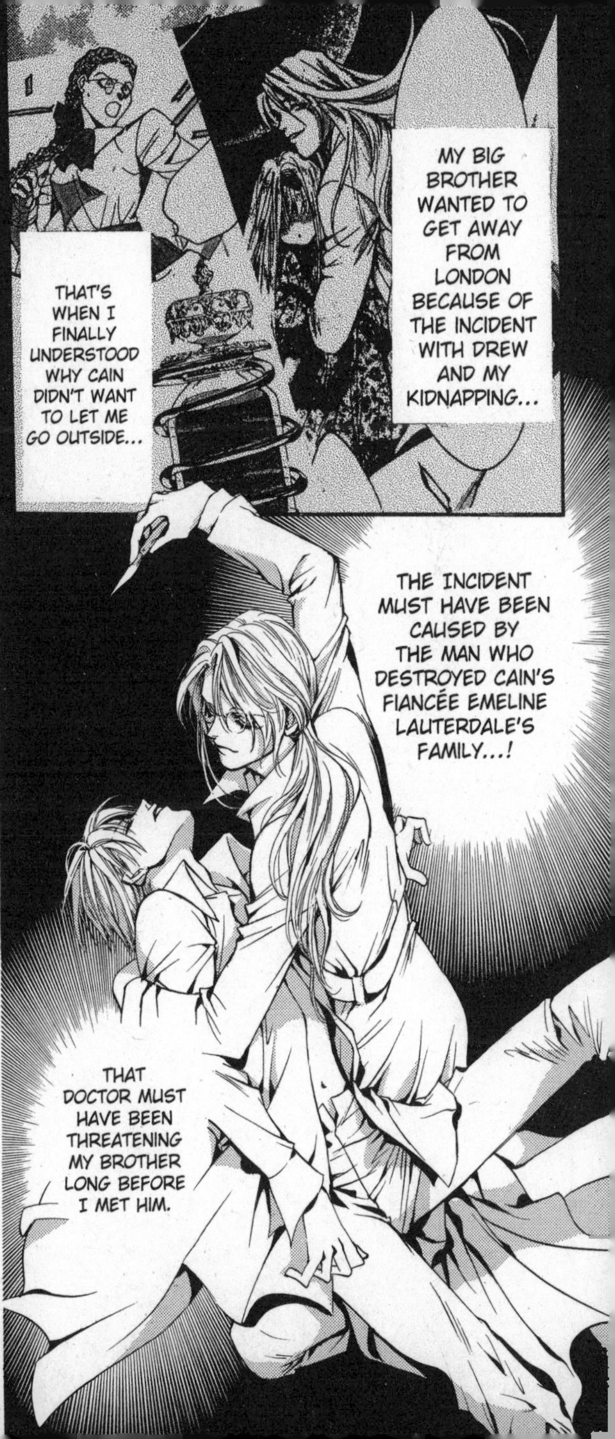
MY BIG BROTHER WANTED TO GET AWAY FROM LONDON BECAUSE OF THE INCIDENT WITH DREW AND MY KIDNAPPING...
THAT'S WHEN I FINALLY UNDERSTOOD WHY CAIN DIDN'T WANT TO LET ME GO OUTSIDE...
THE INCIDENT MUST HAVE BEEN CAUSED BY THE MAN WHO DESTROYED CAIN'S FIANCÉE EMELINE LAUTERDALE'S FAMILY...!
THAT DOCTOR MUST HAVE BEEN THREATENING MY BROTHER LONG BEFORE I MET HIM.

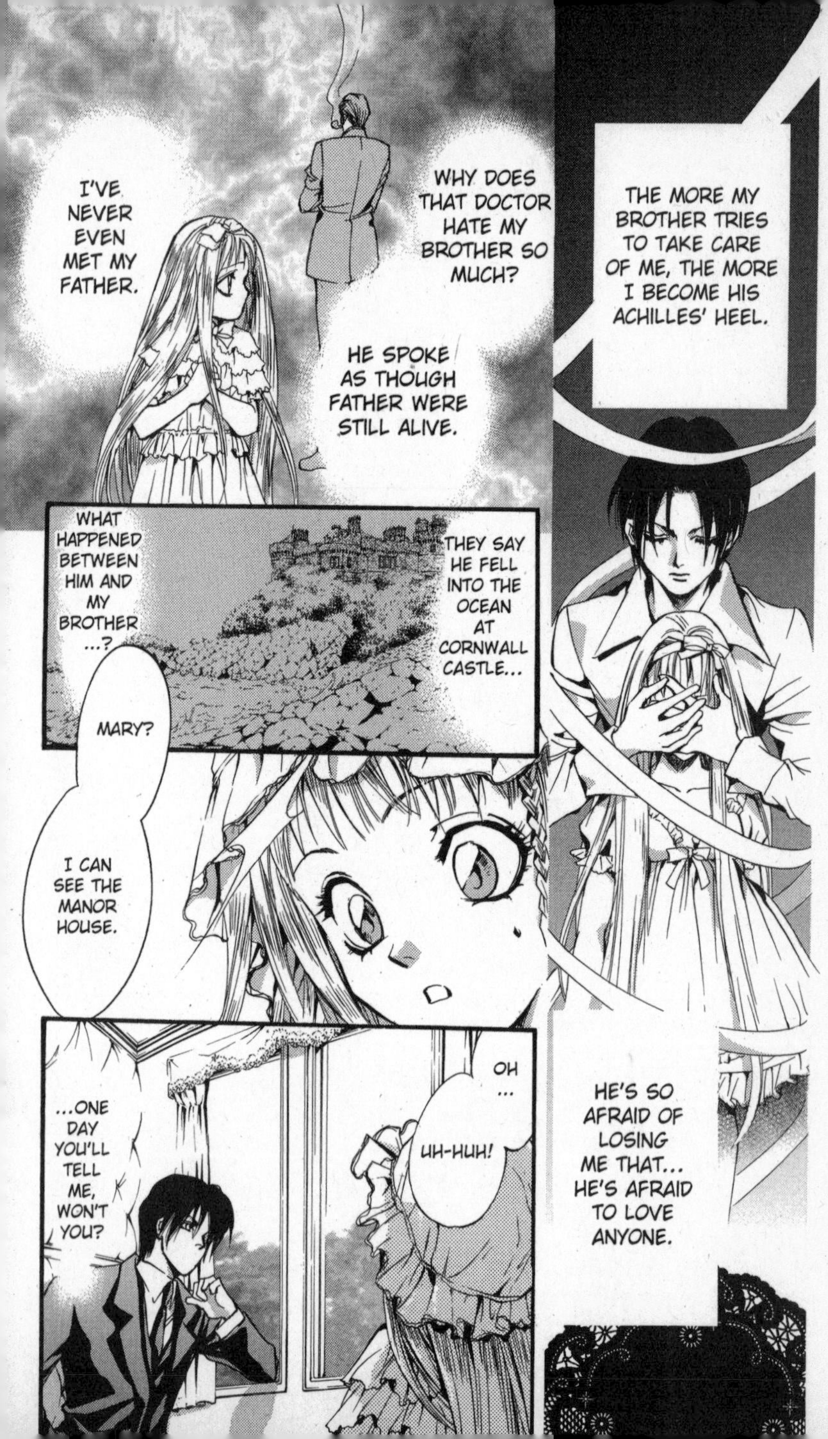
THE MORE MY BROTHER TRIES TO TAKE CARE OF ME, THE MORE I BECOME HIS ACHILLES' HEEL.
HE'S SO AFRAID OF LOSING ME THAT... HE'S AFRAID TO LOVE ANYONE.
WHY DOES THAT DOCTOR HATE MY BROTHER SO MUCH?
I'VE NEVER EVEN MET MY FATHER.
HE SPOKE AS THOUGH FATHER WERE STILL ALIVE.
THEY SAY HE FELL INTO THE OCEAN AT CORNWALL CASTLE...
WHAT HAPPENED BETWEEN HIM AND MY BROTHER ...?
MARY?
I CAN SEE THE MANOR HOUSE.
OH ...
UH-HUH!
...ONE DAY YOU'LL TELL ME, WON'T YOU?

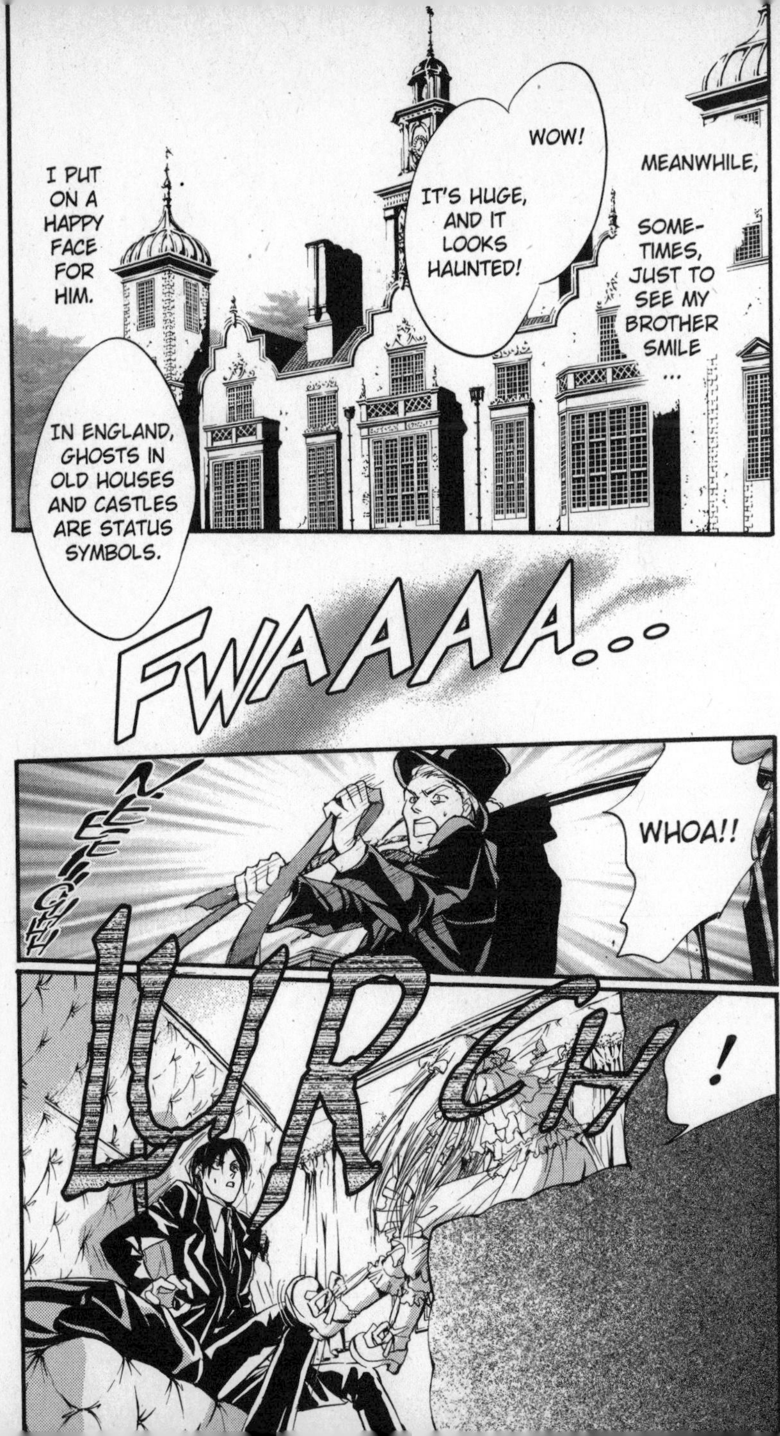
MEANWHILE,
SOMETIMES, JUST TO SEE MY BROTHER SMILE...
WOW!
IT'S HUGE, AND IT LOOKS HAUNTED!
I PUT ON A HAPPY FACE FOR HIM.
IN ENGLAND, GHOSTS IN OLD HOUSES AND CASTLES ARE STATUS SYMBOLS.
FWAAAA...
WHOA!!
NEEEIGHH
LURCH
!

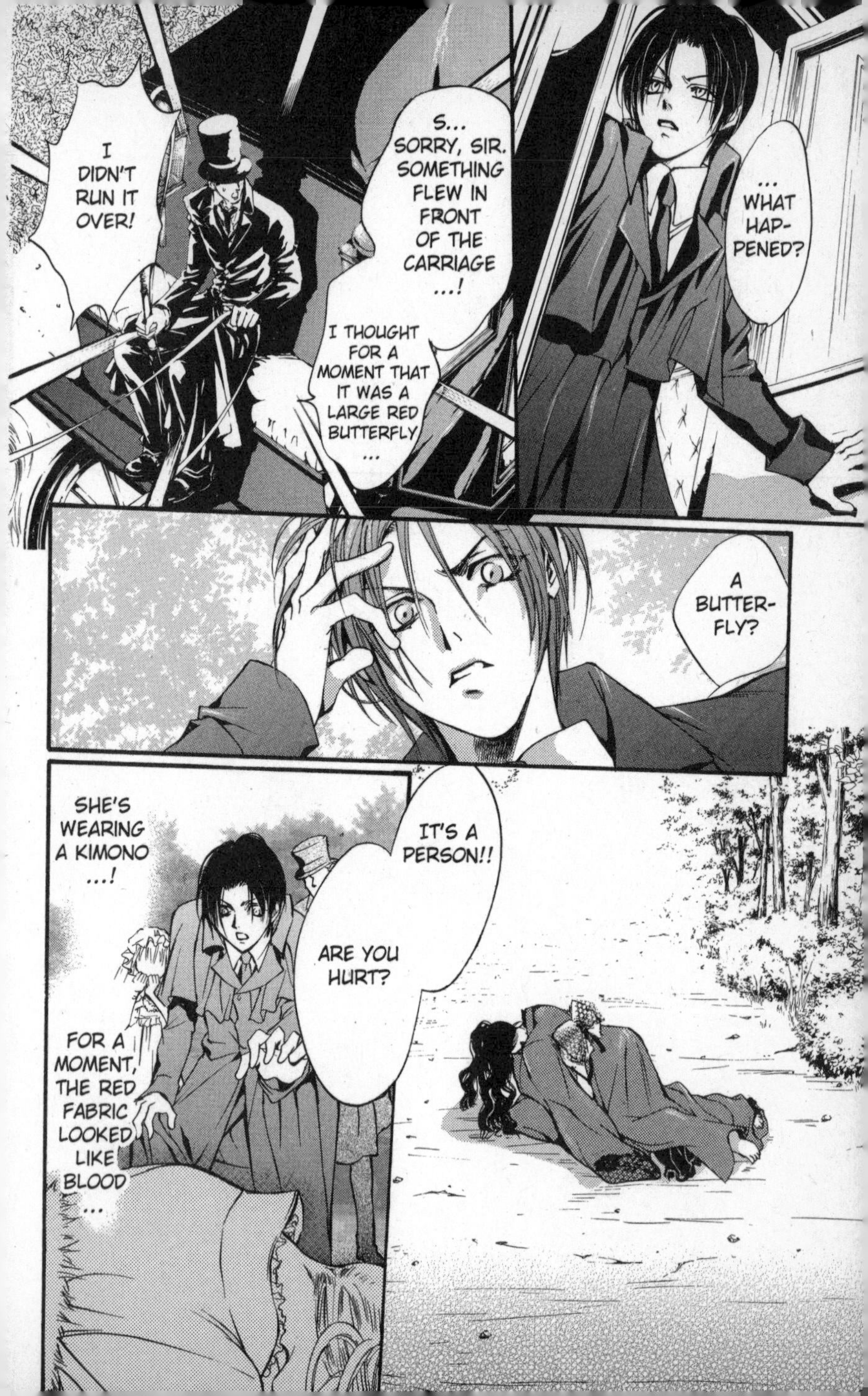
...WHAT HAPPENED?
S... SORRY, SIR. SOMETHING FLEW IN FRONT OF THE CARRIAGE ...!
I THOUGHT FOR A MOMENT THAT IT WAS A LARGE RED BUTTERFLY ...
I DIDN'T RUN IT OVER!
A BUTTERFLY?
IT'S A PERSON!!
ARE YOU HURT?
SHE'S WEARING A KIMONO ...!
FOR A MOMENT, THE RED FABRIC LOOKED LIKE BLOOD ...

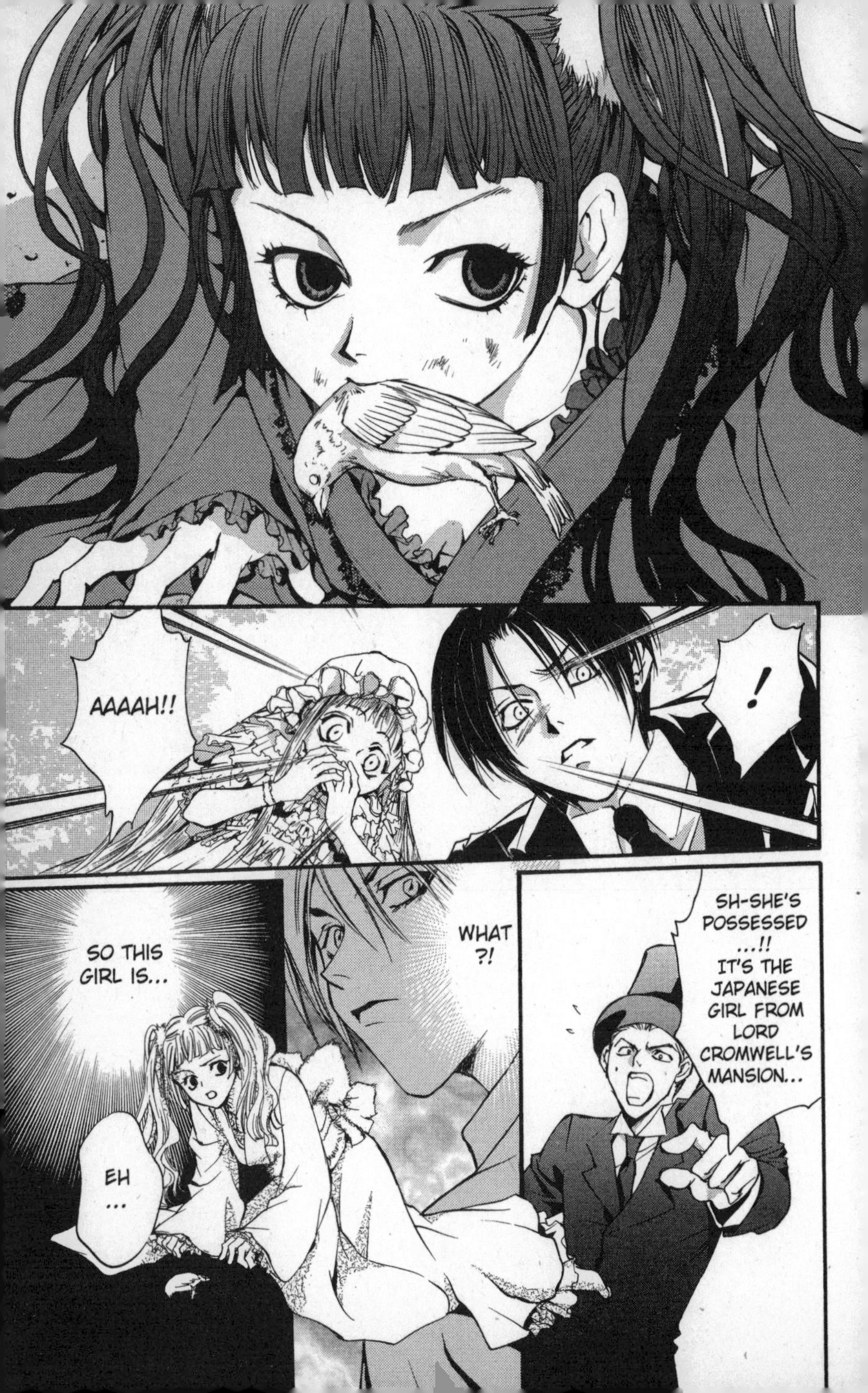
!
AAAAH!!
SH-SHE'S POSSESSED ...!! IT'S THE JAPANESE GIRL FROM LORD CROMWELL'S MANSION...
WHAT ?!
SO THIS GIRL IS...
EH ...

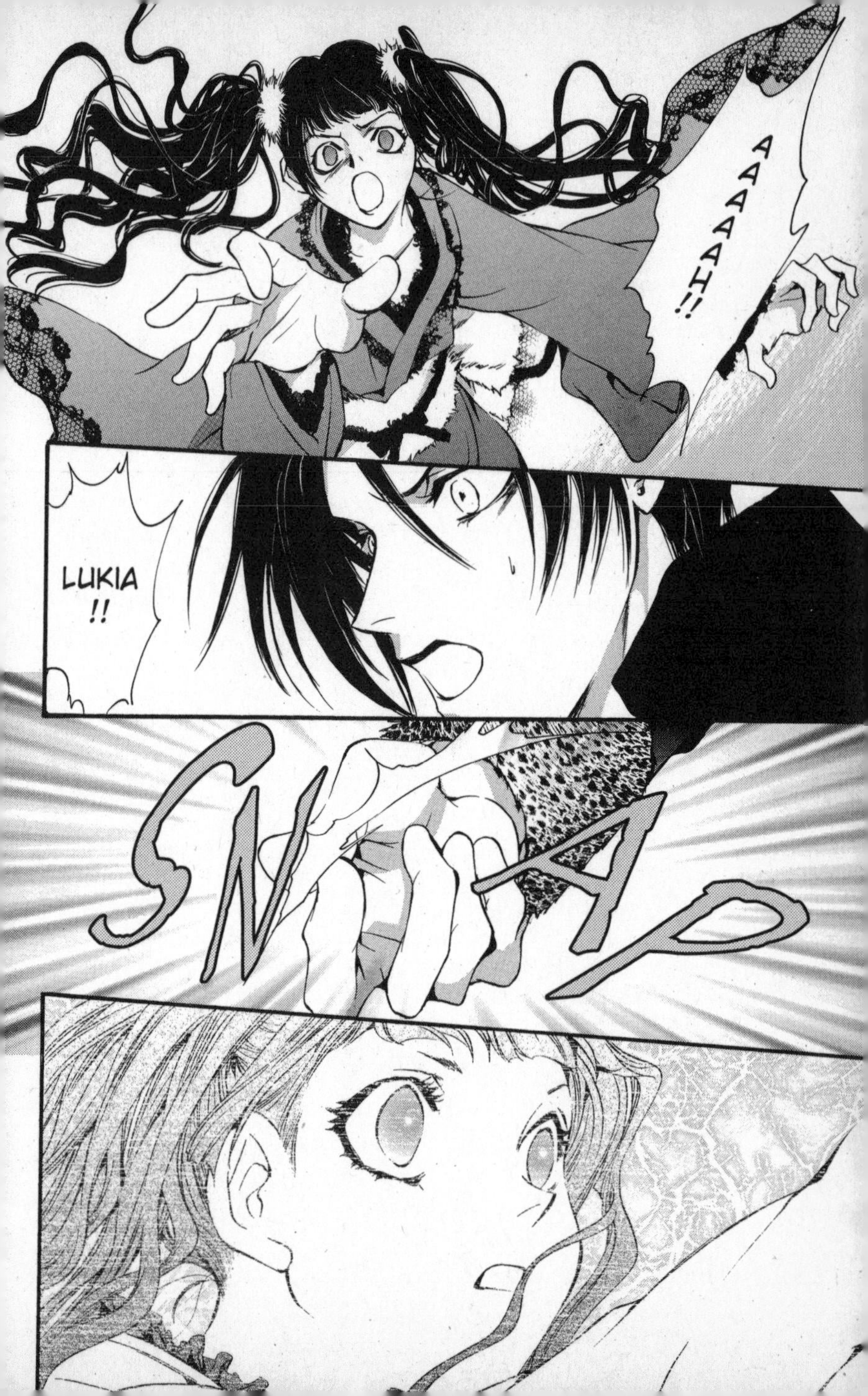
AAAAAAH!!
LUKIA !!
SNAP

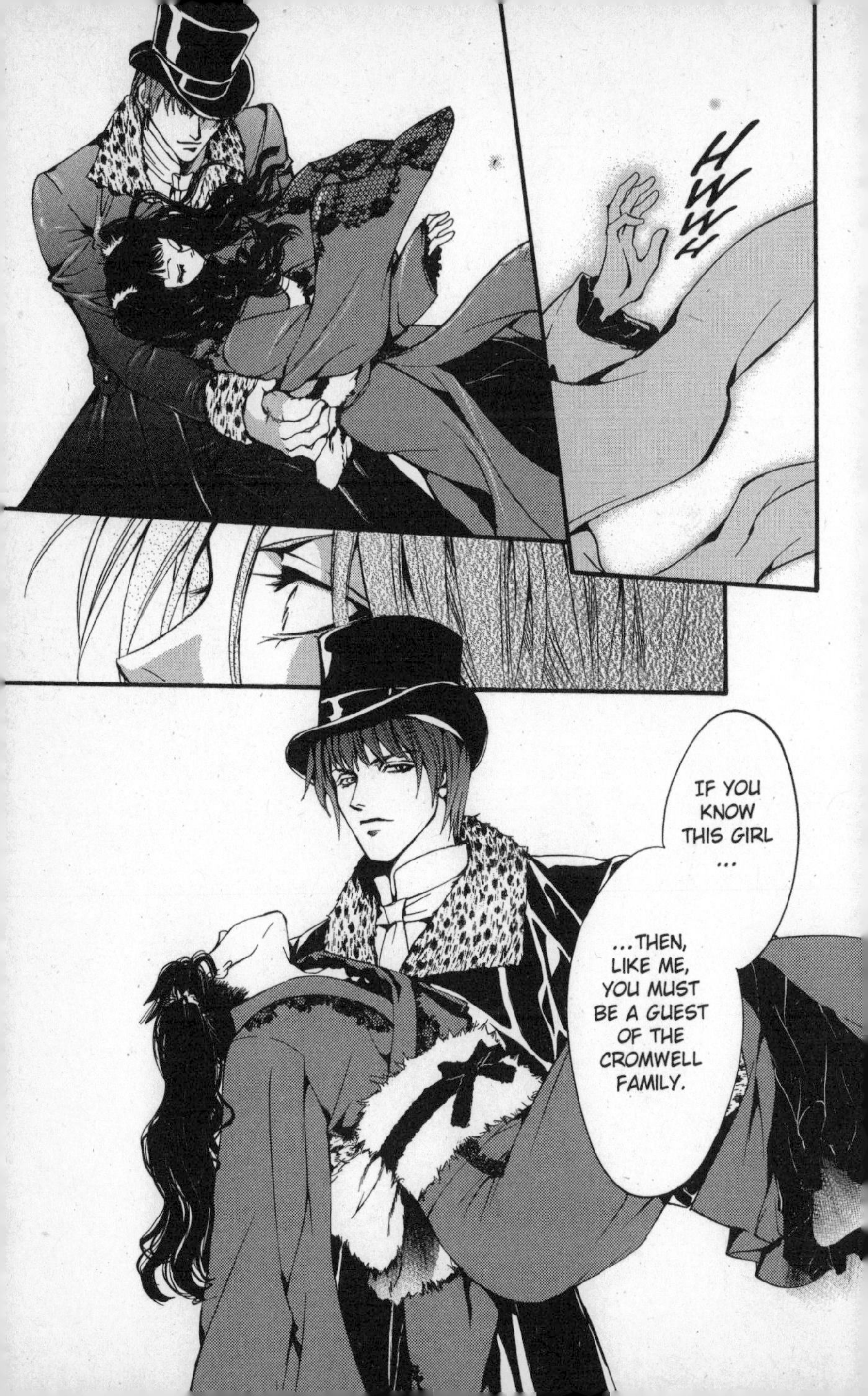
HWWH
IF YOU KNOW THIS GIRL ...
...THEN, LIKE ME, YOU MUST BE A GUEST OF THE CROMWELL FAMILY.

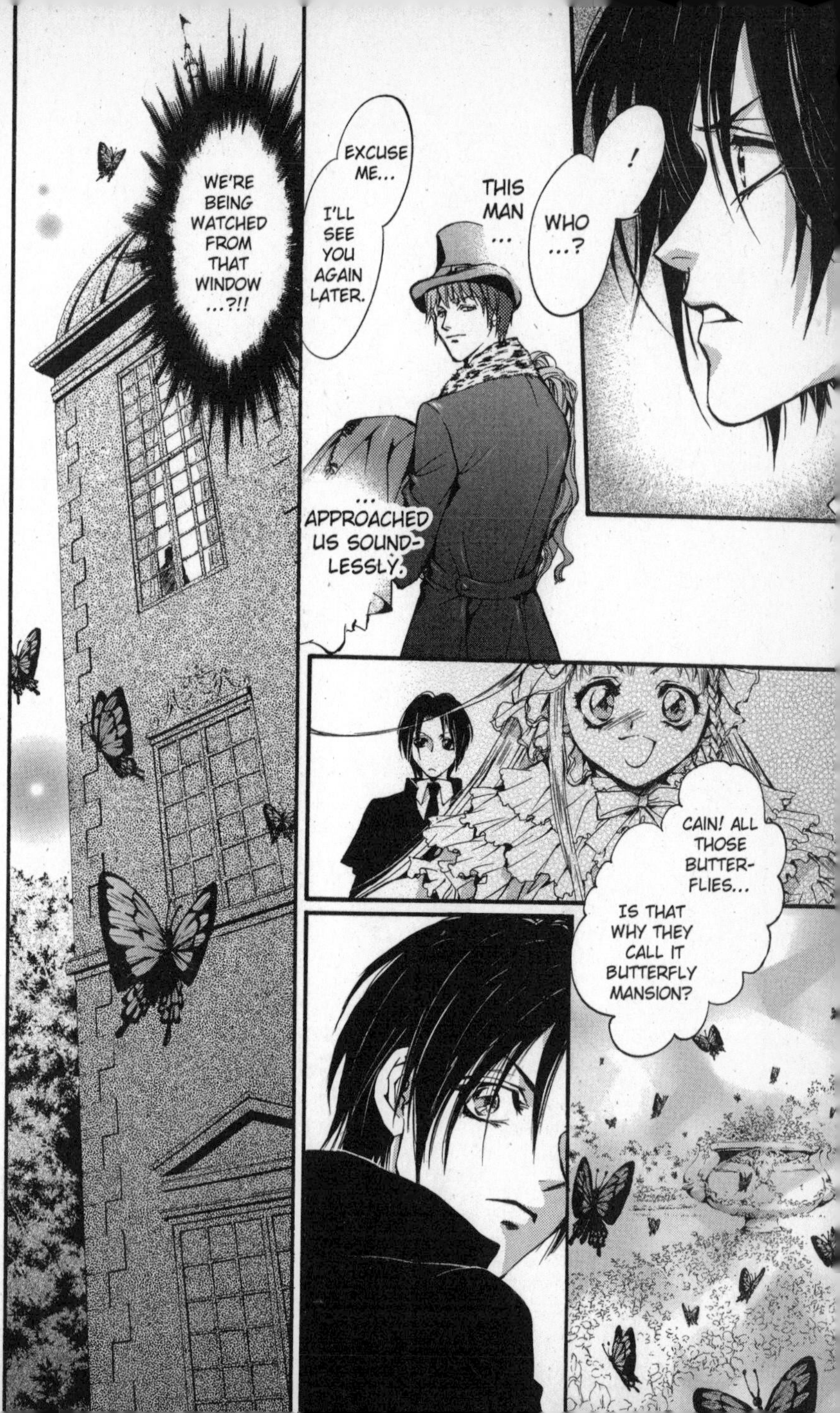
!
WHO ...?
THIS MAN ...
EXCUSE ME...
I'LL SEE YOU AGAIN LATER.
... APPROACHED US SOUNDLESSLY.
CAIN! ALL THOSE BUTTERFLIES...
IS THAT WHY THEY CALL IT BUTTERFLY MANSION?
WE'RE BEING WATCHED FROM THAT WINDOW ...?!!

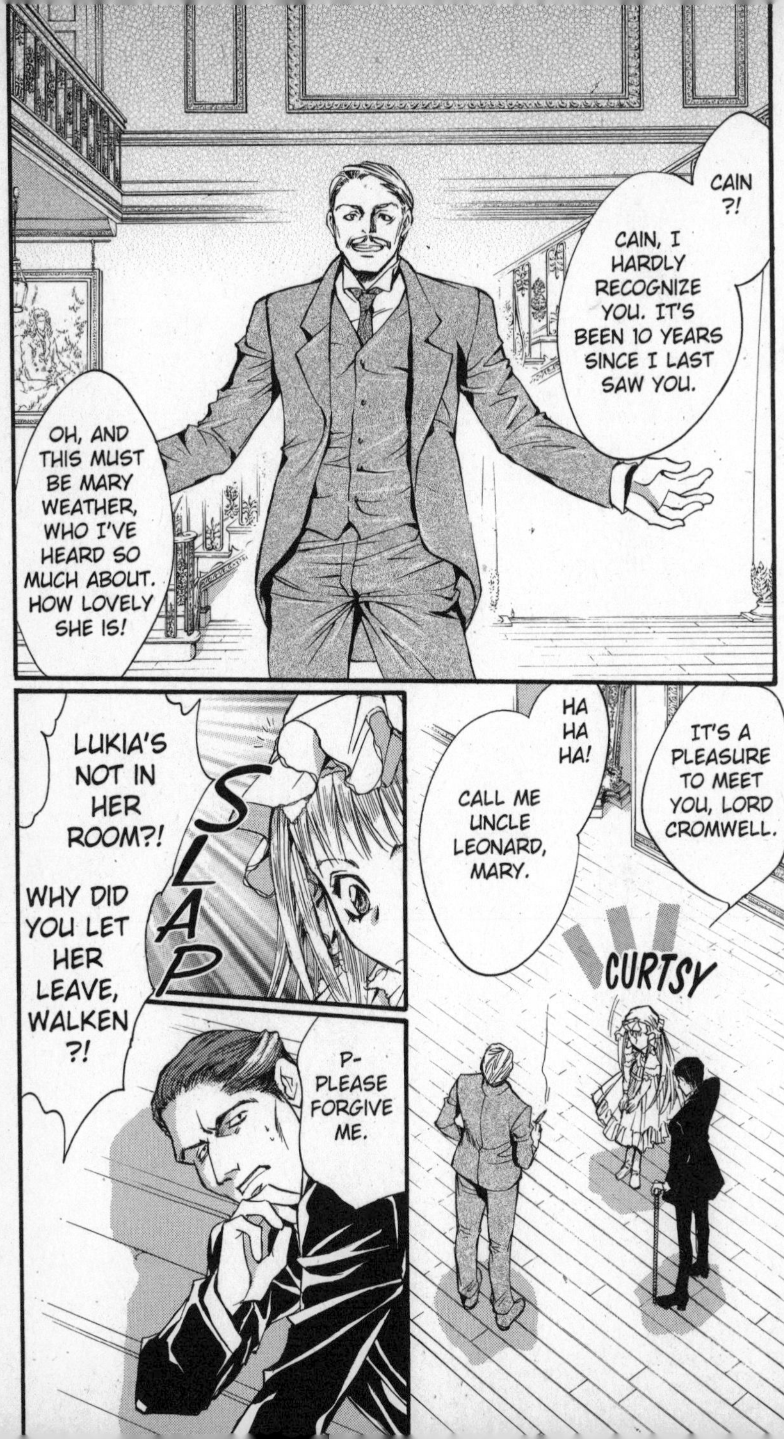
CAIN ?!
CAIN, I HARDLY RECOGNIZE YOU. IT'S BEEN 10 YEARS SINCE I LAST SAW YOU.
OH, AND THIS MUST BE MARY WEATHER, WHO I'VE HEARD SO MUCH ABOUT. HOW LOVELY SHE IS!
IT'S A PLEASURE TO MEET YOU, LORD CROMWELL.
HA HA HA!
CALL ME UNCLE LEONARD, MARY.
CURTSY
LUKIA'S NOT IN HER ROOM?!
SLAP
WHY DID YOU LET HER LEAVE, WALKEN ?!
P- PLEASE FORGIVE ME.

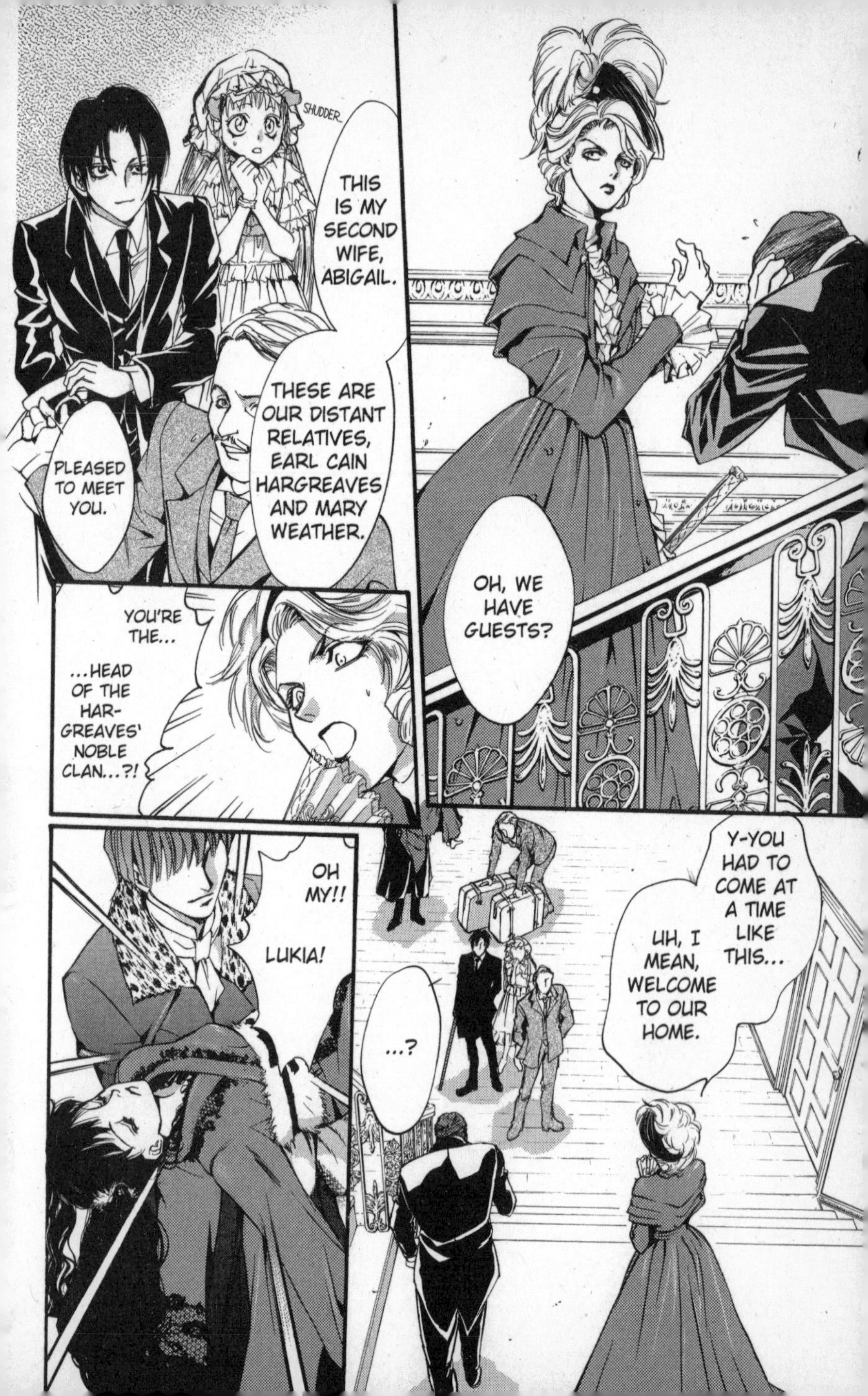

OH, WE HAVE GUESTS?
SHUDDER...
THIS IS MY SECOND WIFE, ABIGAIL.
THESE ARE OUR DISTANT RELATIVES, EARL CAIN HARGREAVES AND MARY WEATHER.
PLEASED TO MEET YOU.
YOU'RE THE...
...HEAD OF THE HAR-GREAVES' NOBLE CLAN...?!
Y-YOU HAD TO COME AT A TIME LIKE THIS...
UH, I MEAN, WELCOME TO OUR HOME.
...?
OH MY!!
LUKIA!

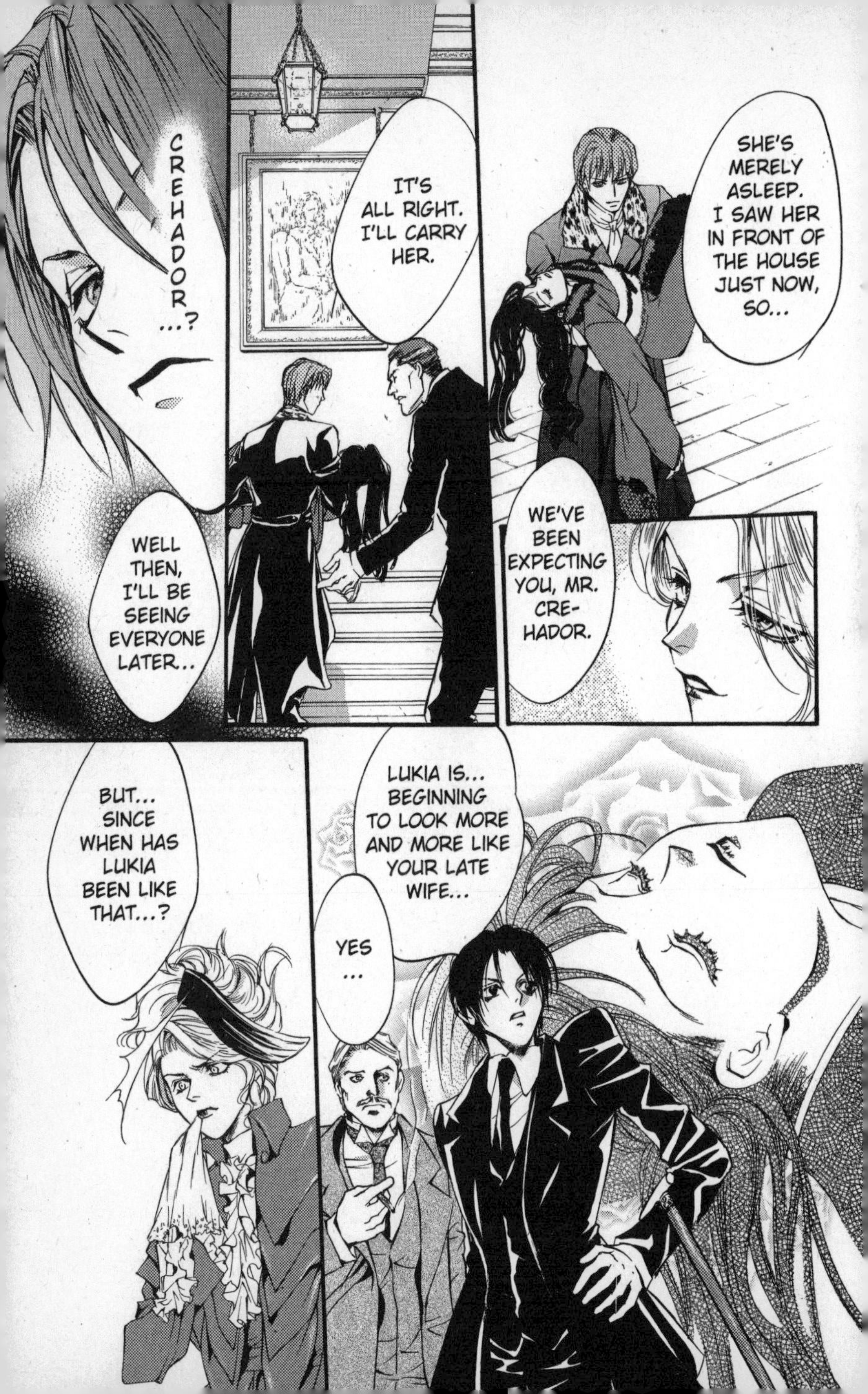
SHE'S MERELY ASLEEP. I SAW HER IN FRONT OF THE HOUSE JUST NOW, SO...
WE'VE BEEN EXPECTING YOU, MR. CRE-HADOR.
IT'S ALL RIGHT. I'LL CARRY HER.
CREHADOR...?
WELL THEN, I'LL BE SEEING EVERYONE LATER...
LUKIA IS... BEGINNING TO LOOK MORE AND MORE LIKE YOUR LATE WIFE...
YES...
BUT... SINCE WHEN HAS LUKIA BEEN LIKE THAT...?

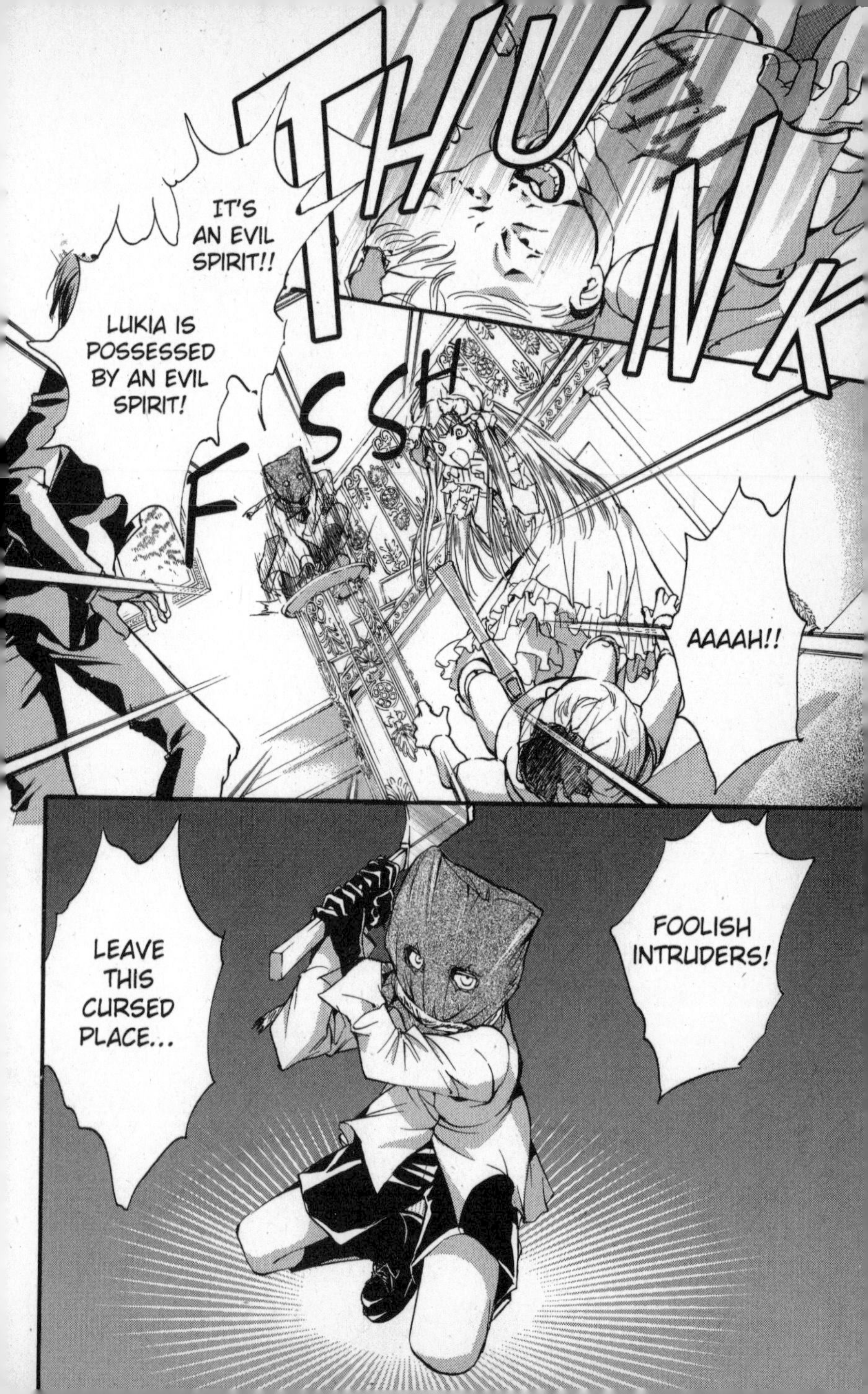
THUNK
IT'S AN EVIL SPIRIT!!
LUKIA IS POSSESSED BY AN EVIL SPIRIT!
FSSH
AAAAH!!
FOOLISH INTRUDERS!
LEAVE THIS CURSED PLACE...

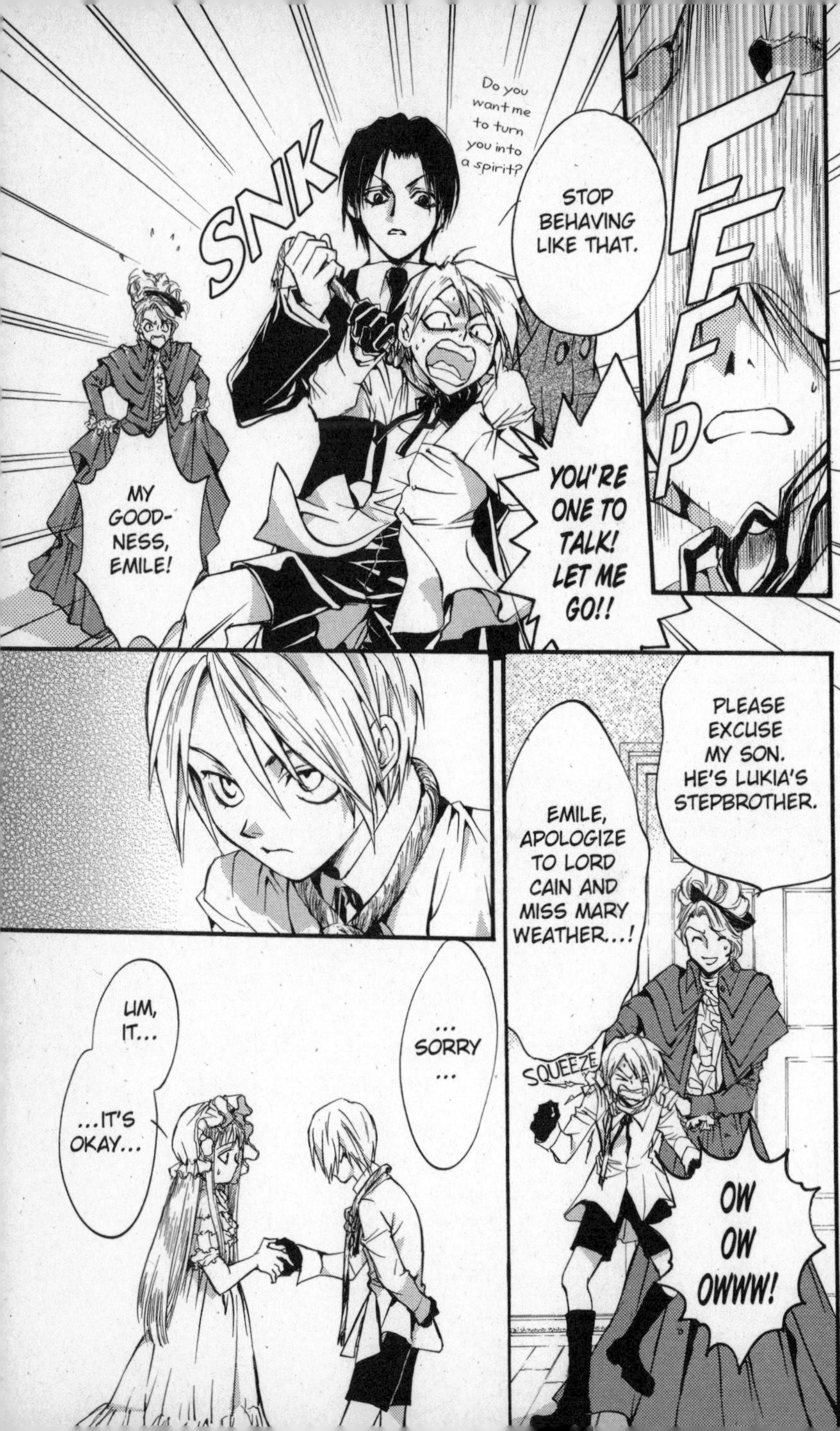
FFFP
SNK
Do you want me to turn you into a spirit?
STOP BEHAVING LIKE THAT.
YOU'RE ONE TO TALK! LET ME GO!!
MY GOODNESS, EMILE!
PLEASE EXCUSE MY SON. HE'S LUKIA'S STEPBROTHER.
EMILE, APOLOGIZE TO LORD CAIN AND MISS MARY WEATHER...!
SQUEEZE
OW OW OWWW!
...SORRY...
UM, IT...
...IT'S OKAY...

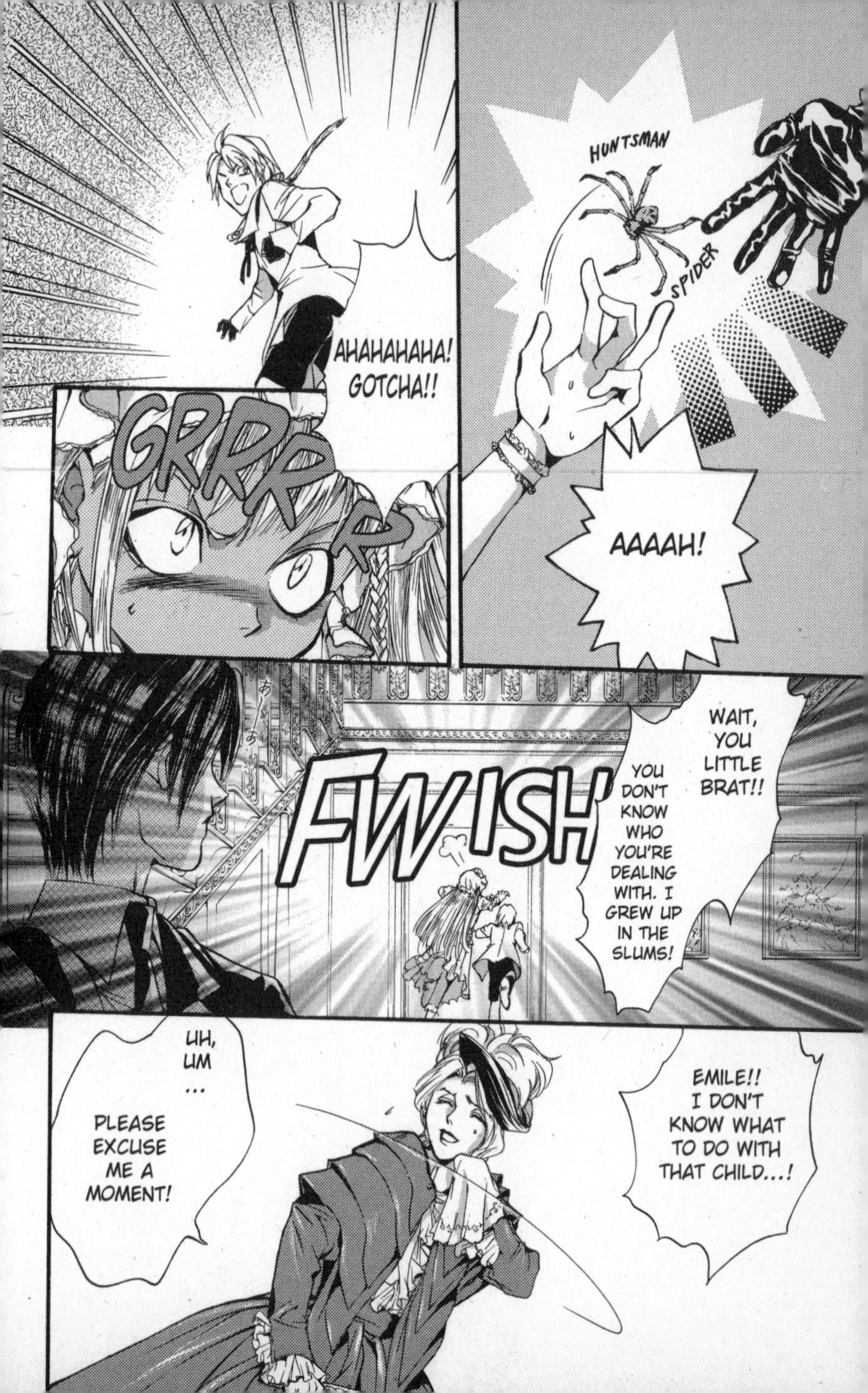
HUNTSMAN
SPIDER
AAAAH!
AHAHAHAHA! GOTCHA!!
GRRRR
WAIT, YOU LITTLE BRAT!!
YOU DON'T KNOW WHO YOU'RE DEALING WITH. I GREW UP IN THE SLUMS!
FWISH
EMILE!! I DON'T KNOW WHAT TO DO WITH THAT CHILD...!
UH, UM ...
PLEASE EXCUSE ME A MOMENT!

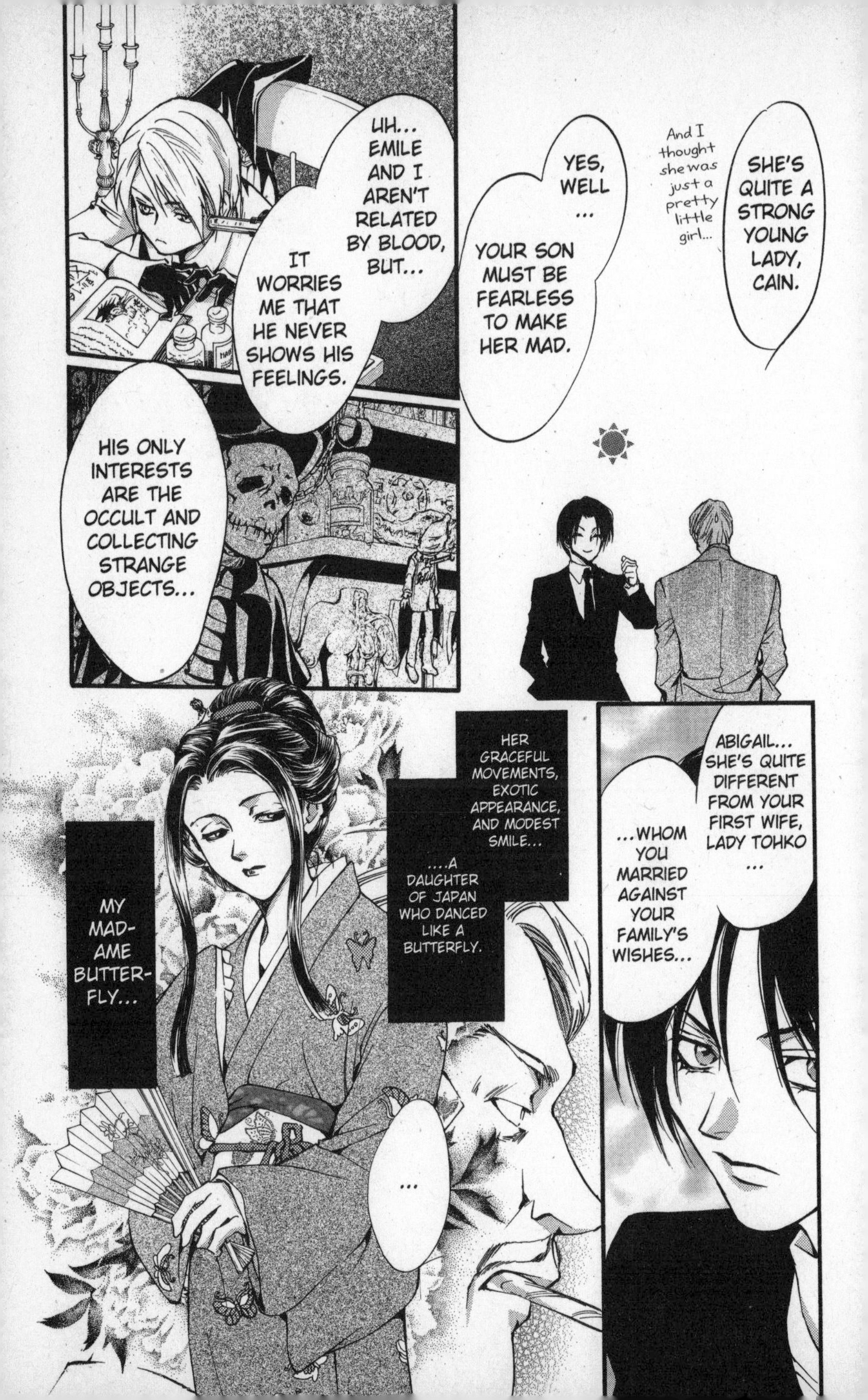
SHE'S QUITE A STRONG YOUNG LADY, CAIN.
And I thought she was just a pretty little girl...
YES, WELL...
YOUR SON MUST BE FEARLESS TO MAKE HER MAD.
UH... EMILE AND I AREN'T RELATED BY BLOOD, BUT...
IT WORRIES ME THAT HE NEVER SHOWS HIS FEELINGS.
HIS ONLY INTERESTS ARE THE OCCULT AND COLLECTING STRANGE OBJECTS...
ABIGAIL... SHE'S QUITE DIFFERENT FROM YOUR FIRST WIFE, LADY TOHKO...
...WHOM YOU MARRIED AGAINST YOUR FAMILY'S WISHES...
...
HER GRACEFUL MOVEMENTS, EXOTIC APPEARANCE, AND MODEST SMILE...
....A DAUGHTER OF JAPAN WHO DANCED LIKE A BUTTERFLY.
MY MAD-AME BUTTER-FLY...

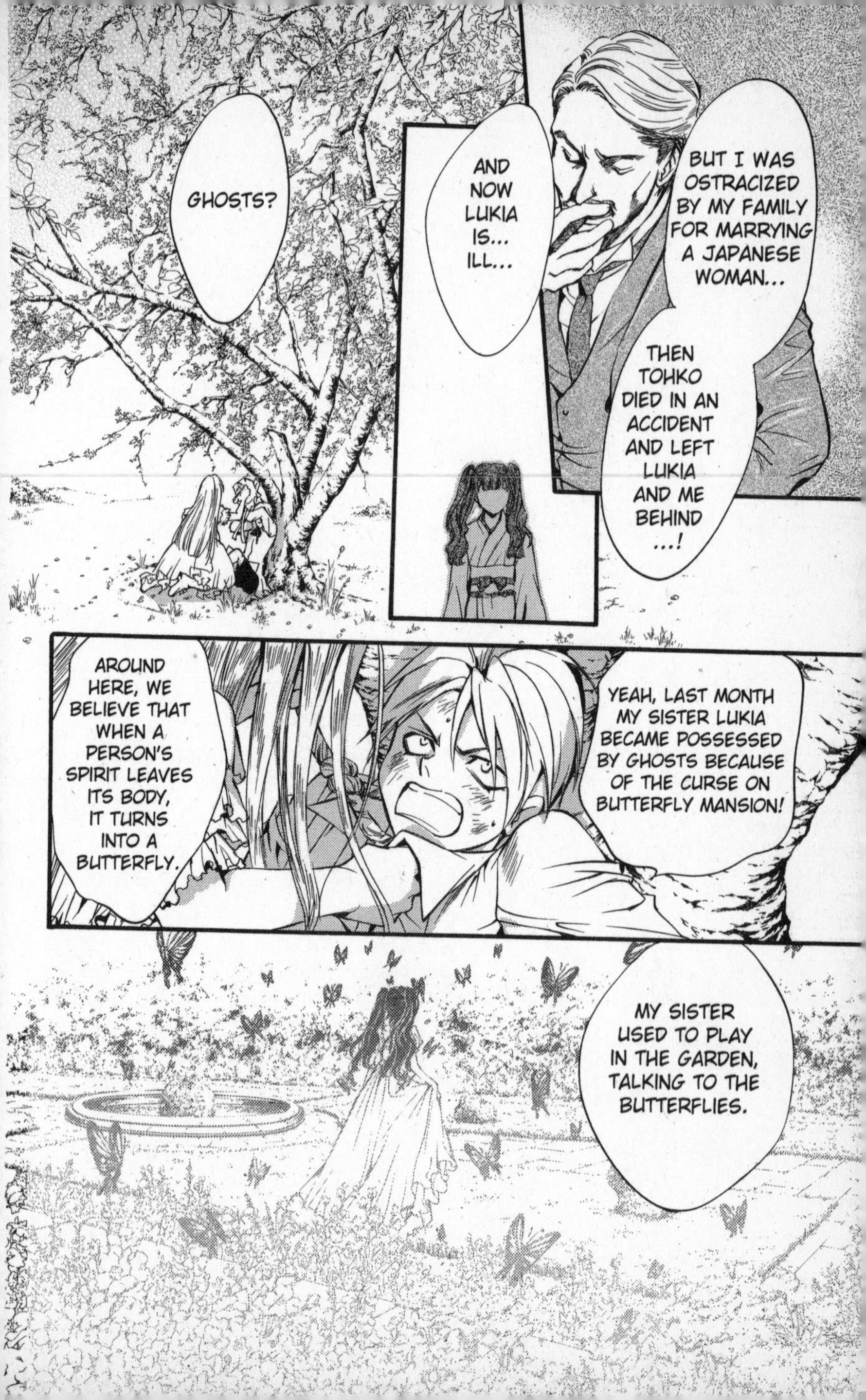
BUT I WAS OSTRACIZED BY MY FAMILY FOR MARRYING A JAPANESE WOMAN...
THEN TOHKO DIED IN AN ACCIDENT AND LEFT LUKIA AND ME BEHIND ...!
AND NOW LUKIA IS... ILL...
GHOSTS?
YEAH, LAST MONTH MY SISTER LUKIA BECAME POSSESSED BY GHOSTS BECAUSE OF THE CURSE ON BUTTERFLY MANSION!
AROUND HERE, WE BELIEVE THAT WHEN A PERSON'S SPIRIT LEAVES ITS BODY, IT TURNS INTO A BUTTERFLY.
MY SISTER USED TO PLAY IN THE GARDEN, TALKING TO THE BUTTERFLIES.

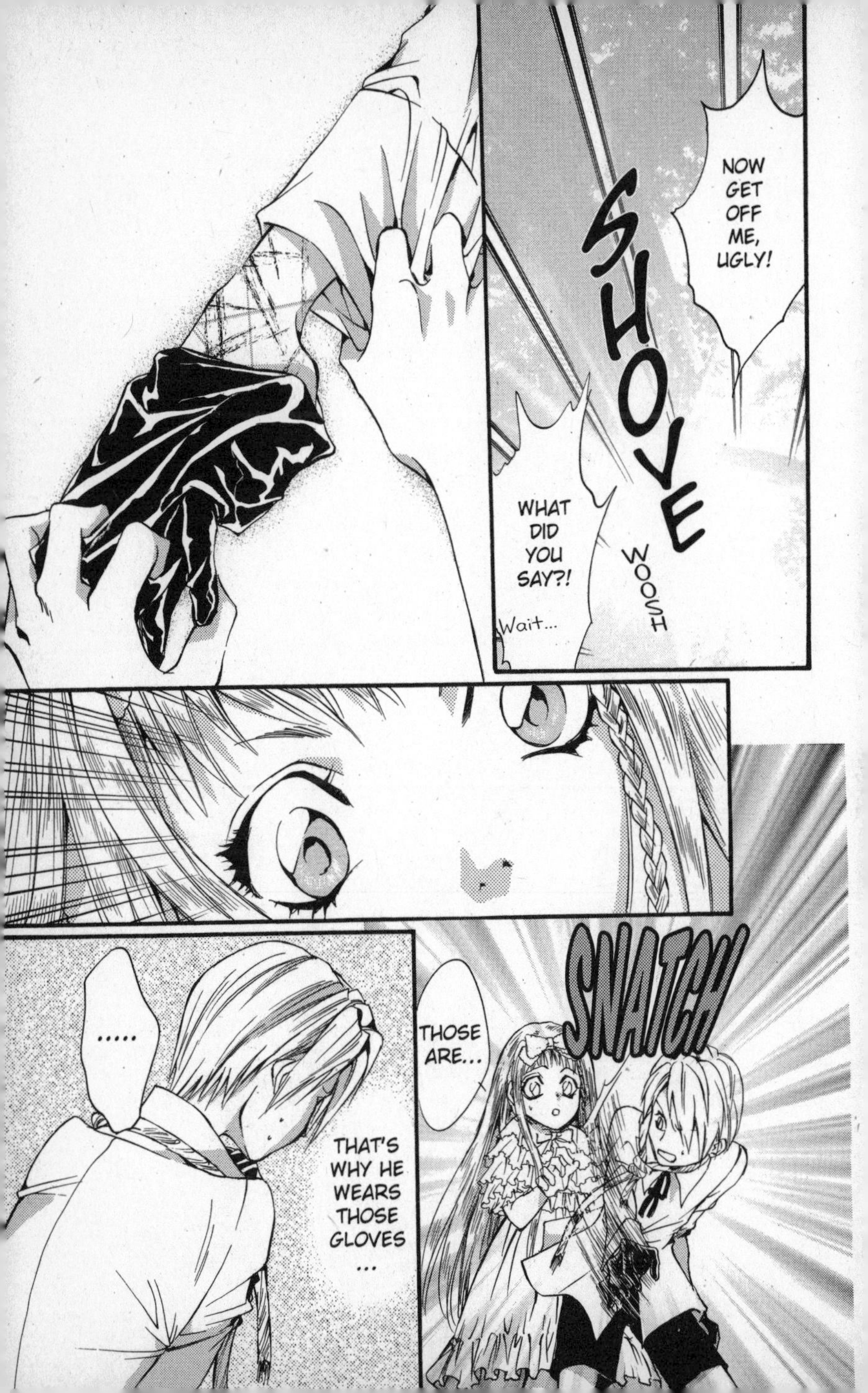
NOW GET OFF ME, UGLY!
SHOVE
WHAT DID YOU SAY?!
WOOSH
Wait...
SNATCH
THOSE ARE...
THAT'S WHY HE WEARS THOSE GLOVES...
.....

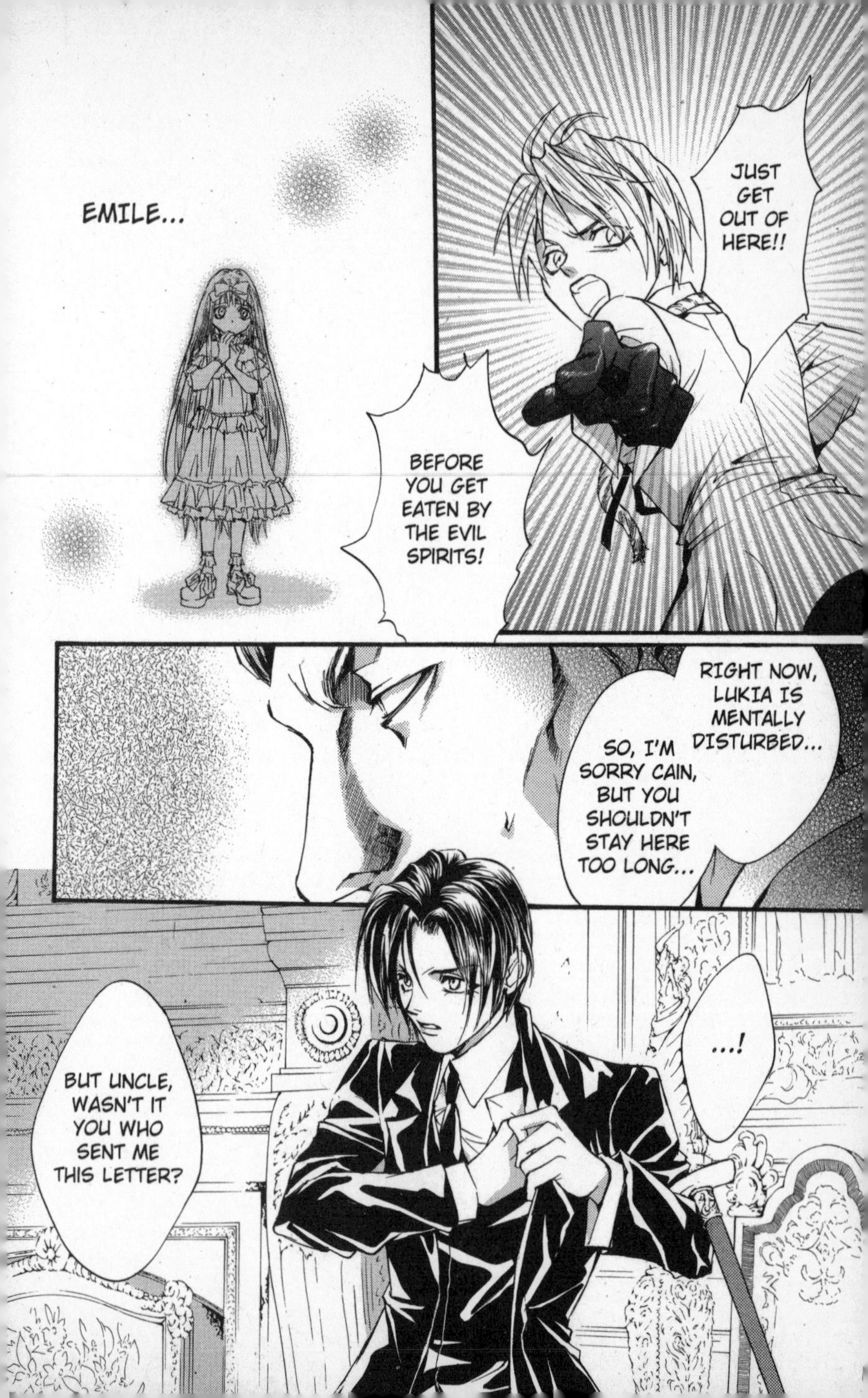
JUST GET OUT OF HERE!!
BEFORE YOU GET EATEN BY THE EVIL SPIRITS!
EMILE...
RIGHT NOW, LUKIA IS MENTALLY DISTURBED...
SO, I'M SORRY CAIN, BUT YOU SHOULDN'T STAY HERE TOO LONG...
...!
BUT UNCLE, WASN'T IT YOU WHO SENT ME THIS LETTER?

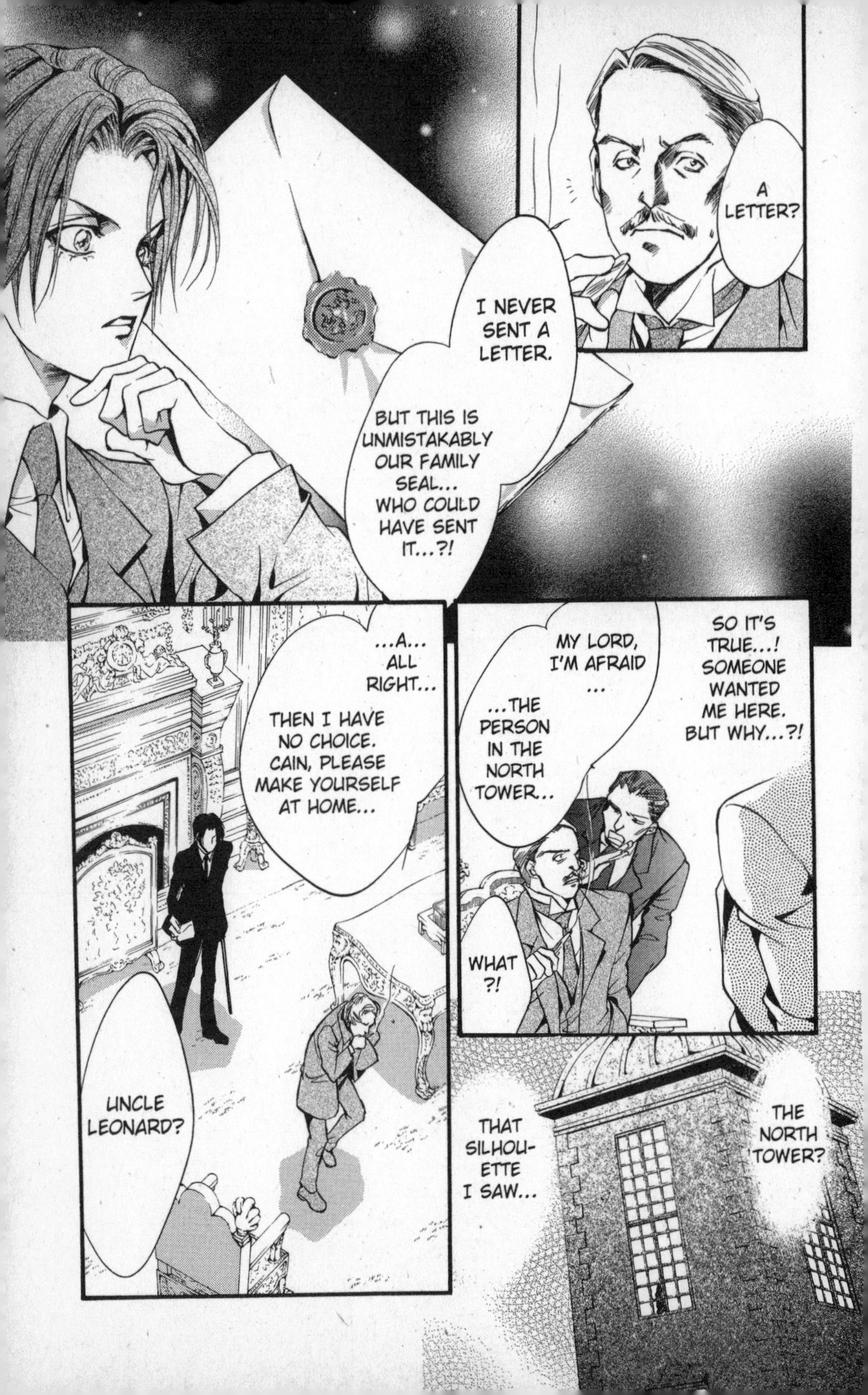
A LETTER?
I NEVER SENT A LETTER.
BUT THIS IS UNMISTAKABLY OUR FAMILY SEAL... WHO COULD HAVE SENT IT...?!
SO IT'S TRUE...! SOMEONE WANTED ME HERE. BUT WHY...?!
MY LORD, I'M AFRAID ...
...THE PERSON IN THE NORTH TOWER...
WHAT ?!
THE NORTH TOWER?
THAT SILHOU- ETTE I SAW...
...A... ALL RIGHT...
THEN I HAVE NO CHOICE. CAIN, PLEASE MAKE YOURSELF AT HOME...
UNCLE LEONARD?

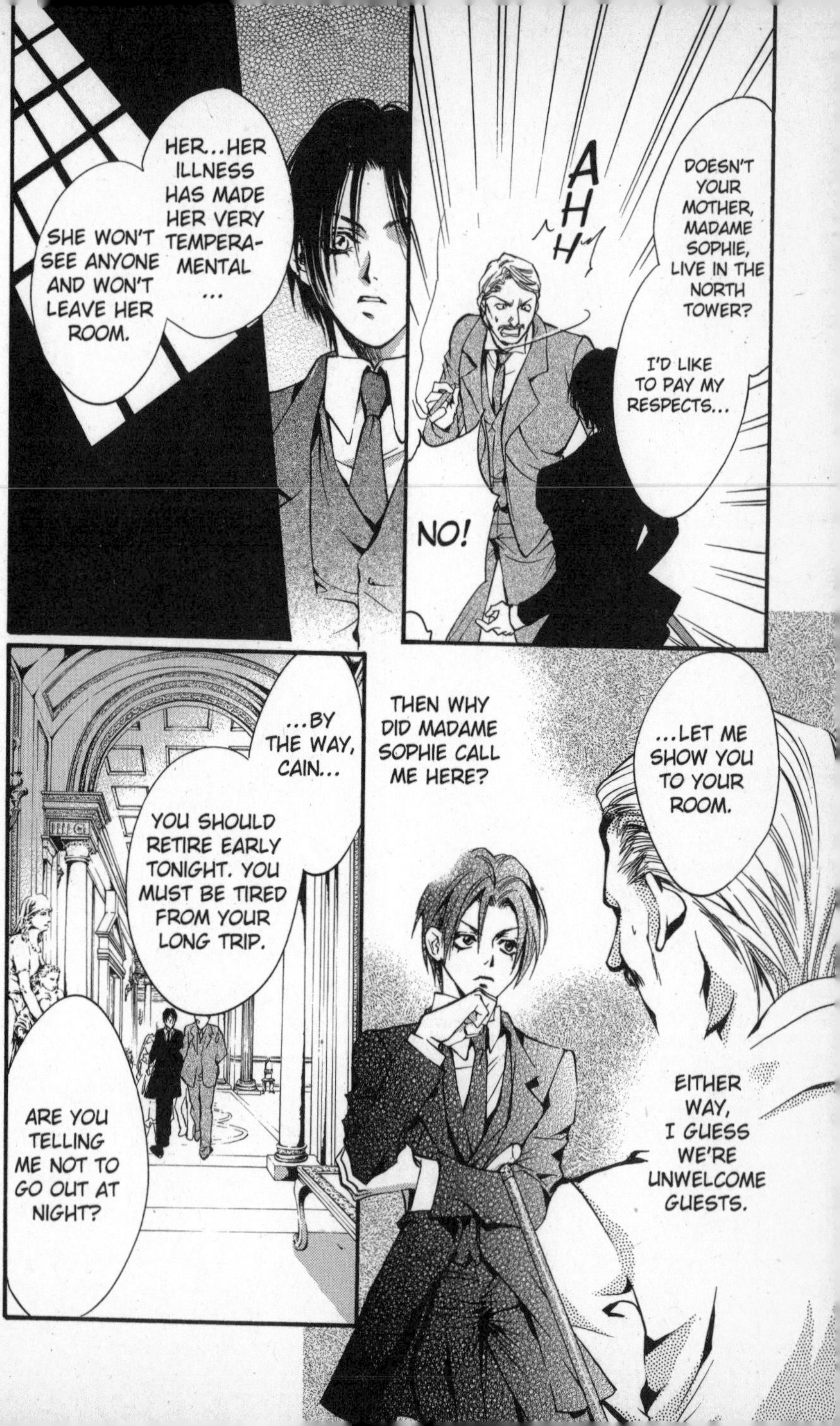
DOESN'T YOUR MOTHER, MADAME SOPHIE, LIVE IN THE NORTH TOWER?
I'D LIKE TO PAY MY RESPECTS...
AHH
NO!
HER...HER ILLNESS HAS MADE HER VERY TEMPERA-MENTAL...
SHE WON'T SEE ANYONE AND WON'T LEAVE HER ROOM.
...LET ME SHOW YOU TO YOUR ROOM.
THEN WHY DID MADAME SOPHIE CALL ME HERE?
...BY THE WAY, CAIN...
YOU SHOULD RETIRE EARLY TONIGHT. YOU MUST BE TIRED FROM YOUR LONG TRIP.
ARE YOU TELLING ME NOT TO GO OUT AT NIGHT?
EITHER WAY, I GUESS WE'RE UNWELCOME GUESTS.

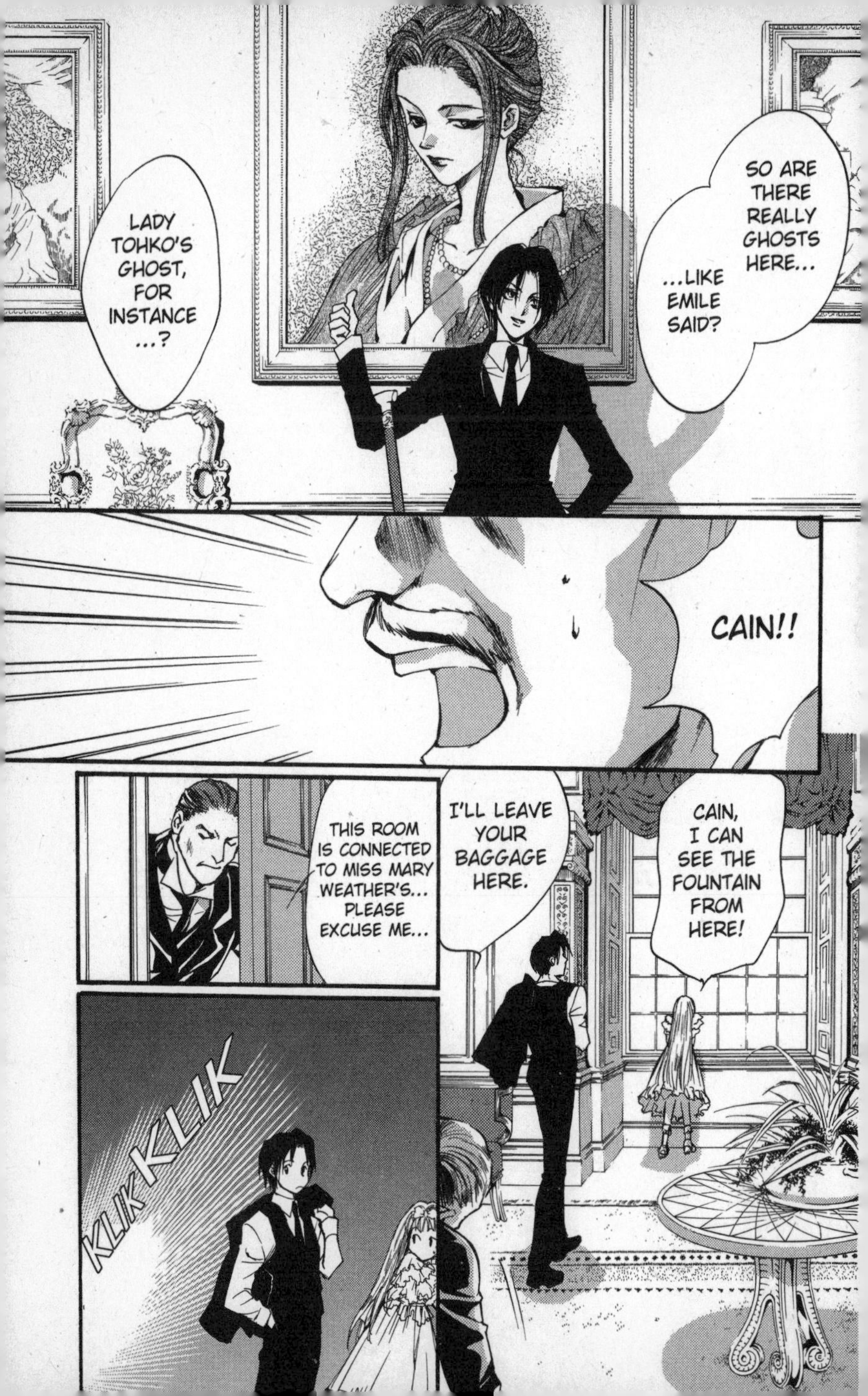
SO ARE THERE REALLY GHOSTS HERE...
...LIKE EMILE SAID?
LADY TOHKO'S GHOST, FOR INSTANCE ...?
CAIN!!
CAIN, I CAN SEE THE FOUNTAIN FROM HERE!
I'LL LEAVE YOUR BAGGAGE HERE.
THIS ROOM IS CONNECTED TO MISS MARY WEATHER'S... PLEASE EXCUSE ME...
KLIK KLIK

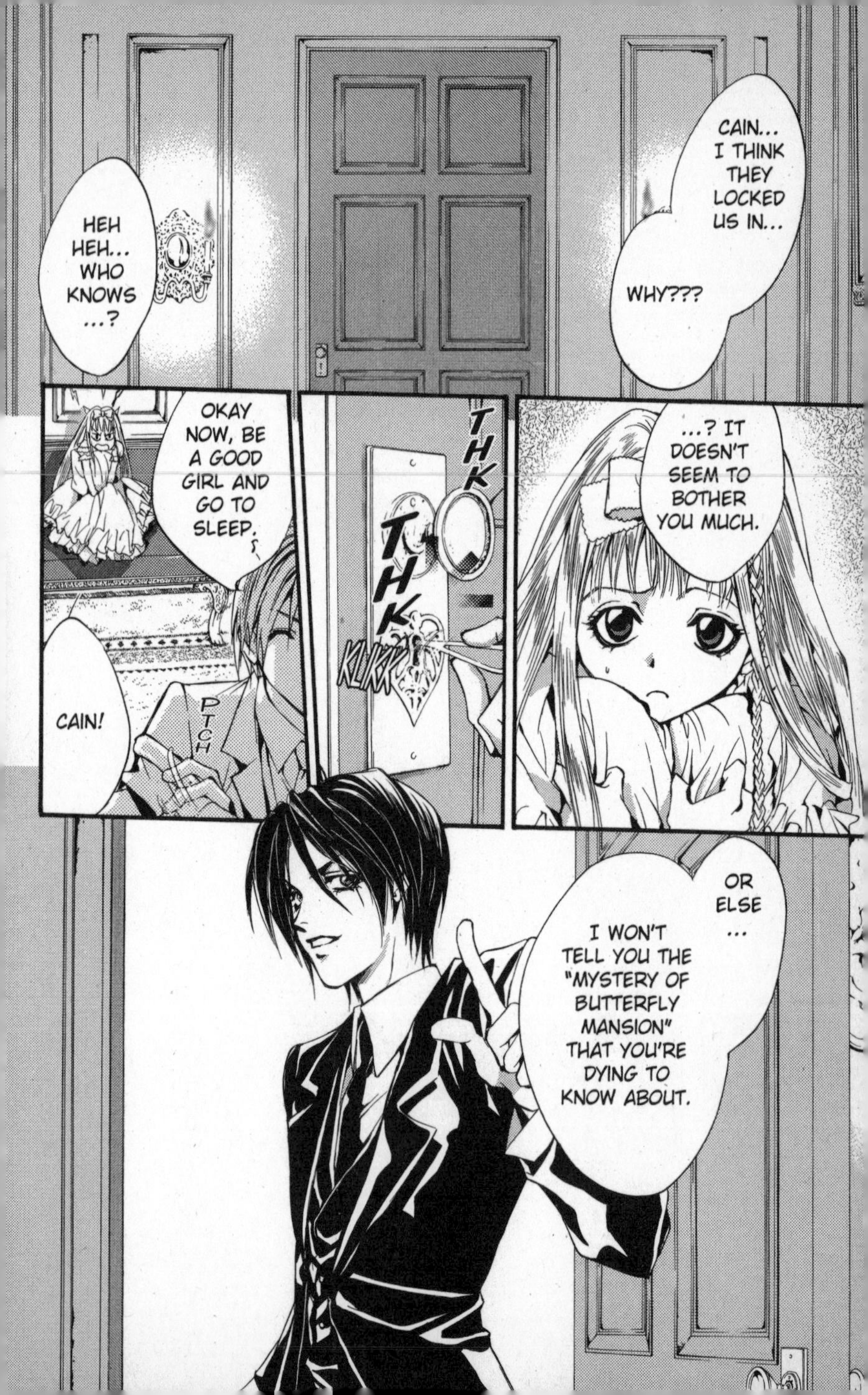
CAIN... I THINK THEY LOCKED US IN...
WHY???
HEH HEH... WHO KNOWS ...?
...? IT DOESN'T SEEM TO BOTHER YOU MUCH.
THK
THK
KLIKK
OKAY NOW, BE A GOOD GIRL AND GO TO SLEEP.
CAIN!
PTCH
OR ELSE ...
I WON'T TELL YOU THE "MYSTERY OF BUTTERFLY MANSION" THAT YOU'RE DYING TO KNOW ABOUT.

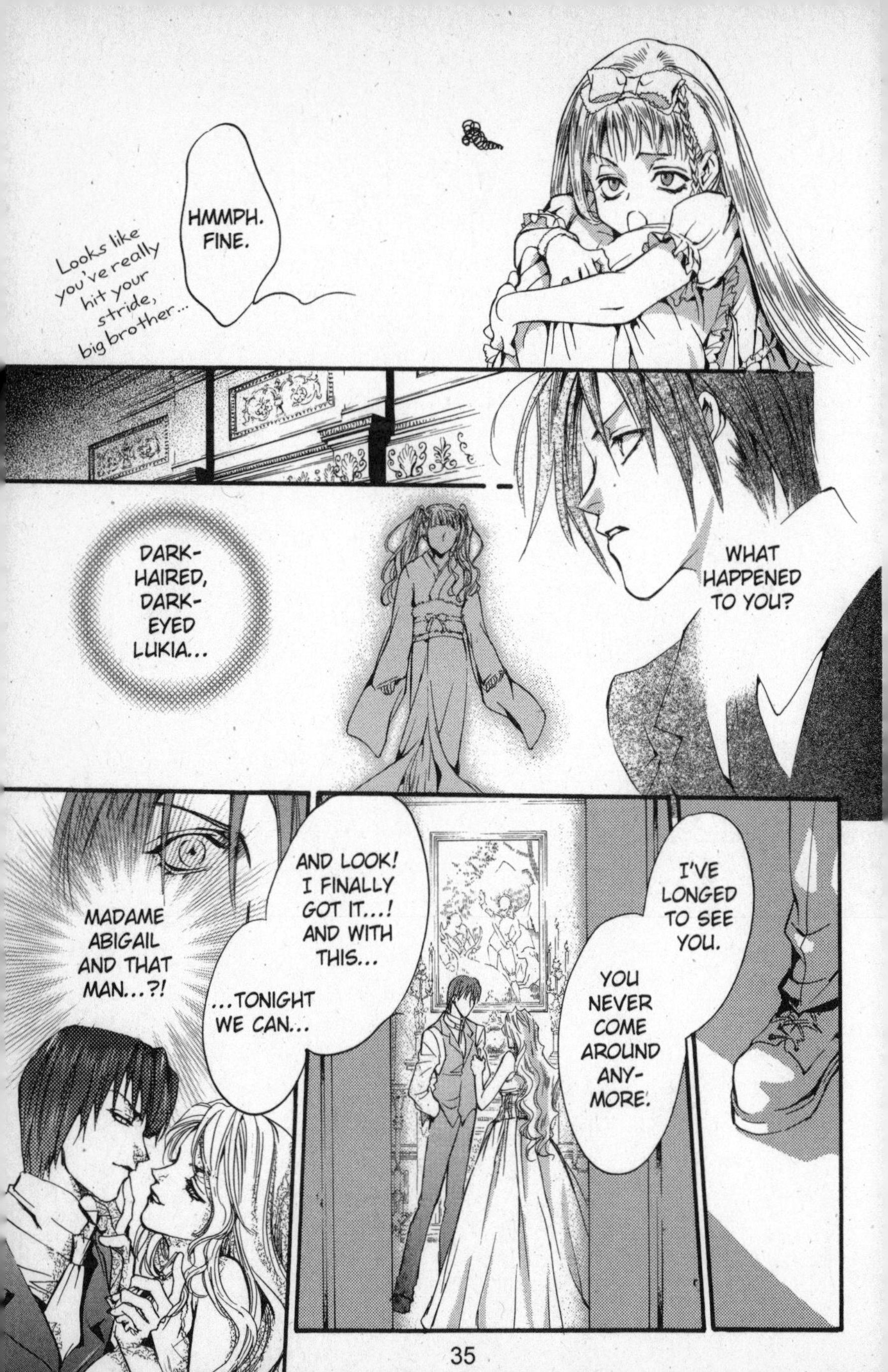
HMMPH. FINE.
Looks like you've really hit your stride, big brother...
WHAT HAPPENED TO YOU?
DARK-HAIRED, DARK-EYED LUKIA...
I'VE LONGED TO SEE YOU.
YOU NEVER COME AROUND ANYMORE.
AND LOOK! I FINALLY GOT IT...! AND WITH THIS...
...TONIGHT WE CAN...
MADAME ABIGAIL AND THAT MAN...?!

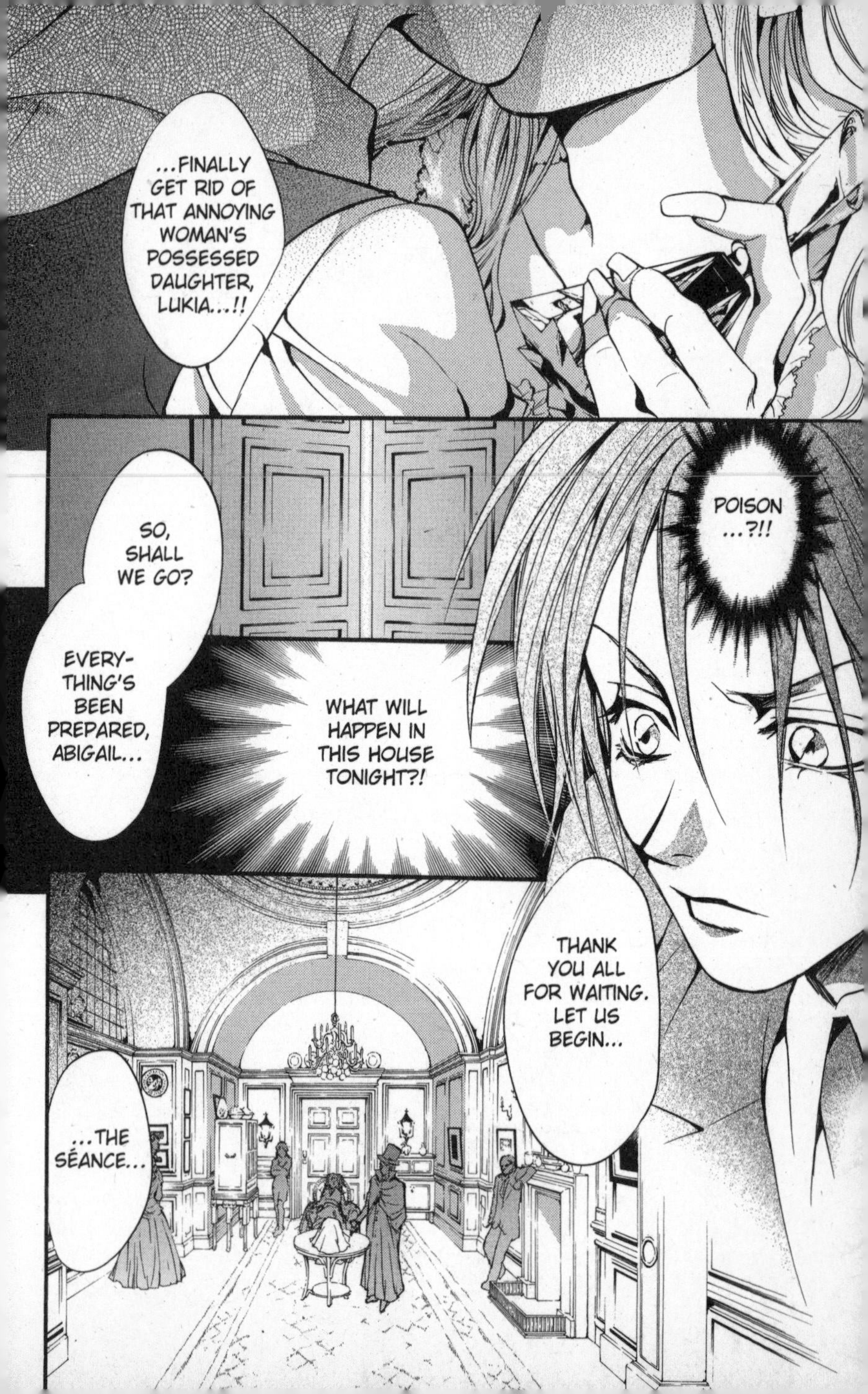
...FINALLY GET RID OF THAT ANNOYING WOMAN'S POSSESSED DAUGHTER, LUKIA...!!
POISON ...?!!
SO, SHALL WE GO?
EVERY-THING'S BEEN PREPARED, ABIGAIL...
WHAT WILL HAPPEN IN THIS HOUSE TONIGHT?!
THANK YOU ALL FOR WAITING. LET US BEGIN...
...THE SÉANCE...

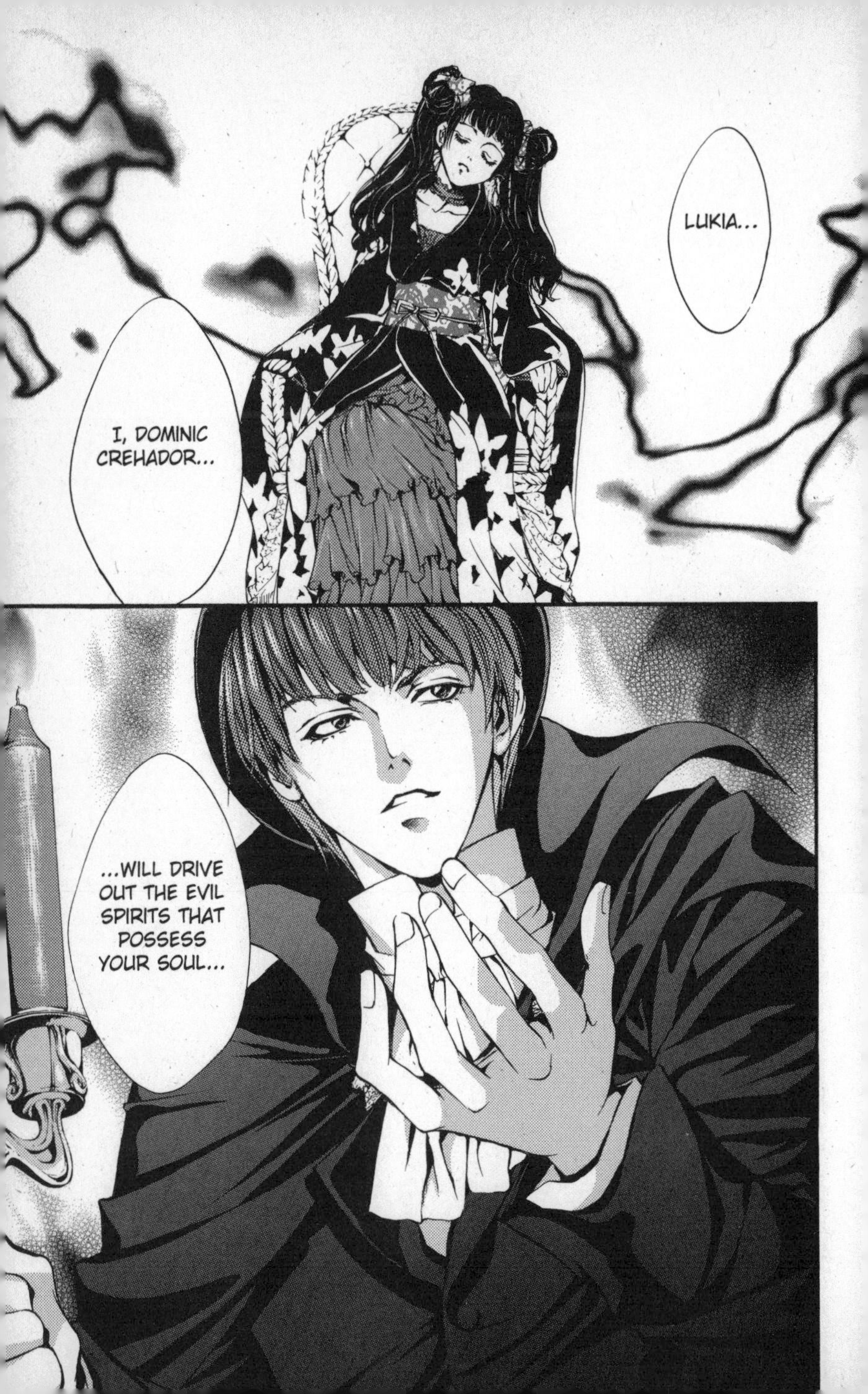
LUKIA...
I, DOMINIC CREHADOR...
...WILL DRIVE OUT THE EVIL SPIRITS THAT POSSESS YOUR SOUL...

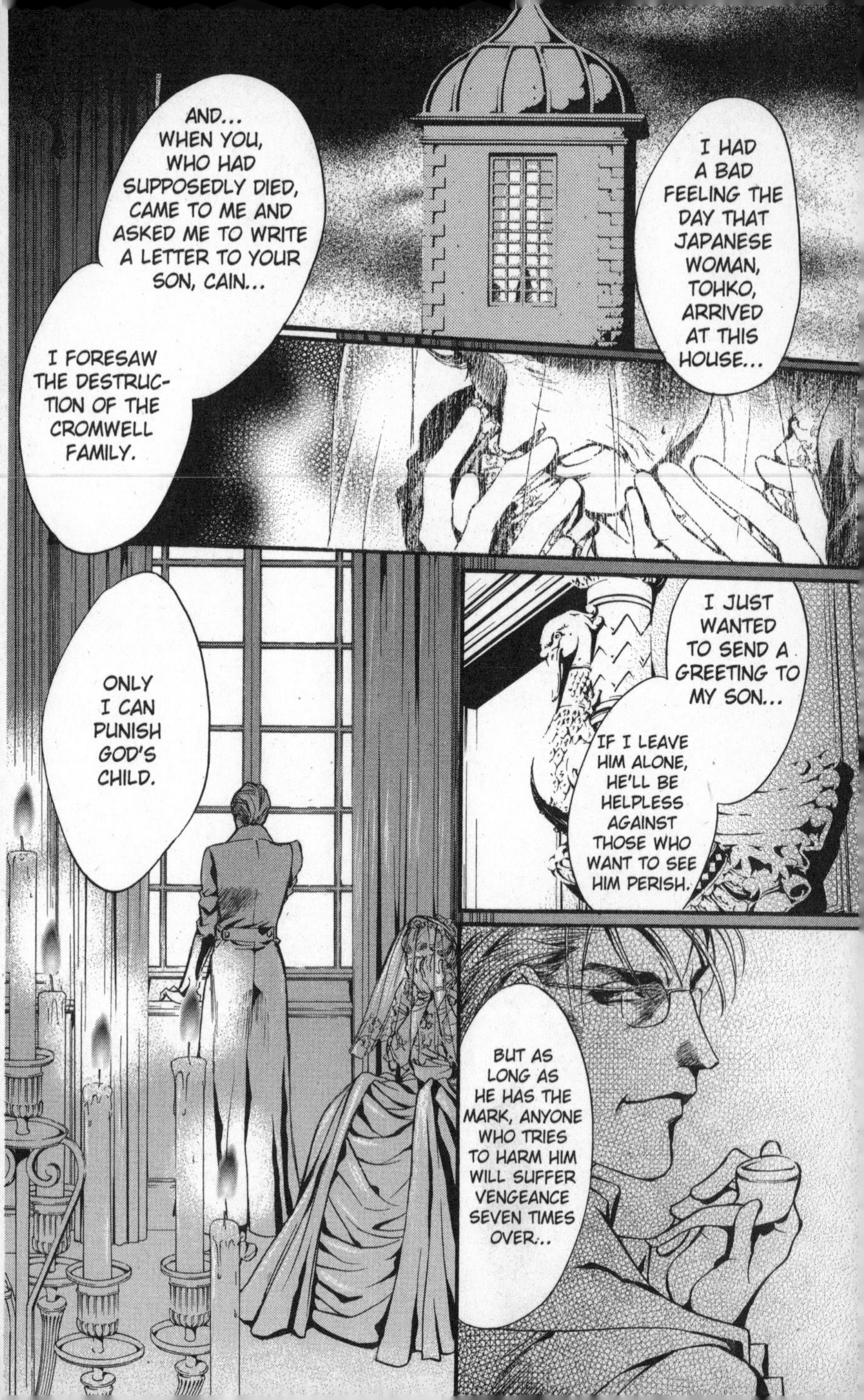
I HAD A BAD FEELING THE DAY THAT JAPANESE WOMAN, TOHKO, ARRIVED AT THIS HOUSE...
AND... WHEN YOU, WHO HAD SUPPOSEDLY DIED, CAME TO ME AND ASKED ME TO WRITE A LETTER TO YOUR SON, CAIN...
I FORESAW THE DESTRUCTION OF THE CROMWELL FAMILY.
I JUST WANTED TO SEND A GREETING TO MY SON...
IF I LEAVE HIM ALONE, HE'LL BE HELPLESS AGAINST THOSE WHO WANT TO SEE HIM PERISH.
BUT AS LONG AS HE HAS THE MARK, ANYONE WHO TRIES TO HARM HIM WILL SUFFER VENGEANCE SEVEN TIMES OVER...
ONLY I CAN PUNISH GOD'S CHILD.

"ONE SUNNY DAY, IN THE DISTANT SKY..."

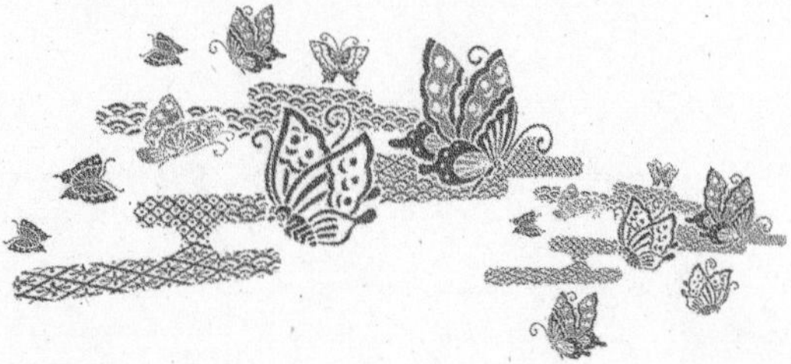

ALMOST LIKE A FLUTTERING RED BUTTERFLY.

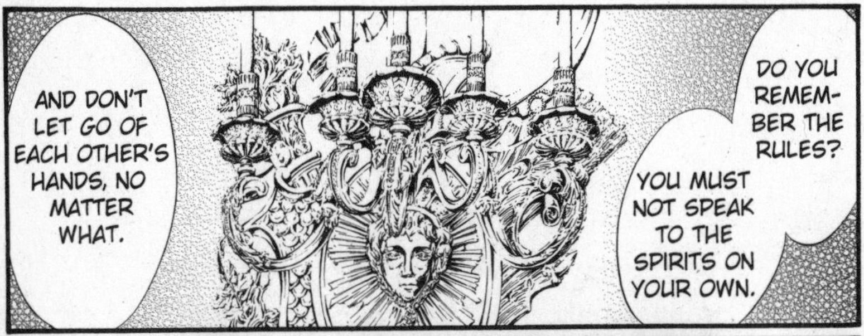
DO YOU REMEMBER THE RULES?
YOU MUST NOT SPEAK TO THE SPIRITS ON YOUR OWN.
AND DON'T LET GO OF EACH OTHER'S HANDS, NO MATTER WHAT.

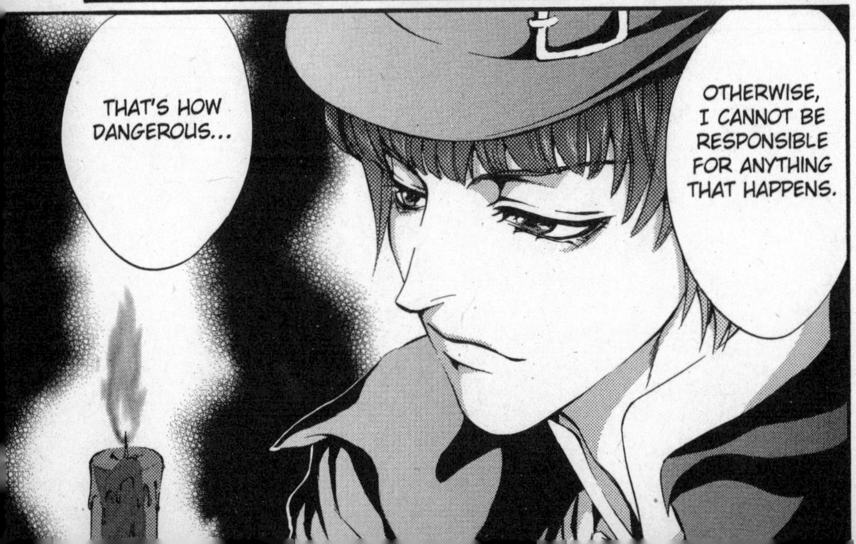
OTHERWISE, I CANNOT BE RESPONSIBLE FOR ANYTHING THAT HAPPENS.
THAT'S HOW DANGEROUS...

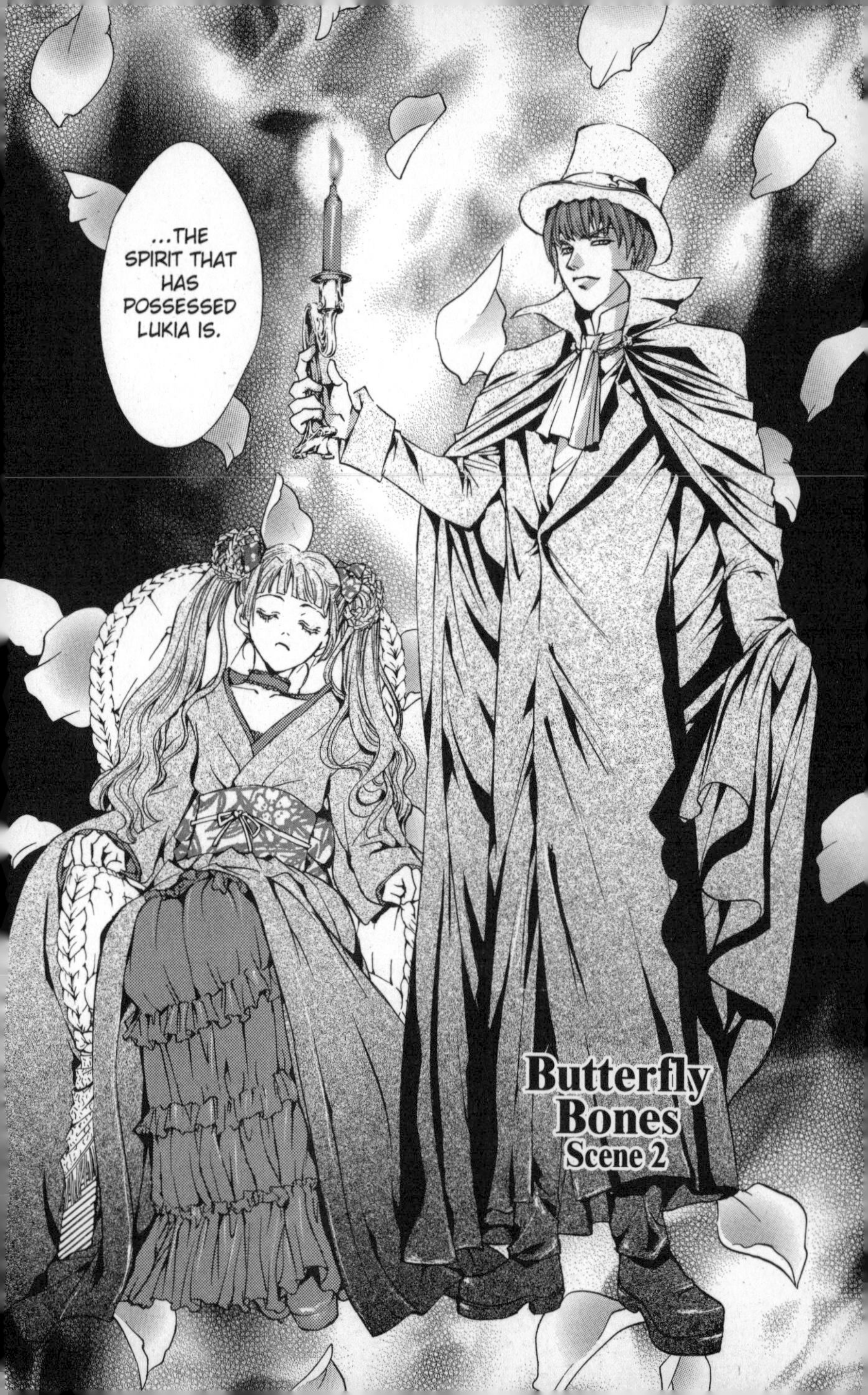
...THE SPIRIT THAT HAS POSSESSED LUKIA IS.
Butterfly Bones
Scene 2

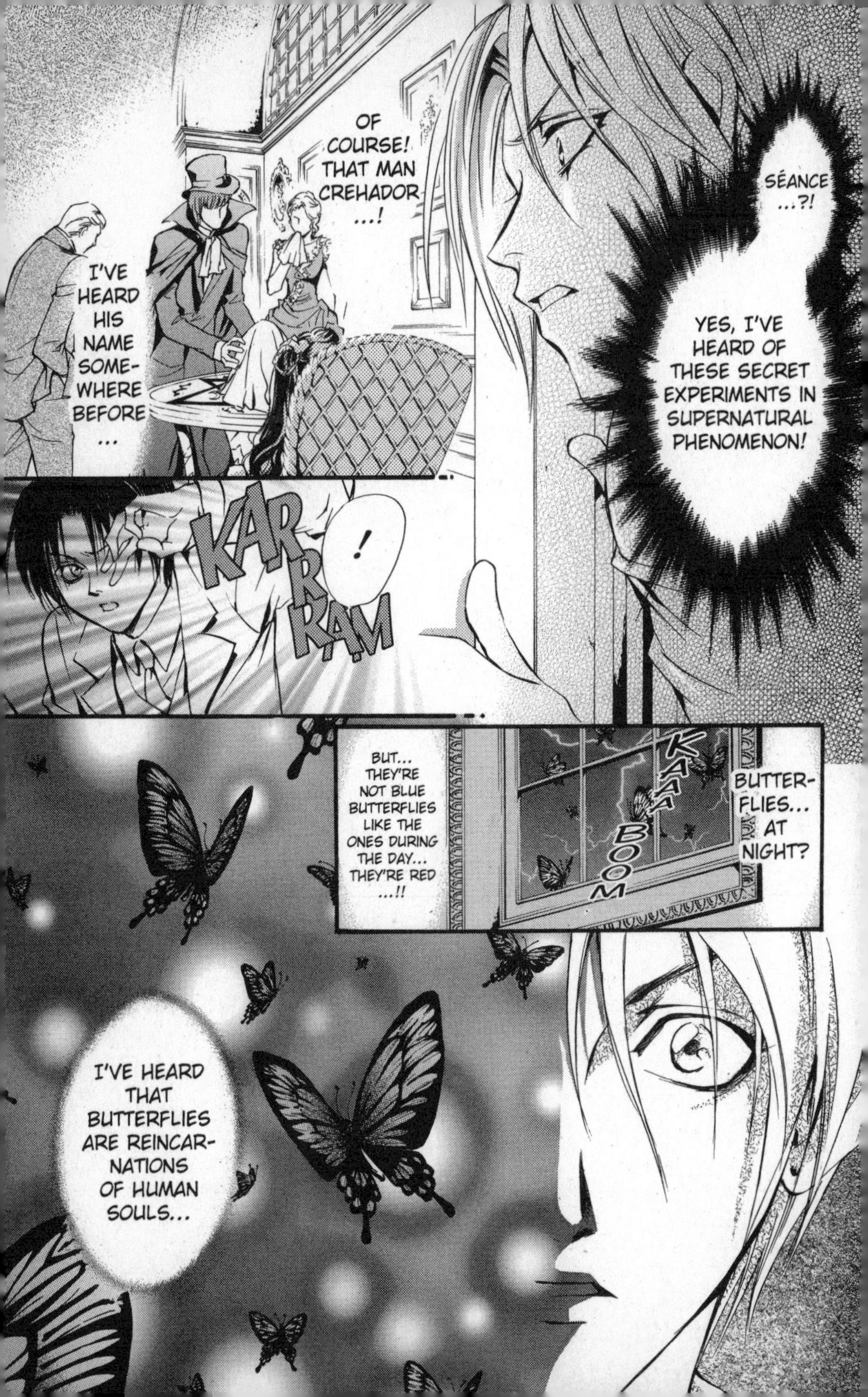
SÉANCE ...?!
YES, I'VE HEARD OF THESE SECRET EXPERIMENTS IN SUPERNATURAL PHENOMENON!
OF COURSE! THAT MAN CREHADOR ...!
I'VE HEARD HIS NAME SOME-WHERE BEFORE ...
!
KARRRAM
BUTTER-FLIES... AT NIGHT?
KAAAA BOOM
BUT... THEY'RE NOT BLUE BUTTERFLIES LIKE THE ONES DURING THE DAY... THEY'RE RED ...!!
I'VE HEARD THAT BUTTERFLIES ARE REINCAR-NATIONS OF HUMAN SOULS...

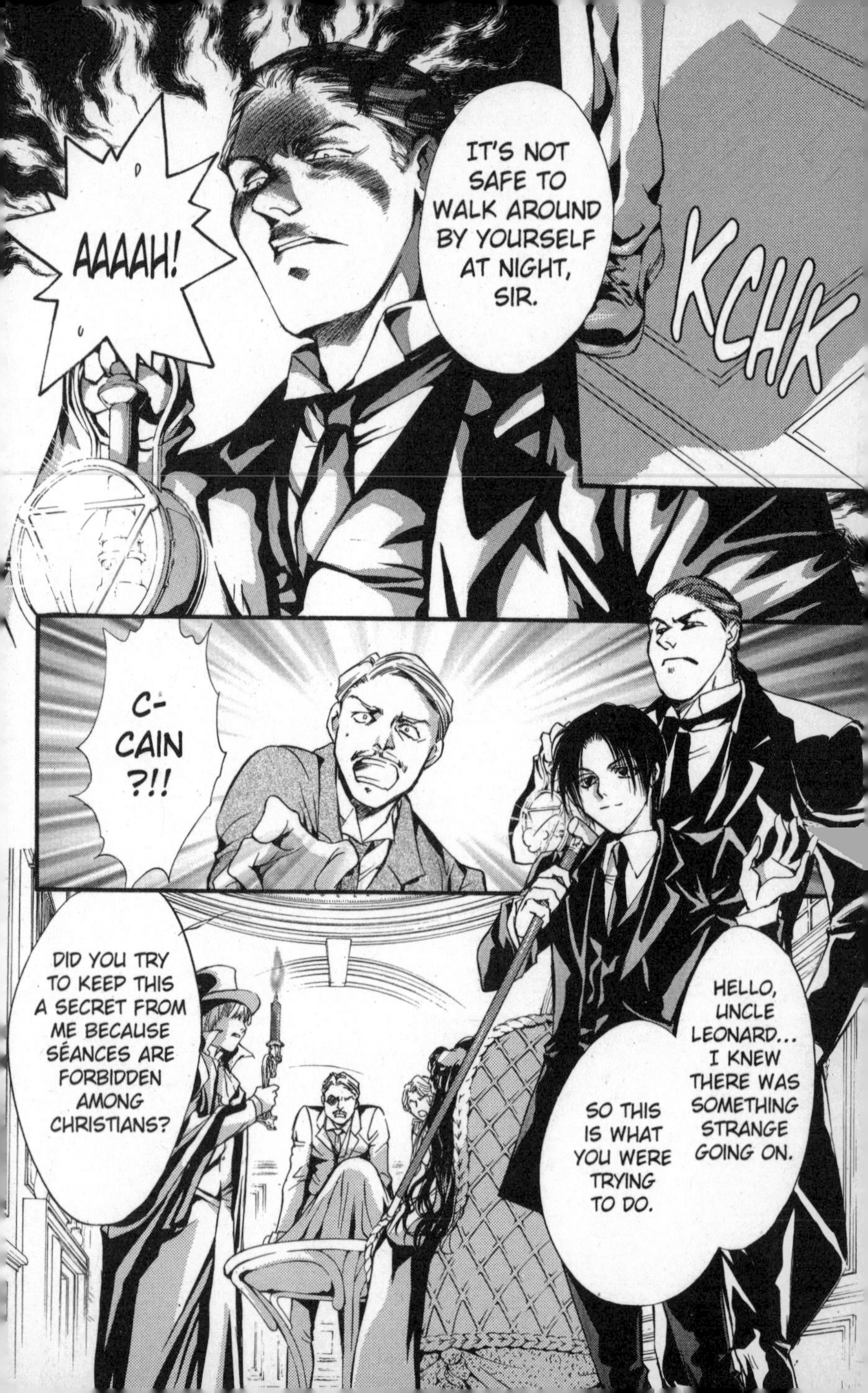
KCHK
IT'S NOT SAFE TO WALK AROUND BY YOURSELF AT NIGHT, SIR.
AAAAH!
C-CAIN ?!!
HELLO, UNCLE LEONARD... I KNEW THERE WAS SOMETHING STRANGE GOING ON.
SO THIS IS WHAT YOU WERE TRYING TO DO.
DID YOU TRY TO KEEP THIS A SECRET FROM ME BECAUSE SÉANCES ARE FORBIDDEN AMONG CHRISTIANS?

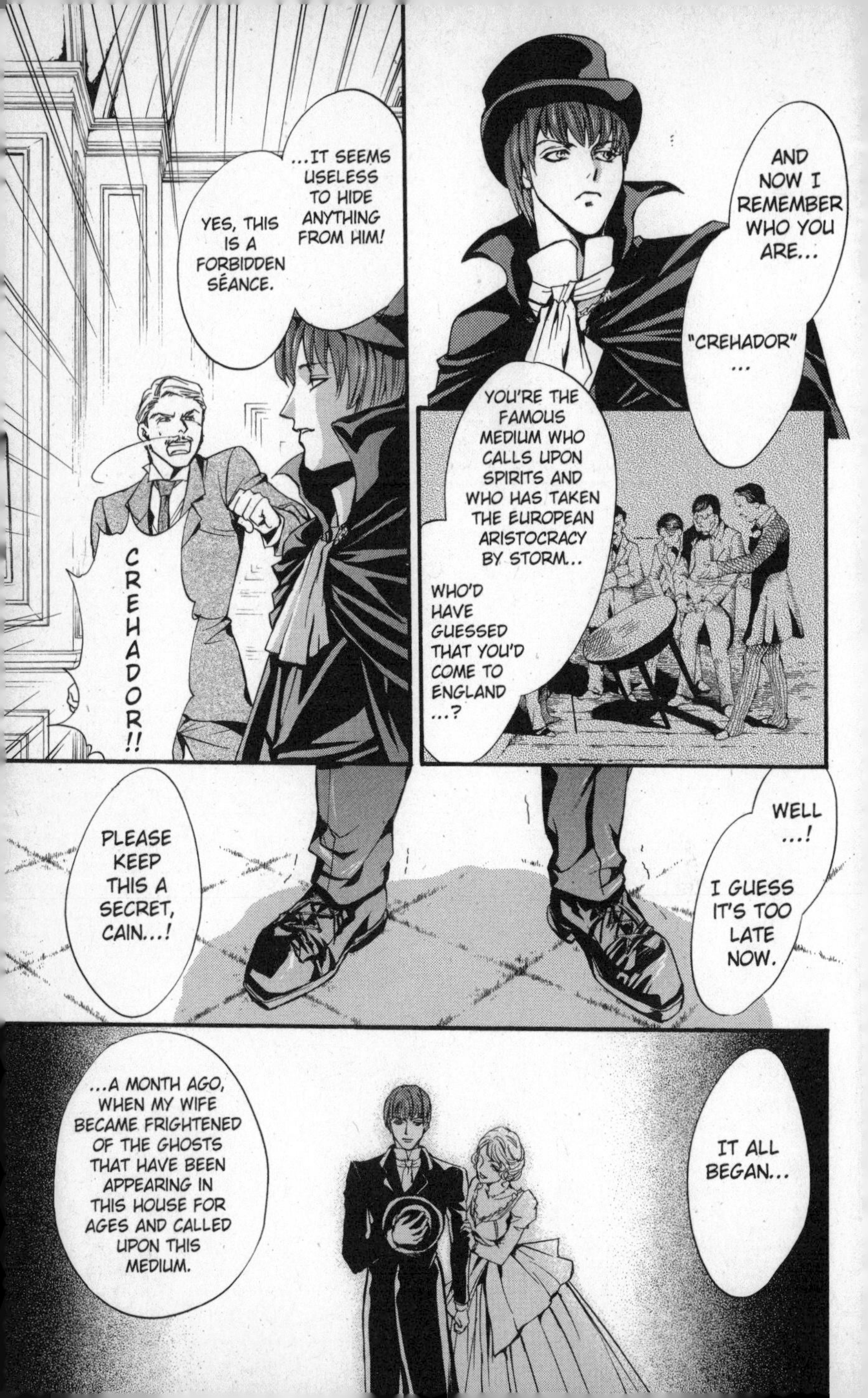
AND NOW I REMEMBER WHO YOU ARE...
"CREHADOR" ...
YOU'RE THE FAMOUS MEDIUM WHO CALLS UPON SPIRITS AND WHO HAS TAKEN THE EUROPEAN ARISTOCRACY BY STORM...
WHO'D HAVE GUESSED THAT YOU'D COME TO ENGLAND ...?
...IT SEEMS USELESS TO HIDE ANYTHING FROM HIM!
YES, THIS IS A FORBIDDEN SÉANCE.
CREHADOR!!
WELL ...!
I GUESS IT'S TOO LATE NOW.
PLEASE KEEP THIS A SECRET, CAIN...!
IT ALL BEGAN...
...A MONTH AGO, WHEN MY WIFE BECAME FRIGHTENED OF THE GHOSTS THAT HAVE BEEN APPEARING IN THIS HOUSE FOR AGES AND CALLED UPON THIS MEDIUM.

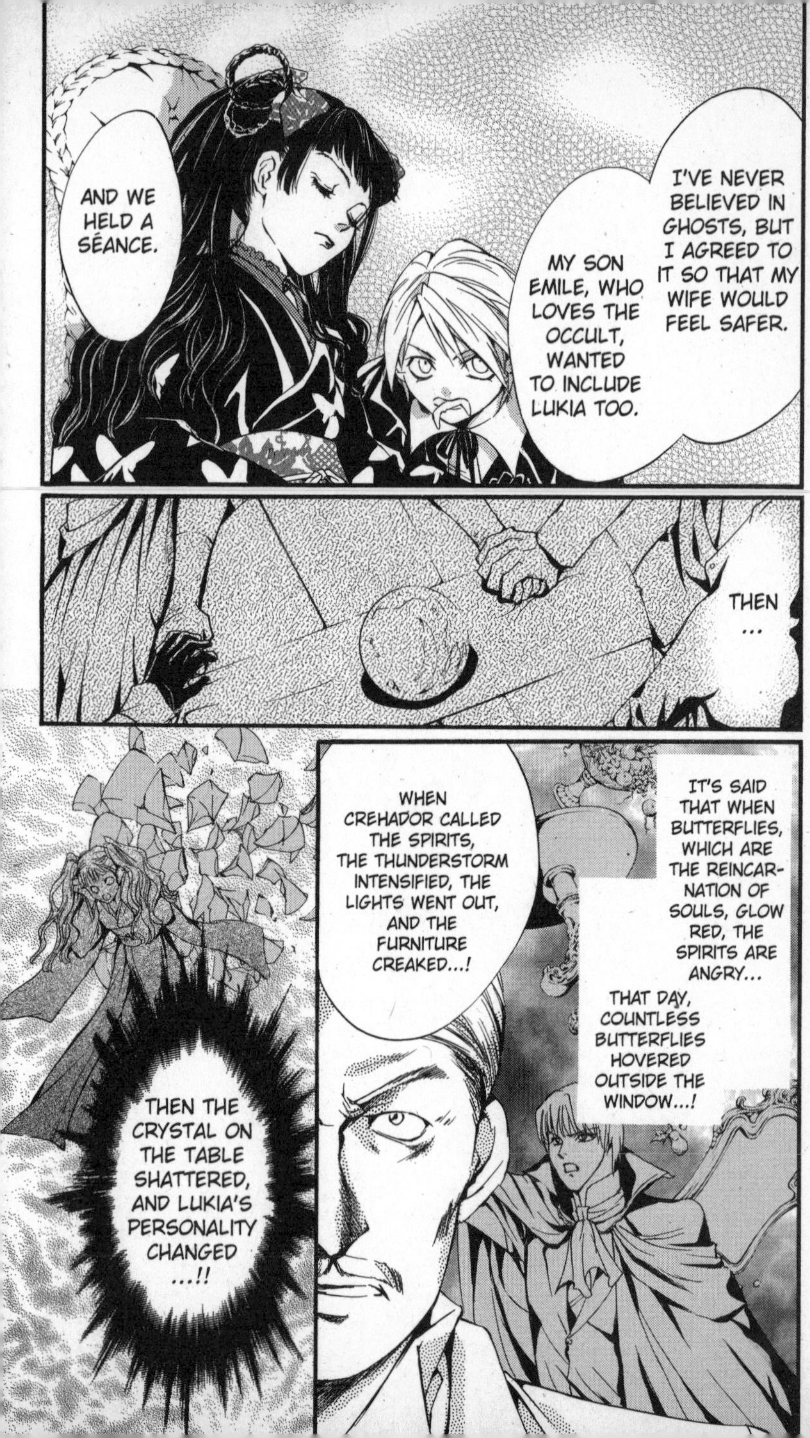
I'VE NEVER BELIEVED IN GHOSTS, BUT I AGREED TO IT SO THAT MY WIFE WOULD FEEL SAFER.
MY SON EMILE, WHO LOVES THE OCCULT, WANTED TO INCLUDE LUKIA TOO.
AND WE HELD A SÉANCE.
THEN ...
IT'S SAID THAT WHEN BUTTERFLIES, WHICH ARE THE REINCARNATION OF SOULS, GLOW RED, THE SPIRITS ARE ANGRY...
THAT DAY, COUNTLESS BUTTERFLIES HOVERED OUTSIDE THE WINDOW...!
WHEN CREHADOR CALLED THE SPIRITS, THE THUNDERSTORM INTENSIFIED, THE LIGHTS WENT OUT, AND THE FURNITURE CREAKED...!
THEN THE CRYSTAL ON THE TABLE SHATTERED, AND LUKIA'S PERSONALITY CHANGED ...!!

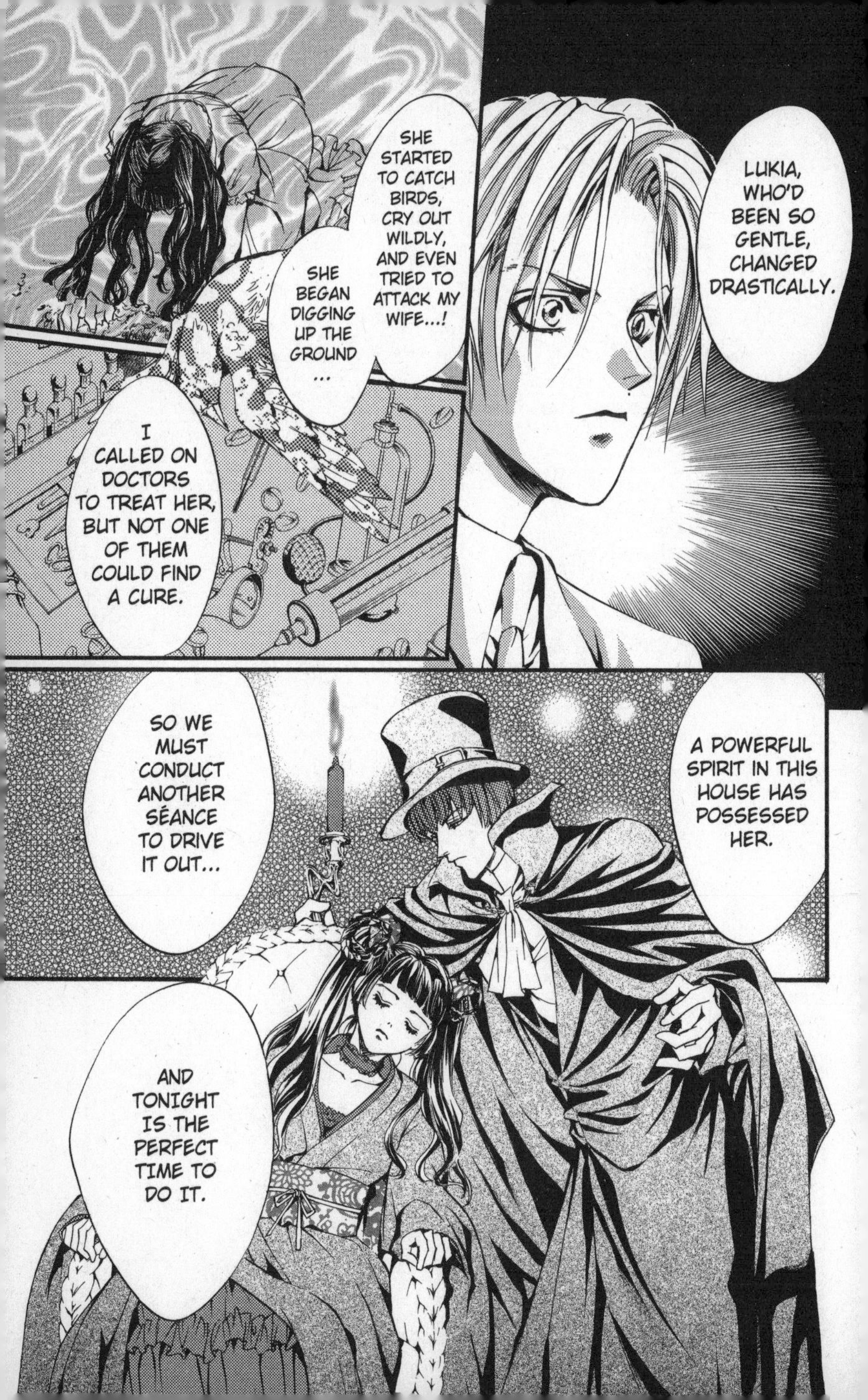
LUKIA, WHO'D BEEN SO GENTLE, CHANGED DRASTICALLY.
SHE STARTED TO CATCH BIRDS, CRY OUT WILDLY, AND EVEN TRIED TO ATTACK MY WIFE...!
SHE BEGAN DIGGING UP THE GROUND...
I CALLED ON DOCTORS TO TREAT HER, BUT NOT ONE OF THEM COULD FIND A CURE.
A POWERFUL SPIRIT IN THIS HOUSE HAS POSSESSED HER.
SO WE MUST CONDUCT ANOTHER SÉANCE TO DRIVE IT OUT...
AND TONIGHT IS THE PERFECT TIME TO DO IT.

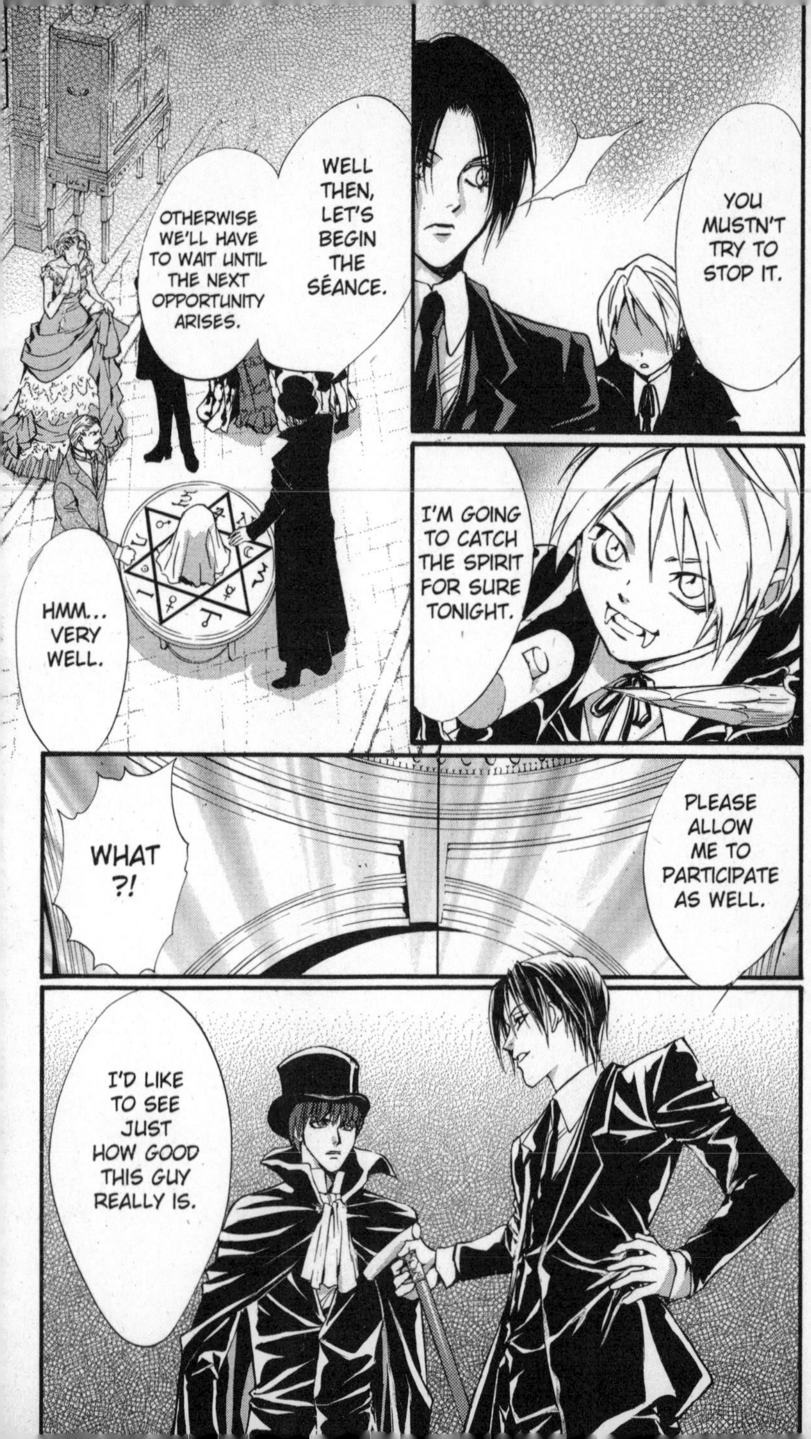
YOU MUSTN'T TRY TO STOP IT.
I'M GOING TO CATCH THE SPIRIT FOR SURE TONIGHT.
WELL THEN, LET'S BEGIN THE SÉANCE.
OTHERWISE WE'LL HAVE TO WAIT UNTIL THE NEXT OPPORTUNITY ARISES.
HMM... VERY WELL.
PLEASE ALLOW ME TO PARTICIPATE AS WELL.
WHAT ?!
I'D LIKE TO SEE JUST HOW GOOD THIS GUY REALLY IS.

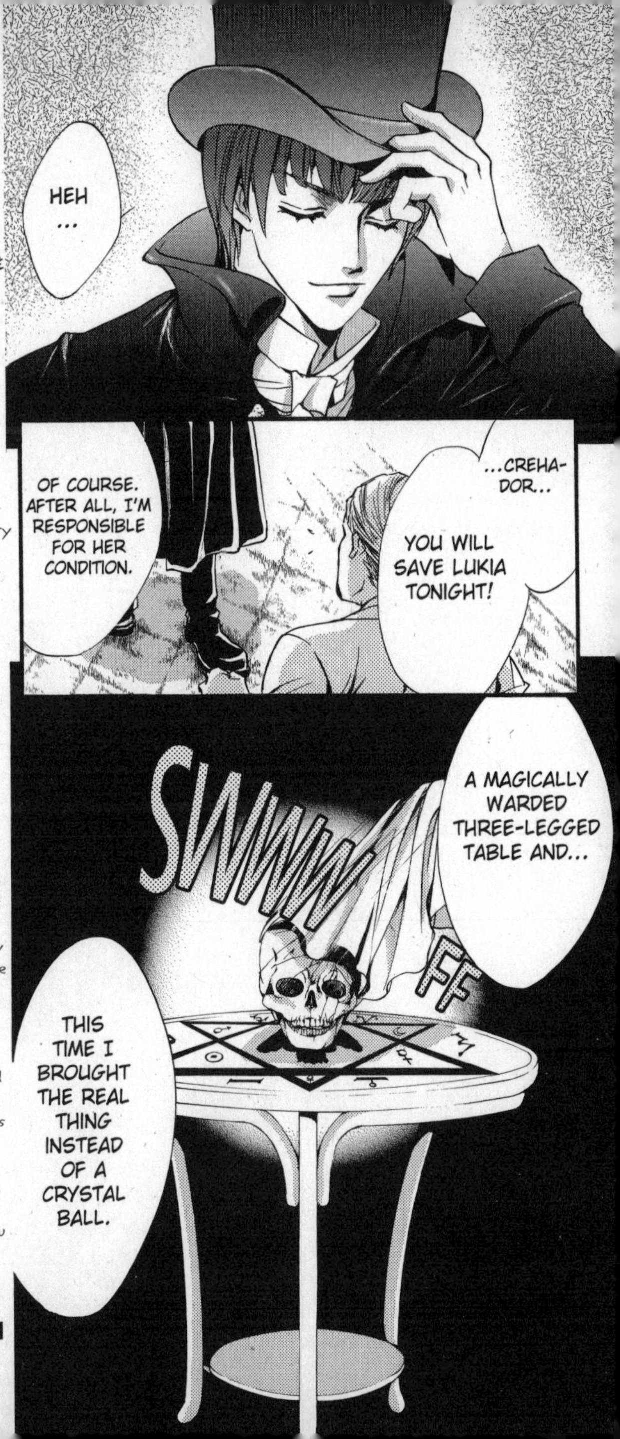
HEH ...
...CREHA-DOR...
YOU WILL SAVE LUKIA TONIGHT!
OF COURSE. AFTER ALL, I'M RESPONSIBLE FOR HER CONDITION.
A MAGICALLY WARDED THREE-LEGGED TABLE AND...
SWWWW
FF
THIS TIME I BROUGHT THE REAL THING INSTEAD OF A CRYSTAL BALL.

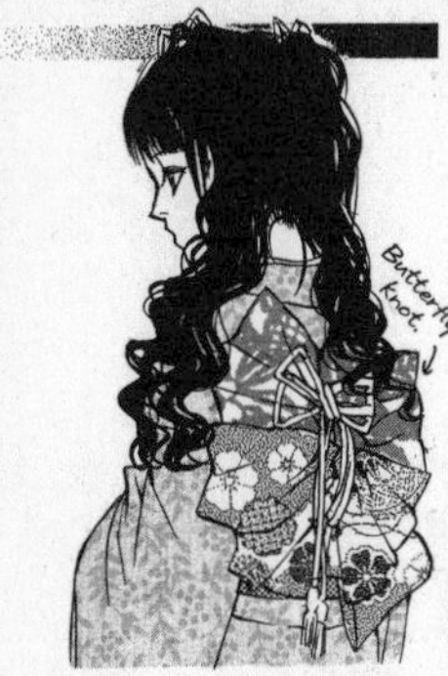
Butterfly knot.

There's no particular reason why I decided to introduce a Japanese character into this story except that shortly before this story takes place, there was a sudden fascination with Japan in England in the form of "Japan Village" expositions and the opera "Mikado." I thought it would be fun to include some of the misconceptions Europeans had regarding Japanese kimonos, so I played around quite a bit with Lukia's kimono and her hairstyle. I also wanted to do a little bit of research on butterflies and was pleasantly surprised to find out the many varieties that exist. I really learned a lot. But it took me longer than I expected to design a Europeanized kimono. It was worth it, though, because readers loved Lukia's fashion. But if I had asked people's opinions back in those days they would probably have said, "You gotta be kidding!" It was probably just plain wrong.

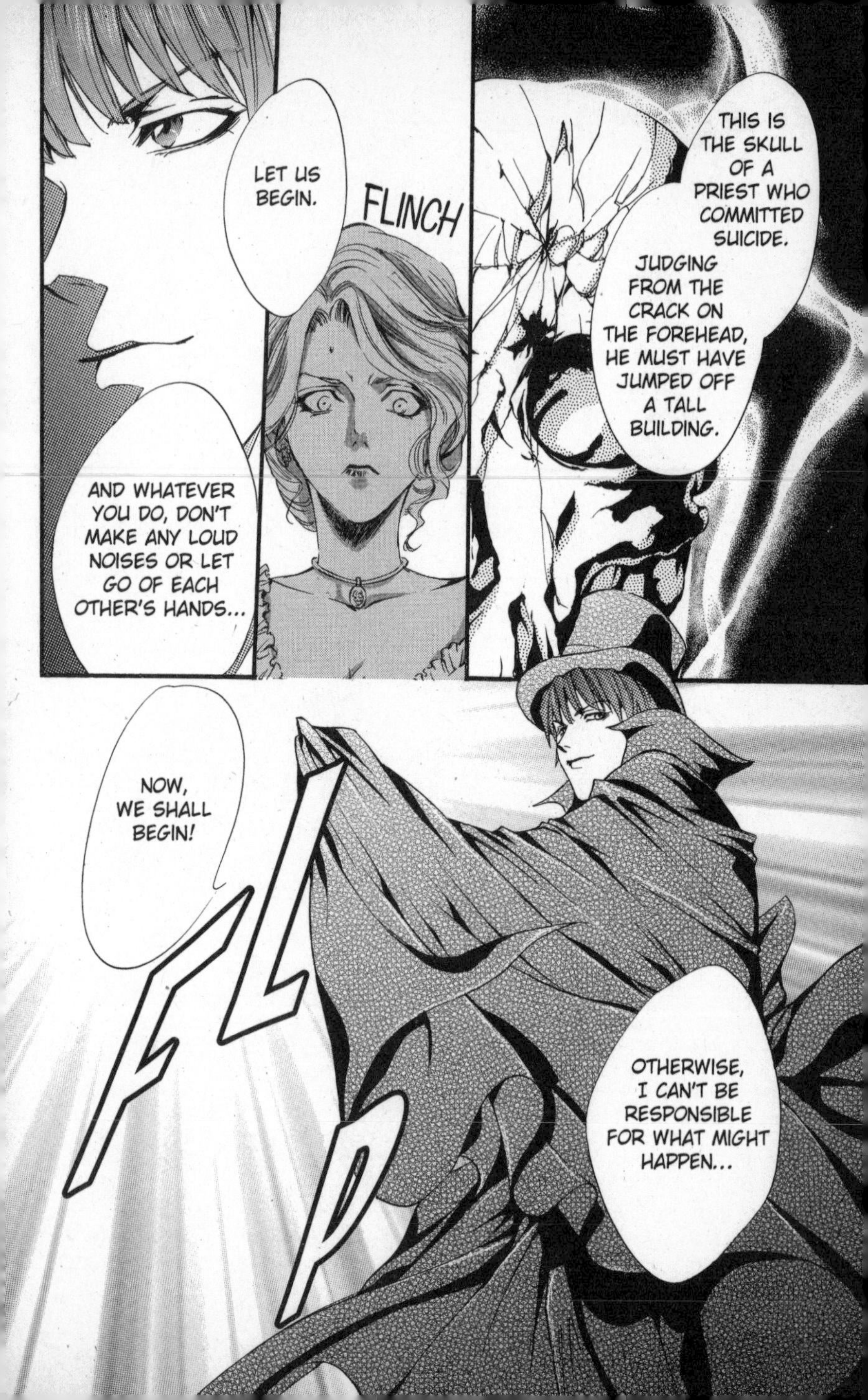

THIS IS THE SKULL OF A PRIEST WHO COMMITTED SUICIDE.
JUDGING FROM THE CRACK ON THE FOREHEAD, HE MUST HAVE JUMPED OFF A TALL BUILDING.
FLINCH
LET US BEGIN.
AND WHATEVER YOU DO, DON'T MAKE ANY LOUD NOISES OR LET GO OF EACH OTHER'S HANDS...
OTHERWISE, I CAN'T BE RESPONSIBLE FOR WHAT MIGHT HAPPEN...
FLIP
NOW, WE SHALL BEGIN!

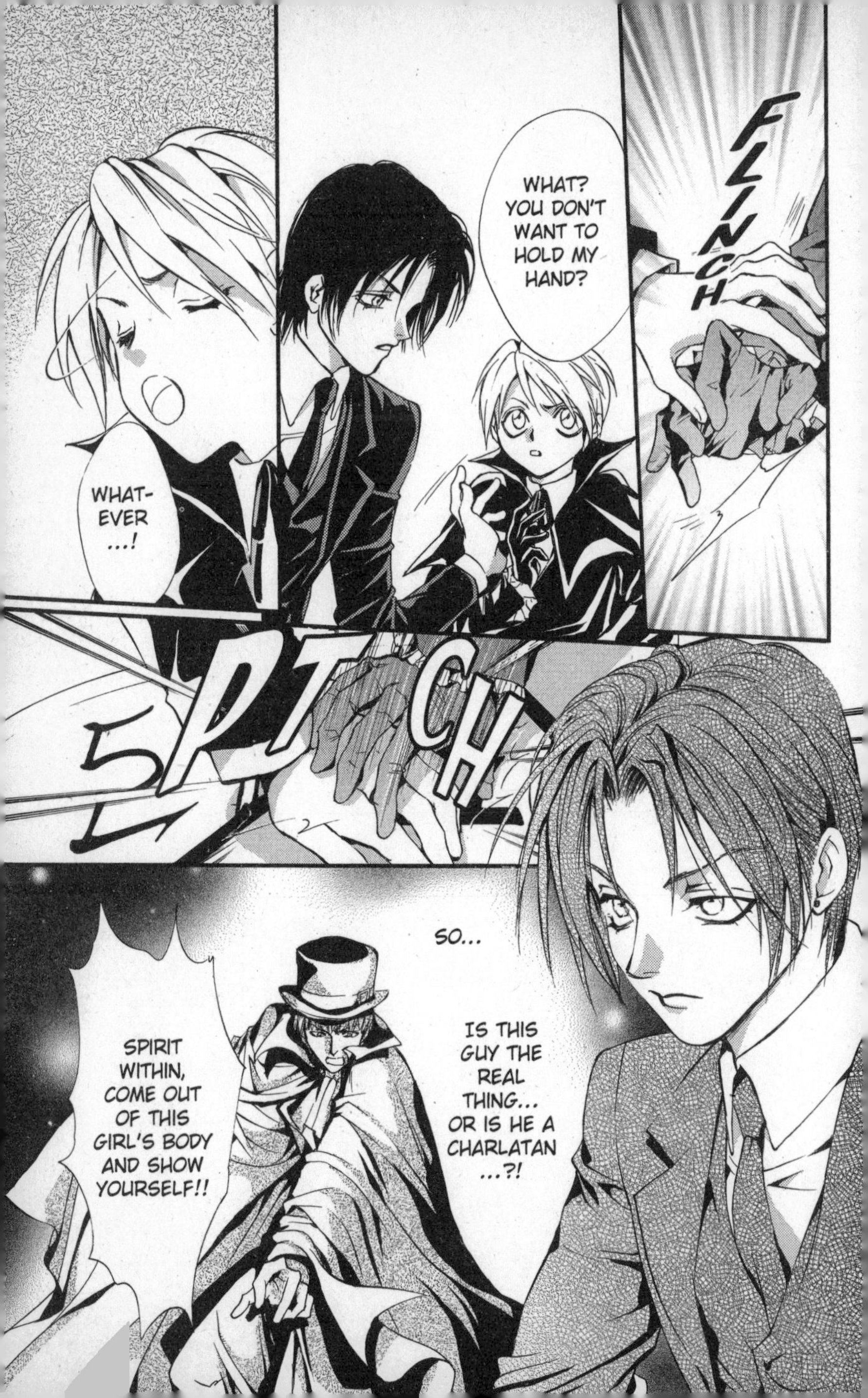
FLINCH
WHAT? YOU DON'T WANT TO HOLD MY HAND?
WHAT-EVER ...!
SPITCH
SO...
IS THIS GUY THE REAL THING... OR IS HE A CHARLATAN ...?!
SPIRIT WITHIN, COME OUT OF THIS GIRL'S BODY AND SHOW YOURSELF!!

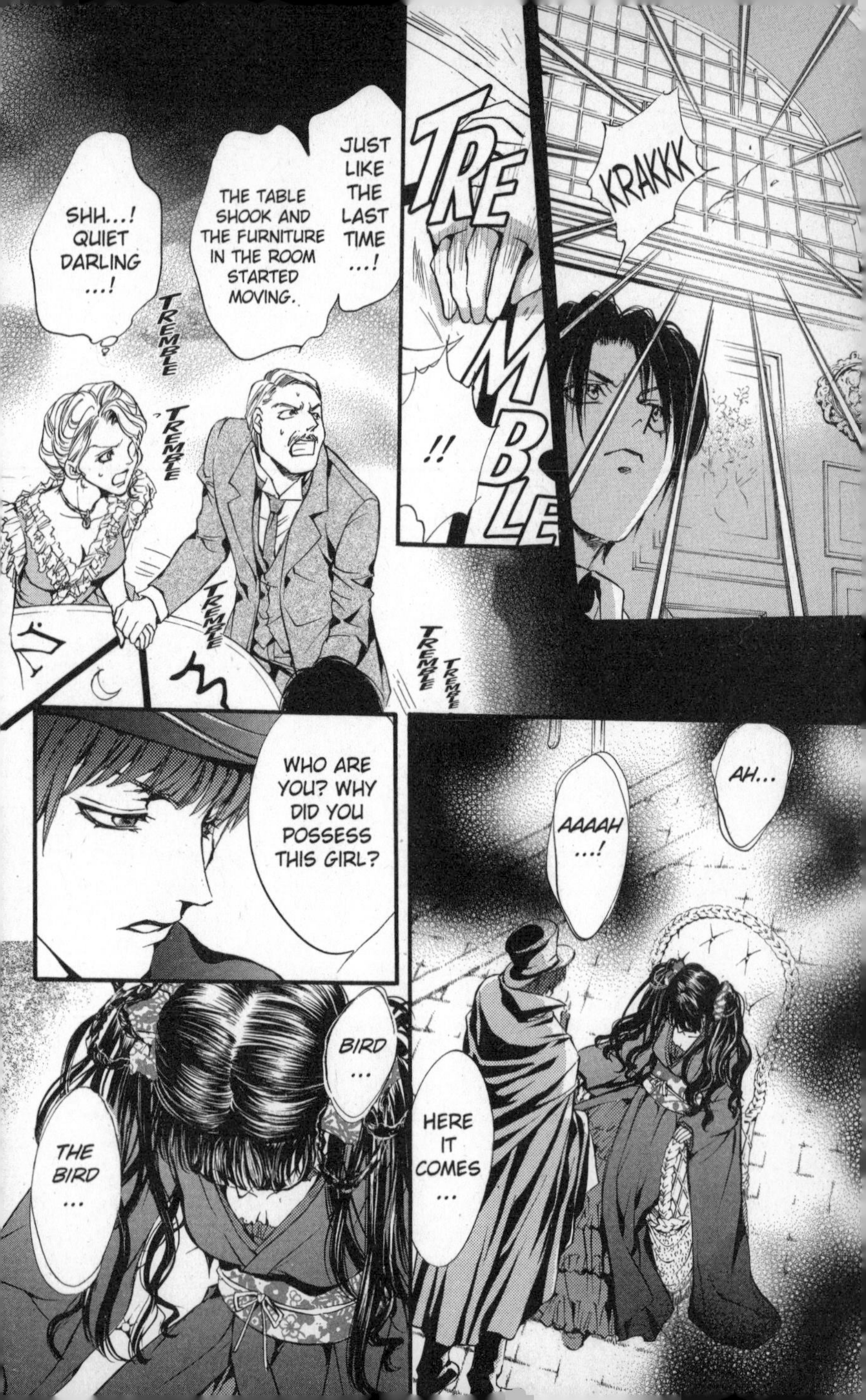
KRAKKK
TREMBLE
!!
JUST LIKE THE LAST TIME ...!
THE TABLE SHOOK AND THE FURNITURE IN THE ROOM STARTED MOVING.
SHH...! QUIET DARLING ...!
TREMBLE
TREMBLE
TREMBLE
TREMBLE
TREMBLE
AH...
AAAAH ...!
HERE IT COMES ...
WHO ARE YOU? WHY DID YOU POSSESS THIS GIRL?
BIRD ...
THE BIRD ...

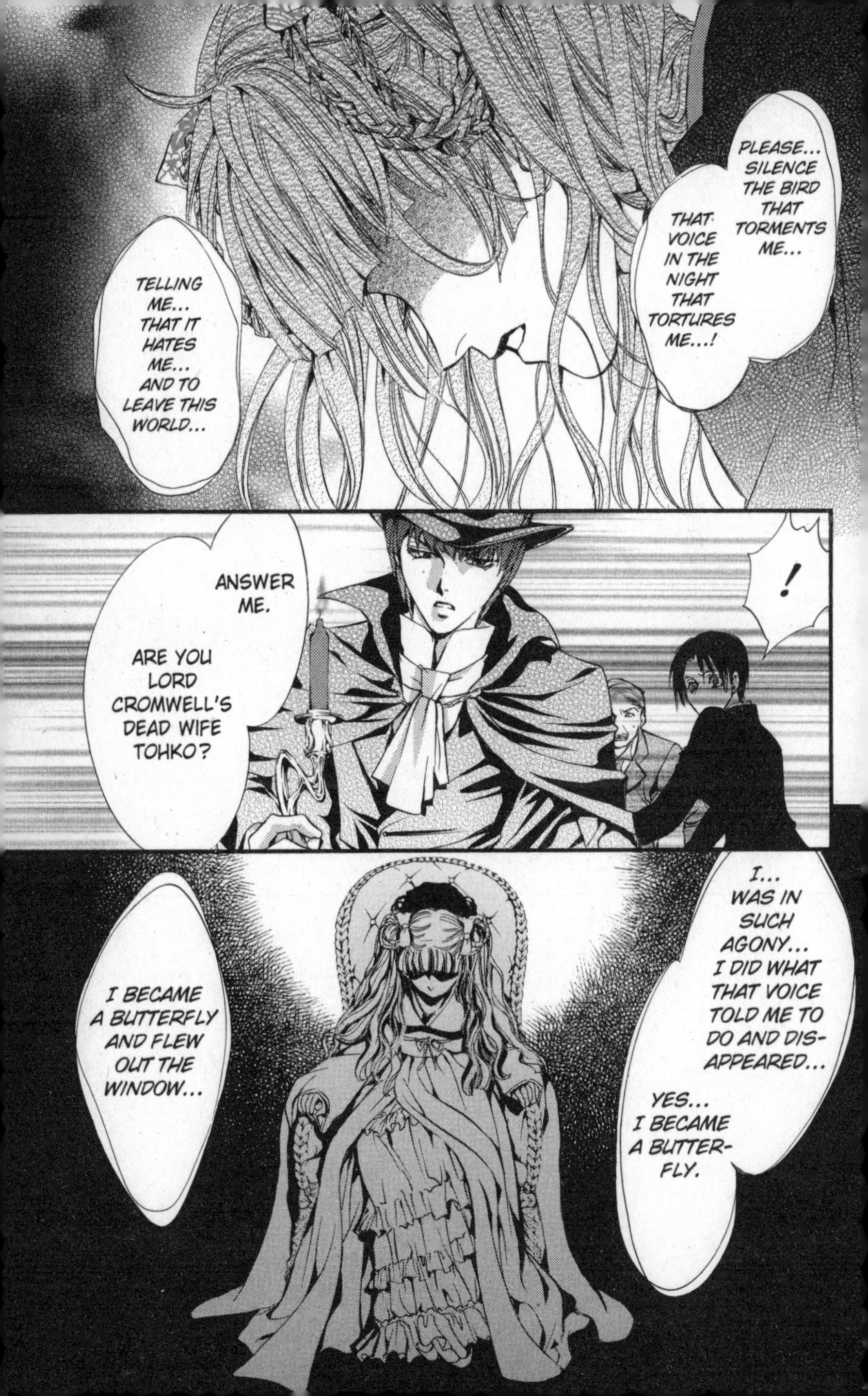
PLEASE... SILENCE THE BIRD THAT TORMENTS ME...
THAT VOICE IN THE NIGHT THAT TORTURES ME...!
TELLING ME... THAT IT HATES ME... AND TO LEAVE THIS WORLD...
!
ANSWER ME.
ARE YOU LORD CROMWELL'S DEAD WIFE TOHKO?
I... WAS IN SUCH AGONY... I DID WHAT THAT VOICE TOLD ME TO DO AND DISAPPEARED...
YES... I BECAME A BUTTERFLY.
I BECAME A BUTTERFLY AND FLEW OUT THE WINDOW...

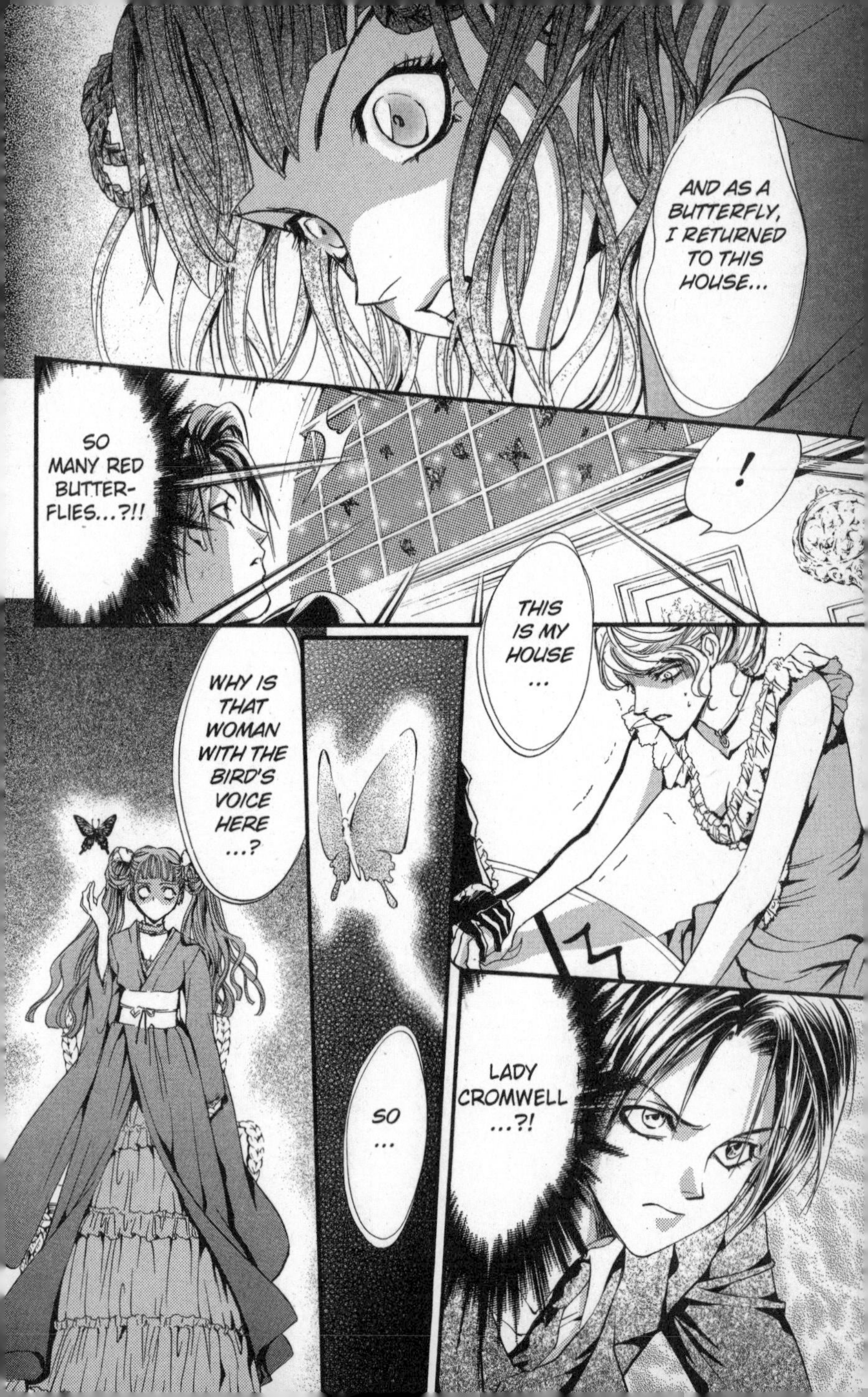
AND AS A BUTTERFLY, I RETURNED TO THIS HOUSE...
!
SO MANY RED BUTTER-FLIES...?!!
THIS IS MY HOUSE ...
LADY CROMWELL ...?!
SO ...
WHY IS THAT WOMAN WITH THE BIRD'S VOICE HERE ...?

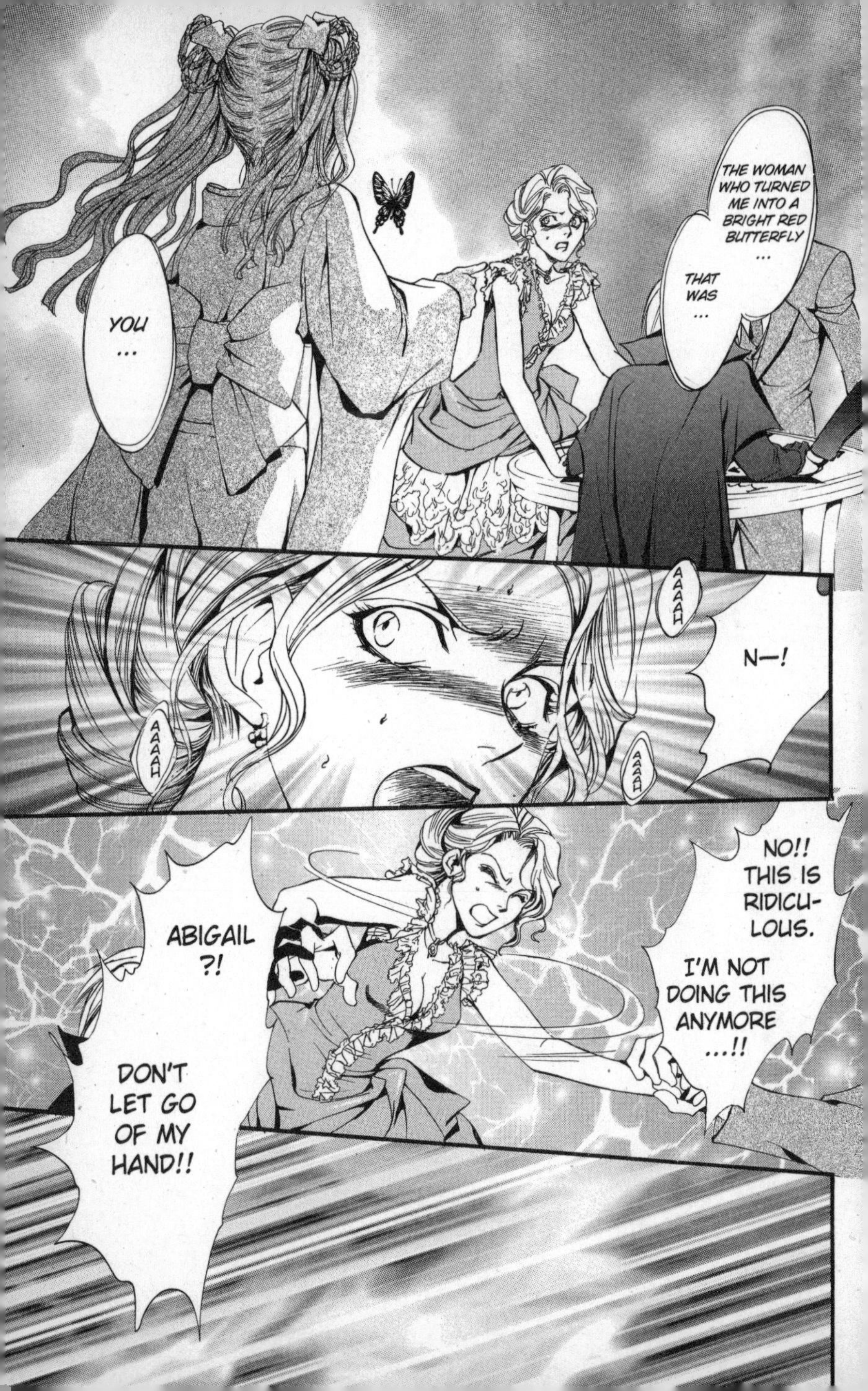
THE WOMAN WHO TURNED ME INTO A BRIGHT RED BUTTERFLY ...
THAT WAS ...
YOU ...
AAAAH
N—!
AAAAH
AAAAH
NO!! THIS IS RIDICU-LOUS.
I'M NOT DOING THIS ANYMORE ...!!
ABIGAIL ?!
DON'T LET GO OF MY HAND!!

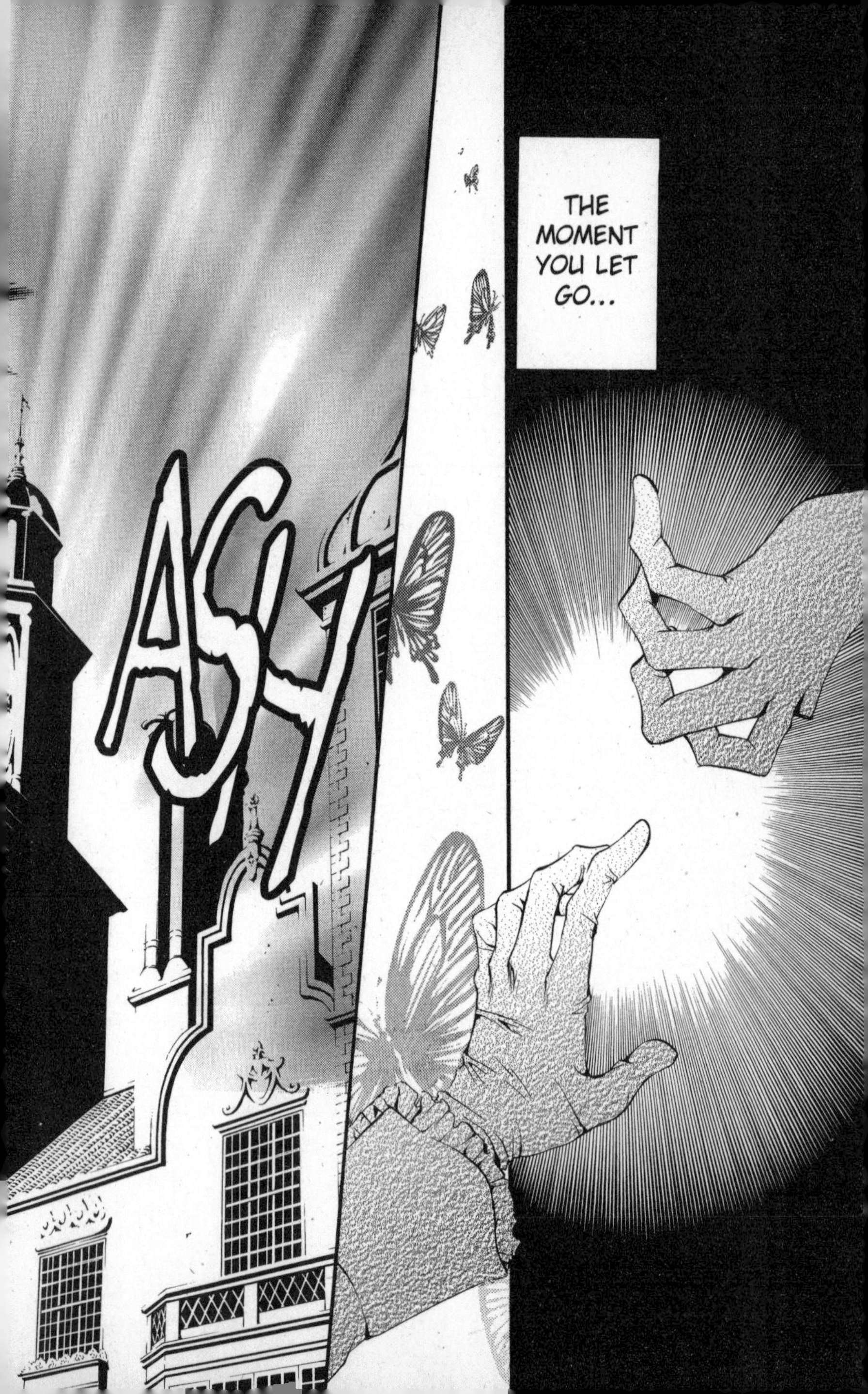
THE MOMENT YOU LET GO...
ASH

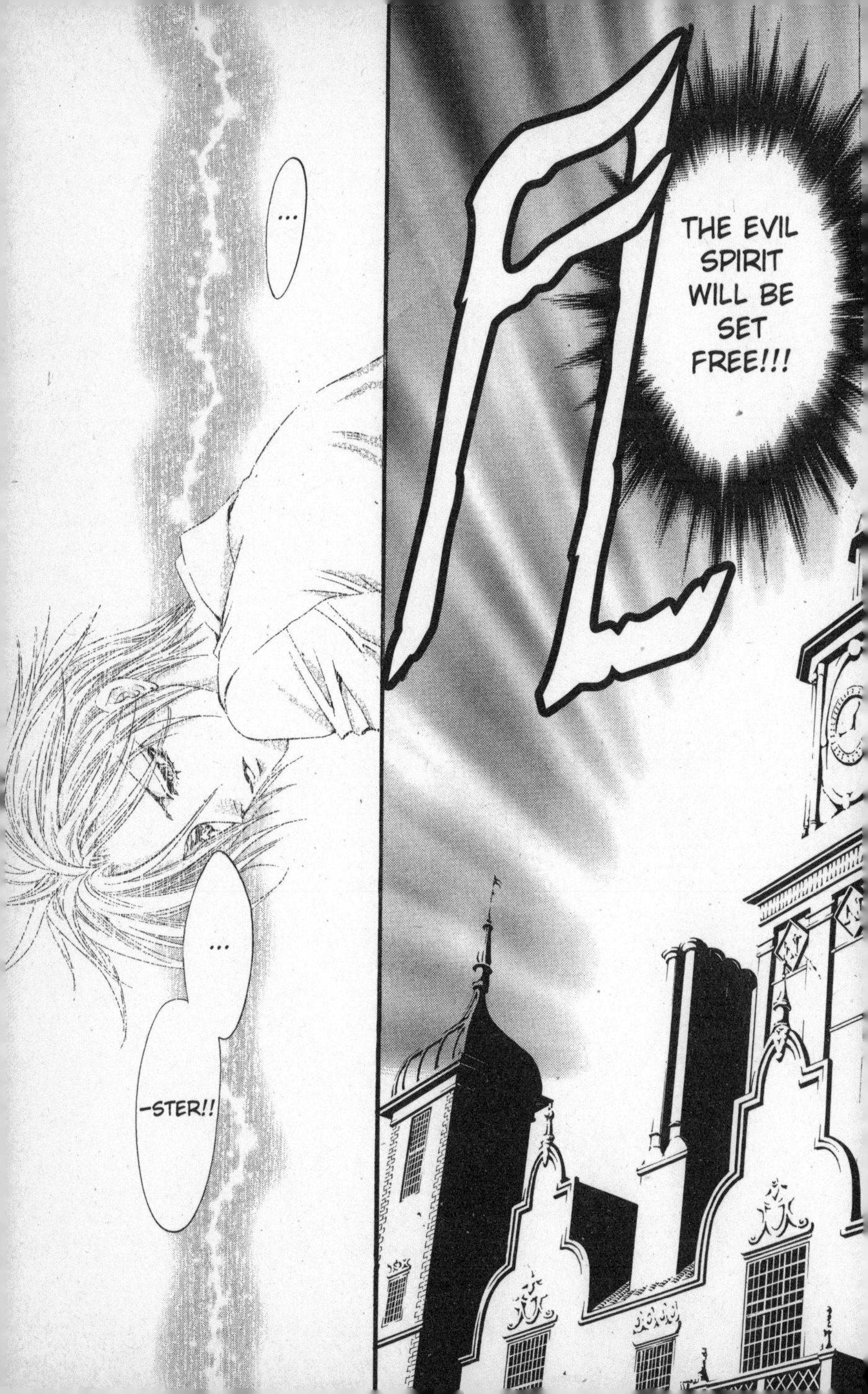
THE EVIL SPIRIT WILL BE SET FREE!!!
...
...
-STER!!

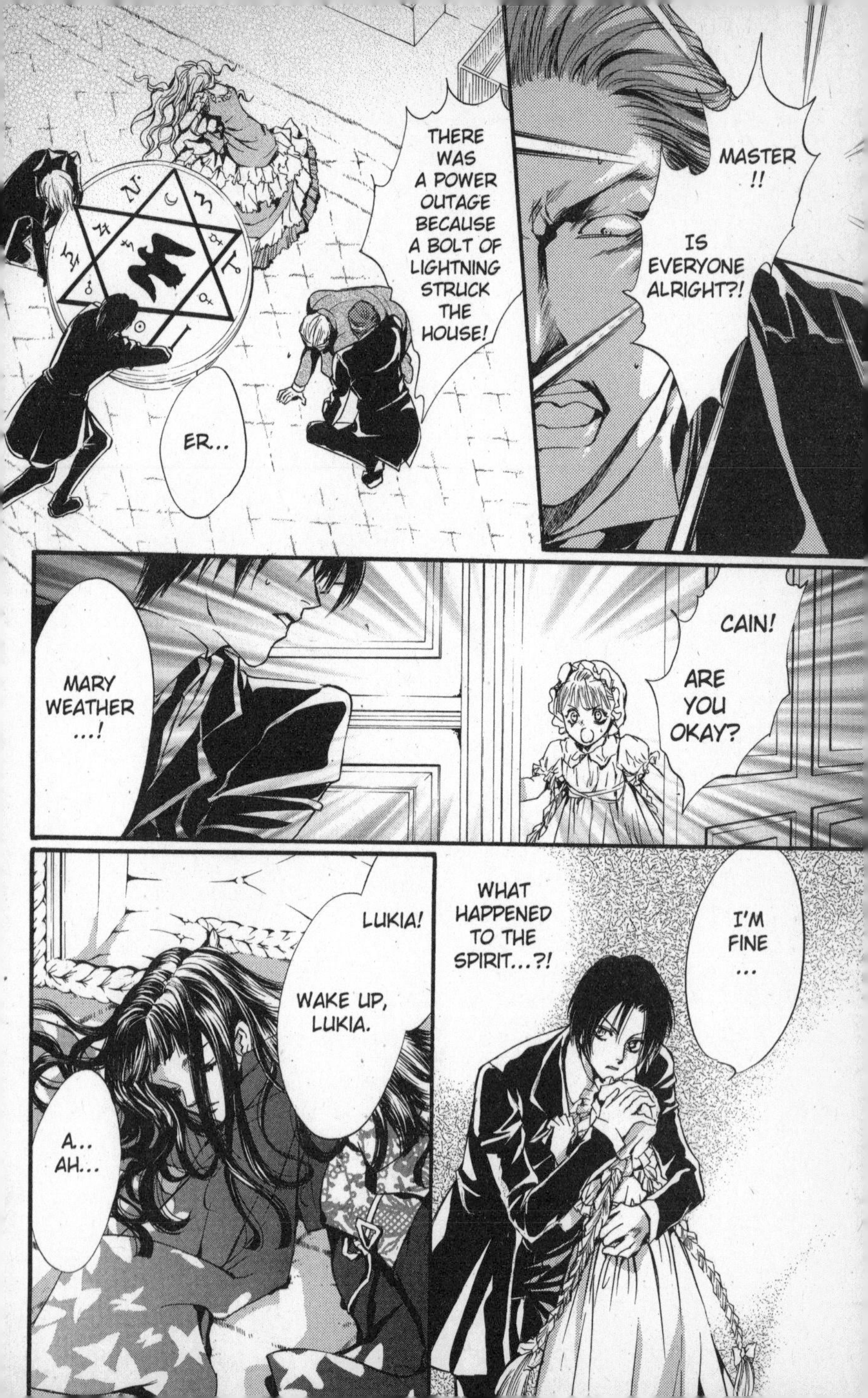
MASTER !!
IS EVERYONE ALRIGHT?!
THERE WAS A POWER OUTAGE BECAUSE A BOLT OF LIGHTNING STRUCK THE HOUSE!
ER...
CAIN!
ARE YOU OKAY?
MARY WEATHER ...!
I'M FINE ...
WHAT HAPPENED TO THE SPIRIT...?!
LUKIA!
WAKE UP, LUKIA.
A... AH...

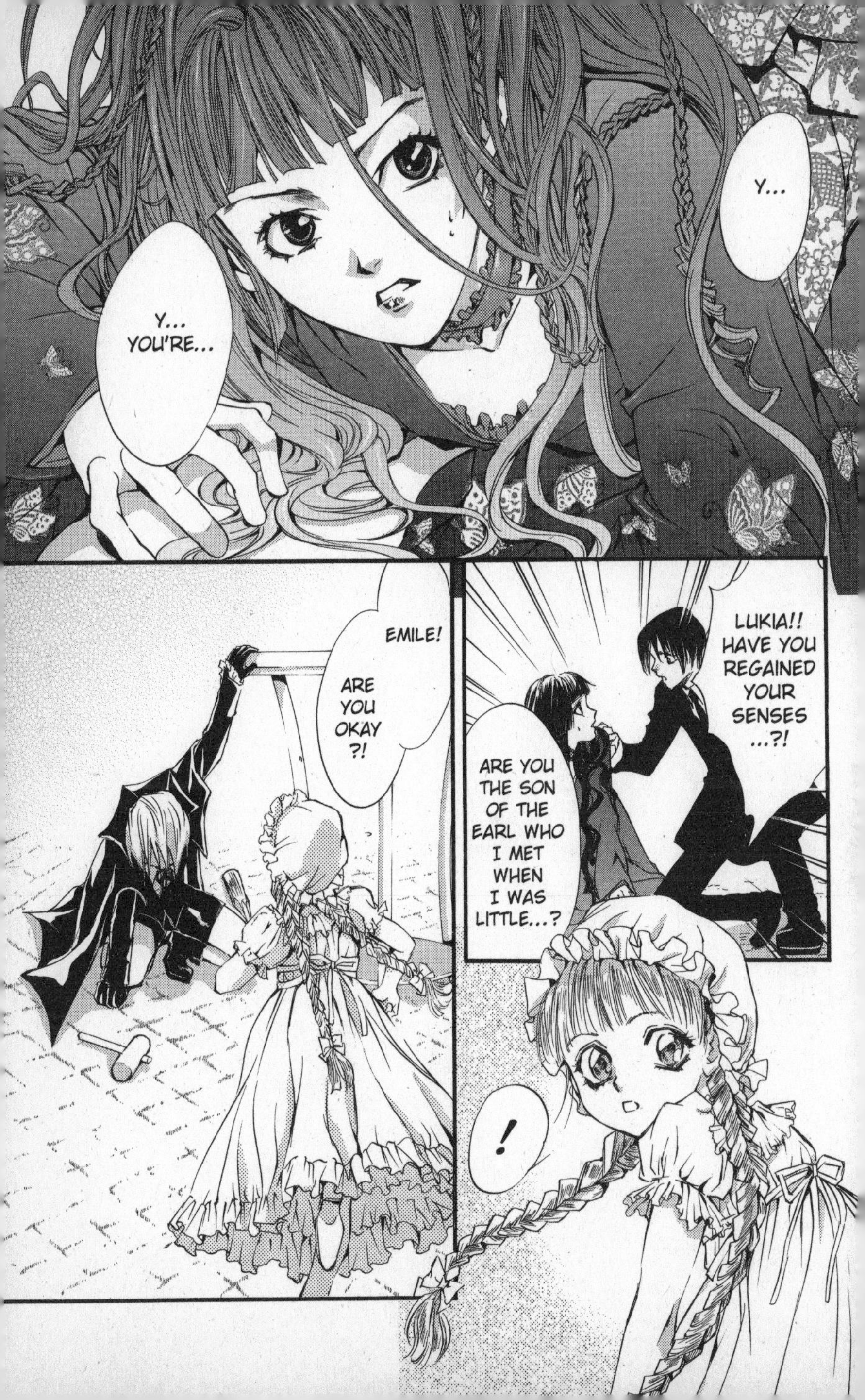
Y...
Y... YOU'RE...
LUKIA!! HAVE YOU REGAINED YOUR SENSES ...?!
ARE YOU THE SON OF THE EARL WHO I MET WHEN I WAS LITTLE...?
!
EMILE!
ARE YOU OKAY ?!

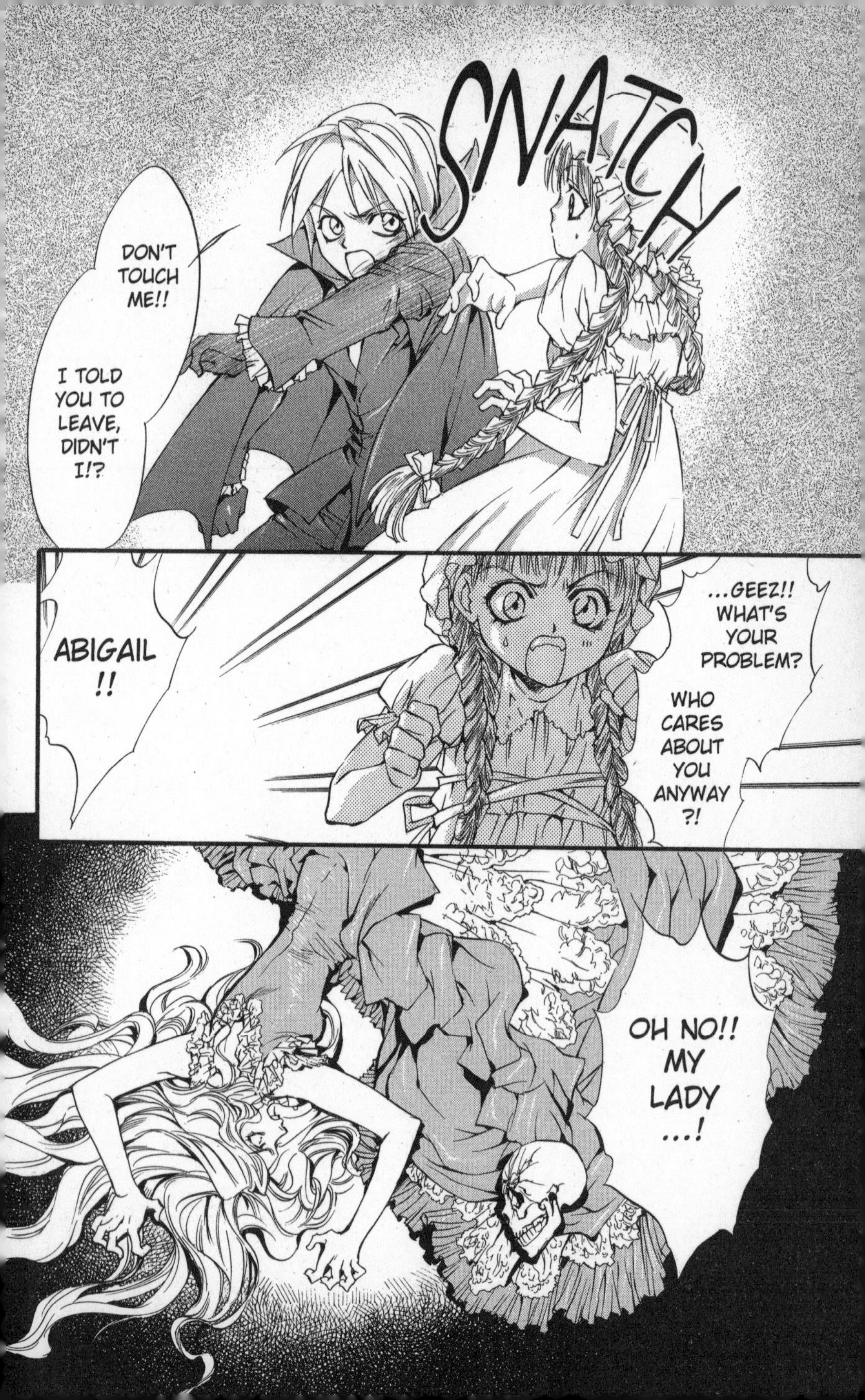
SNATCH
DON'T TOUCH ME!!
I TOLD YOU TO LEAVE, DIDN'T I!?
...GEEZ!! WHAT'S YOUR PROBLEM?
WHO CARES ABOUT YOU ANYWAY ?!
ABIGAIL !!
OH NO!! MY LADY ...!

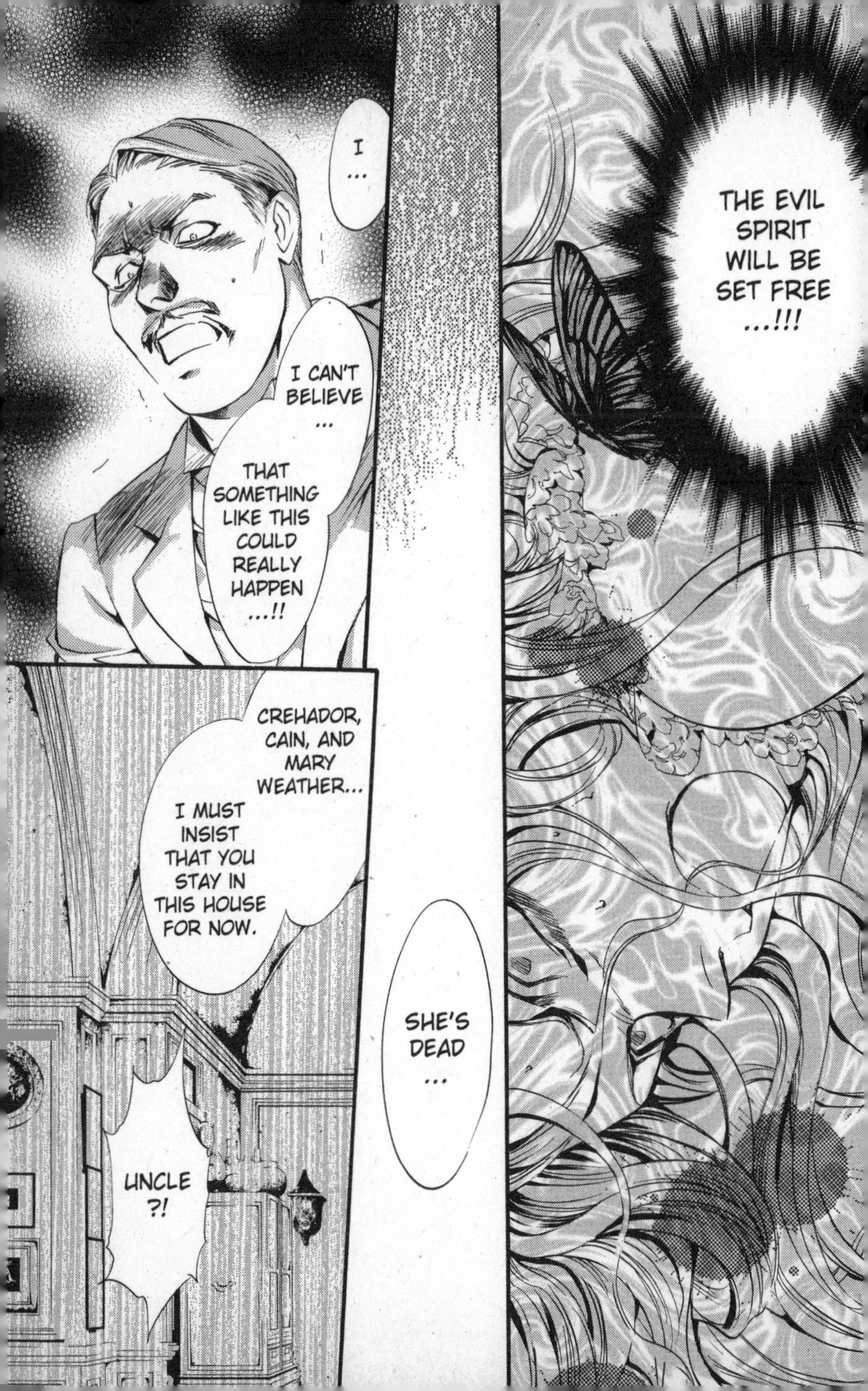
THE EVIL SPIRIT WILL BE SET FREE ...!!!
SHE'S DEAD ...
I ...
I CAN'T BELIEVE ...
THAT SOMETHING LIKE THIS COULD REALLY HAPPEN ...!!
CREHADOR, CAIN, AND MARY WEATHER...
I MUST INSIST THAT YOU STAY IN THIS HOUSE FOR NOW.
UNCLE ?!

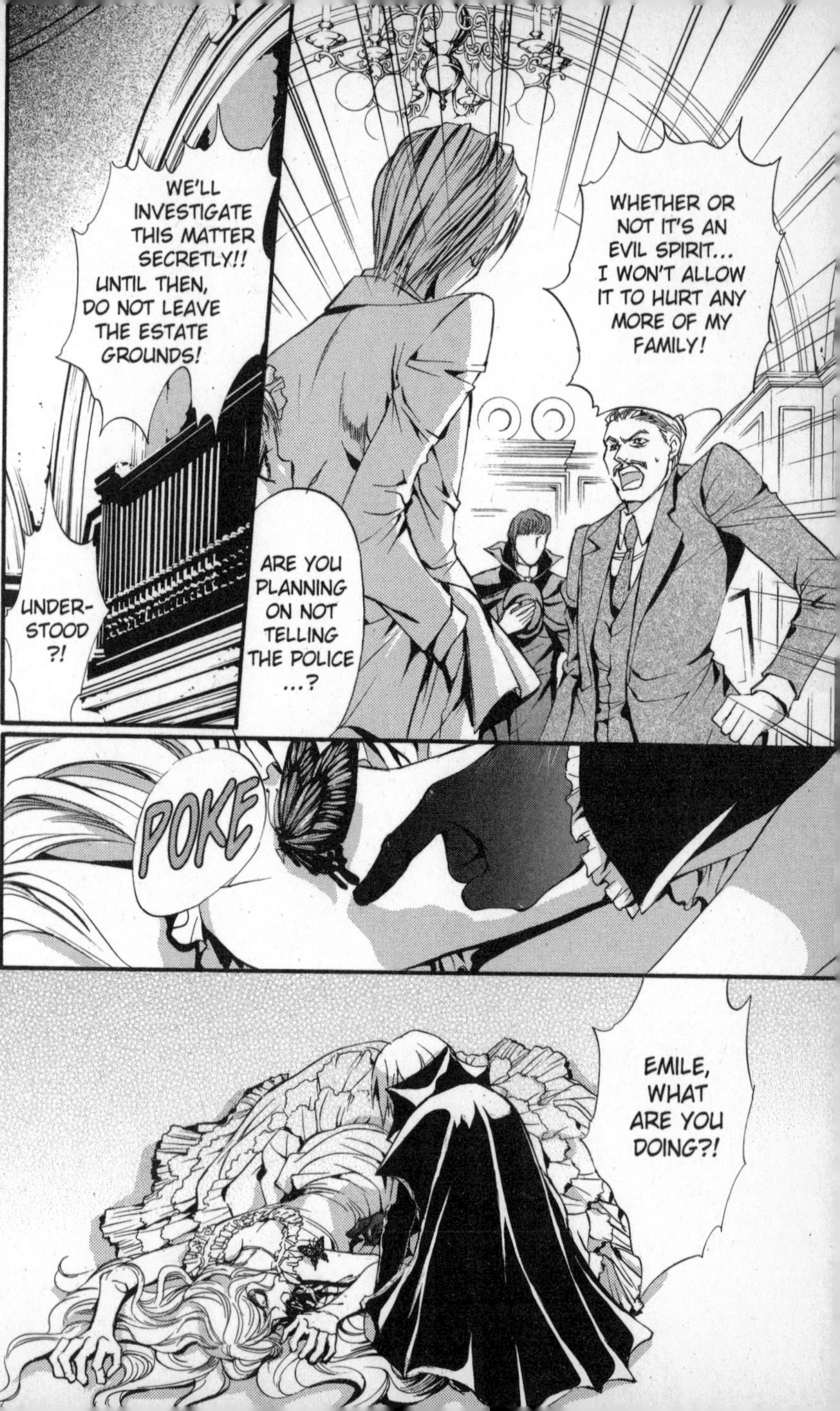
WHETHER OR NOT IT'S AN EVIL SPIRIT... I WON'T ALLOW IT TO HURT ANY MORE OF MY FAMILY!
WE'LL INVESTIGATE THIS MATTER SECRETLY!! UNTIL THEN, DO NOT LEAVE THE ESTATE GROUNDS!
ARE YOU PLANNING ON NOT TELLING THE POLICE ...?
UNDER-STOOD ?!
POKE
EMILE, WHAT ARE YOU DOING?!

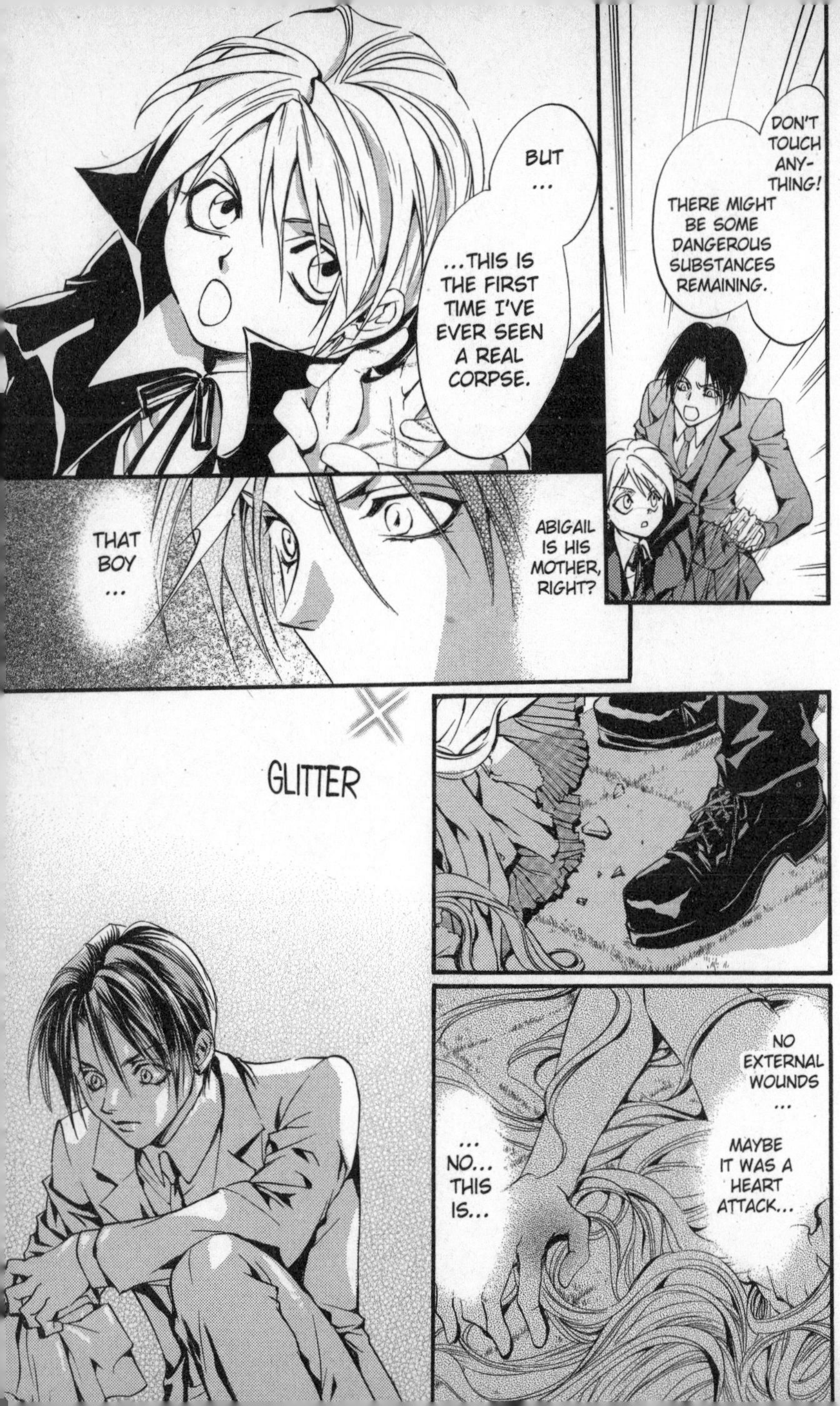
DON'T TOUCH ANY-THING!
THERE MIGHT BE SOME DANGEROUS SUBSTANCES REMAINING.
ABIGAIL IS HIS MOTHER, RIGHT?
BUT ...
...THIS IS THE FIRST TIME I'VE EVER SEEN A REAL CORPSE.
THAT BOY ...
NO EXTERNAL WOUNDS ...
MAYBE IT WAS A HEART ATTACK...
... NO... THIS IS...
GLITTER

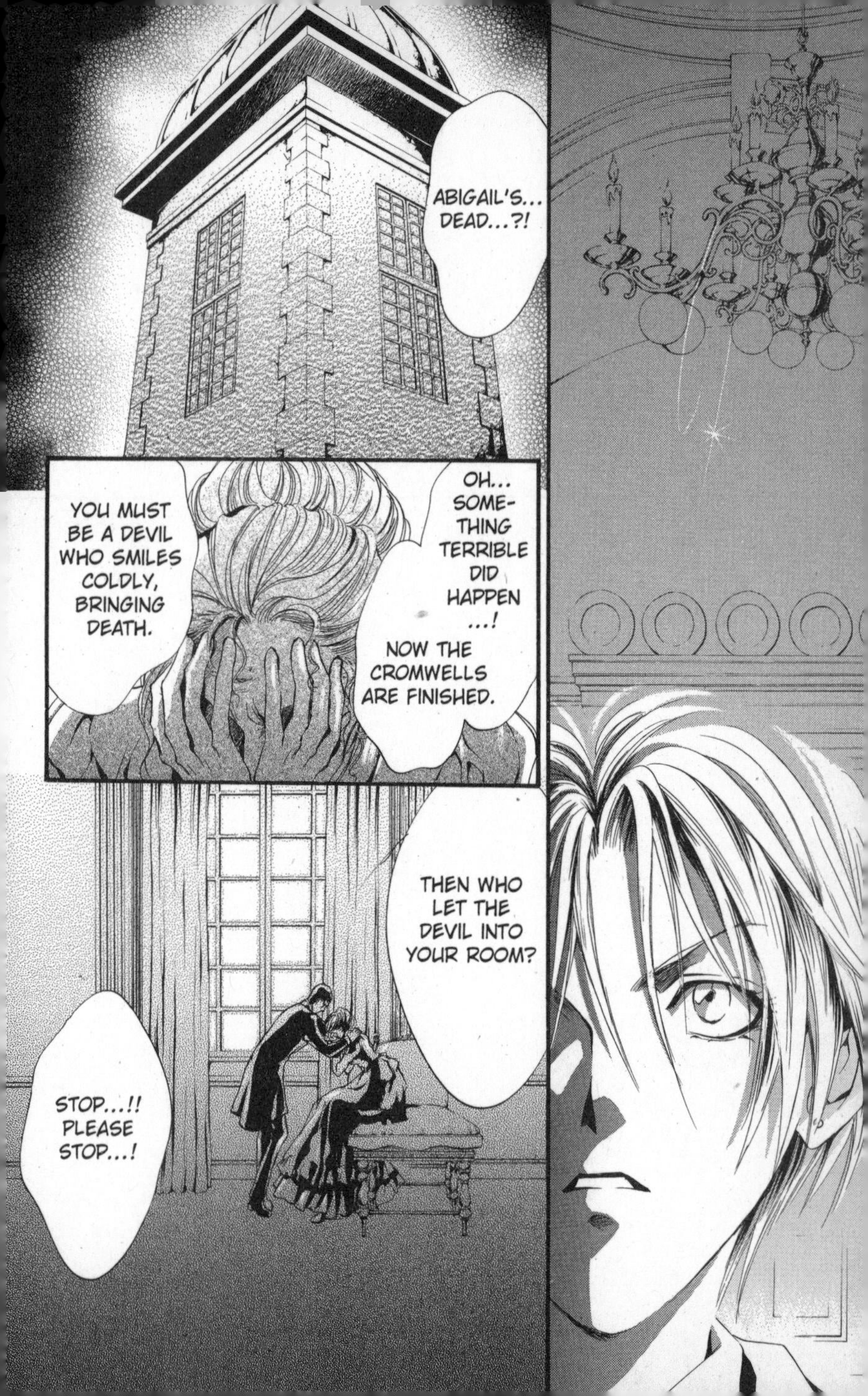
ABIGAIL'S... DEAD...?!
OH... SOME-THING TERRIBLE DID HAPPEN ...!
NOW THE CROMWELLS ARE FINISHED.
YOU MUST BE A DEVIL WHO SMILES COLDLY, BRINGING DEATH.
THEN WHO LET THE DEVIL INTO YOUR ROOM?
STOP...!! PLEASE STOP...!

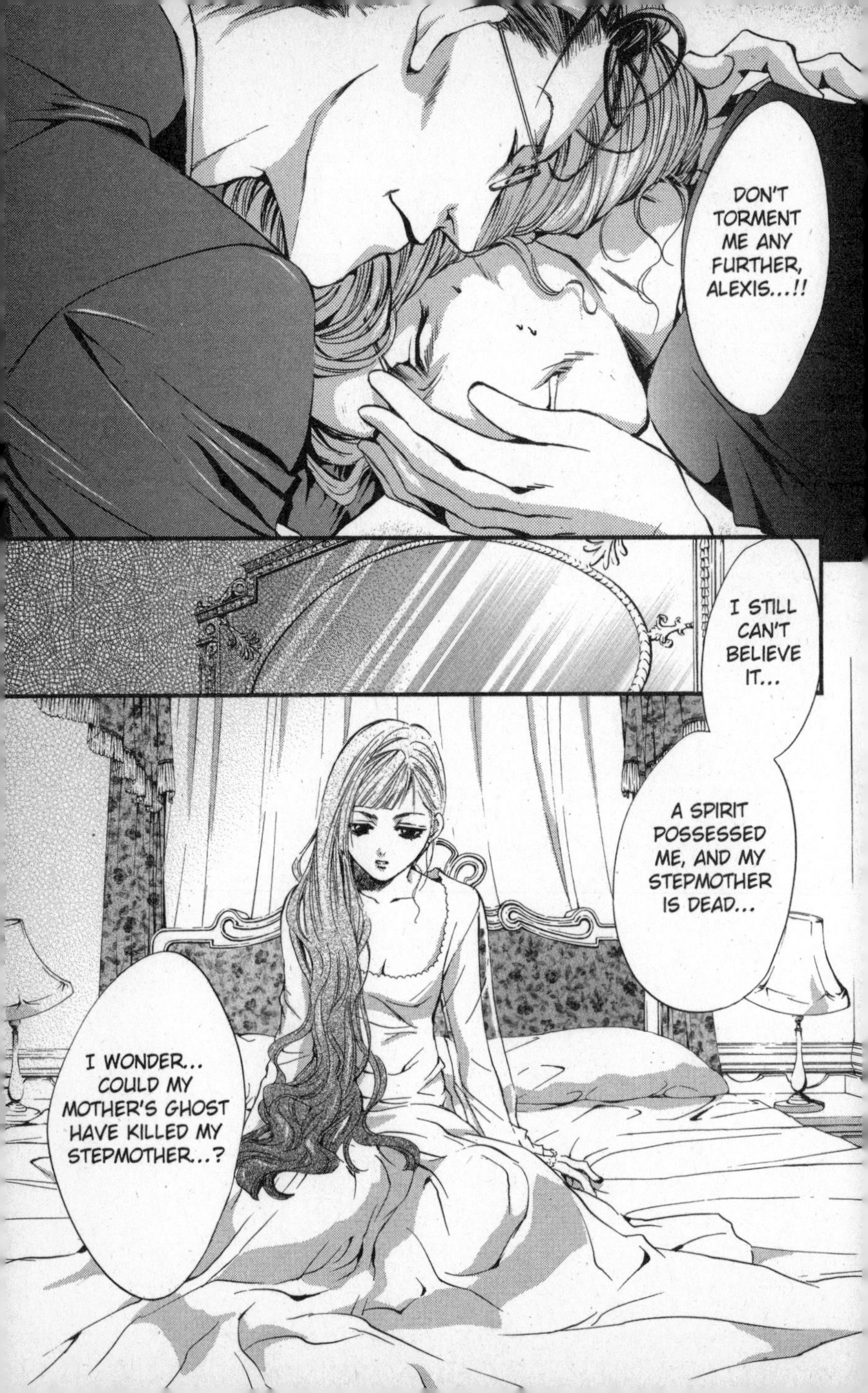
DON'T TORMENT ME ANY FURTHER, ALEXIS...!!
I STILL CAN'T BELIEVE IT...
A SPIRIT POSSESSED ME, AND MY STEPMOTHER IS DEAD...
I WONDER... COULD MY MOTHER'S GHOST HAVE KILLED MY STEPMOTHER...?

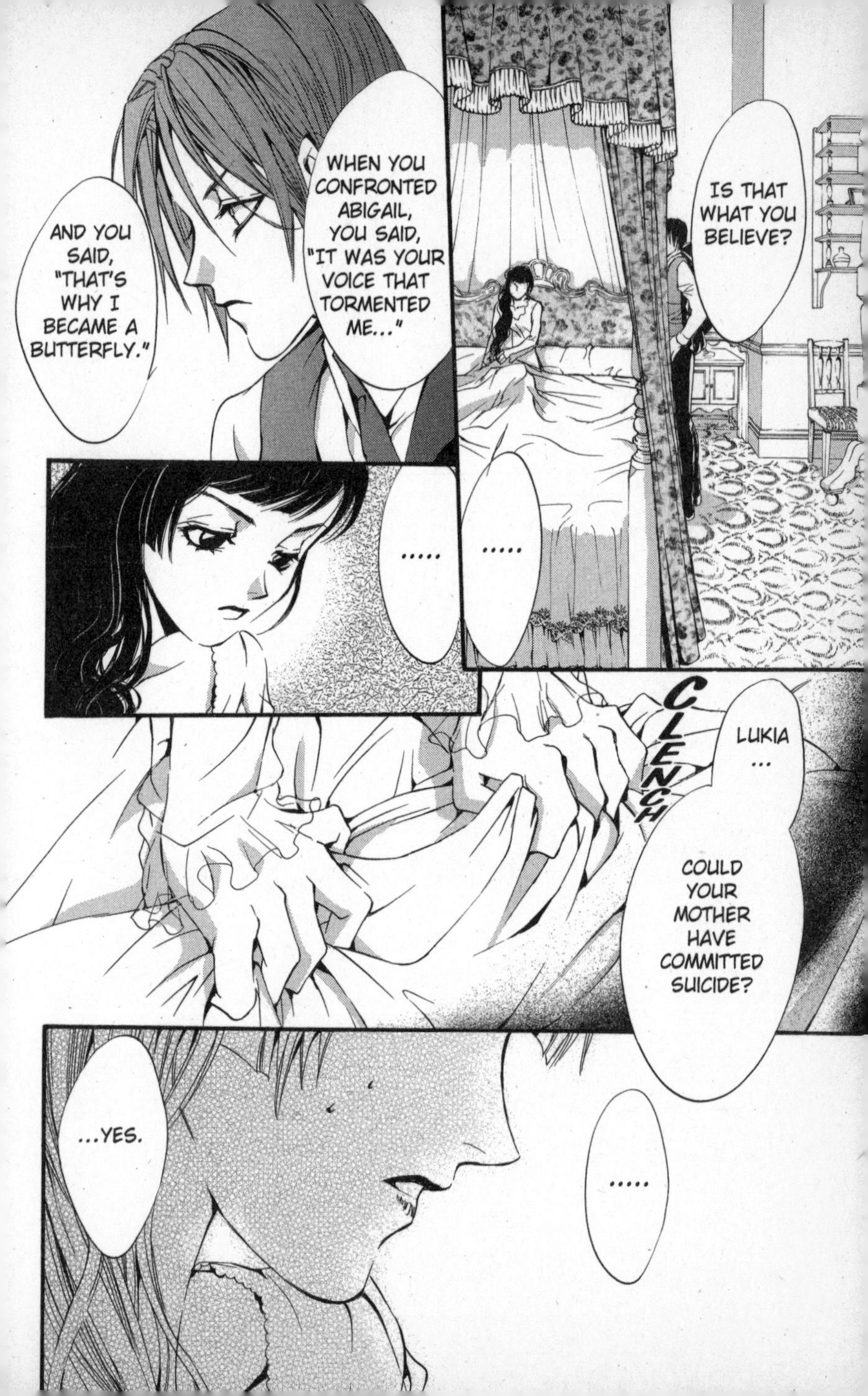
IS THAT WHAT YOU BELIEVE?
.....
WHEN YOU CONFRONTED ABIGAIL, YOU SAID, "IT WAS YOUR VOICE THAT TORMENTED ME..."
AND YOU SAID, "THAT'S WHY I BECAME A BUTTERFLY."
.....
CLENCH
LUKIA ... COULD YOUR MOTHER HAVE COMMITTED SUICIDE?
.....
...YES.

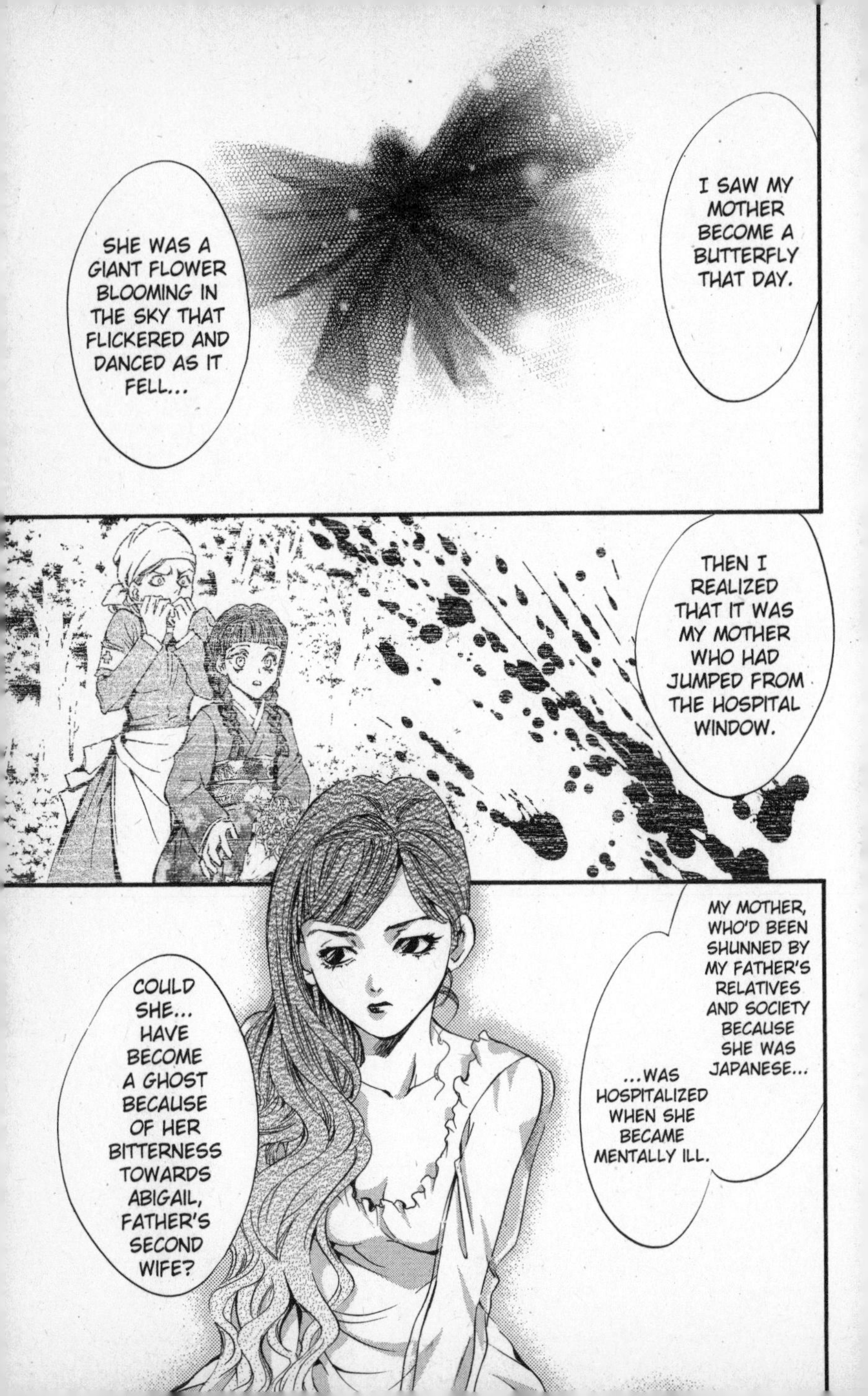
I SAW MY MOTHER BECOME A BUTTERFLY THAT DAY.
SHE WAS A GIANT FLOWER BLOOMING IN THE SKY THAT FLICKERED AND DANCED AS IT FELL...
THEN I REALIZED THAT IT WAS MY MOTHER WHO HAD JUMPED FROM THE HOSPITAL WINDOW.
MY MOTHER, WHO'D BEEN SHUNNED BY MY FATHER'S RELATIVES AND SOCIETY BECAUSE SHE WAS JAPANESE...
...WAS HOSPITALIZED WHEN SHE BECAME MENTALLY ILL.
COULD SHE... HAVE BECOME A GHOST BECAUSE OF HER BITTERNESS TOWARDS ABIGAIL, FATHER'S SECOND WIFE?

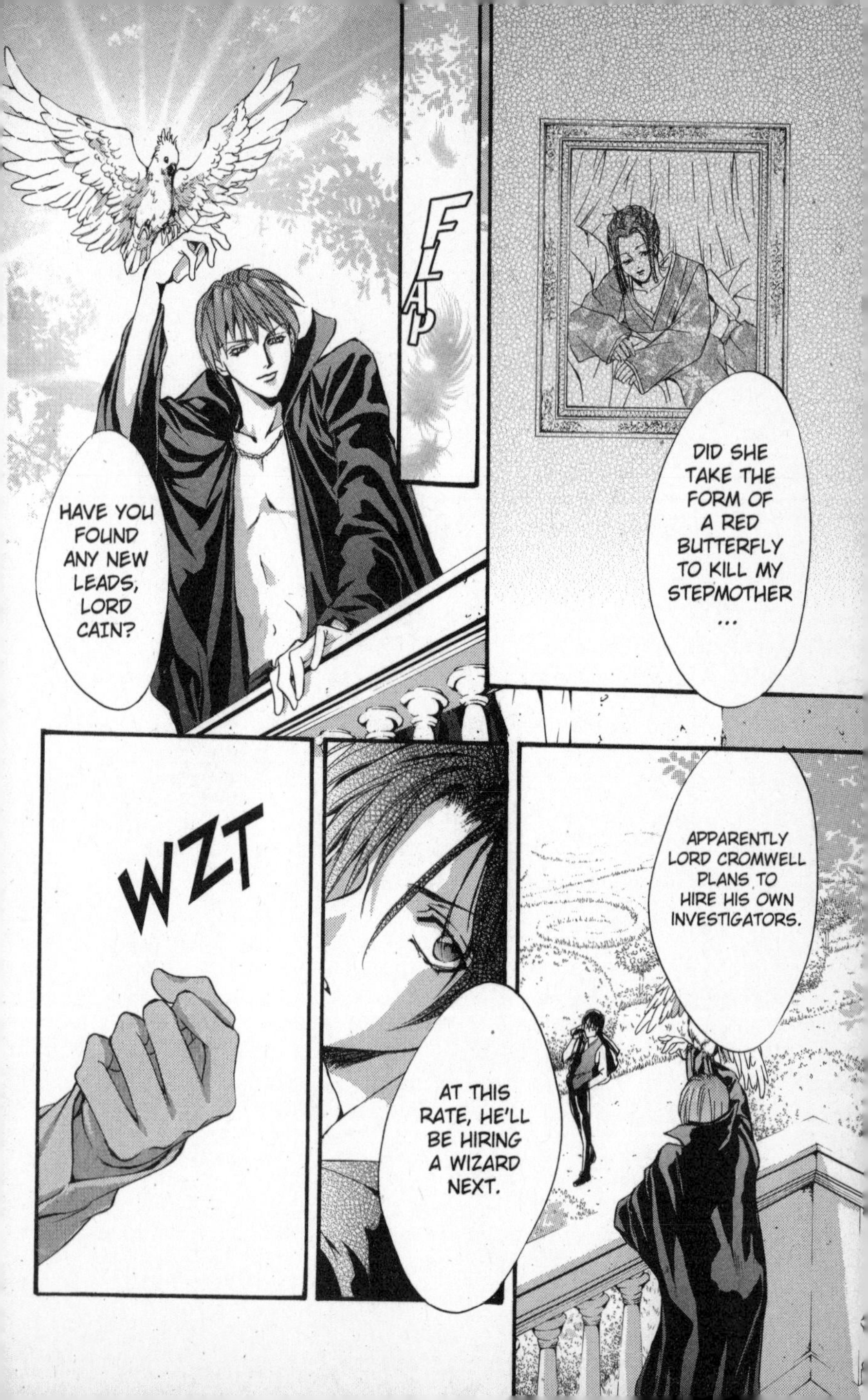
DID SHE TAKE THE FORM OF A RED BUTTERFLY TO KILL MY STEPMOTHER ...
FLAP
HAVE YOU FOUND ANY NEW LEADS, LORD CAIN?
APPARENTLY LORD CROMWELL PLANS TO HIRE HIS OWN INVESTIGATORS.
AT THIS RATE, HE'LL BE HIRING A WIZARD NEXT.
WZT

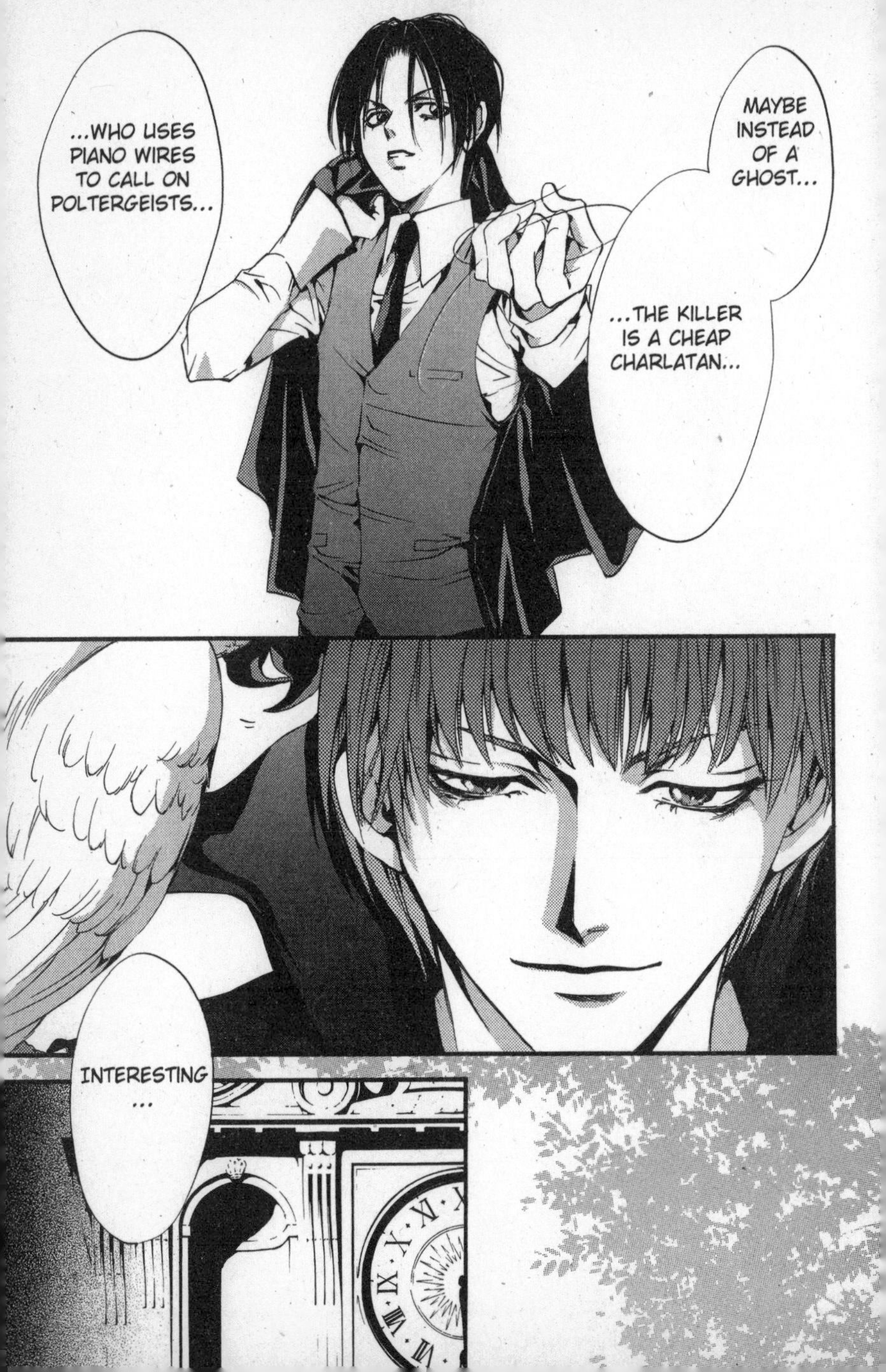
MAYBE INSTEAD OF A GHOST...
...THE KILLER IS A CHEAP CHARLATAN...
...WHO USES PIANO WIRES TO CALL ON POLTERGEISTS...
INTERESTING ...

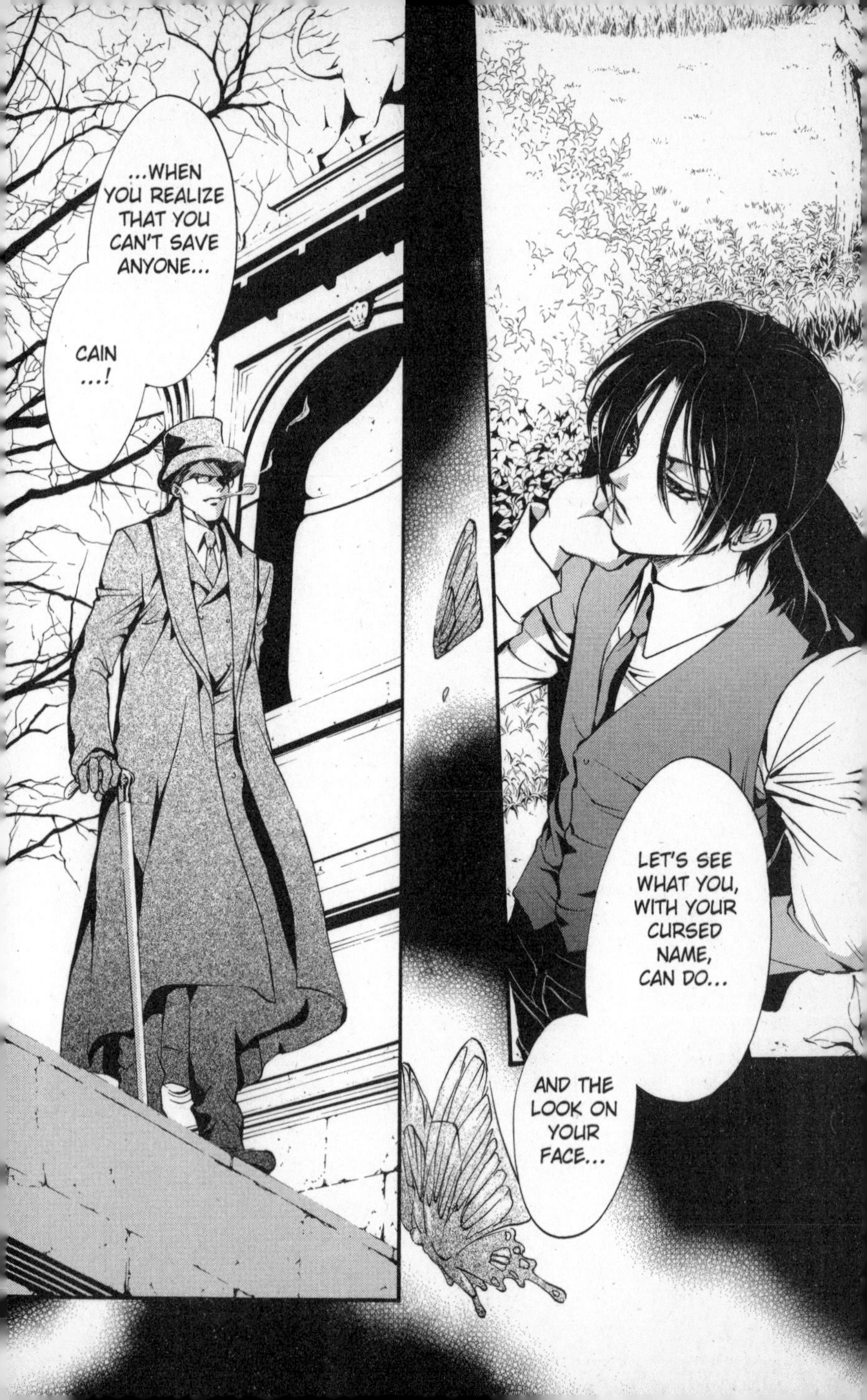
LET'S SEE WHAT YOU, WITH YOUR CURSED NAME, CAN DO...
AND THE LOOK ON YOUR FACE...
...WHEN YOU REALIZE THAT YOU CAN'T SAVE ANYONE...
CAIN ...!

Butterfly Bones
Scene 3

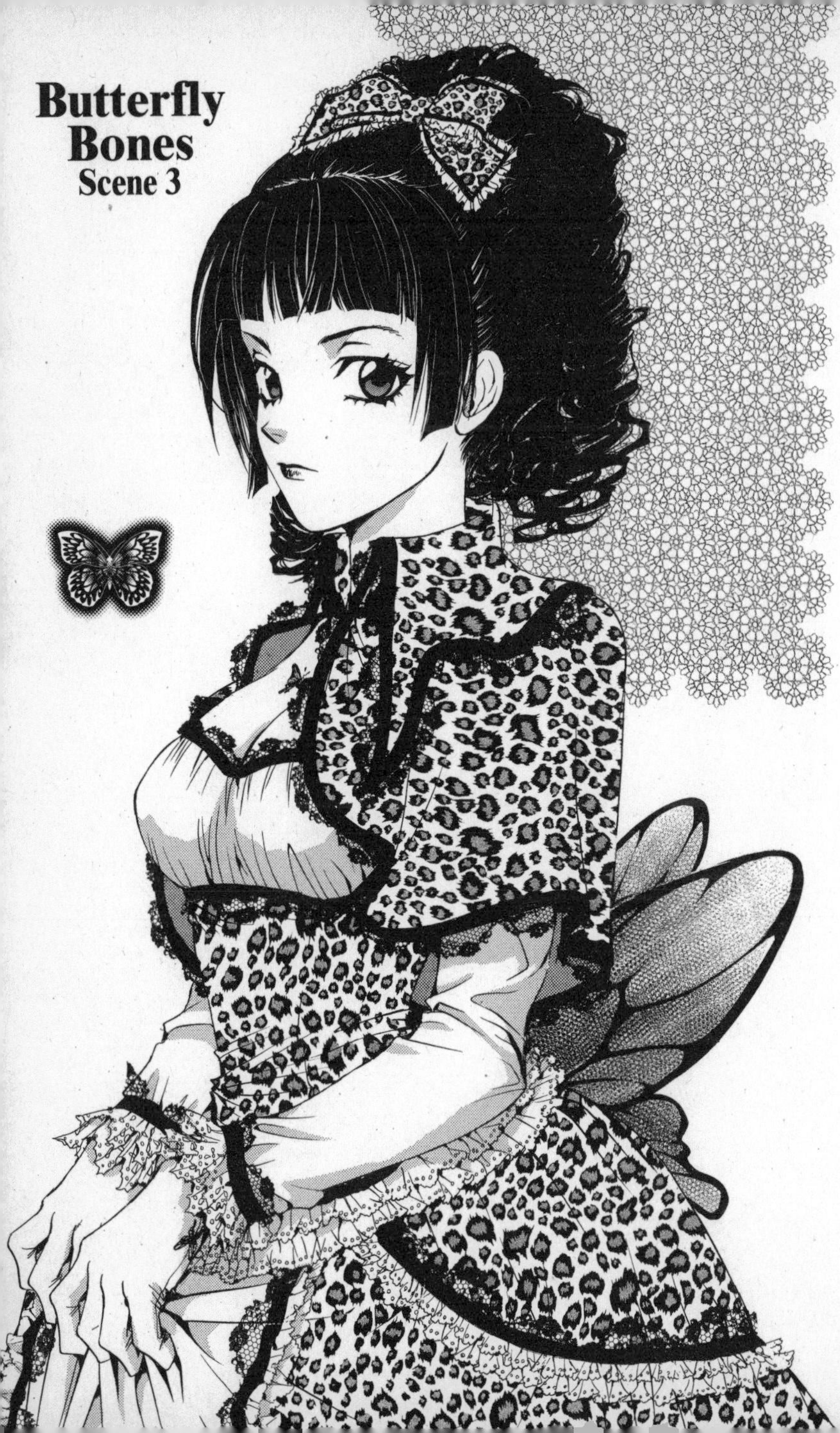

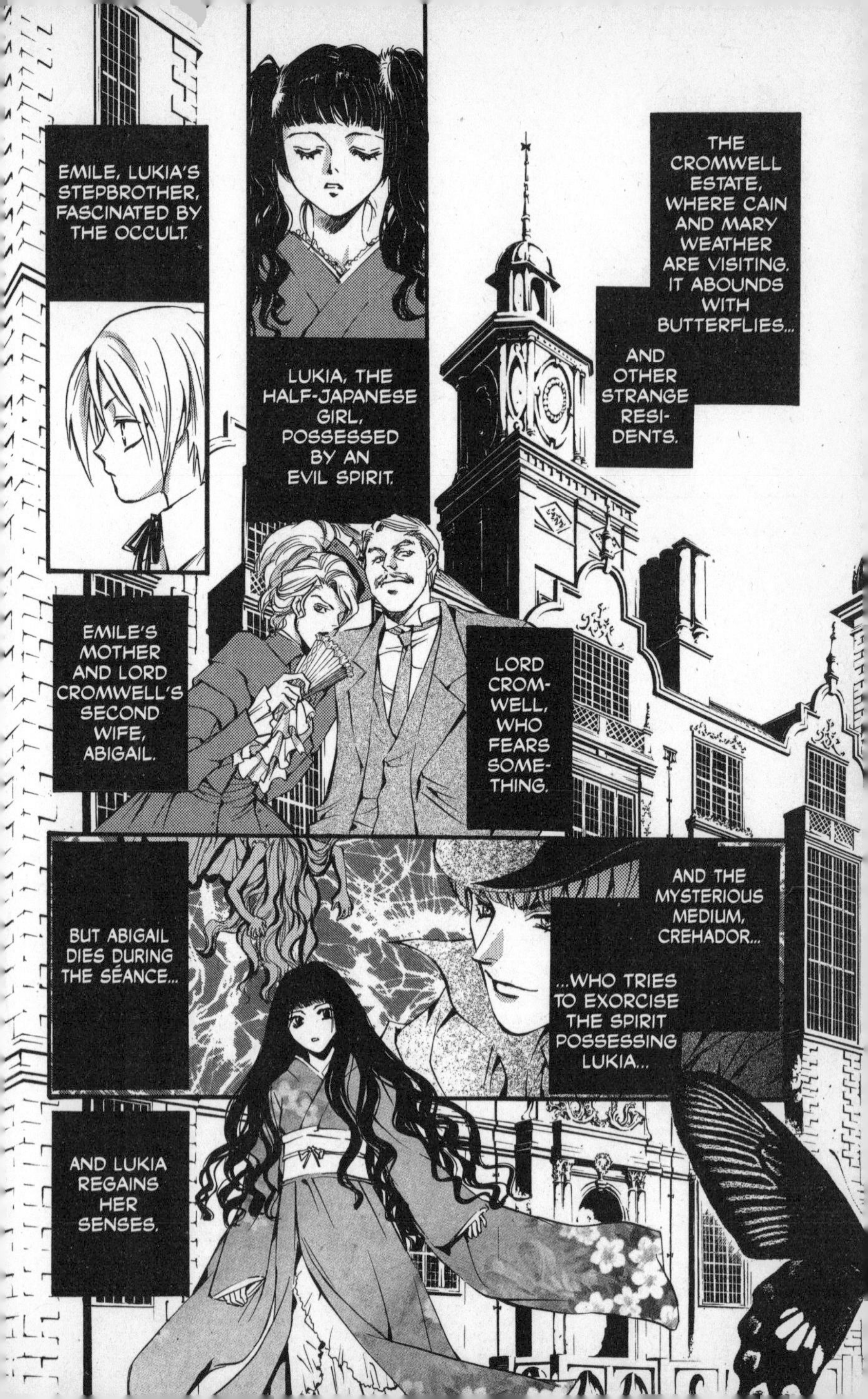
THE CROMWELL ESTATE, WHERE CAIN AND MARY WEATHER ARE VISITING. IT ABOUNDS WITH BUTTERFLIES...
AND OTHER STRANGE RESI-DENTS.
LUKIA, THE HALF-JAPANESE GIRL, POSSESSED BY AN EVIL SPIRIT.
EMILE, LUKIA'S STEPBROTHER, FASCINATED BY THE OCCULT.
LORD CROM-WELL, WHO FEARS SOME-THING.
EMILE'S MOTHER AND LORD CROMWELL'S SECOND WIFE, ABIGAIL.
AND THE MYSTERIOUS MEDIUM, CREHADOR...
...WHO TRIES TO EXORCISE THE SPIRIT POSSESSING LUKIA...
BUT ABIGAIL DIES DURING THE SÉANCE...
AND LUKIA REGAINS HER SENSES.

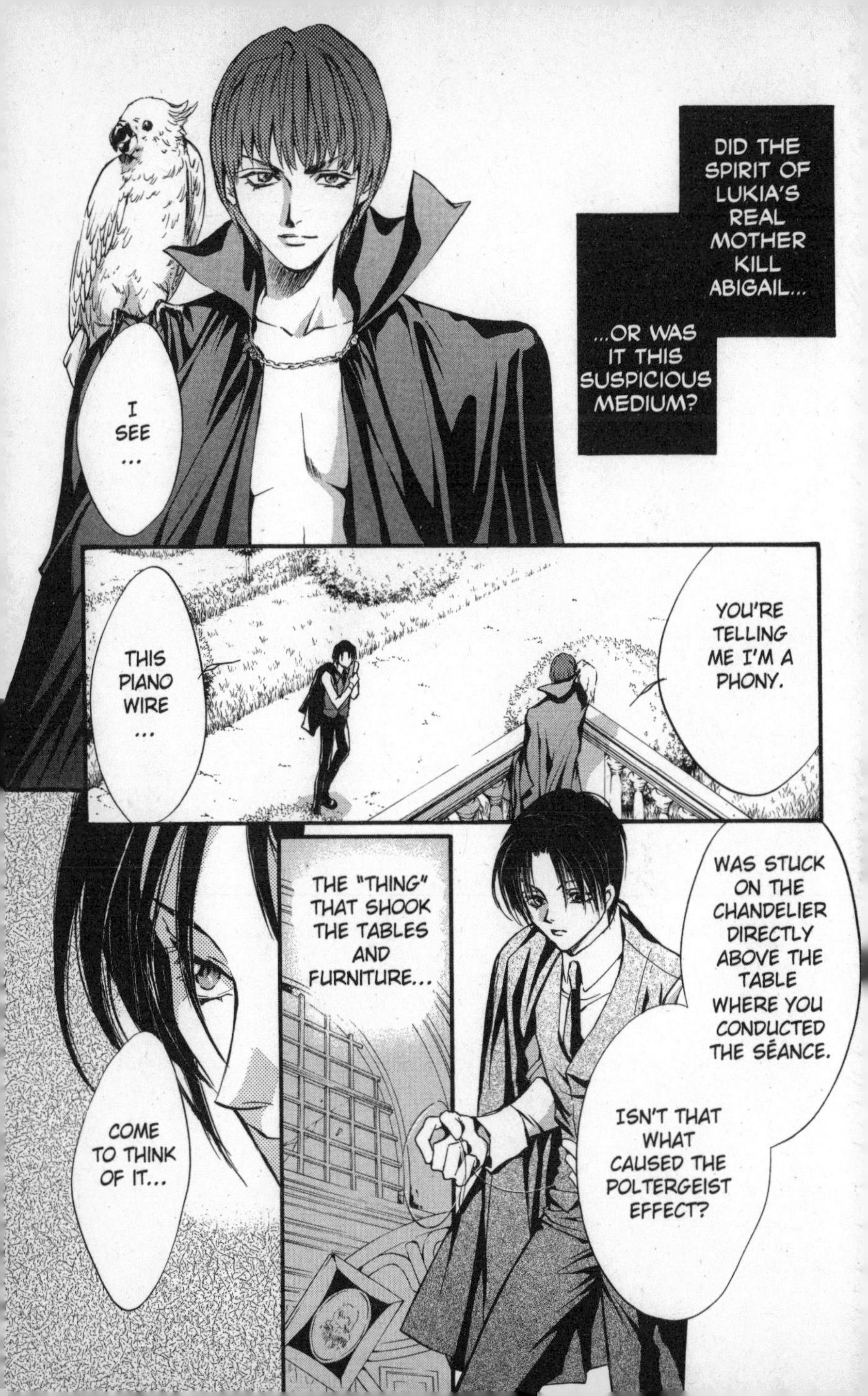
DID THE SPIRIT OF LUKIA'S REAL MOTHER KILL ABIGAIL...
...OR WAS IT THIS SUSPICIOUS MEDIUM?
I SEE ...
YOU'RE TELLING ME I'M A PHONY.
THIS PIANO WIRE ...
WAS STUCK ON THE CHANDELIER DIRECTLY ABOVE THE TABLE WHERE YOU CONDUCTED THE SÉANCE.
ISN'T THAT WHAT CAUSED THE POLTERGEIST EFFECT?
THE "THING" THAT SHOOK THE TABLES AND FURNITURE...
COME TO THINK OF IT...

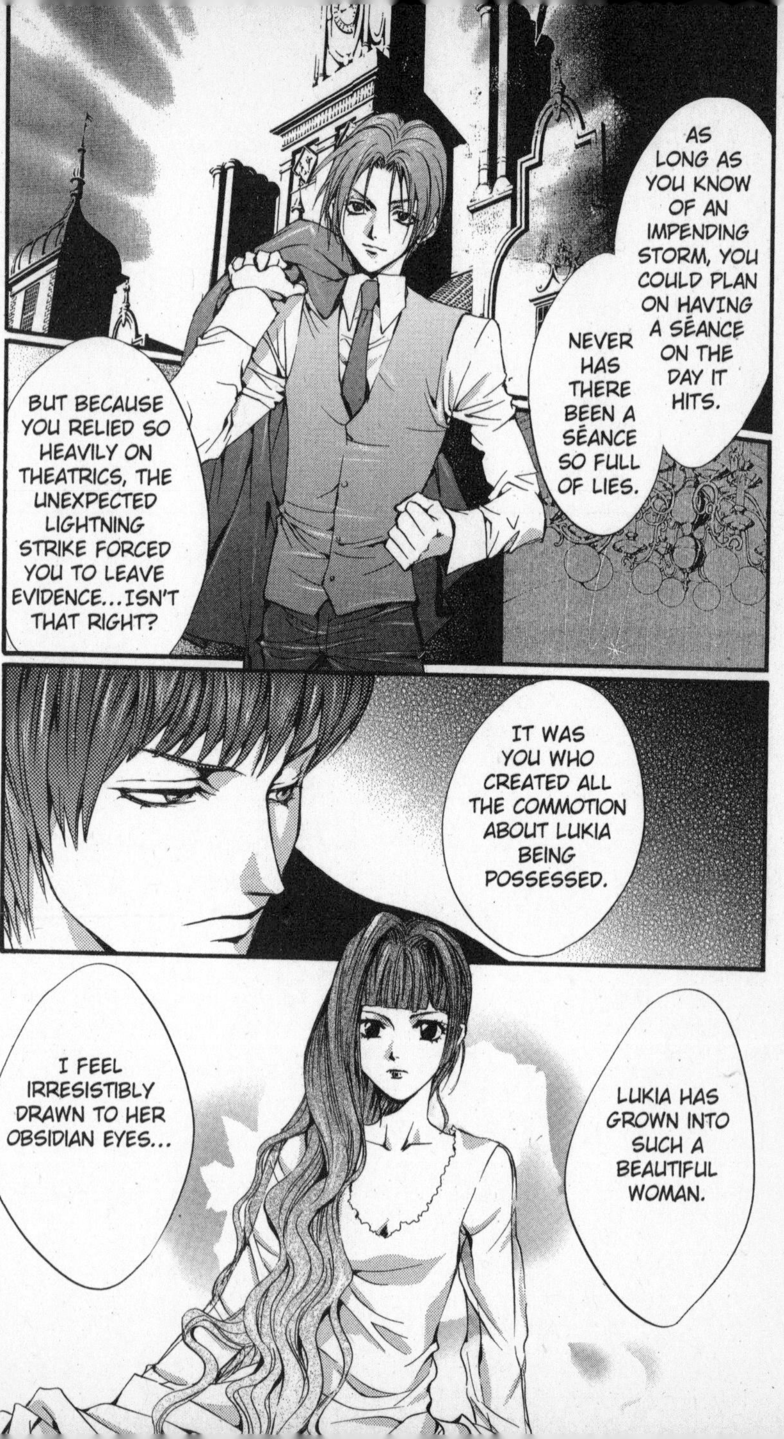
AS LONG AS YOU KNOW OF AN IMPENDING STORM, YOU COULD PLAN ON HAVING A SÉANCE ON THE DAY IT HITS.
NEVER HAS THERE BEEN A SÉANCE SO FULL OF LIES.
BUT BECAUSE YOU RELIED SO HEAVILY ON THEATRICS, THE UNEXPECTED LIGHTNING STRIKE FORCED YOU TO LEAVE EVIDENCE...ISN'T THAT RIGHT?
IT WAS YOU WHO CREATED ALL THE COMMOTION ABOUT LUKIA BEING POSSESSED.
LUKIA HAS GROWN INTO SUCH A BEAUTIFUL WOMAN.
I FEEL IRRESISTIBLY DRAWN TO HER OBSIDIAN EYES...

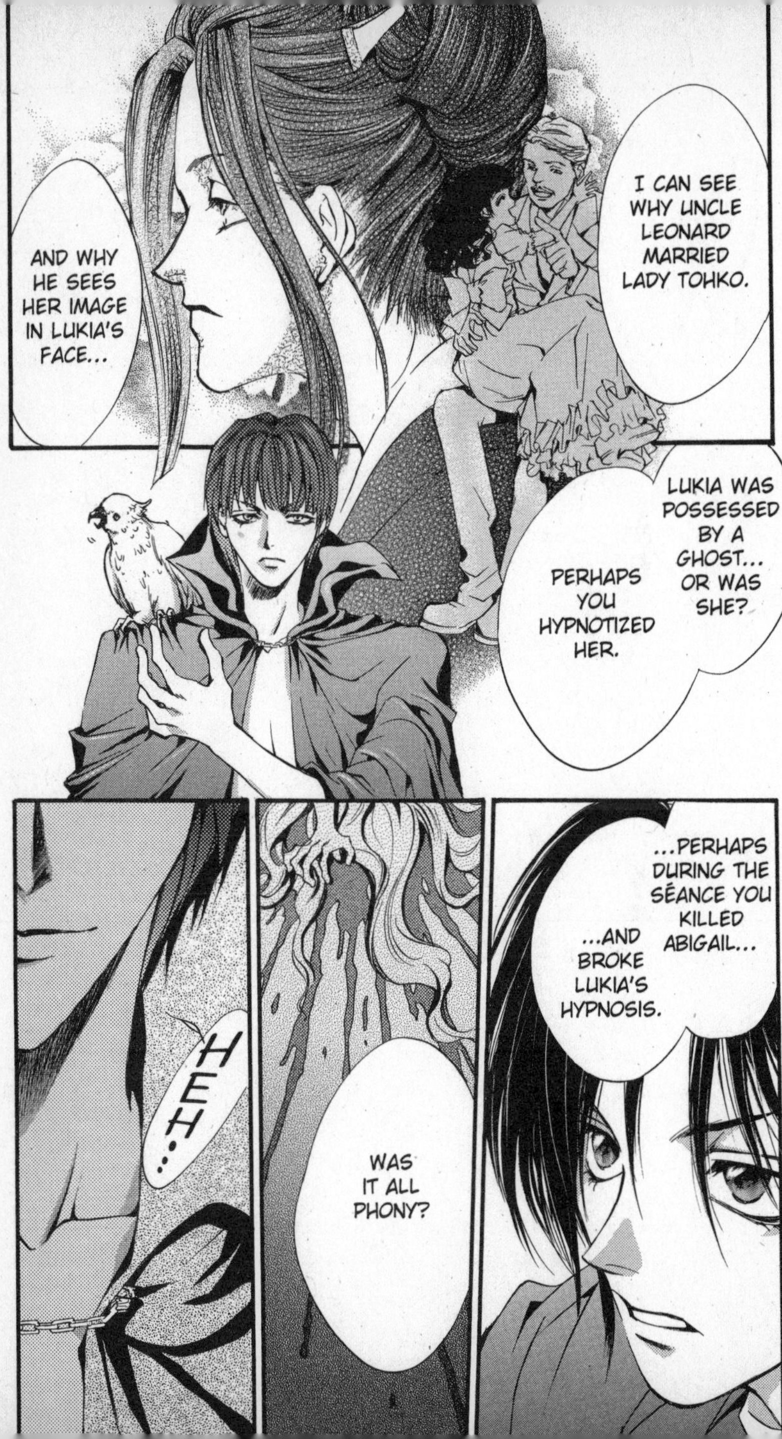
I CAN SEE WHY UNCLE LEONARD MARRIED LADY TOHKO.
AND WHY HE SEES HER IMAGE IN LUKIA'S FACE...
LUKIA WAS POSSESSED BY A GHOST... OR WAS SHE?
PERHAPS YOU HYPNOTIZED HER.
...PERHAPS DURING THE SÉANCE YOU KILLED ABIGAIL...
...AND BROKE LUKIA'S HYPNOSIS.
WAS IT ALL PHONY?
HEH...

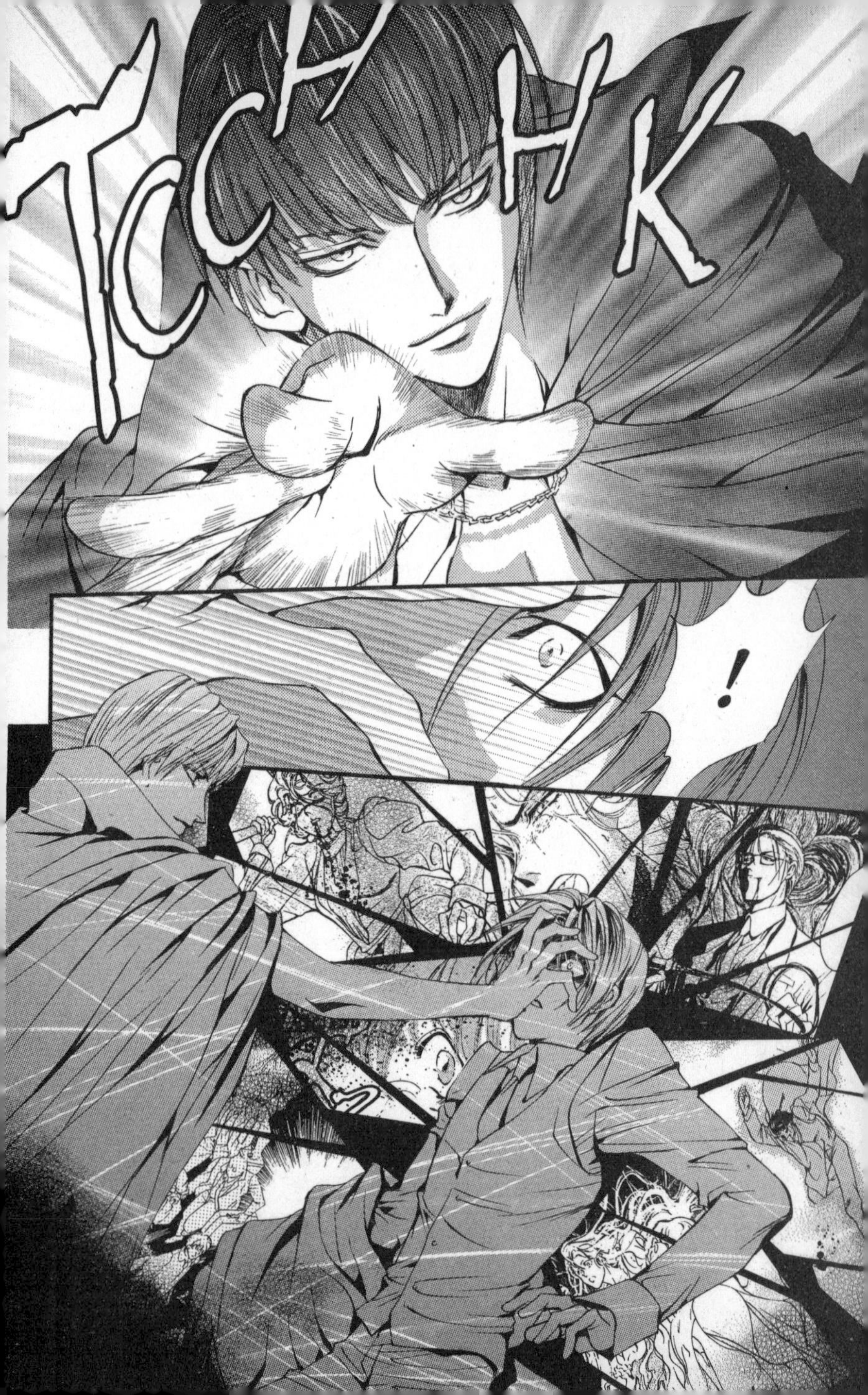
TCCHHK
!

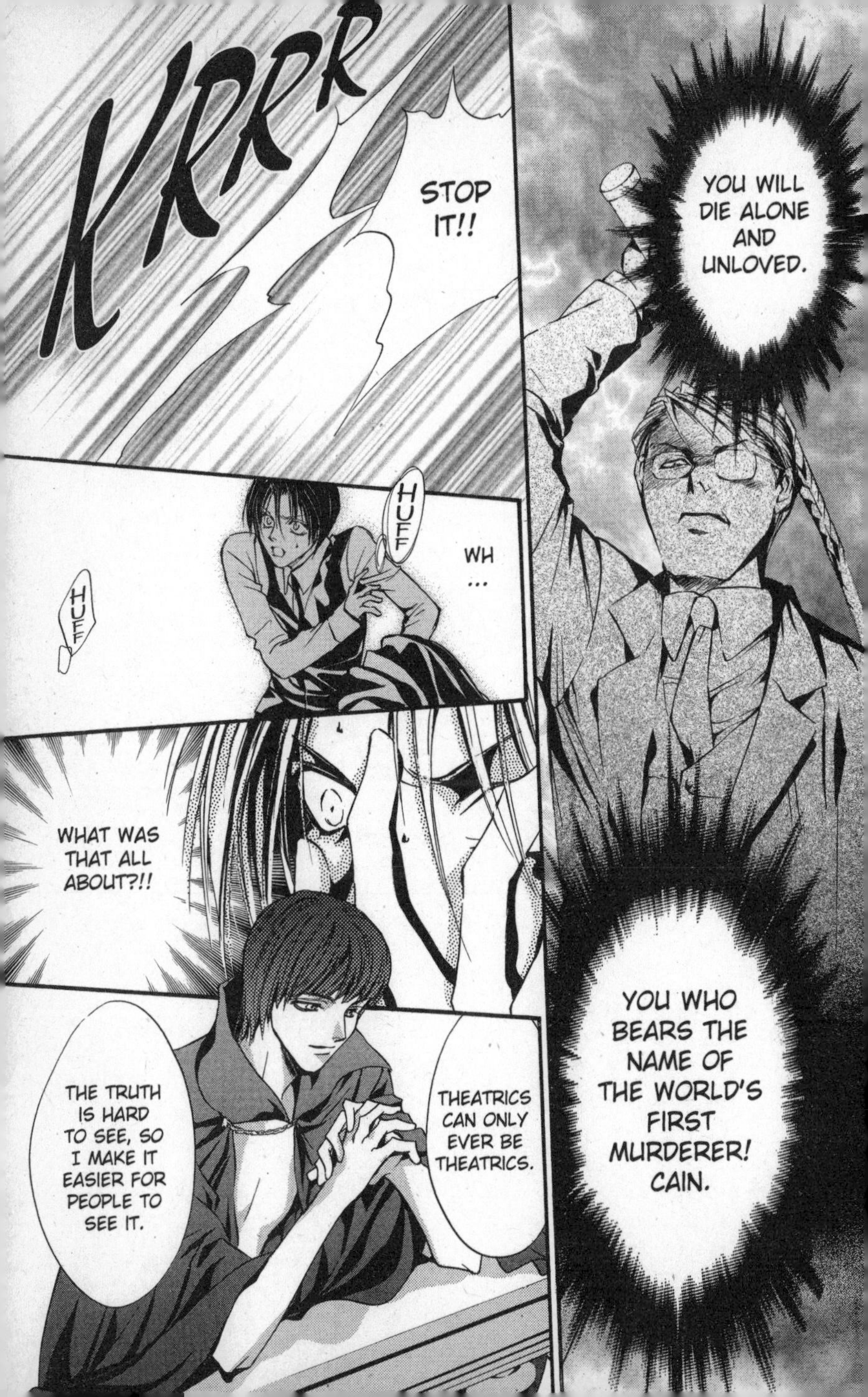
YOU WILL DIE ALONE AND UNLOVED.
YOU WHO BEARS THE NAME OF THE WORLD'S FIRST MURDERER! CAIN.
KRRRR
STOP IT!!
WH...
HUFF
HUFF
WHAT WAS THAT ALL ABOUT?!!
THEATRICS CAN ONLY EVER BE THEATRICS.
THE TRUTH IS HARD TO SEE, SO I MAKE IT EASIER FOR PEOPLE TO SEE IT.

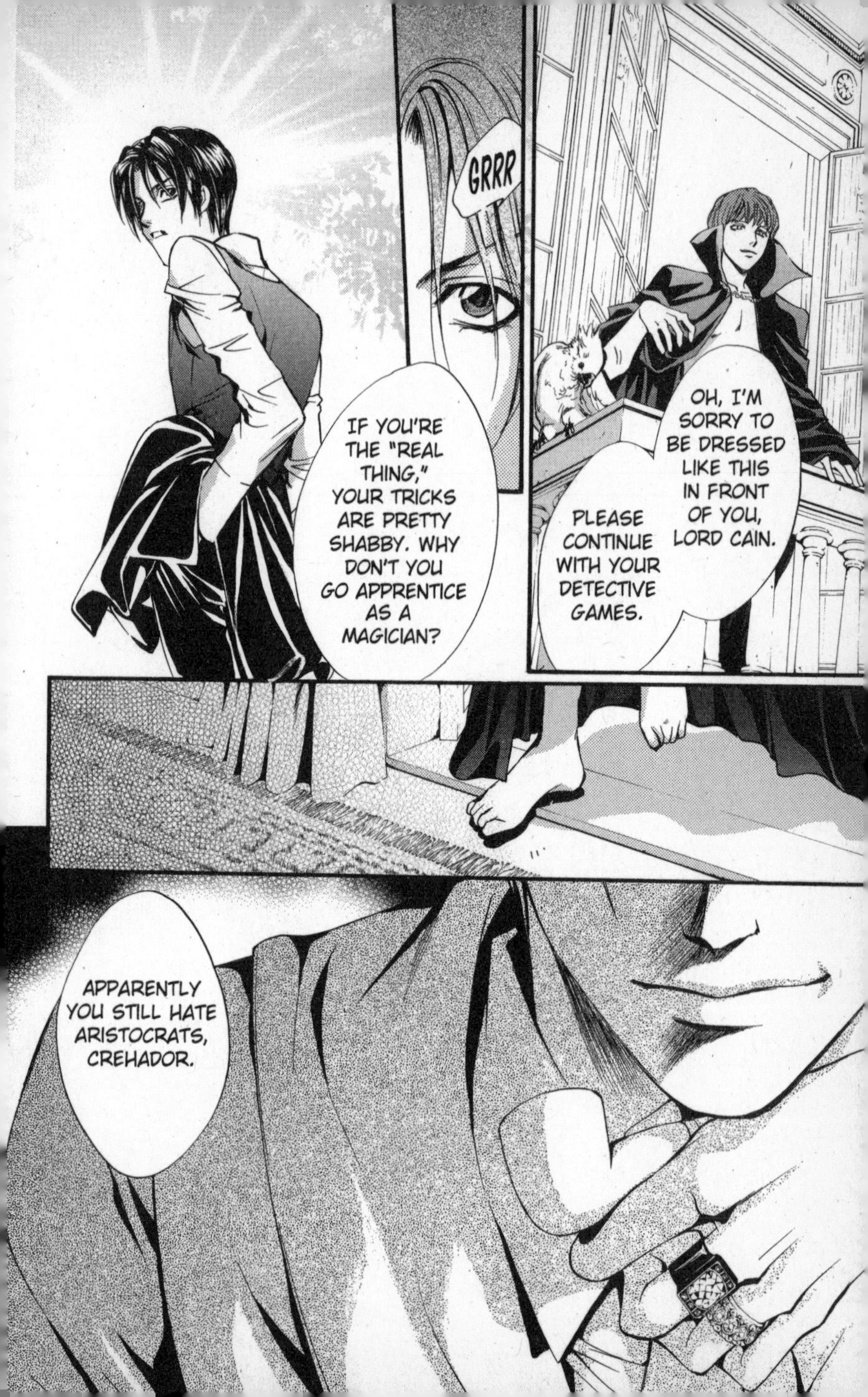
OH, I'M SORRY TO BE DRESSED LIKE THIS IN FRONT OF YOU, LORD CAIN.
PLEASE CONTINUE WITH YOUR DETECTIVE GAMES.
GRRR
IF YOU'RE THE "REAL THING," YOUR TRICKS ARE PRETTY SHABBY. WHY DON'T YOU GO APPRENTICE AS A MAGICIAN?
APPARENTLY YOU STILL HATE ARISTOCRATS, CREHADOR.

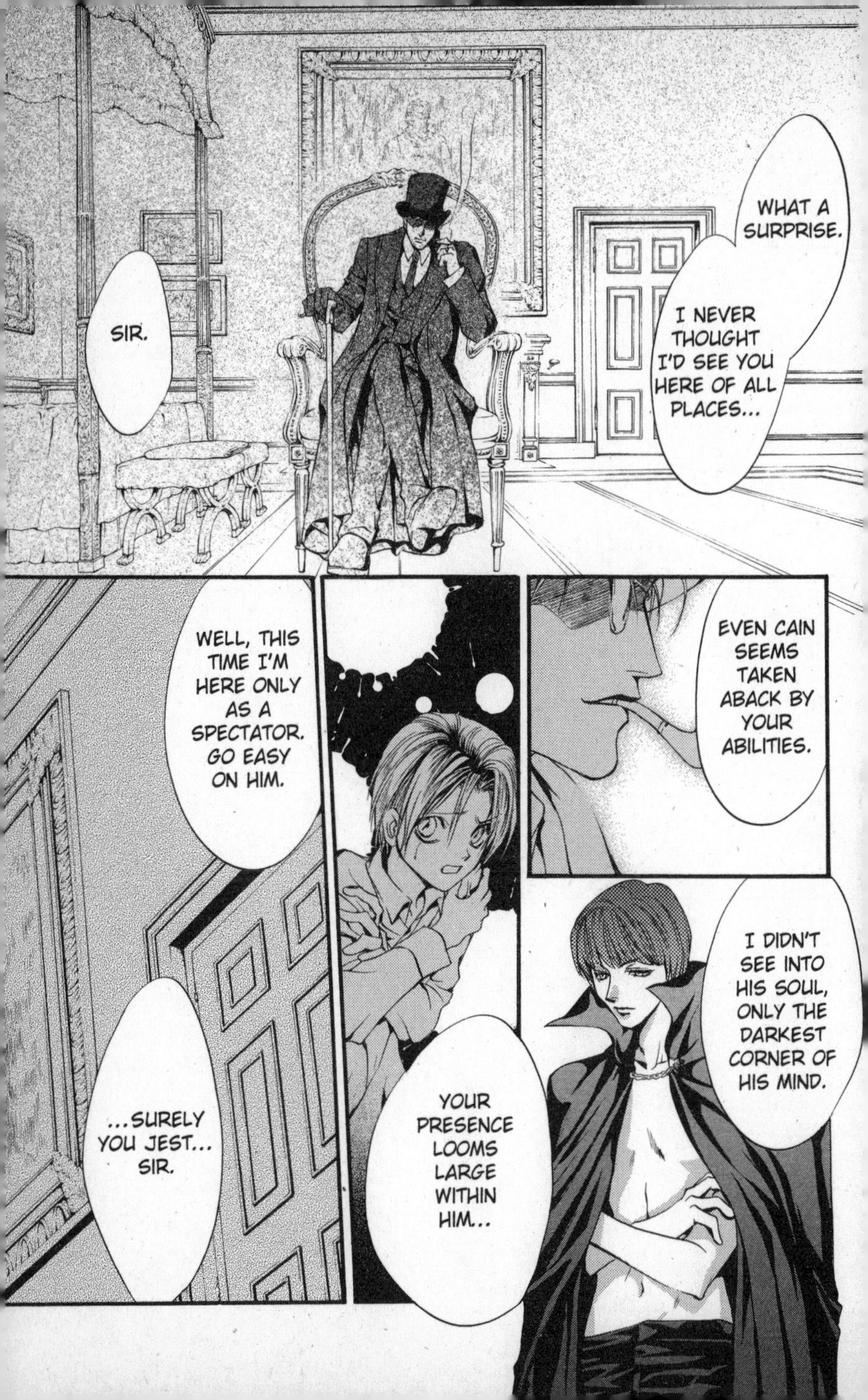
WHAT A SURPRISE.
I NEVER THOUGHT I'D SEE YOU HERE OF ALL PLACES...
SIR.
EVEN CAIN SEEMS TAKEN ABACK BY YOUR ABILITIES.
WELL, THIS TIME I'M HERE ONLY AS A SPECTATOR. GO EASY ON HIM.
...SURELY YOU JEST... SIR.
I DIDN'T SEE INTO HIS SOUL, ONLY THE DARKEST CORNER OF HIS MIND.
YOUR PRESENCE LOOMS LARGE WITHIN HIM...

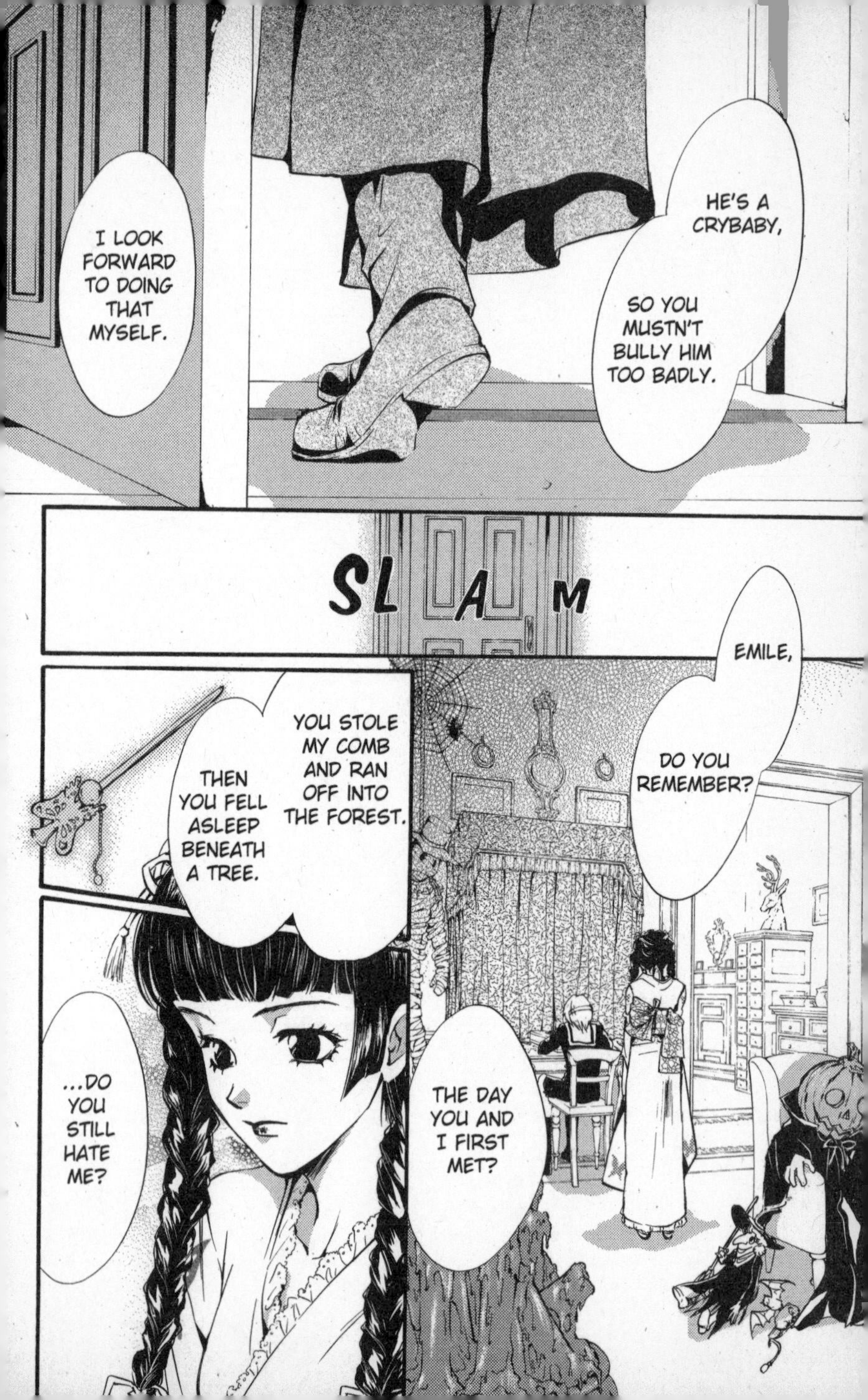
HE'S A CRYBABY,
SO YOU MUSTN'T BULLY HIM TOO BADLY.
I LOOK FORWARD TO DOING THAT MYSELF.
SLAM
EMILE,
DO YOU REMEMBER?
THE DAY YOU AND I FIRST MET?
YOU STOLE MY COMB AND RAN OFF INTO THE FOREST.
THEN YOU FELL ASLEEP BENEATH A TREE.
...DO YOU STILL HATE ME?

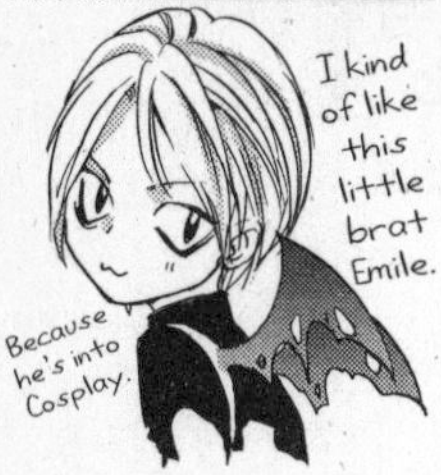

I kind of like this little brat Emile.
Because he's into Cosplay.

I always wanted to write about séances. Crehador seems to have his own style of doing it. This is something that fascinated even Sir Arthur Conan Doyle. It must have been a time when modernization was taking place at an amazing speed, yet interest in the occult still existed. Another way of doing a séance was with a cloth with letters on it placed on a three-legged table. Sometimes the spirits would answer with a knock or make the table float. There were many kinds of séances, but there must have been lots of phonies. It was a little awkward to draw Cain happily holding hands with everyone, but...

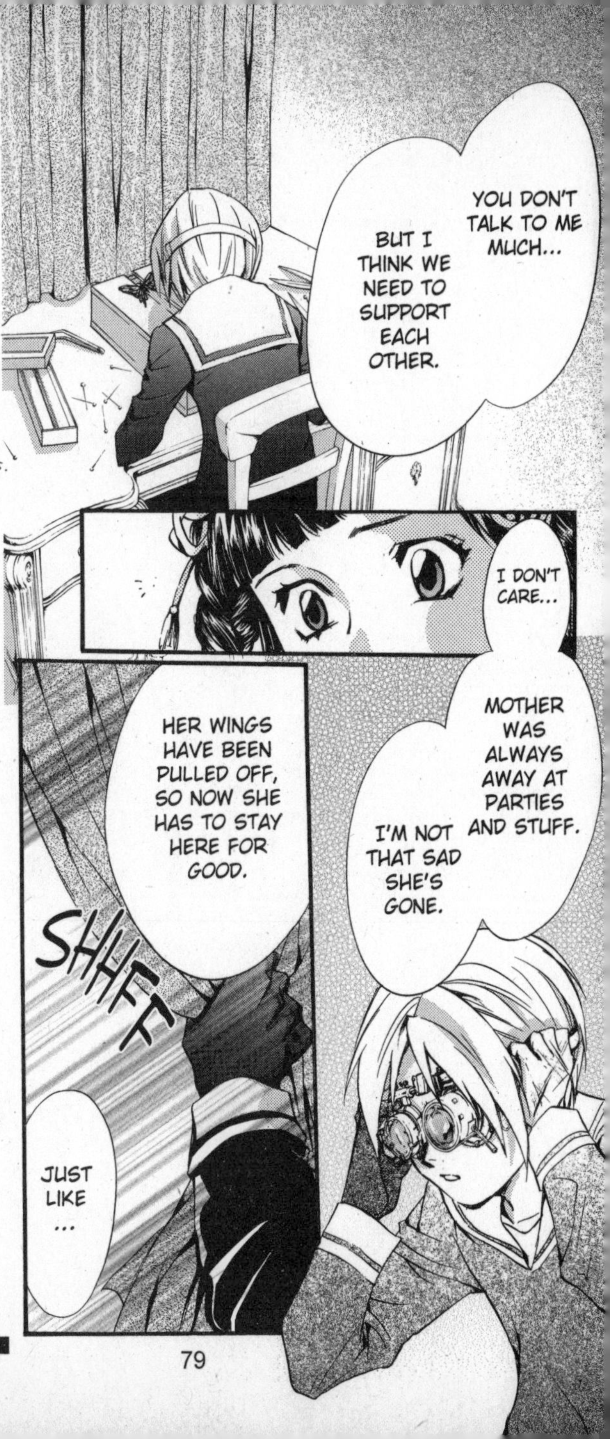

YOU DON'T TALK TO ME MUCH...
BUT I THINK WE NEED TO SUPPORT EACH OTHER.
I DON'T CARE...
MOTHER WAS ALWAYS AWAY AT PARTIES AND STUFF.
I'M NOT THAT SAD SHE'S GONE.
HER WINGS HAVE BEEN PULLED OFF, SO NOW SHE HAS TO STAY HERE FOR GOOD.
SHHFF
JUST LIKE ...

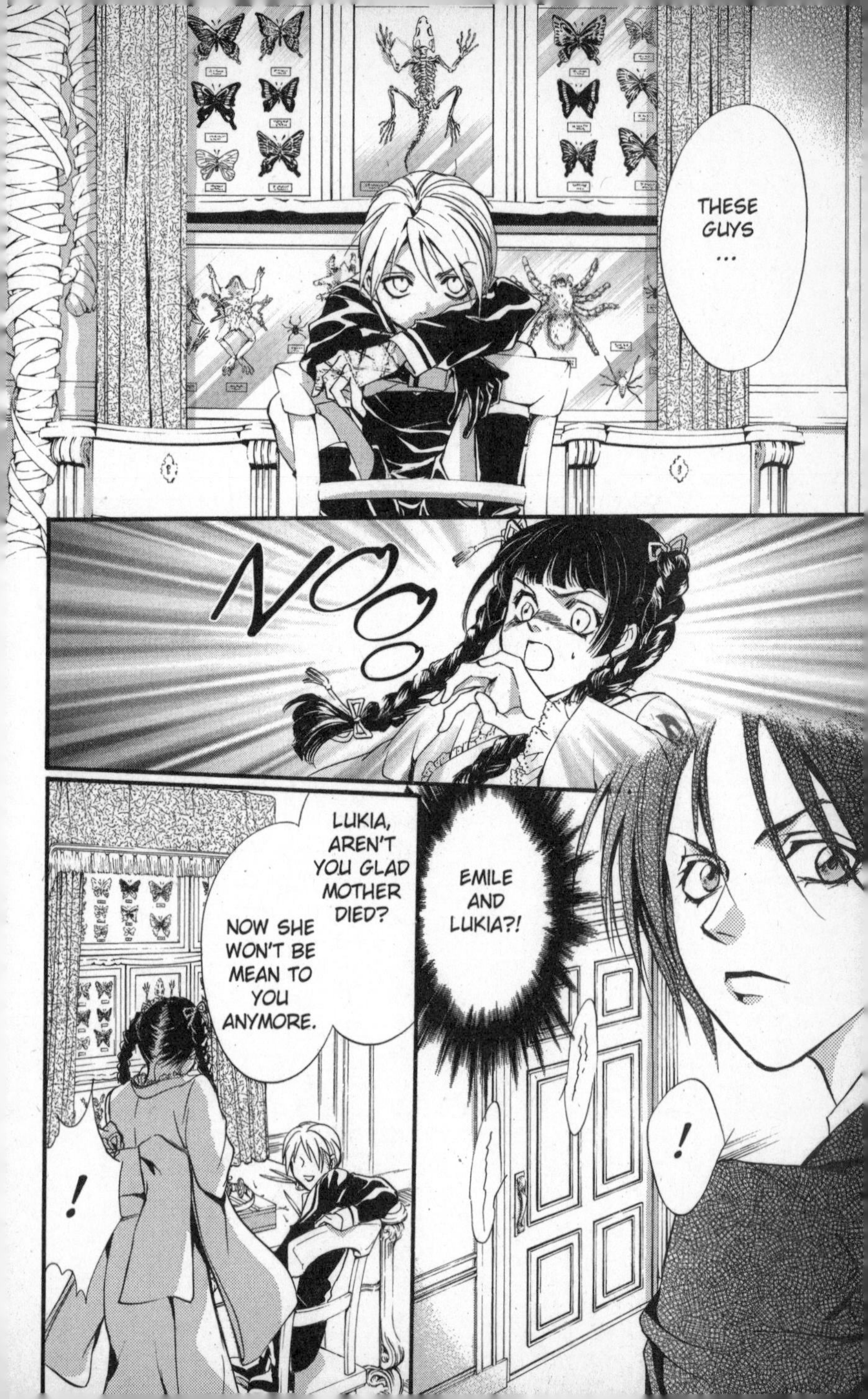
THESE GUYS ...
NOOO
EMILE AND LUKIA?!
!
LUKIA, AREN'T YOU GLAD MOTHER DIED?
NOW SHE WON'T BE MEAN TO YOU ANYMORE.
!

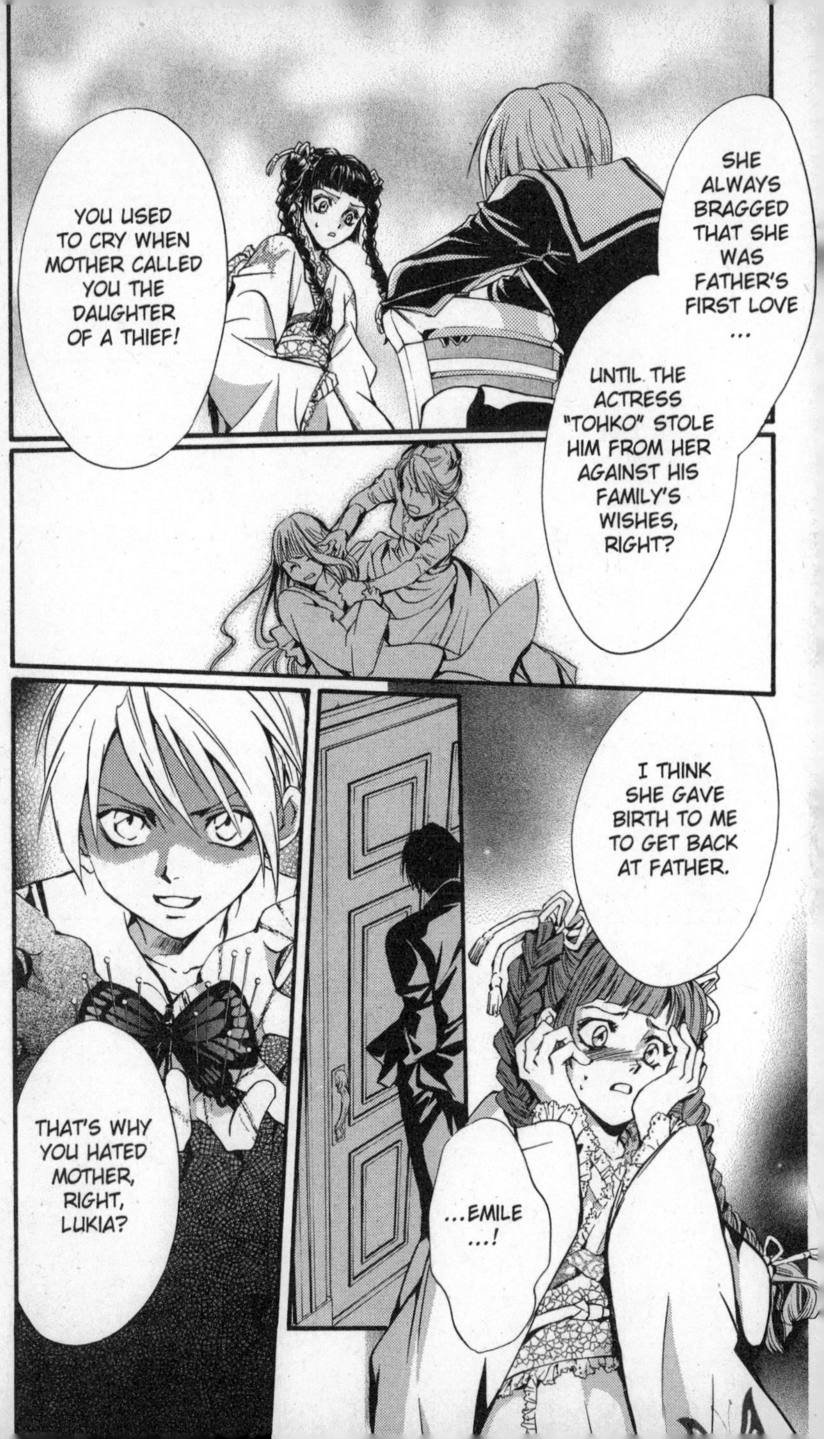
SHE ALWAYS BRAGGED THAT SHE WAS FATHER'S FIRST LOVE ...
UNTIL THE ACTRESS "TOHKO" STOLE HIM FROM HER AGAINST HIS FAMILY'S WISHES, RIGHT?
YOU USED TO CRY WHEN MOTHER CALLED YOU THE DAUGHTER OF A THIEF!
I THINK SHE GAVE BIRTH TO ME TO GET BACK AT FATHER.
...EMILE ...!
THAT'S WHY YOU HATED MOTHER, RIGHT, LUKIA?

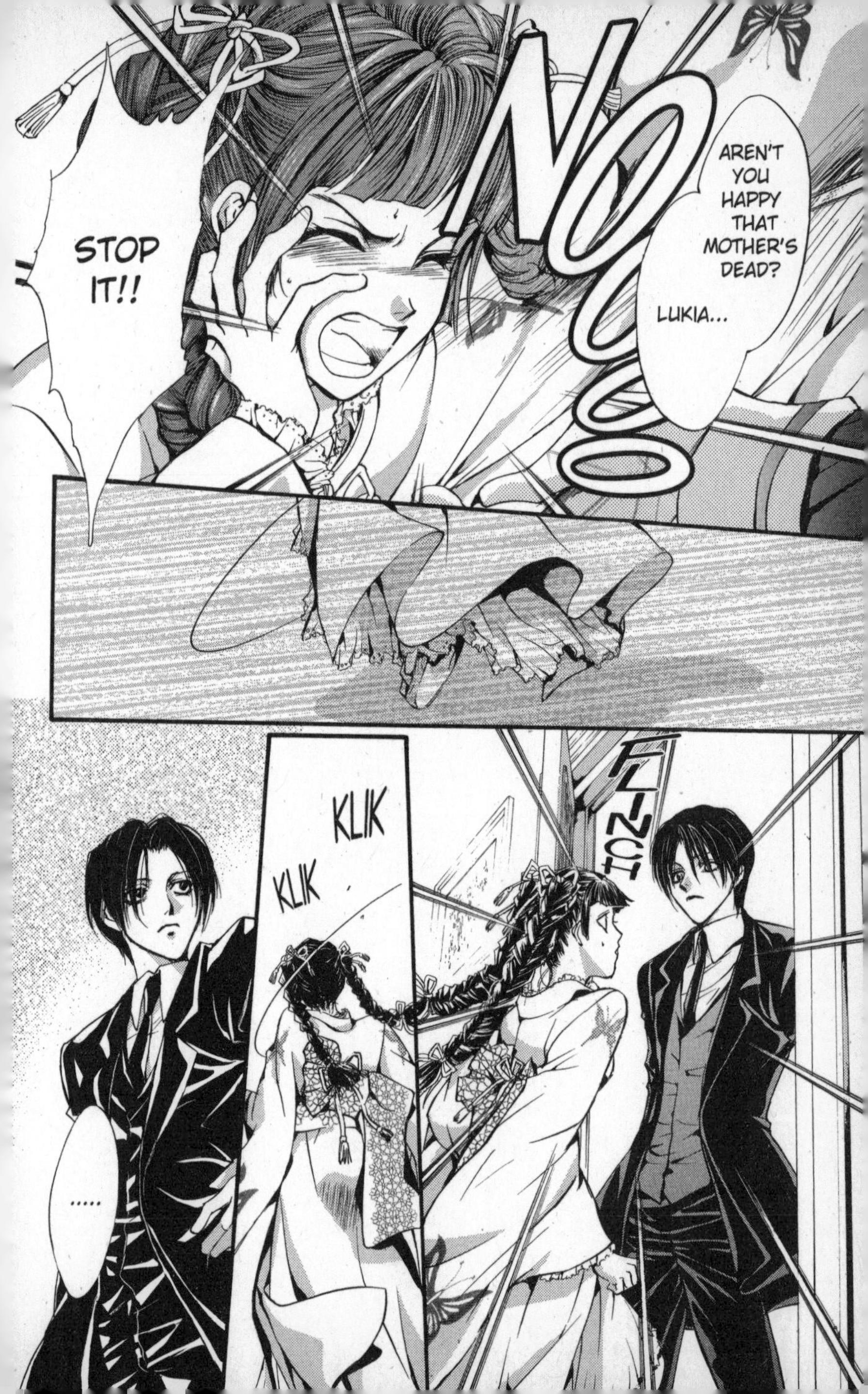
AREN'T YOU HAPPY THAT MOTHER'S DEAD?
LUKIA...
NOOOOOO
STOP IT!!
FLINCH
KLIK
KLIK
.....

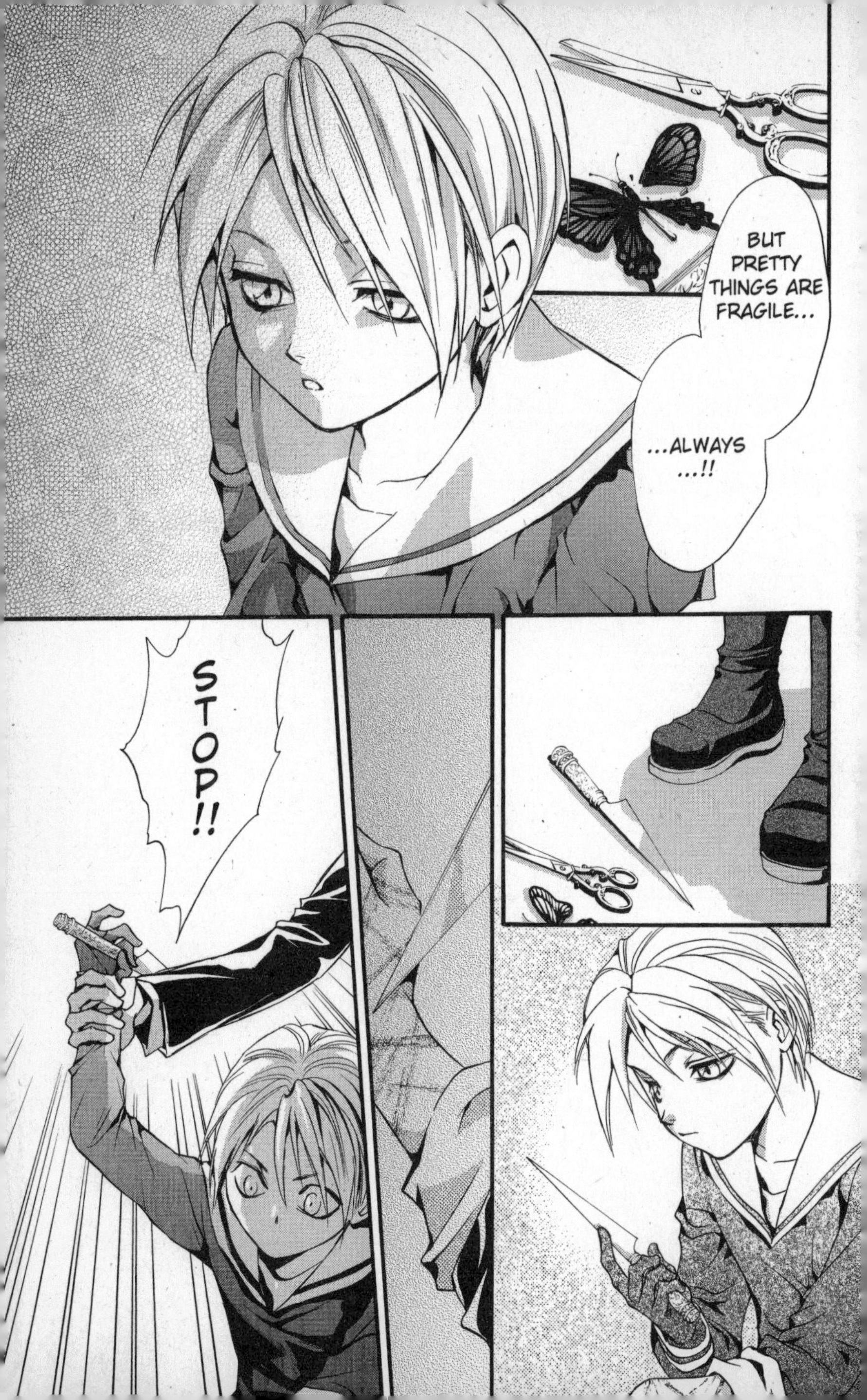
BUT PRETTY THINGS ARE FRAGILE...
...ALWAYS ...!!
STOP!!

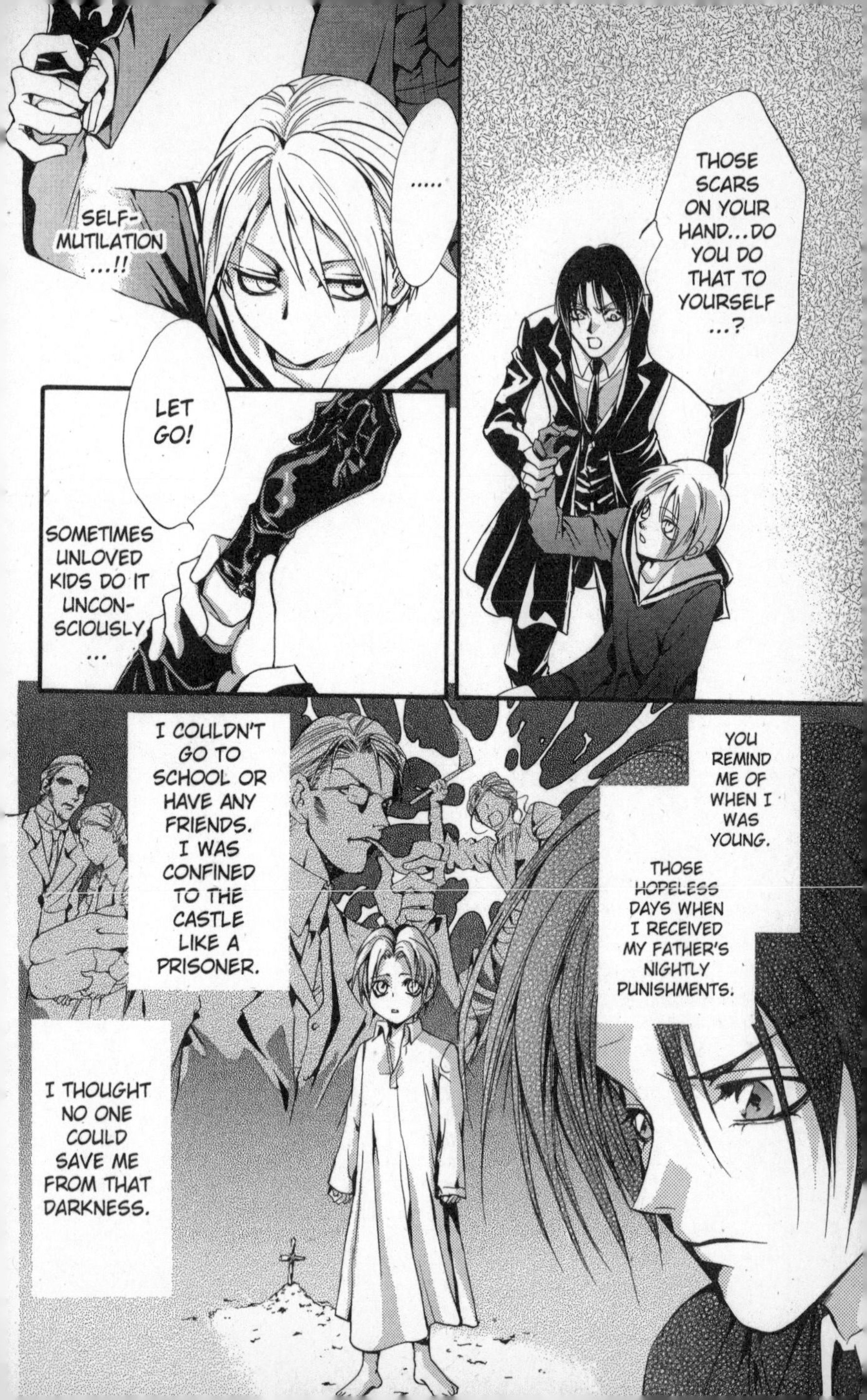

THOSE SCARS ON YOUR HAND...DO YOU DO THAT TO YOURSELF ...?
.....
SELF-MUTILATION ...!!
LET GO!
SOMETIMES UNLOVED KIDS DO IT UNCONSCIOUSLY ...
YOU REMIND ME OF WHEN I WAS YOUNG.
THOSE HOPELESS DAYS WHEN I RECEIVED MY FATHER'S NIGHTLY PUNISHMENTS.
I COULDN'T GO TO SCHOOL OR HAVE ANY FRIENDS. I WAS CONFINED TO THE CASTLE LIKE A PRISONER.
I THOUGHT NO ONE COULD SAVE ME FROM THAT DARKNESS.

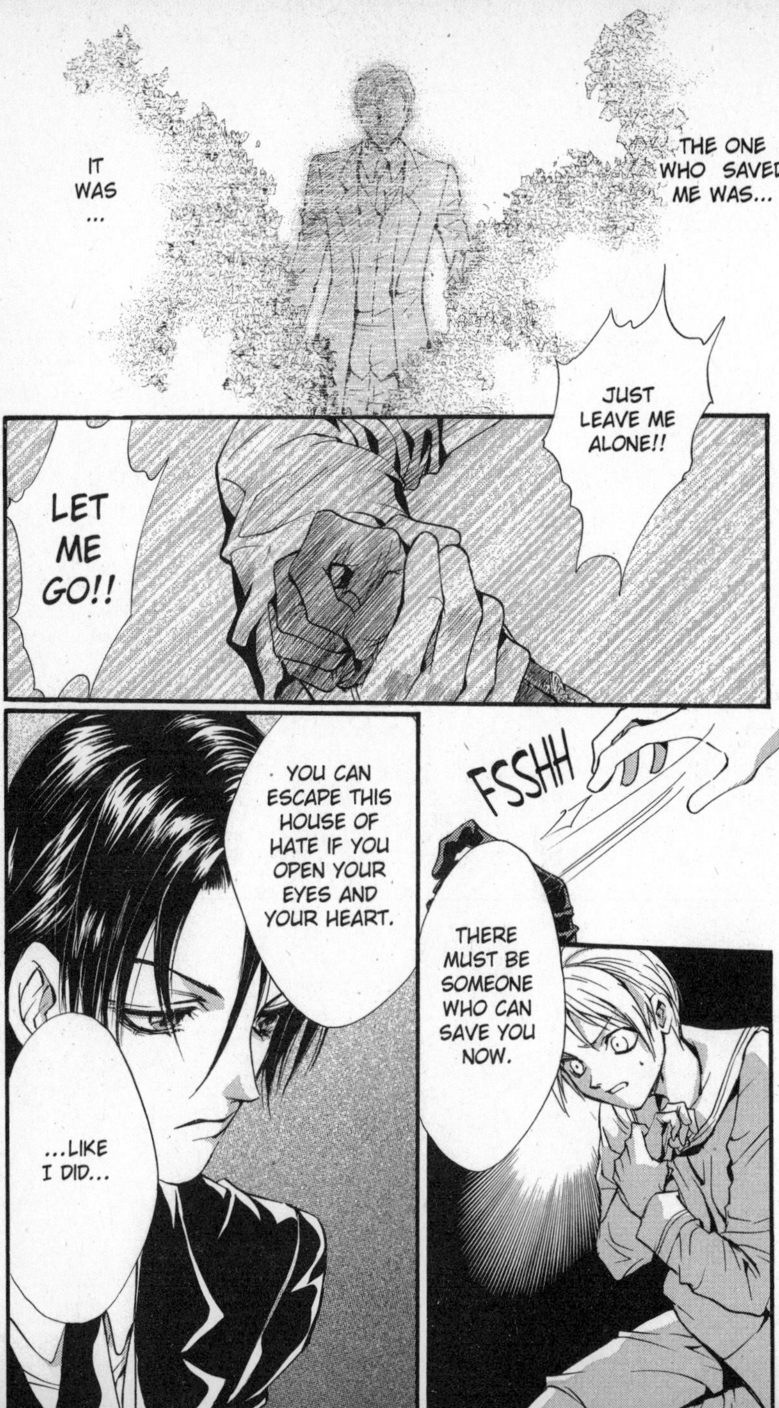
THE ONE WHO SAVED ME WAS...
IT WAS ...
JUST LEAVE ME ALONE!!
LET ME GO!!
FSSHH
THERE MUST BE SOMEONE WHO CAN SAVE YOU NOW.
YOU CAN ESCAPE THIS HOUSE OF HATE IF YOU OPEN YOUR EYES AND YOUR HEART.
...LIKE I DID...

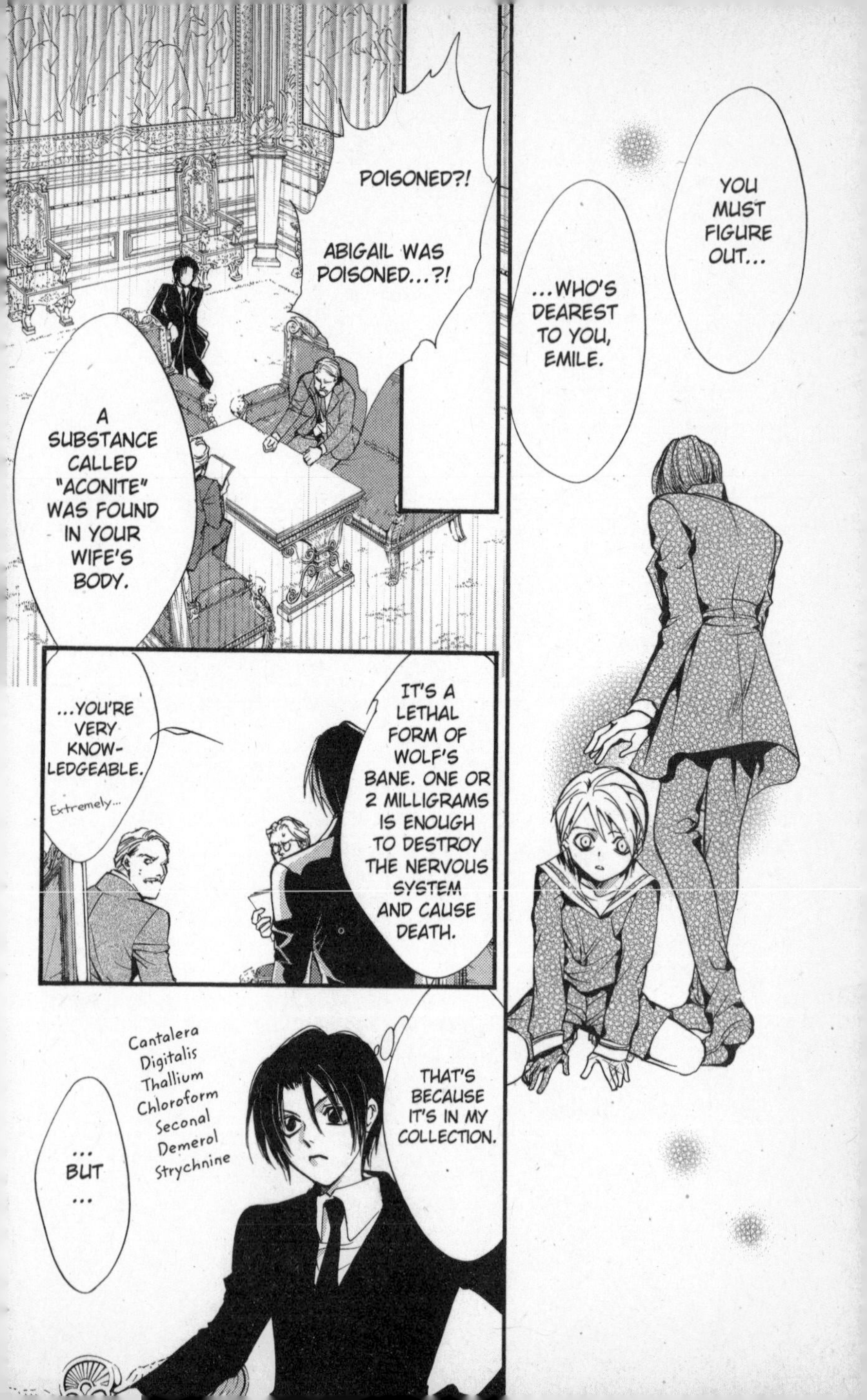
YOU MUST FIGURE OUT...
...WHO'S DEAREST TO YOU, EMILE.
POISONED?!
ABIGAIL WAS POISONED...?!
A SUBSTANCE CALLED "ACONITE" WAS FOUND IN YOUR WIFE'S BODY.
IT'S A LETHAL FORM OF WOLF'S BANE. ONE OR 2 MILLIGRAMS IS ENOUGH TO DESTROY THE NERVOUS SYSTEM AND CAUSE DEATH.
...YOU'RE VERY KNOW-LEDGEABLE.
Extremely...
THAT'S BECAUSE IT'S IN MY COLLECTION.
Cantalera
Digitalis
Thallium
Chloroform
Seconal
Demerol
Strychnine
...BUT...

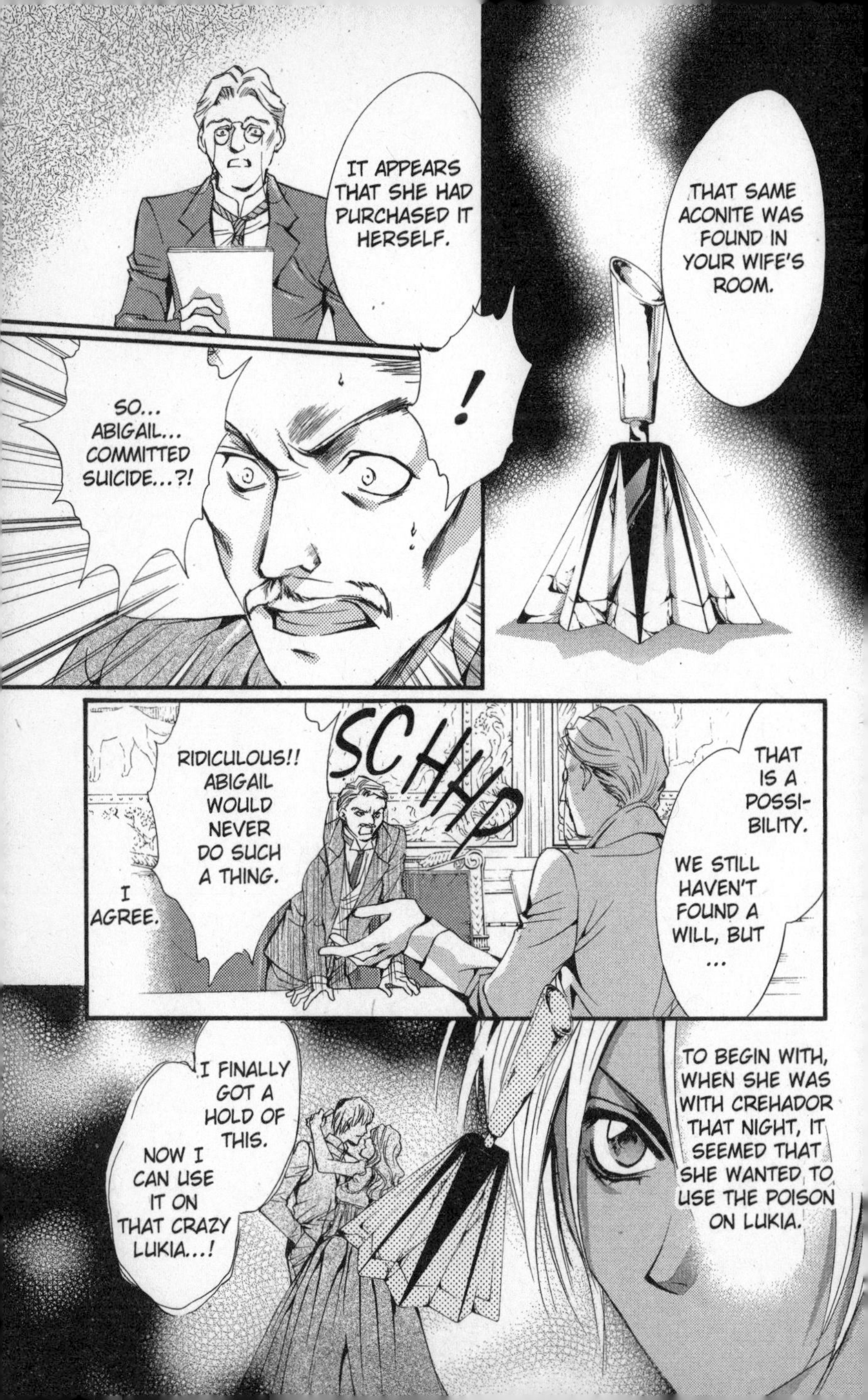
THAT SAME ACONITE WAS FOUND IN YOUR WIFE'S ROOM.
IT APPEARS THAT SHE HAD PURCHASED IT HERSELF.
!
SO... ABIGAIL... COMMITTED SUICIDE...?!
THAT IS A POSSIBILITY.
WE STILL HAVEN'T FOUND A WILL, BUT ...
SCHHP
RIDICULOUS!! ABIGAIL WOULD NEVER DO SUCH A THING.
I AGREE.
TO BEGIN WITH, WHEN SHE WAS WITH CREHADOR THAT NIGHT, IT SEEMED THAT SHE WANTED TO USE THE POISON ON LUKIA.
I FINALLY GOT A HOLD OF THIS.
NOW I CAN USE IT ON THAT CRAZY LUKIA...!

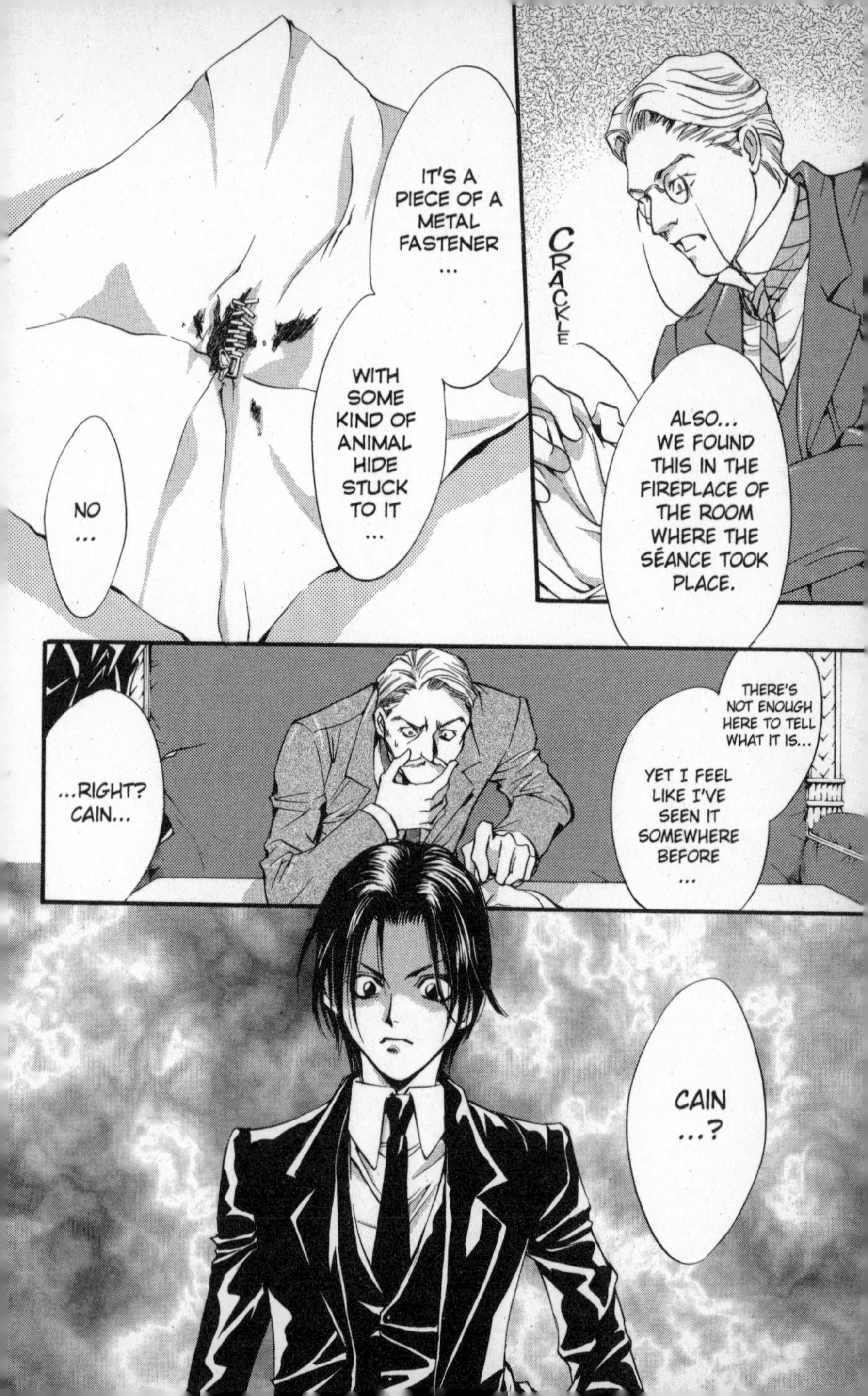
CRACKLE
ALSO... WE FOUND THIS IN THE FIREPLACE OF THE ROOM WHERE THE SÉANCE TOOK PLACE.
IT'S A PIECE OF A METAL FASTENER ...
WITH SOME KIND OF ANIMAL HIDE STUCK TO IT ...
NO ...
THERE'S NOT ENOUGH HERE TO TELL WHAT IT IS...
YET I FEEL LIKE I'VE SEEN IT SOMEWHERE BEFORE ...
...RIGHT? CAIN...
CAIN ...?

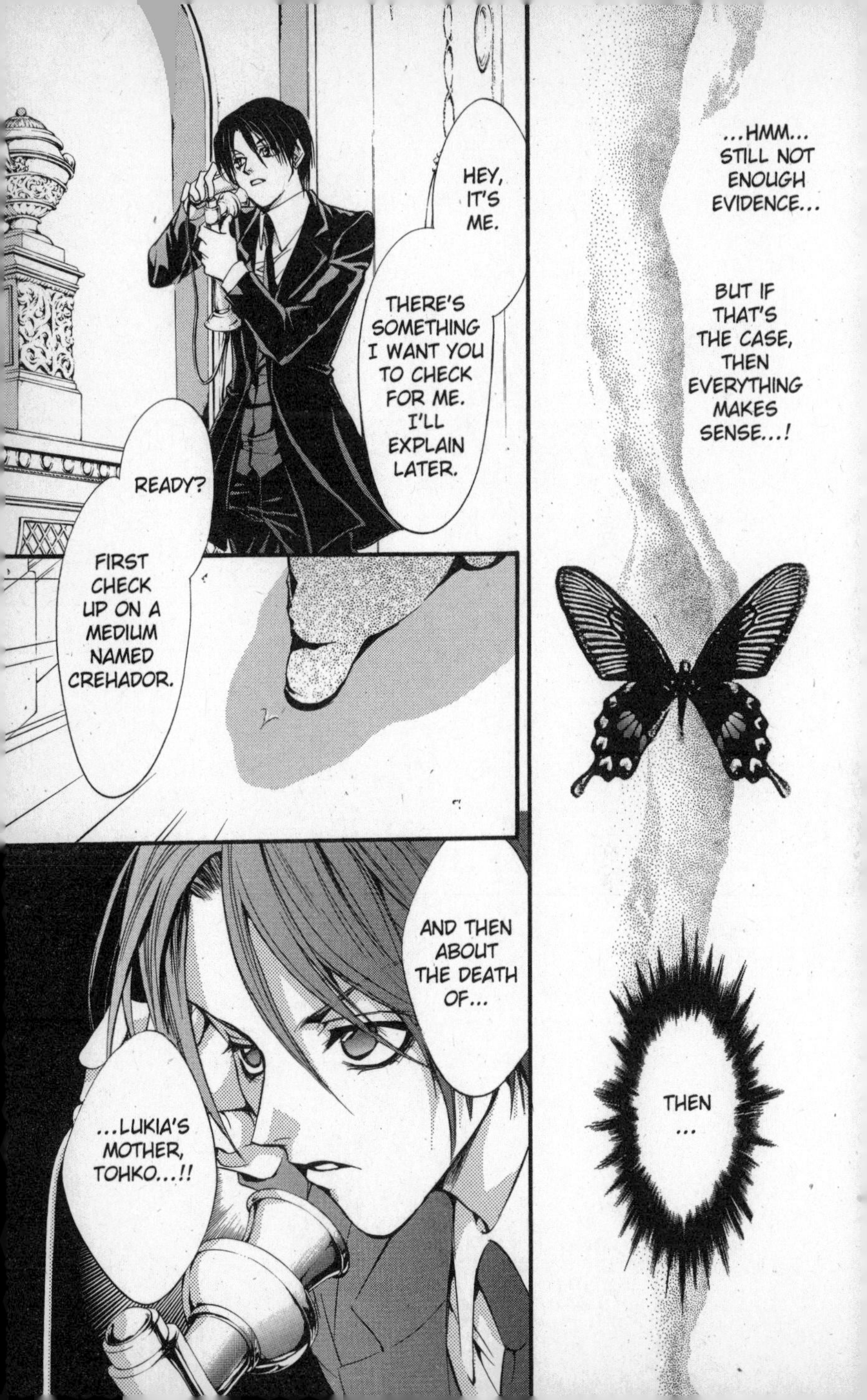
...HMM... STILL NOT ENOUGH EVIDENCE...
BUT IF THAT'S THE CASE, THEN EVERYTHING MAKES SENSE...!
THEN ...
HEY, IT'S ME.
THERE'S SOMETHING I WANT YOU TO CHECK FOR ME. I'LL EXPLAIN LATER.
READY?
FIRST CHECK UP ON A MEDIUM NAMED CREHADOR.
AND THEN ABOUT THE DEATH OF...
...LUKIA'S MOTHER, TOHKO...!!

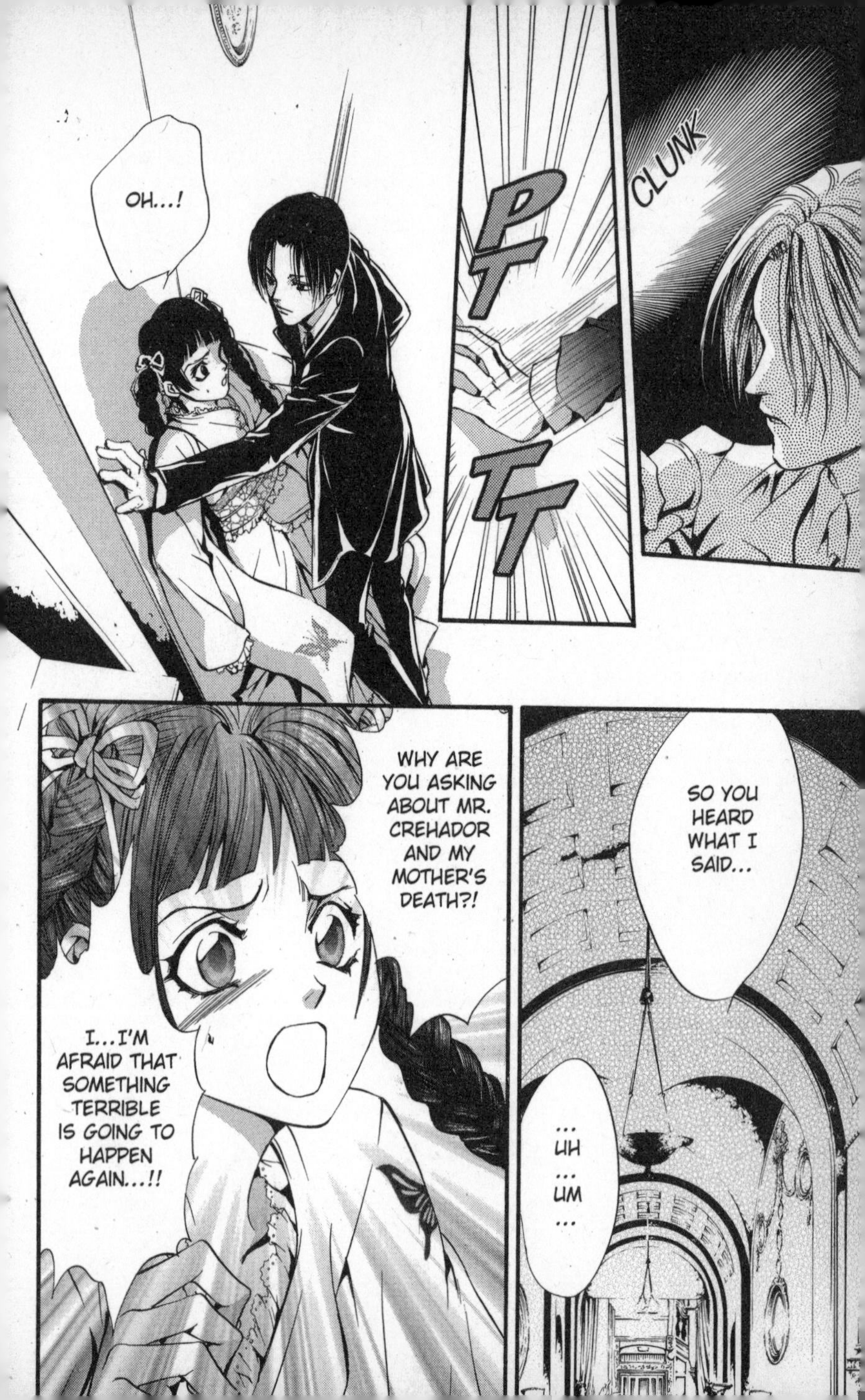
CLUNK
PTTT
OH...!
SO YOU HEARD WHAT I SAID...
...UH...UM...
WHY ARE YOU ASKING ABOUT MR. CREHADOR AND MY MOTHER'S DEATH?!
I...I'M AFRAID THAT SOMETHING TERRIBLE IS GOING TO HAPPEN AGAIN...!!

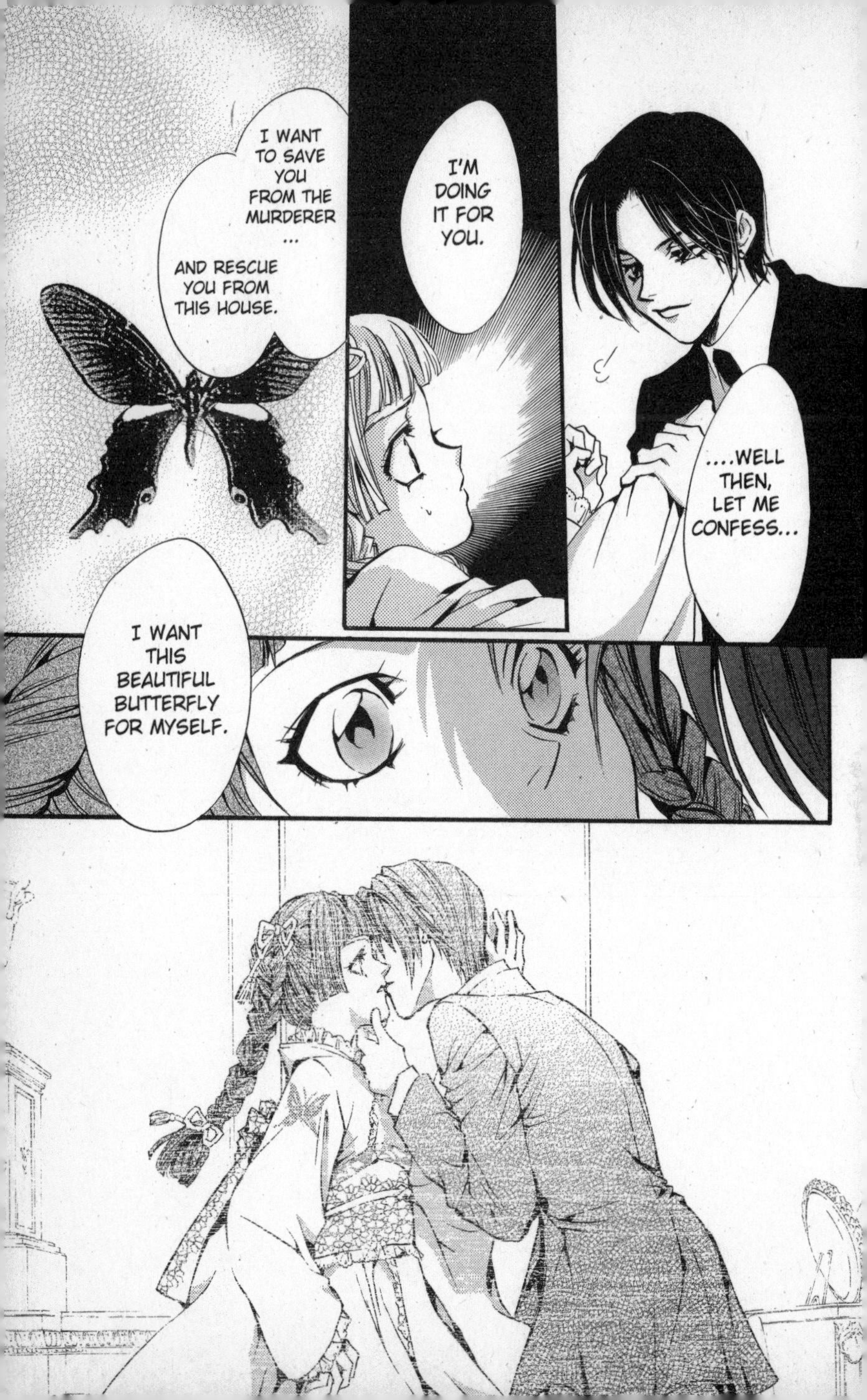
....WELL THEN, LET ME CONFESS...
I'M DOING IT FOR YOU.
I WANT TO SAVE YOU FROM THE MURDERER ...
AND RESCUE YOU FROM THIS HOUSE.
I WANT THIS BEAUTIFUL BUTTERFLY FOR MYSELF.

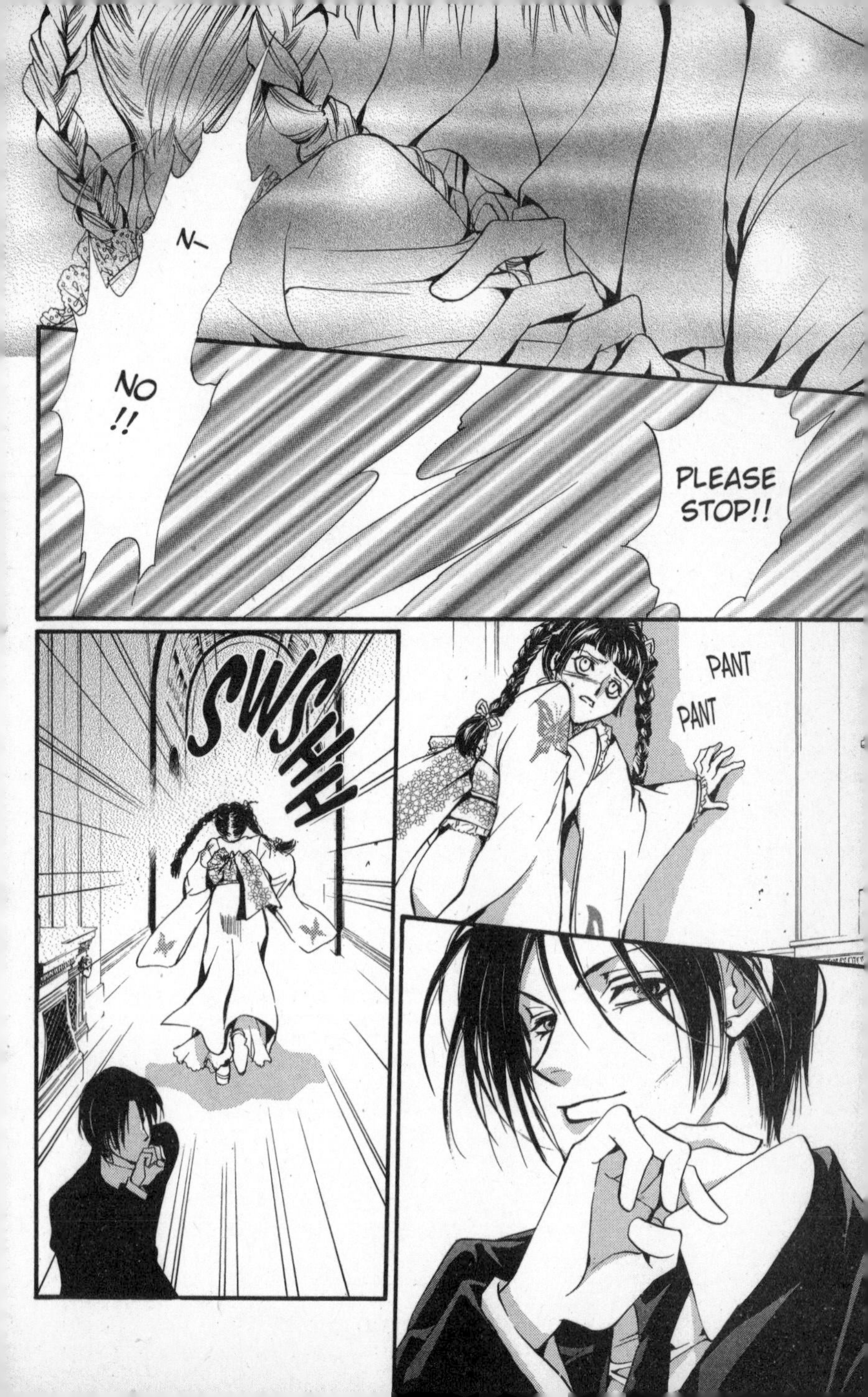
N–
NO!!
PLEASE STOP!!
PANT
PANT
SWSHH

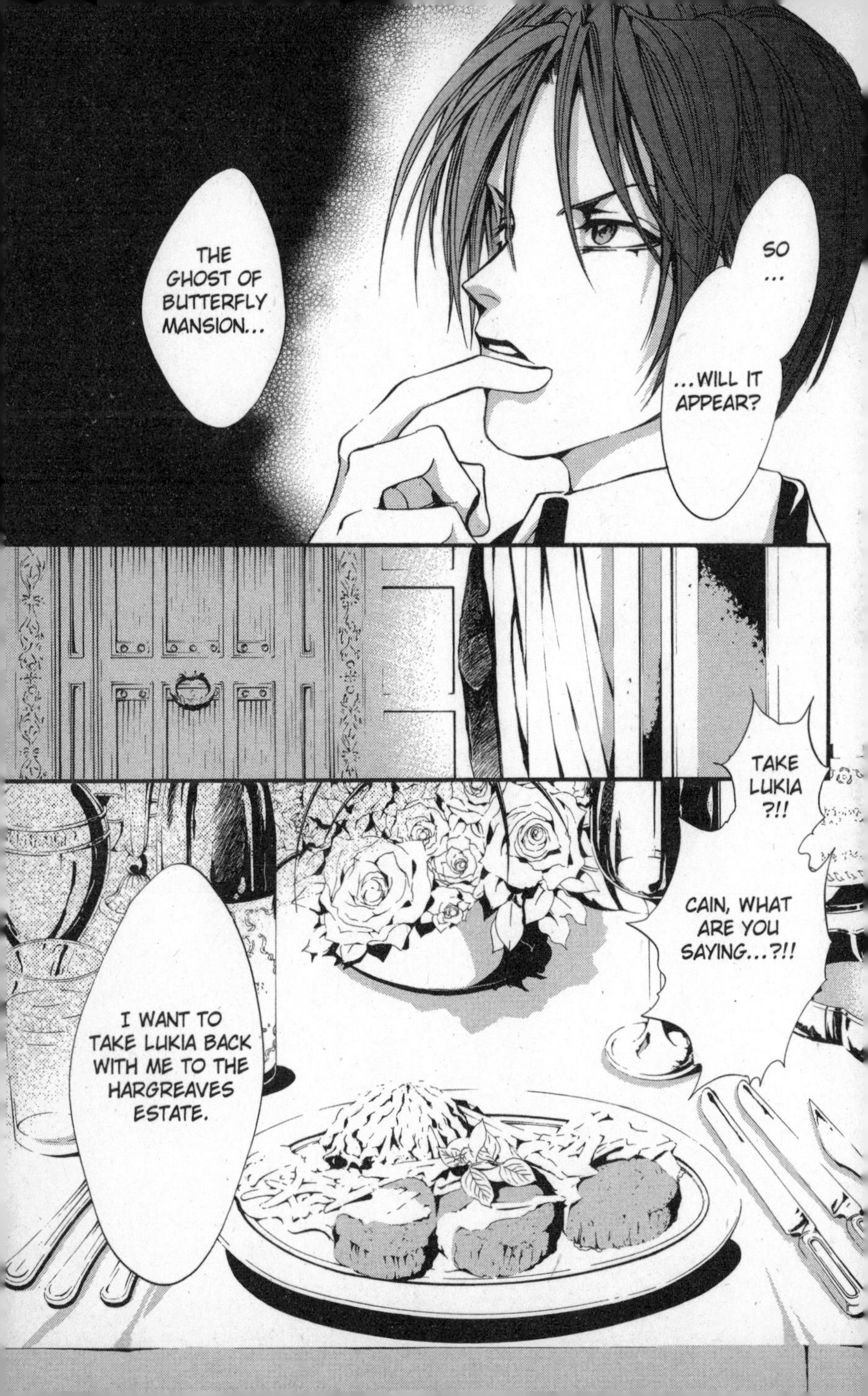
SO ...
...WILL IT APPEAR?
THE GHOST OF BUTTERFLY MANSION...
I WANT TO TAKE LUKIA BACK WITH ME TO THE HARGREAVES ESTATE.
TAKE LUKIA ?!!
CAIN, WHAT ARE YOU SAYING...?!!

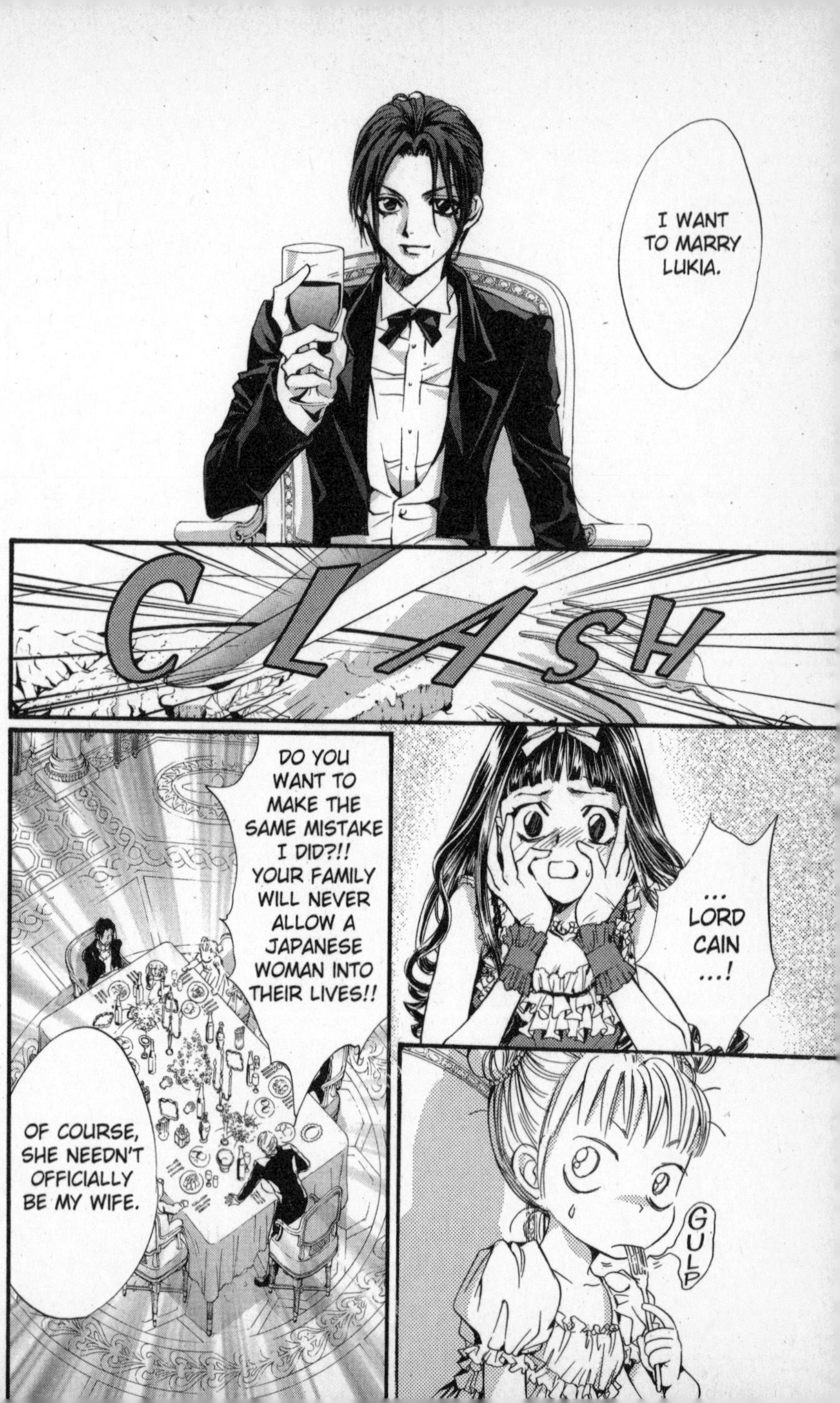
I WANT TO MARRY LUKIA.
CLASH
... LORD CAIN ...!
GULP
DO YOU WANT TO MAKE THE SAME MISTAKE I DID?!! YOUR FAMILY WILL NEVER ALLOW A JAPANESE WOMAN INTO THEIR LIVES!!
OF COURSE, SHE NEEDN'T OFFICIALLY BE MY WIFE.

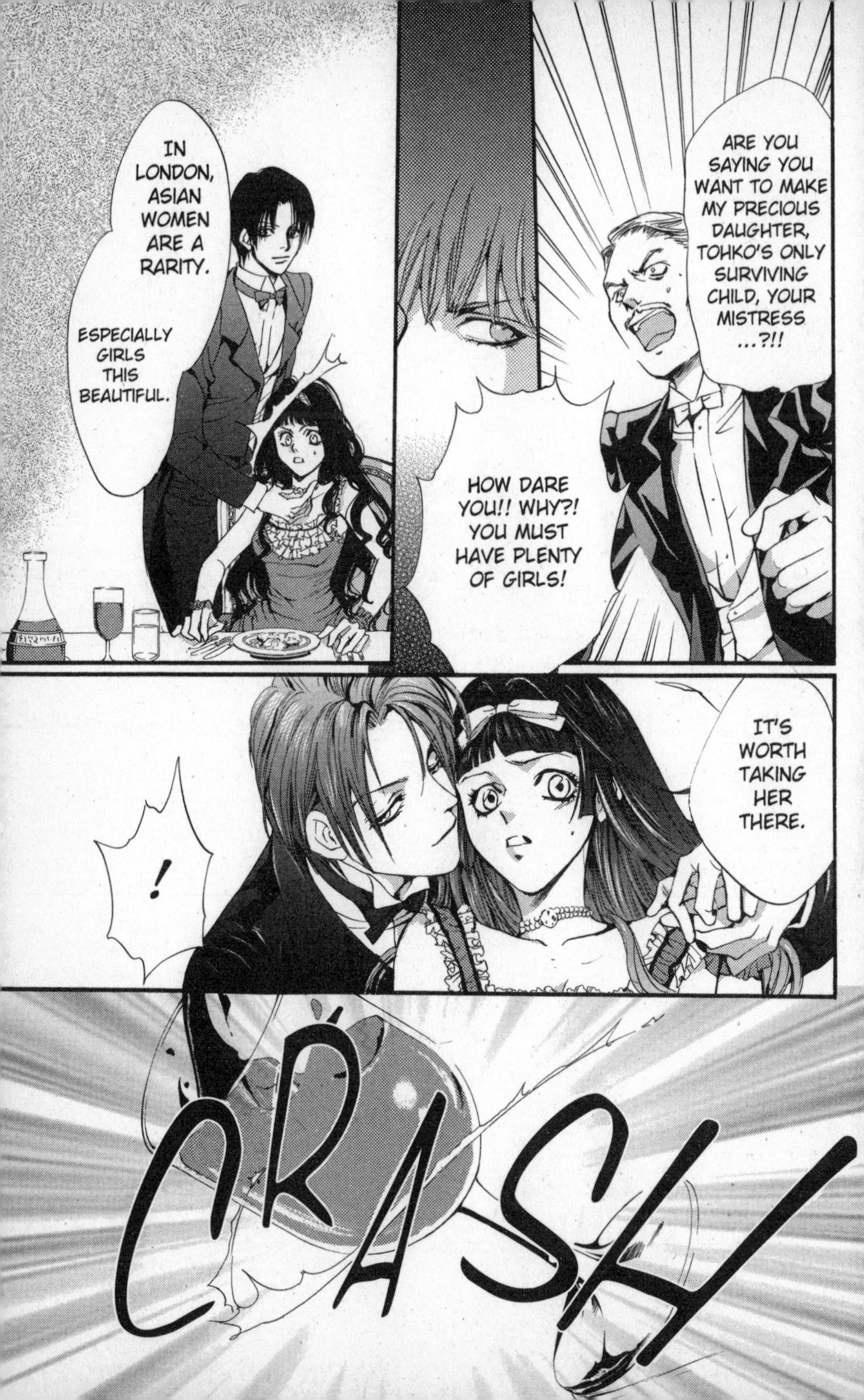
ARE YOU SAYING YOU WANT TO MAKE MY PRECIOUS DAUGHTER, TOHKO'S ONLY SURVIVING CHILD, YOUR MISTRESS ...?!!
HOW DARE YOU!! WHY?! YOU MUST HAVE PLENTY OF GIRLS!
IN LONDON, ASIAN WOMEN ARE A RARITY.
ESPECIALLY GIRLS THIS BEAUTIFUL.
IT'S WORTH TAKING HER THERE.
!
CRASH

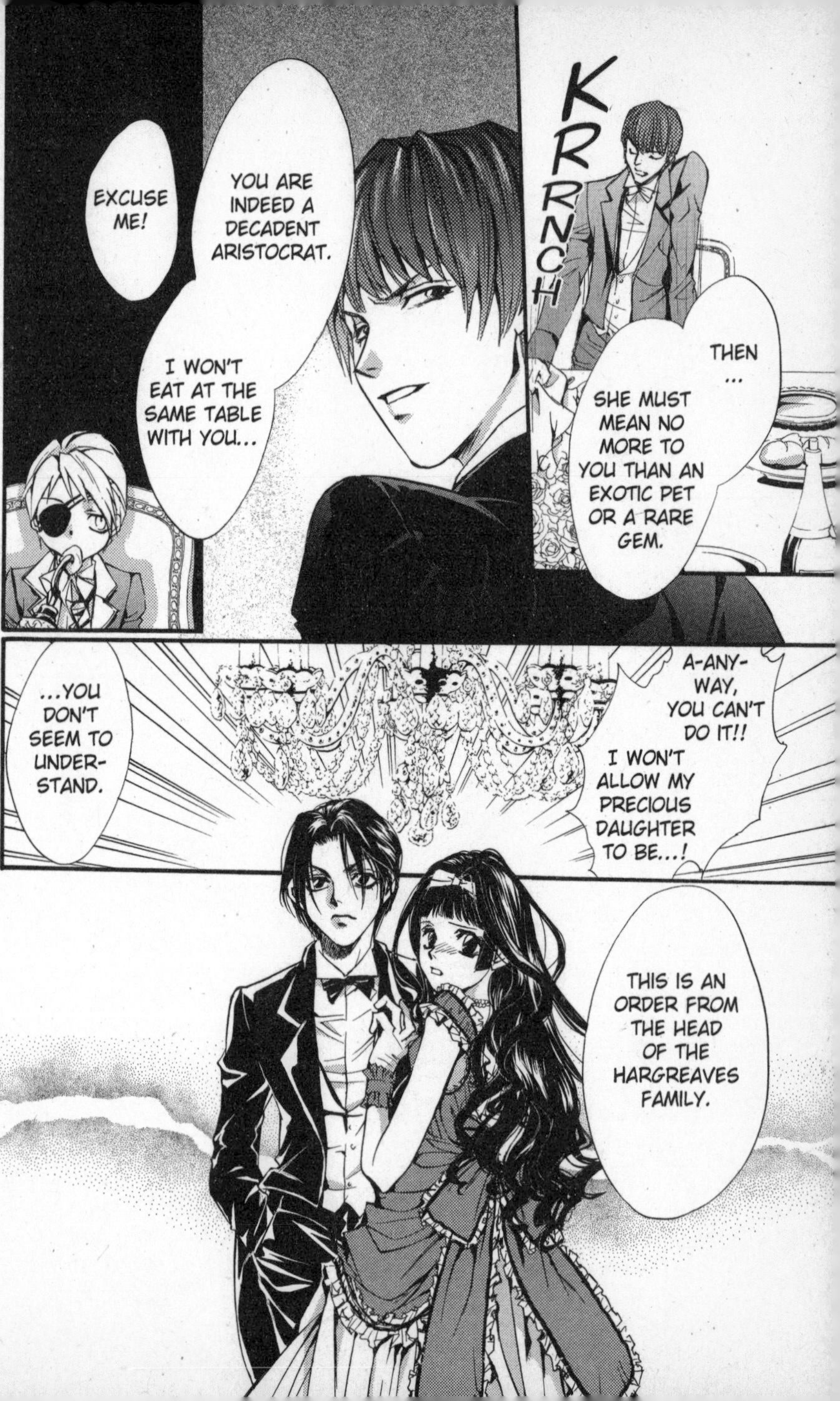
KRRNCH
THEN...
SHE MUST MEAN NO MORE TO YOU THAN AN EXOTIC PET OR A RARE GEM.
YOU ARE INDEED A DECADENT ARISTOCRAT.
I WON'T EAT AT THE SAME TABLE WITH YOU...
EXCUSE ME!
A-ANY-WAY, YOU CAN'T DO IT!!
I WON'T ALLOW MY PRECIOUS DAUGHTER TO BE...!
...YOU DON'T SEEM TO UNDER-STAND.
THIS IS AN ORDER FROM THE HEAD OF THE HARGREAVES FAMILY.

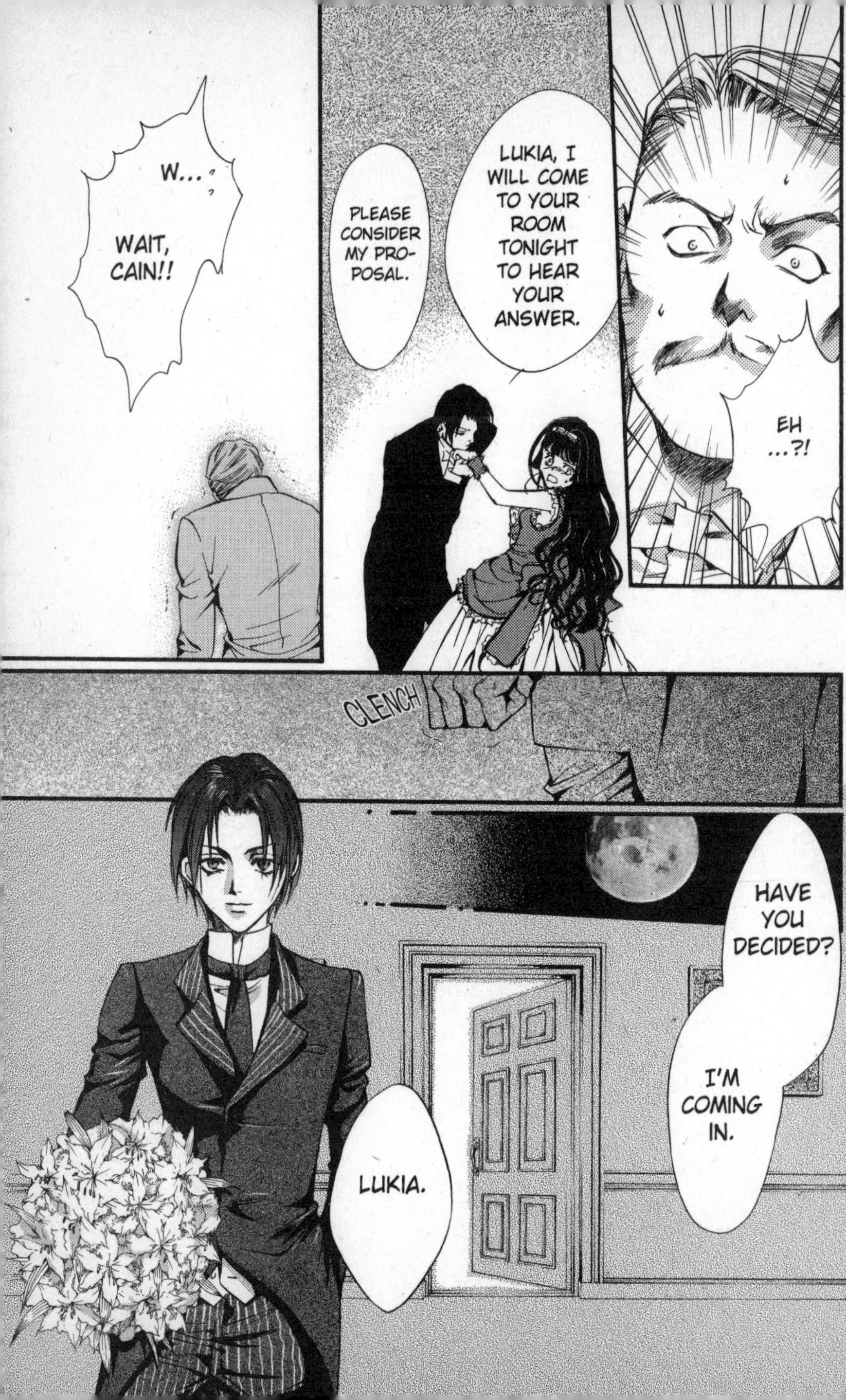
EH ...?!
LUKIA, I WILL COME TO YOUR ROOM TONIGHT TO HEAR YOUR ANSWER.
PLEASE CONSIDER MY PRO-POSAL.
W...?
WAIT, CAIN!!
CLENCH
HAVE YOU DECIDED?
I'M COMING IN.
LUKIA.

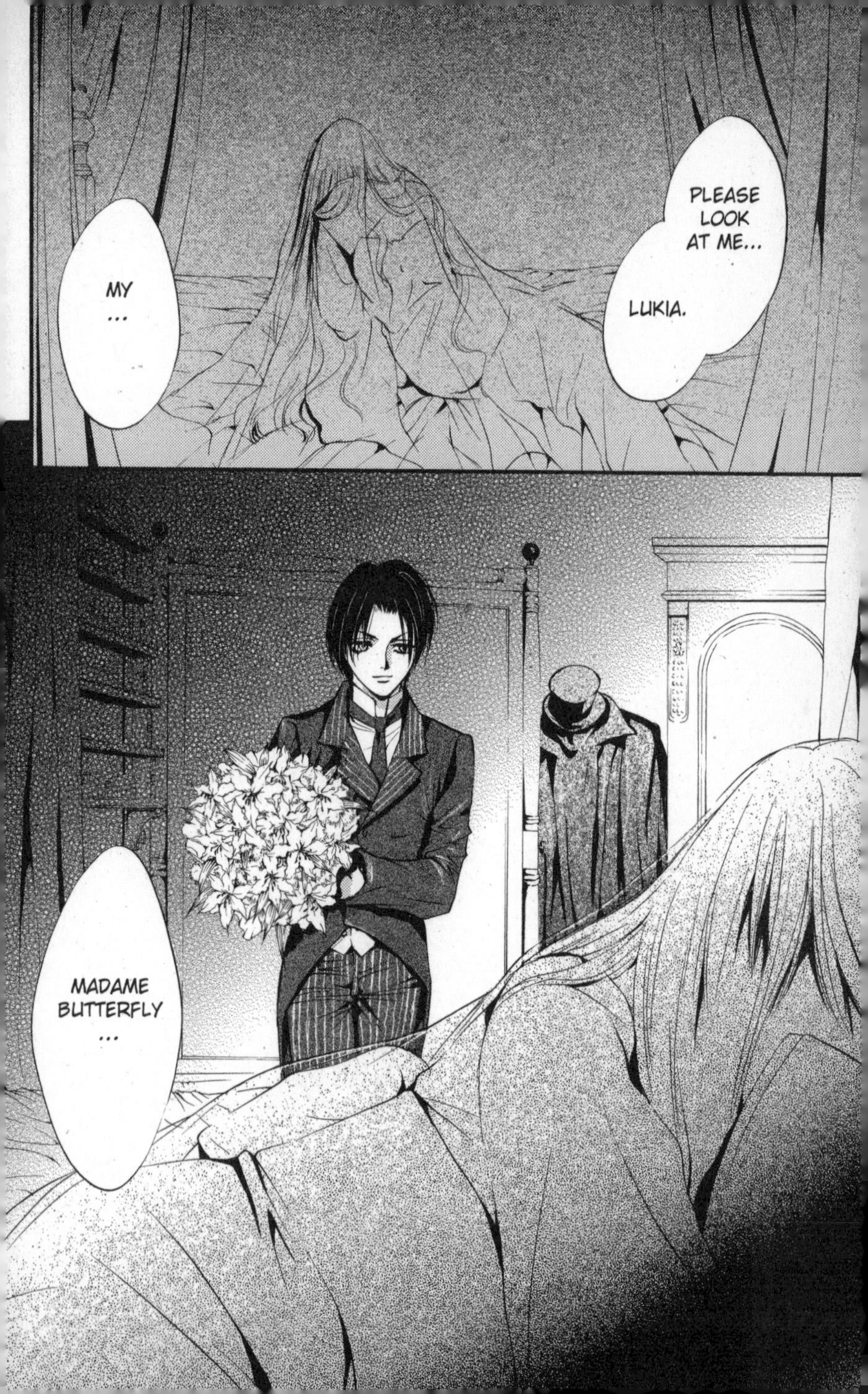
PLEASE LOOK AT ME...
LUKIA.
MY ...
MADAME BUTTERFLY ...

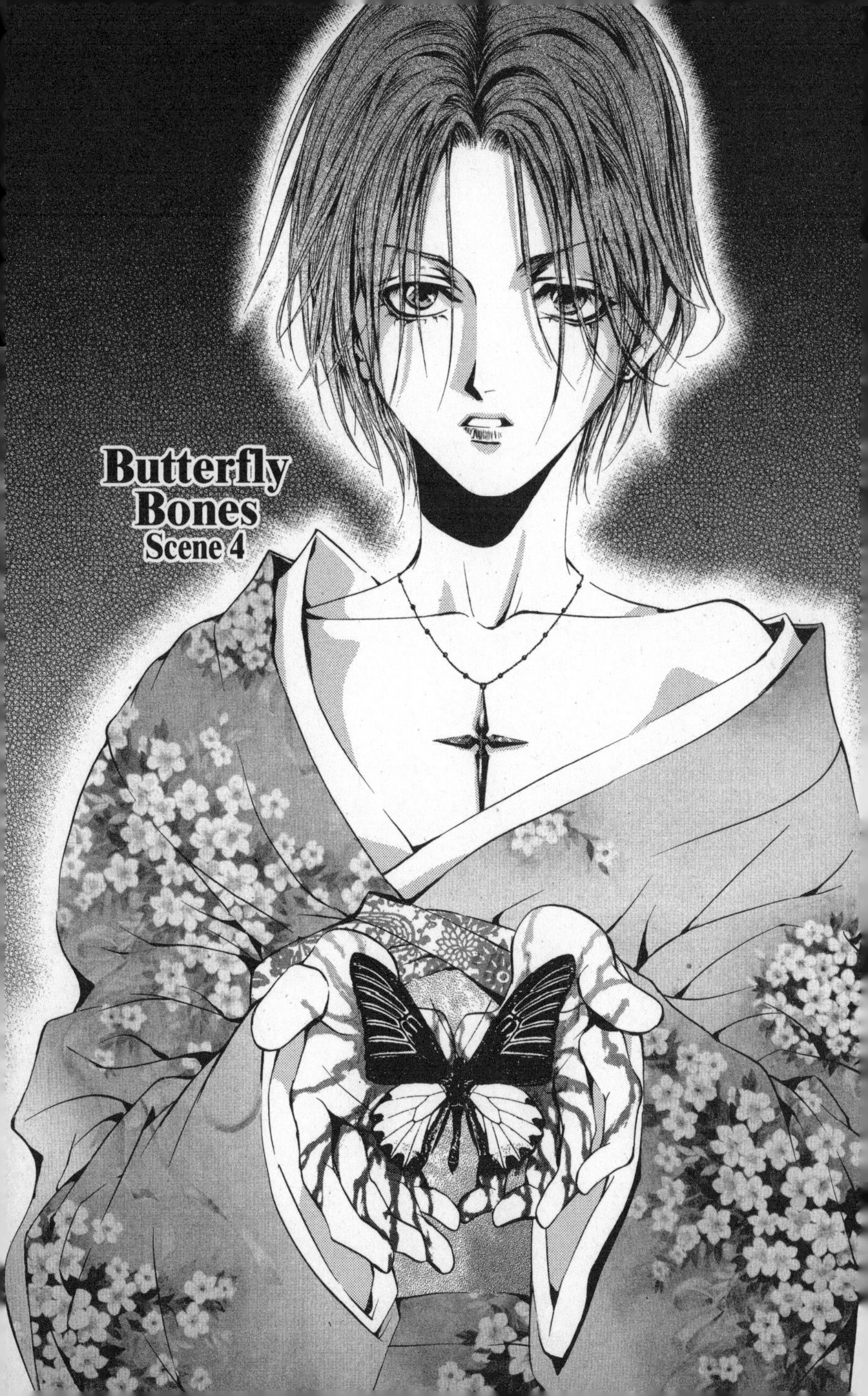
Butterfly Bones
Scene 4

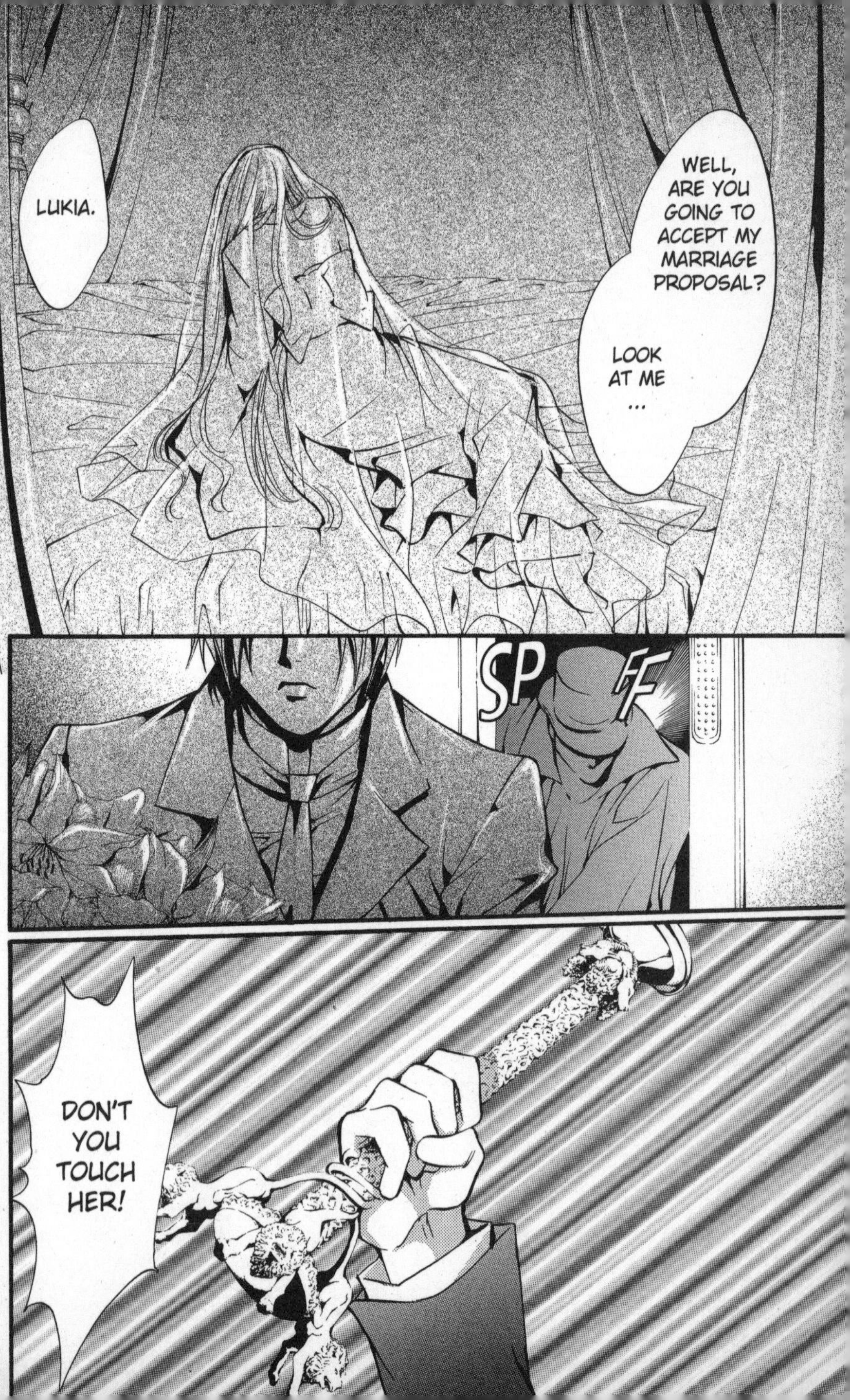
WELL, ARE YOU GOING TO ACCEPT MY MARRIAGE PROPOSAL?
LOOK AT ME ...
LUKIA.
SPFF
DON'T YOU TOUCH HER!

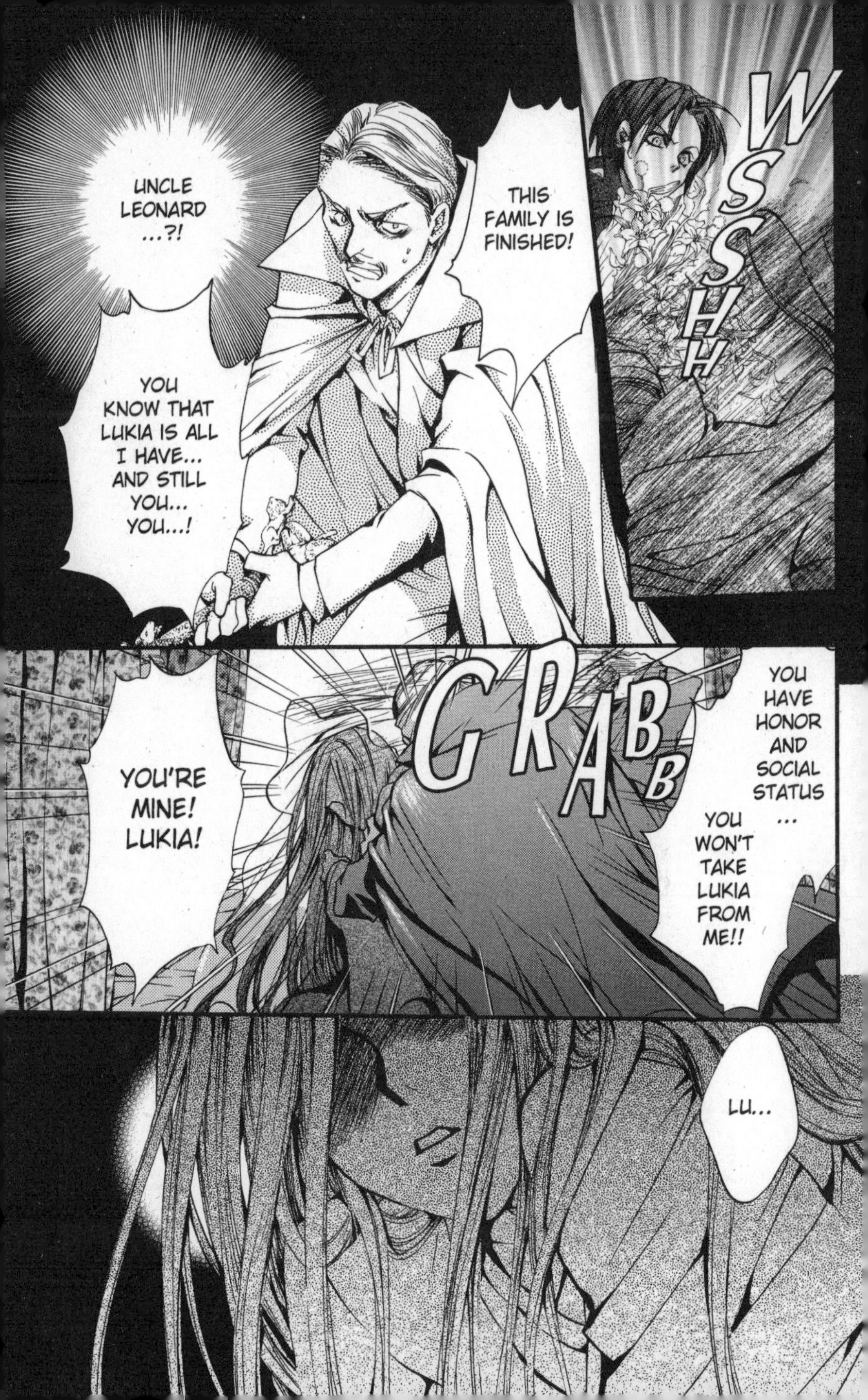
WSSHH
THIS FAMILY IS FINISHED!
UNCLE LEONARD ...?!
YOU KNOW THAT LUKIA IS ALL I HAVE... AND STILL YOU... YOU...!
YOU HAVE HONOR AND SOCIAL STATUS ...
YOU WON'T TAKE LUKIA FROM ME!!
GRABB
YOU'RE MINE! LUKIA!
LU...

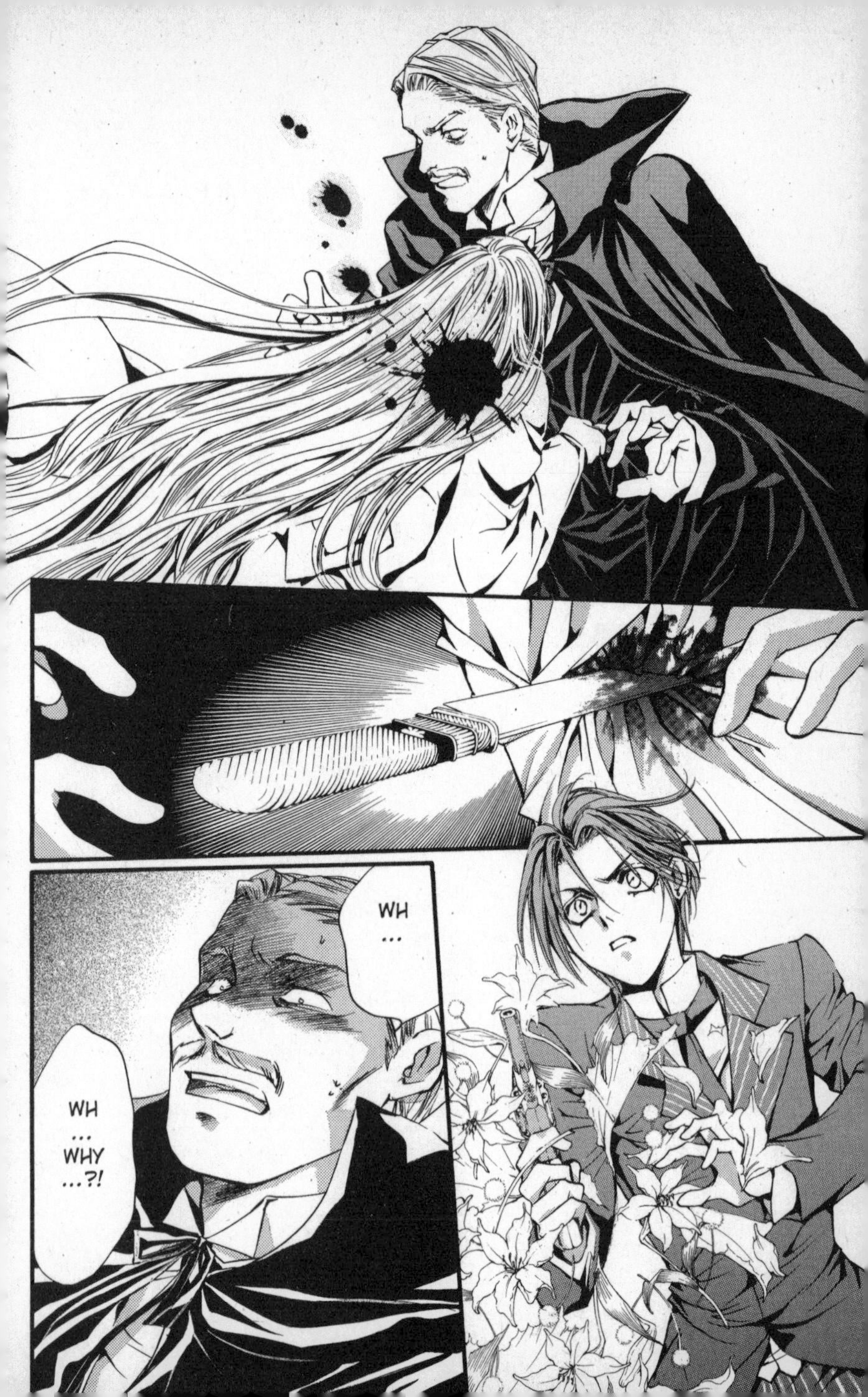
WH ...
WH ... WHY ...?!

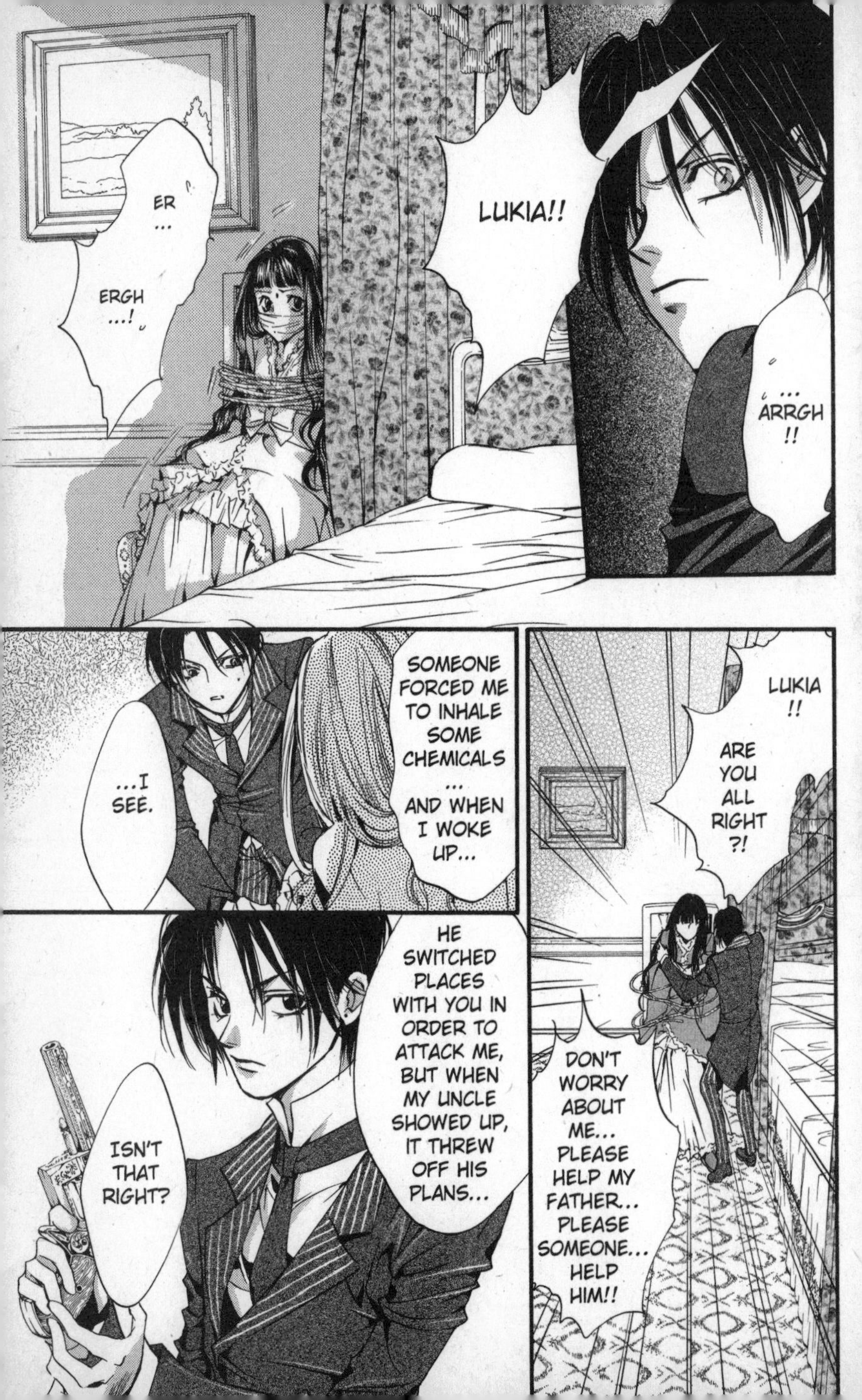
LUKIA!!
... ARRGH !!
ER ...
ERGH ...!
LUKIA !!
ARE YOU ALL RIGHT ?!
DON'T WORRY ABOUT ME... PLEASE HELP MY FATHER... PLEASE SOMEONE... HELP HIM!!
SOMEONE FORCED ME TO INHALE SOME CHEMICALS ... AND WHEN I WOKE UP...
...I SEE.
HE SWITCHED PLACES WITH YOU IN ORDER TO ATTACK ME, BUT WHEN MY UNCLE SHOWED UP, IT THREW OFF HIS PLANS...
ISN'T THAT RIGHT?

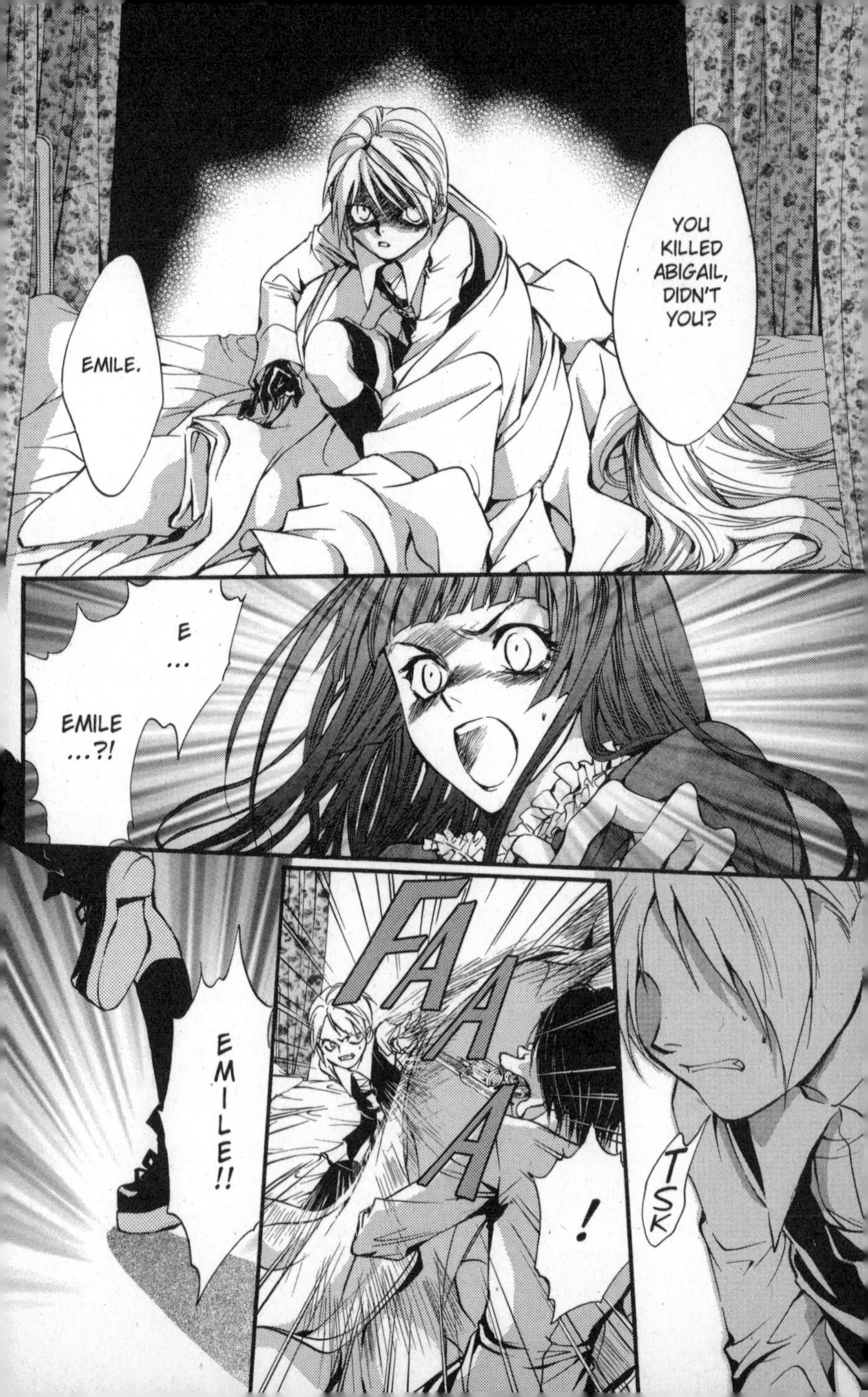
YOU KILLED ABIGAIL, DIDN'T YOU?
EMILE.
E ...
EMILE ...?!
TSK
!
FAAA
EMILE!!

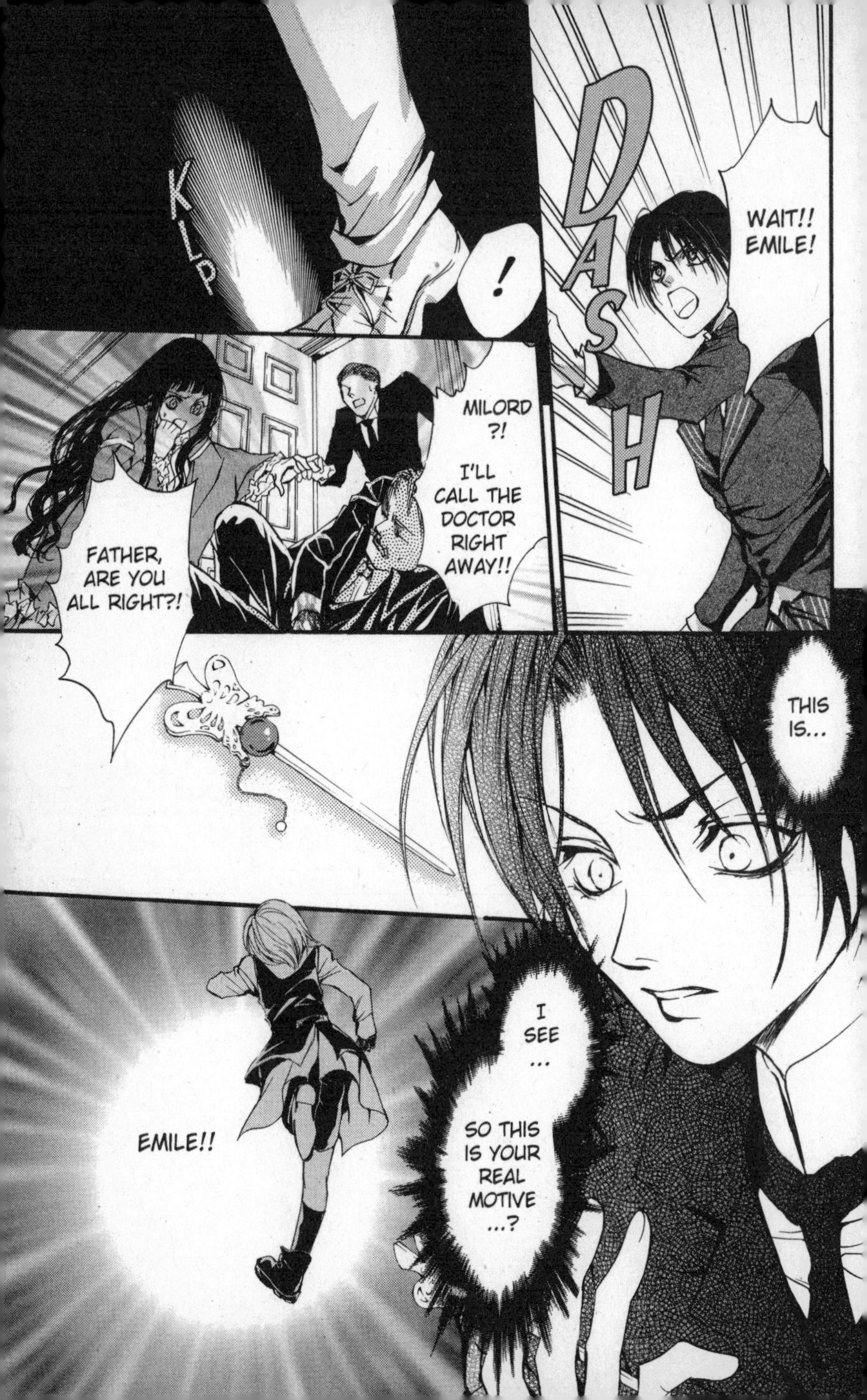
DASH
WAIT!! EMILE!
KLP
!
MILORD ?!
I'LL CALL THE DOCTOR RIGHT AWAY!!
FATHER, ARE YOU ALL RIGHT?!
THIS IS...
I SEE ...
SO THIS IS YOUR REAL MOTIVE ...?
EMILE!!

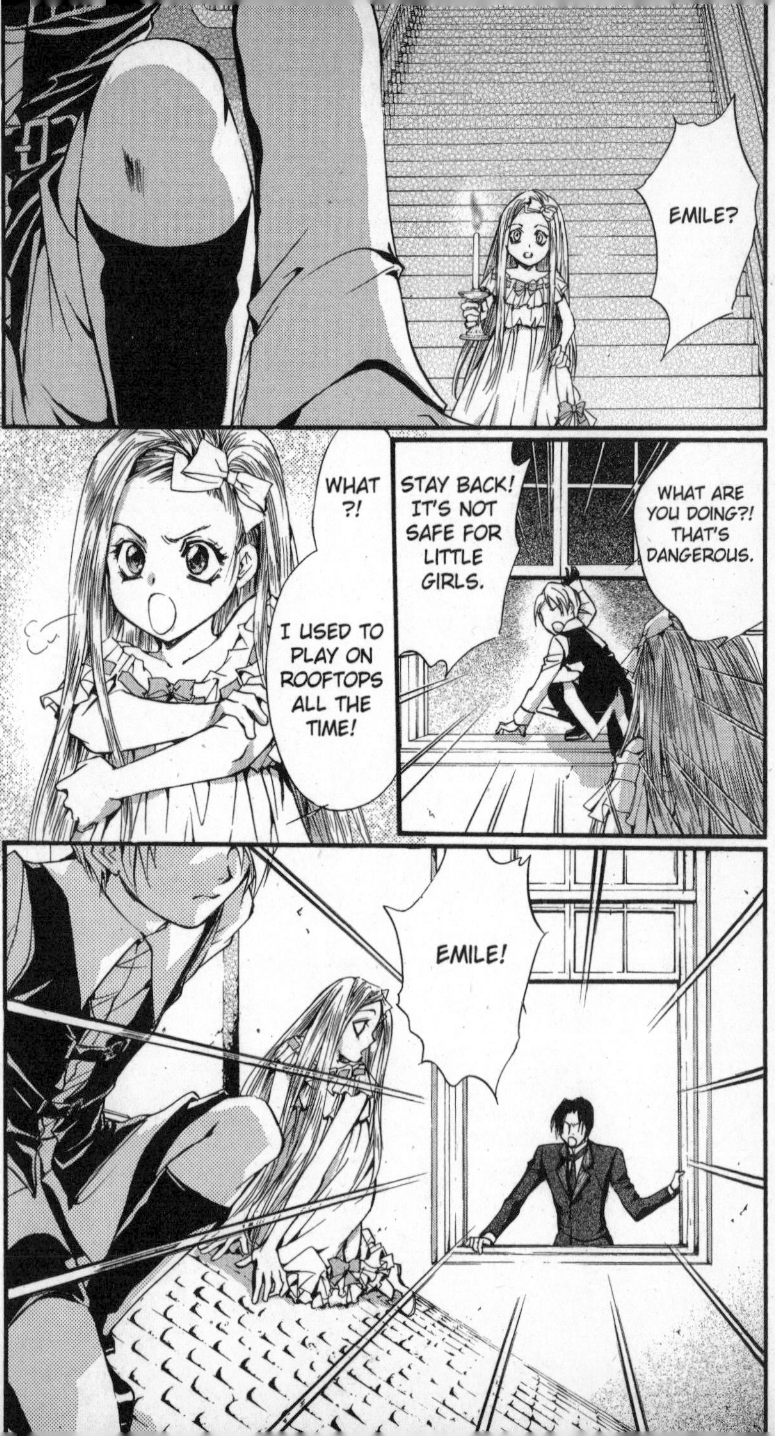
EMILE?
WHAT ARE YOU DOING?! THAT'S DANGEROUS.
STAY BACK! IT'S NOT SAFE FOR LITTLE GIRLS.
WHAT?!
I USED TO PLAY ON ROOFTOPS ALL THE TIME!
EMILE!

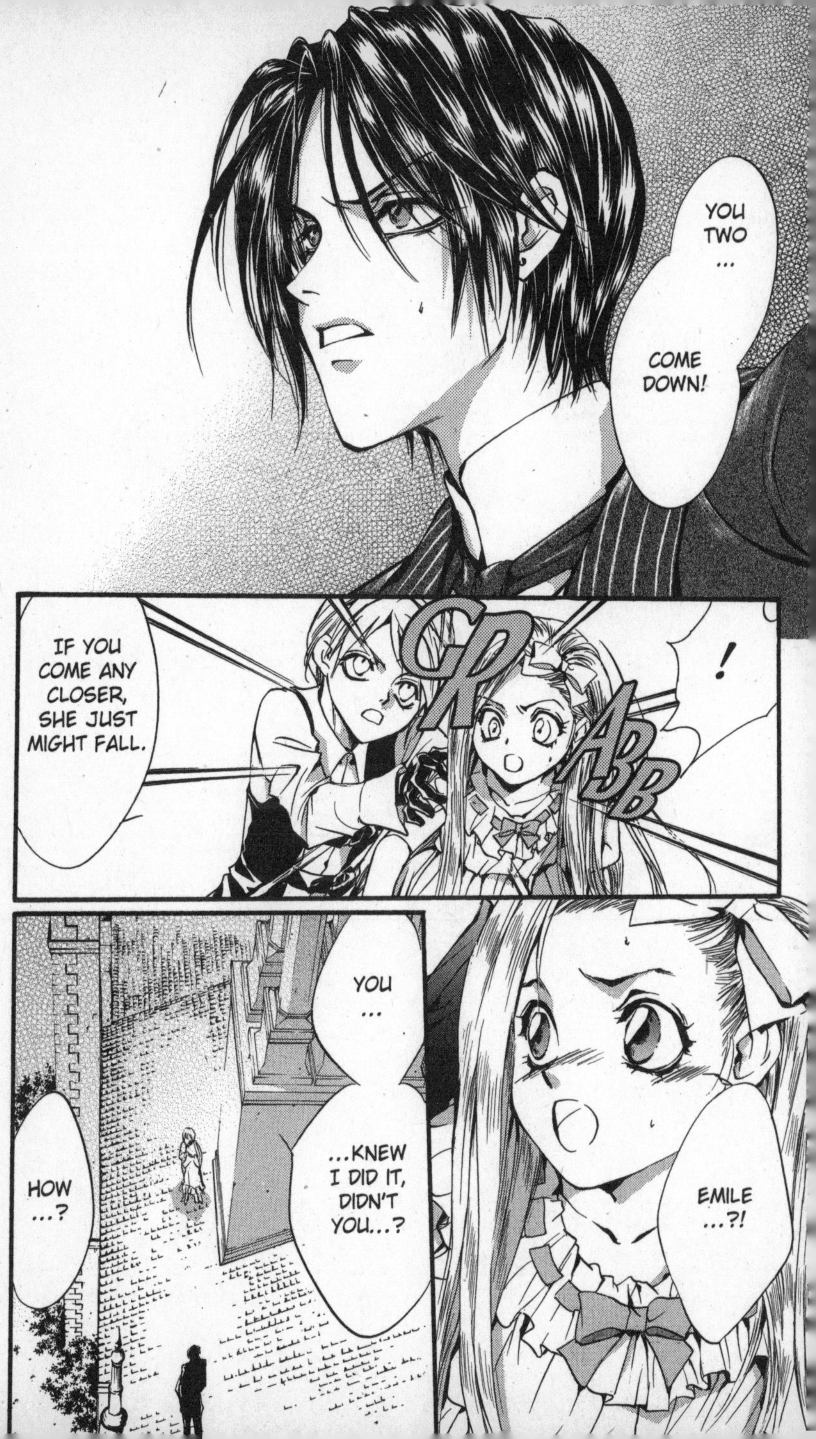
YOU TWO ...
COME DOWN!
!
GRABB
IF YOU COME ANY CLOSER, SHE JUST MIGHT FALL.
EMILE ...?!
YOU ...
...KNEW I DID IT, DIDN'T YOU...?
HOW ...?

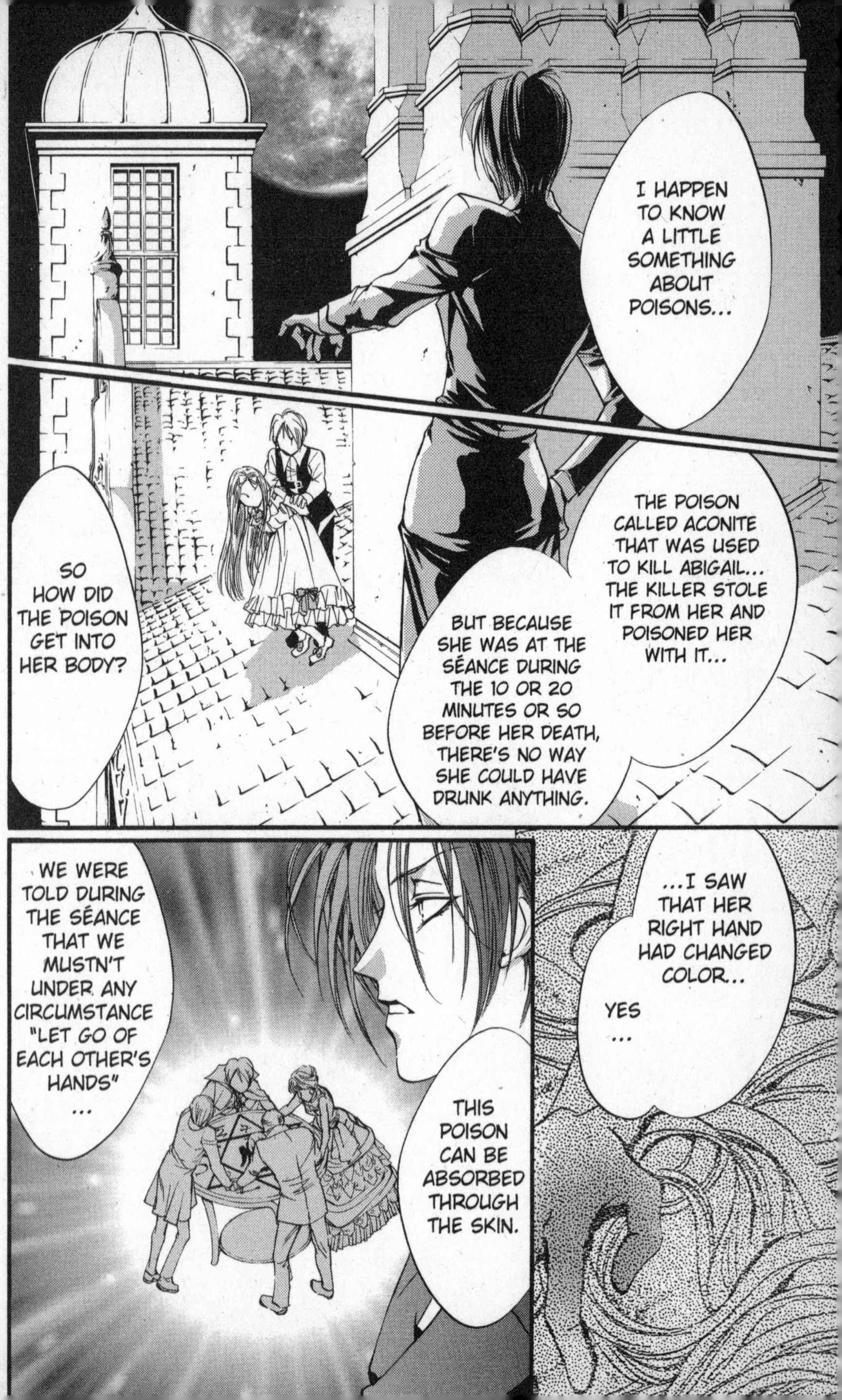
I HAPPEN TO KNOW A LITTLE SOMETHING ABOUT POISONS...
THE POISON CALLED ACONITE THAT WAS USED TO KILL ABIGAIL... THE KILLER STOLE IT FROM HER AND POISONED HER WITH IT...
BUT BECAUSE SHE WAS AT THE SÉANCE DURING THE 10 OR 20 MINUTES OR SO BEFORE HER DEATH, THERE'S NO WAY SHE COULD HAVE DRUNK ANYTHING.
SO HOW DID THE POISON GET INTO HER BODY?
...I SAW THAT HER RIGHT HAND HAD CHANGED COLOR...
YES ...
WE WERE TOLD DURING THE SÉANCE THAT WE MUSTN'T UNDER ANY CIRCUMSTANCE "LET GO OF EACH OTHER'S HANDS" ...
THIS POISON CAN BE ABSORBED THROUGH THE SKIN.

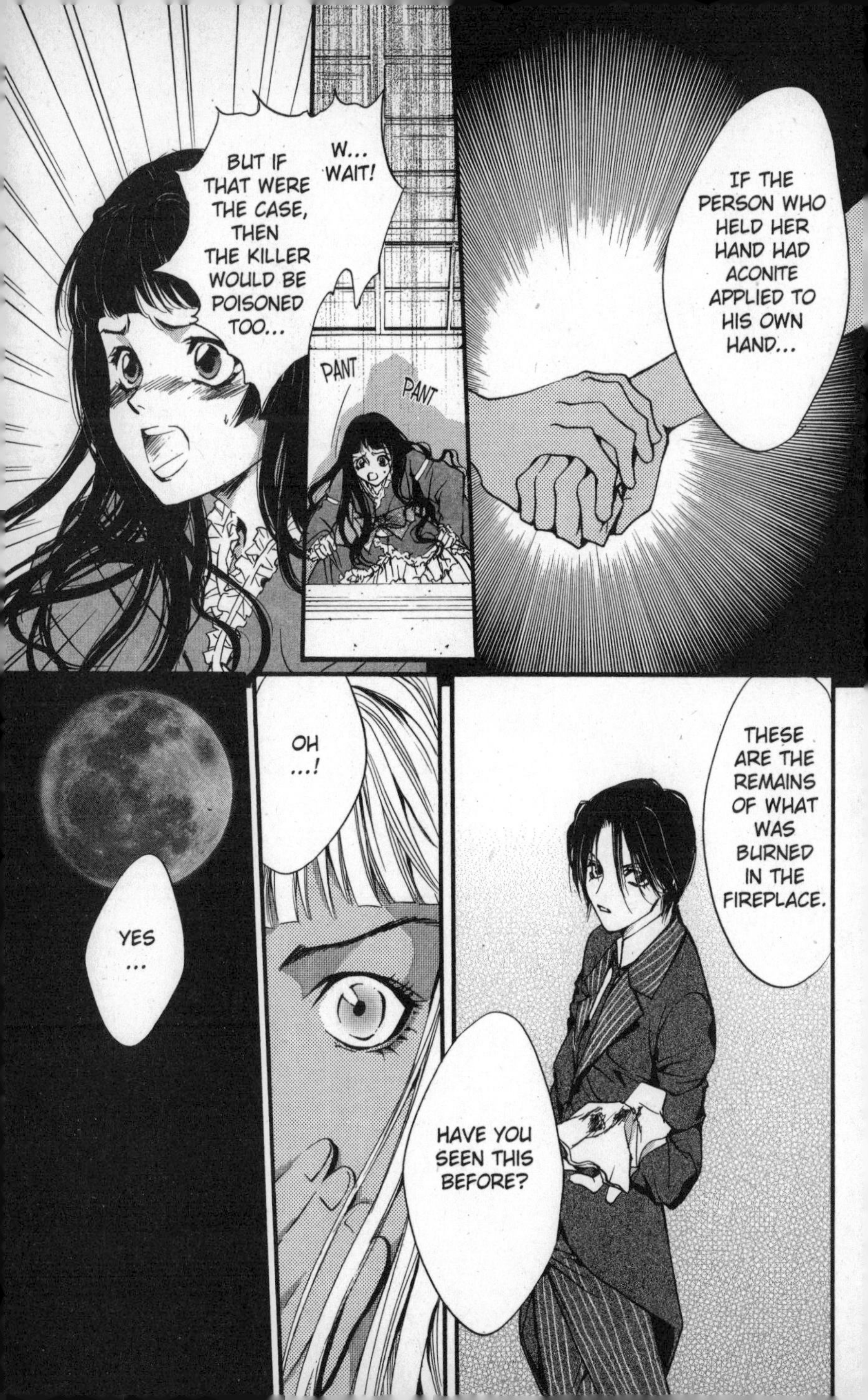
IF THE PERSON WHO HELD HER HAND HAD ACONITE APPLIED TO HIS OWN HAND...
W... WAIT!
PANT
PANT
BUT IF THAT WERE THE CASE, THEN THE KILLER WOULD BE POISONED TOO...
THESE ARE THE REMAINS OF WHAT WAS BURNED IN THE FIREPLACE.
HAVE YOU SEEN THIS BEFORE?
OH ...!
YES ...

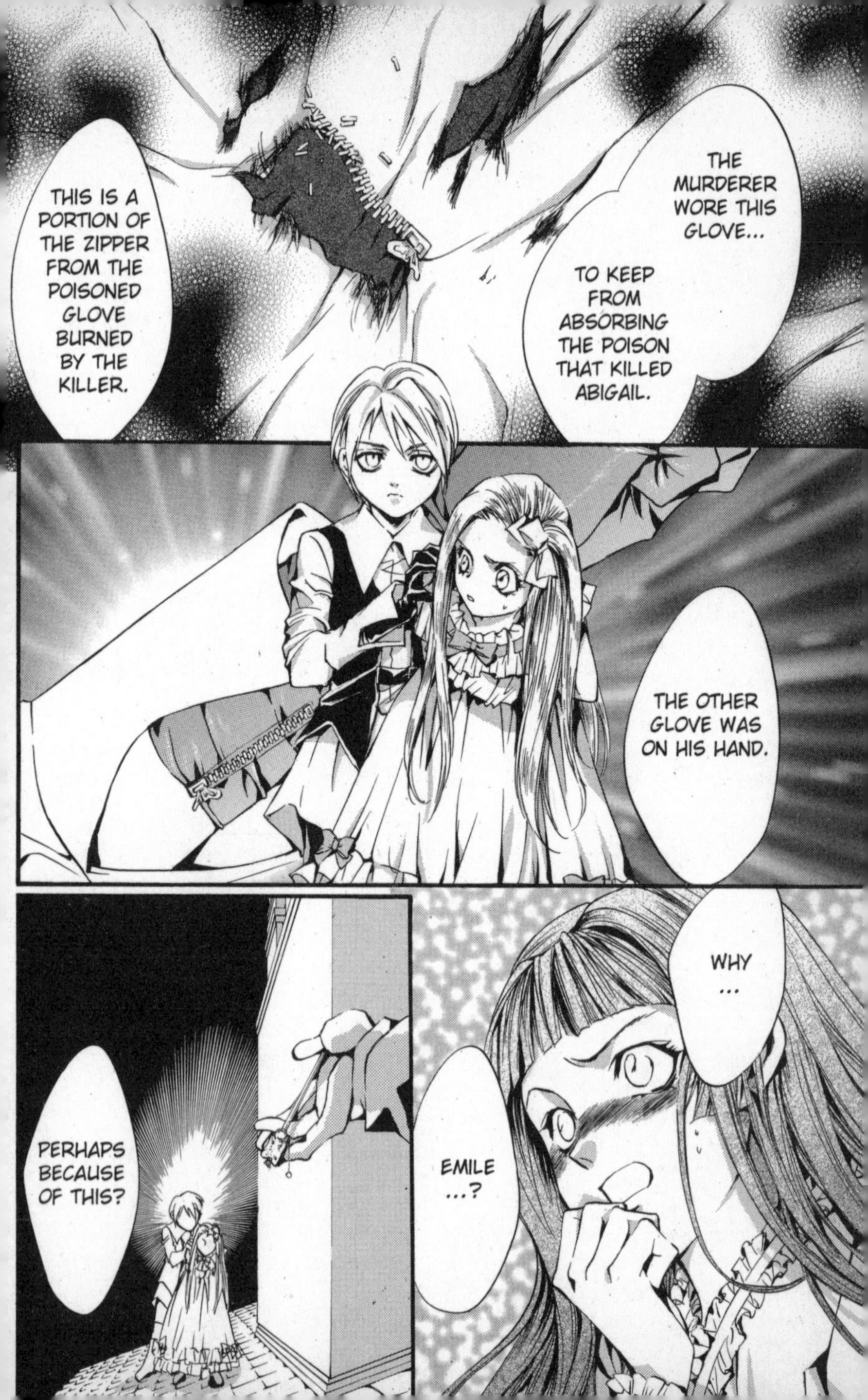
THE MURDERER WORE THIS GLOVE...
TO KEEP FROM ABSORBING THE POISON THAT KILLED ABIGAIL.
THIS IS A PORTION OF THE ZIPPER FROM THE POISONED GLOVE BURNED BY THE KILLER.
THE OTHER GLOVE WAS ON HIS HAND.
WHY ...
EMILE ...?
PERHAPS BECAUSE OF THIS?

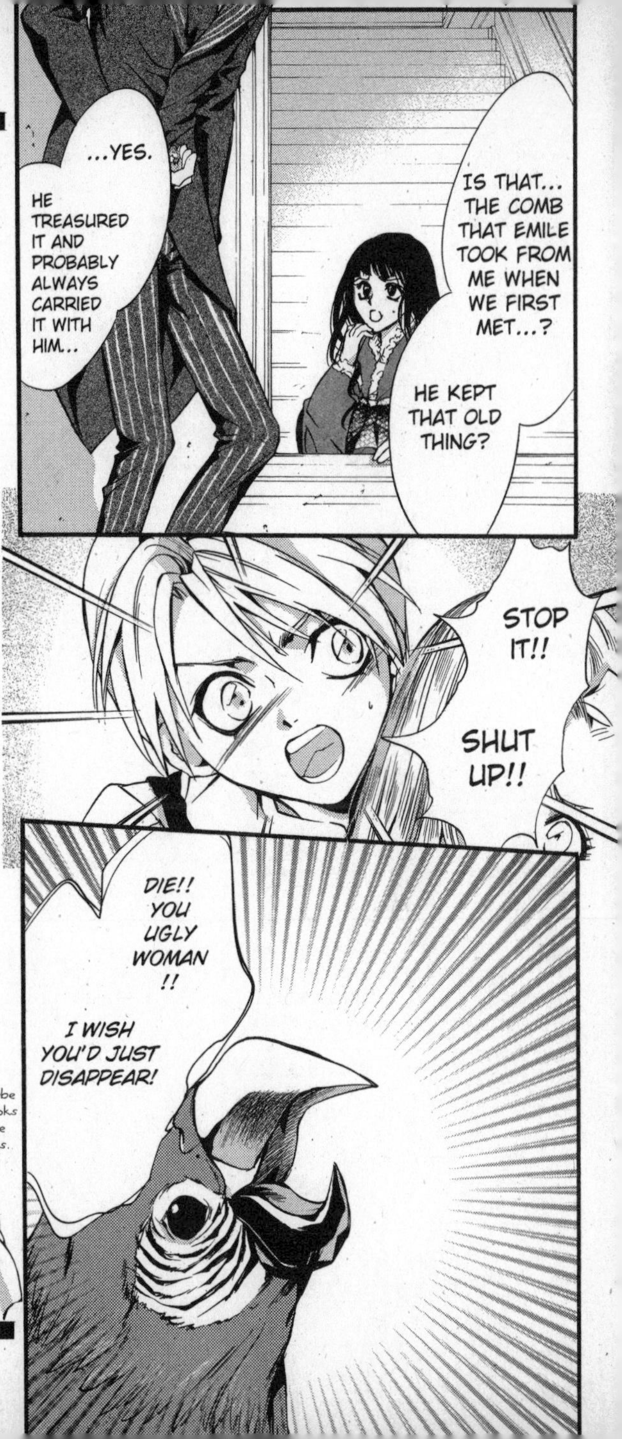
IS THAT... THE COMB THAT EMILE TOOK FROM ME WHEN WE FIRST MET...?
HE KEPT THAT OLD THING?
...YES.
HE TREASURED IT AND PROBABLY ALWAYS CARRIED IT WITH HIM...
STOP IT!!
SHUT UP!!
DIE!! YOU UGLY WOMAN !!
I WISH YOU'D JUST DISAPPEAR!

I think some people seriously wanted to know whether "Cain was really going to marry Lukia." Although Lukia's kind of the quiet type, lots of people said they liked her. Maybe it's because she's Japanese? Maybe not. It's true that if she were a more emotional girl then she might have been Cain's usual type, but maybe since she'd been through so much, she wasn't susceptible to his poisonous charms. Cain seems to prefer girls who aren't too smart. That's the feeling I get when I look back at all the girls from his past. The original Lukia was a Christian martyr in ancient Rome, who took out her own beautiful eyes and sent them to her suitor. In the end she died a tragic death. I would also like to see the paintings that were done on this theme. Apparently, she is portrayed in the paintings holding the eyeballs on a tray. Lukia was kind of creepy.

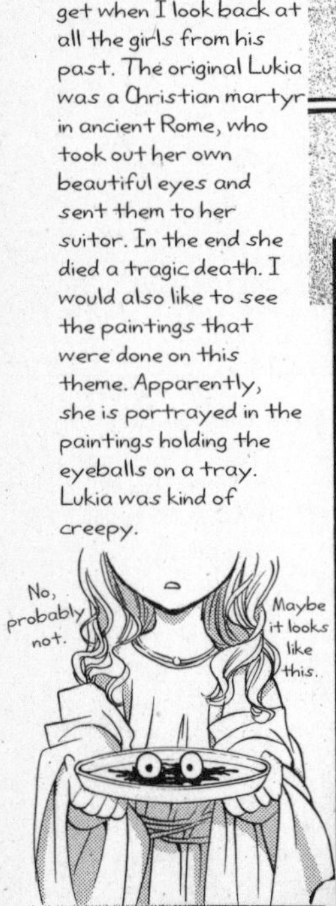
No, probably not.
Maybe it looks like this.

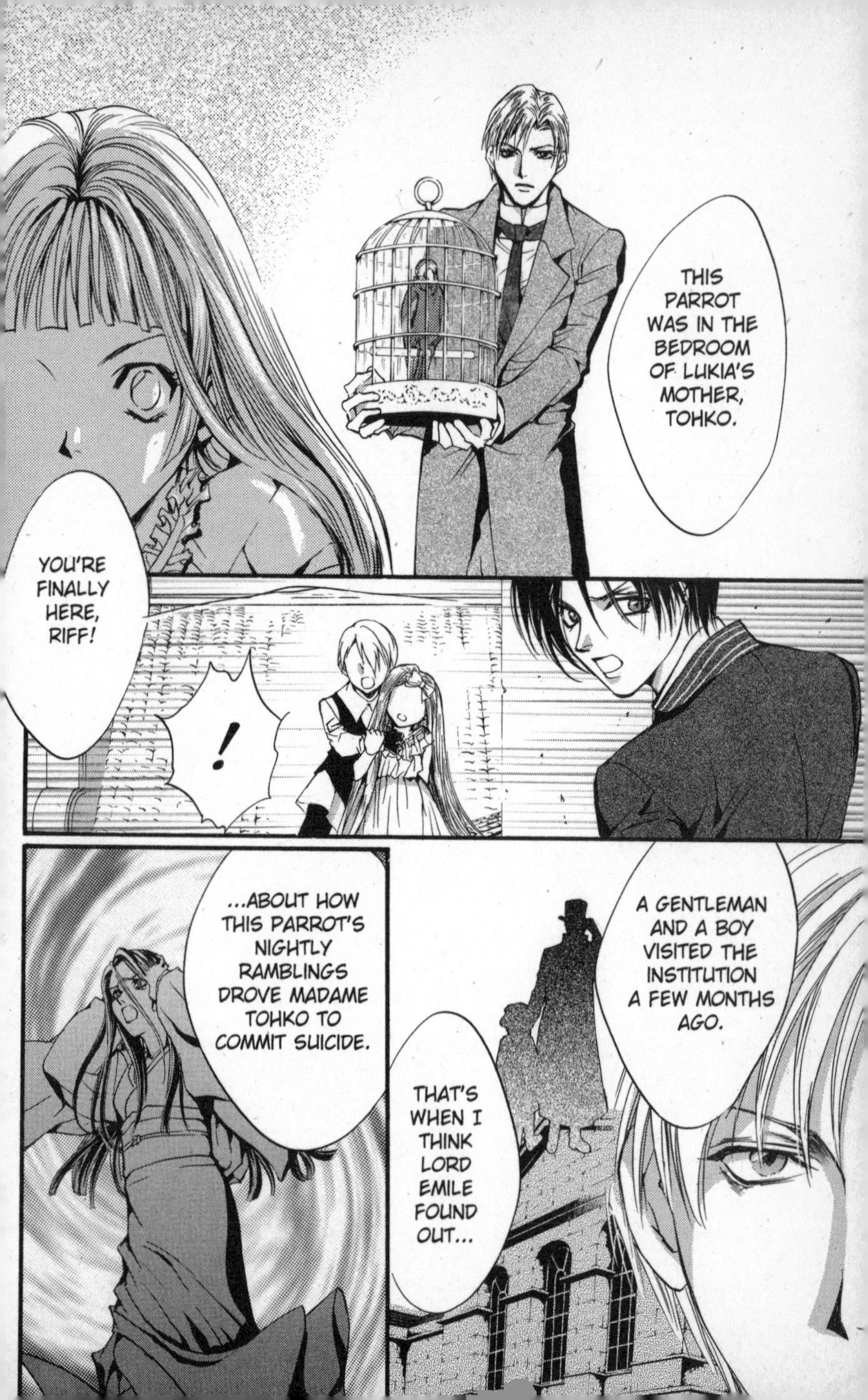
THIS PARROT WAS IN THE BEDROOM OF LUKIA'S MOTHER, TOHKO.
YOU'RE FINALLY HERE, RIFF!
!
A GENTLEMAN AND A BOY VISITED THE INSTITUTION A FEW MONTHS AGO.
THAT'S WHEN I THINK LORD EMILE FOUND OUT...
...ABOUT HOW THIS PARROT'S NIGHTLY RAMBLINGS DROVE MADAME TOHKO TO COMMIT SUICIDE.

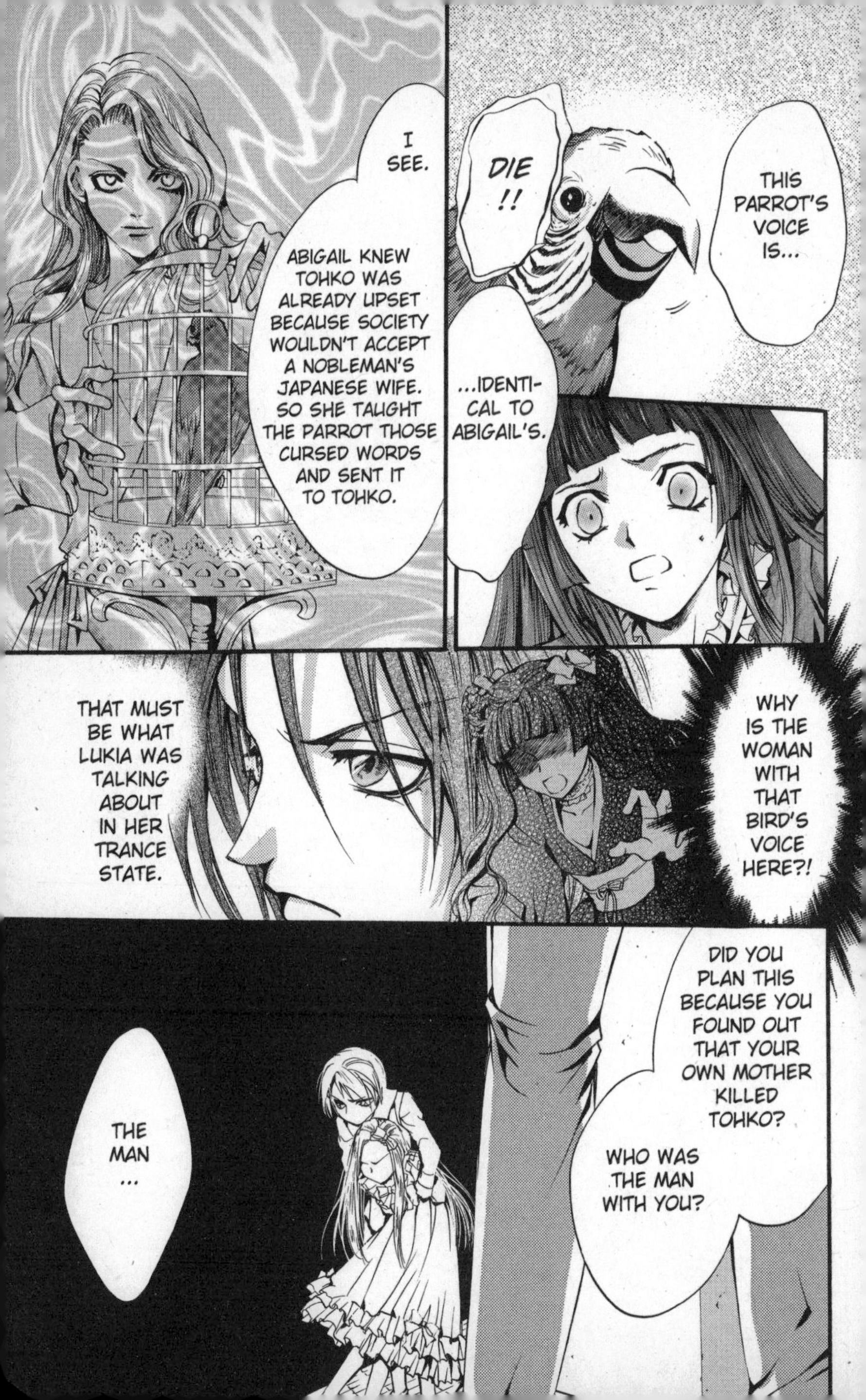
THIS PARROT'S VOICE IS...
DIE !!
...IDENTICAL TO ABIGAIL'S.
I SEE.
ABIGAIL KNEW TOHKO WAS ALREADY UPSET BECAUSE SOCIETY WOULDN'T ACCEPT A NOBLEMAN'S JAPANESE WIFE. SO SHE TAUGHT THE PARROT THOSE CURSED WORDS AND SENT IT TO TOHKO.
WHY IS THE WOMAN WITH THAT BIRD'S VOICE HERE?!
THAT MUST BE WHAT LUKIA WAS TALKING ABOUT IN HER TRANCE STATE.
DID YOU PLAN THIS BECAUSE YOU FOUND OUT THAT YOUR OWN MOTHER KILLED TOHKO?
WHO WAS THE MAN WITH YOU?
THE MAN ...

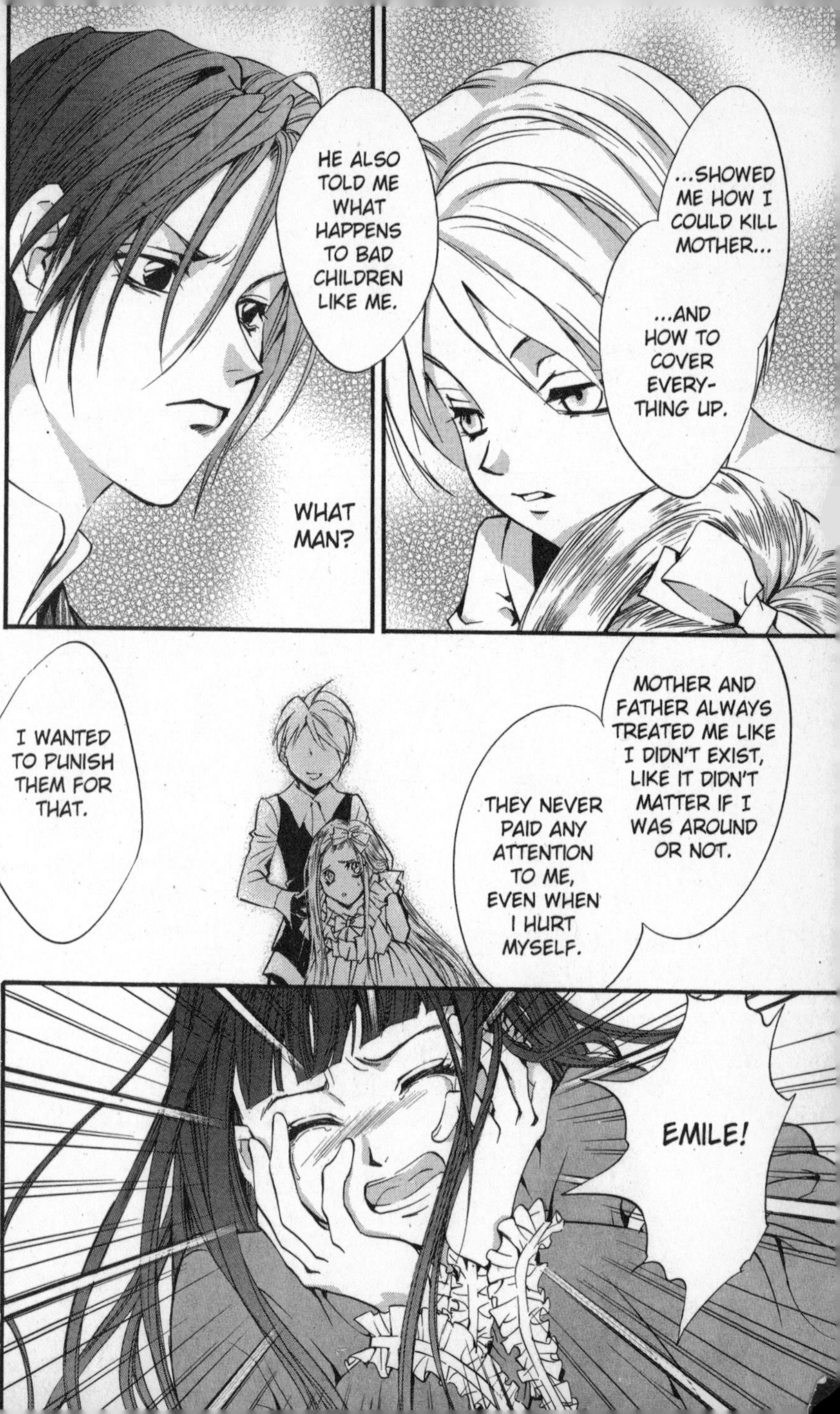
...SHOWED ME HOW I COULD KILL MOTHER...
...AND HOW TO COVER EVERY-THING UP.
HE ALSO TOLD ME WHAT HAPPENS TO BAD CHILDREN LIKE ME.
WHAT MAN?
MOTHER AND FATHER ALWAYS TREATED ME LIKE I DIDN'T EXIST, LIKE IT DIDN'T MATTER IF I WAS AROUND OR NOT.
THEY NEVER PAID ANY ATTENTION TO ME, EVEN WHEN I HURT MYSELF.
I WANTED TO PUNISH THEM FOR THAT.
EMILE!

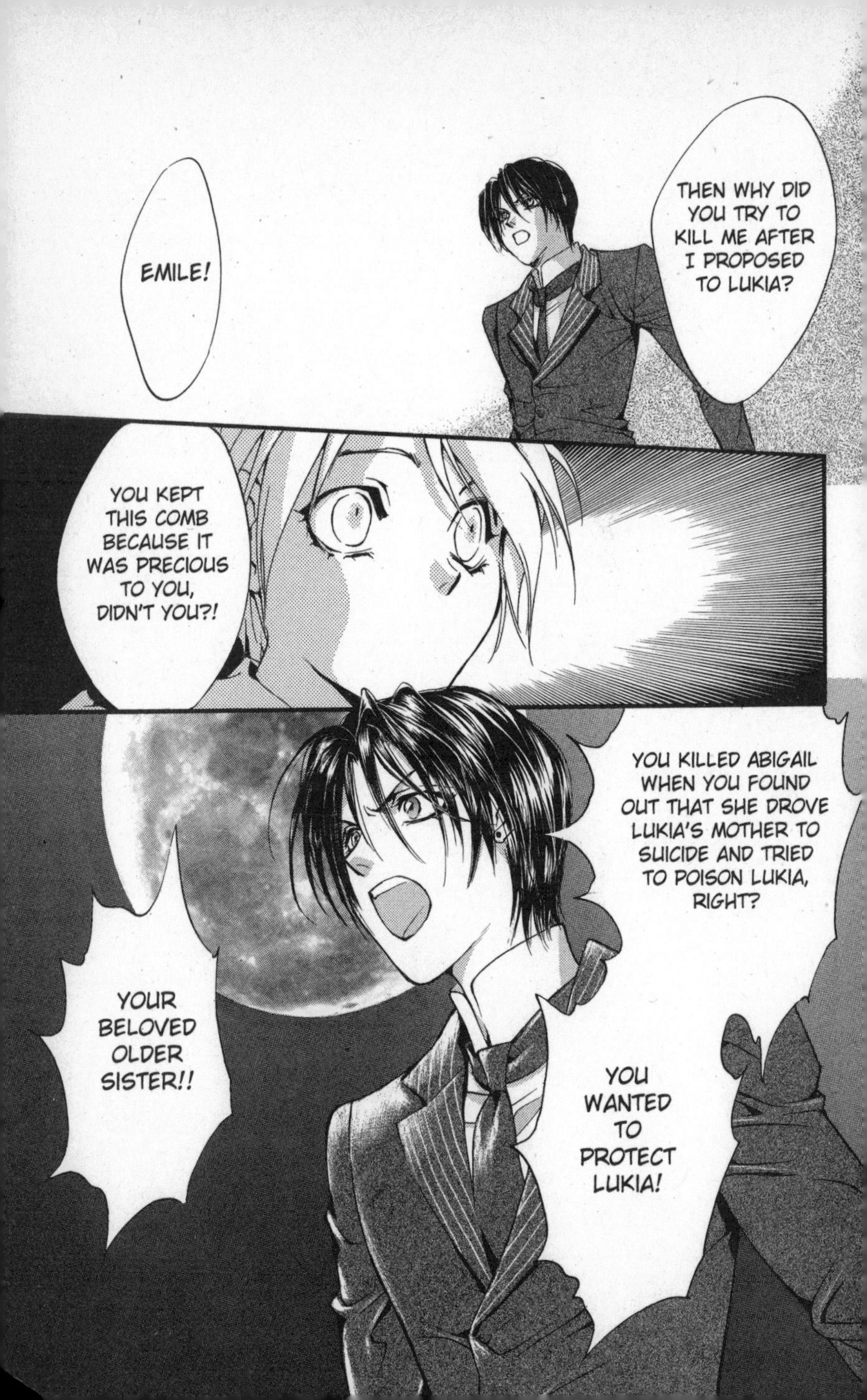
THEN WHY DID YOU TRY TO KILL ME AFTER I PROPOSED TO LUKIA?
EMILE!
YOU KEPT THIS COMB BECAUSE IT WAS PRECIOUS TO YOU, DIDN'T YOU?!
YOU KILLED ABIGAIL WHEN YOU FOUND OUT THAT SHE DROVE LUKIA'S MOTHER TO SUICIDE AND TRIED TO POISON LUKIA, RIGHT?
YOU WANTED TO PROTECT LUKIA!
YOUR BELOVED OLDER SISTER!!

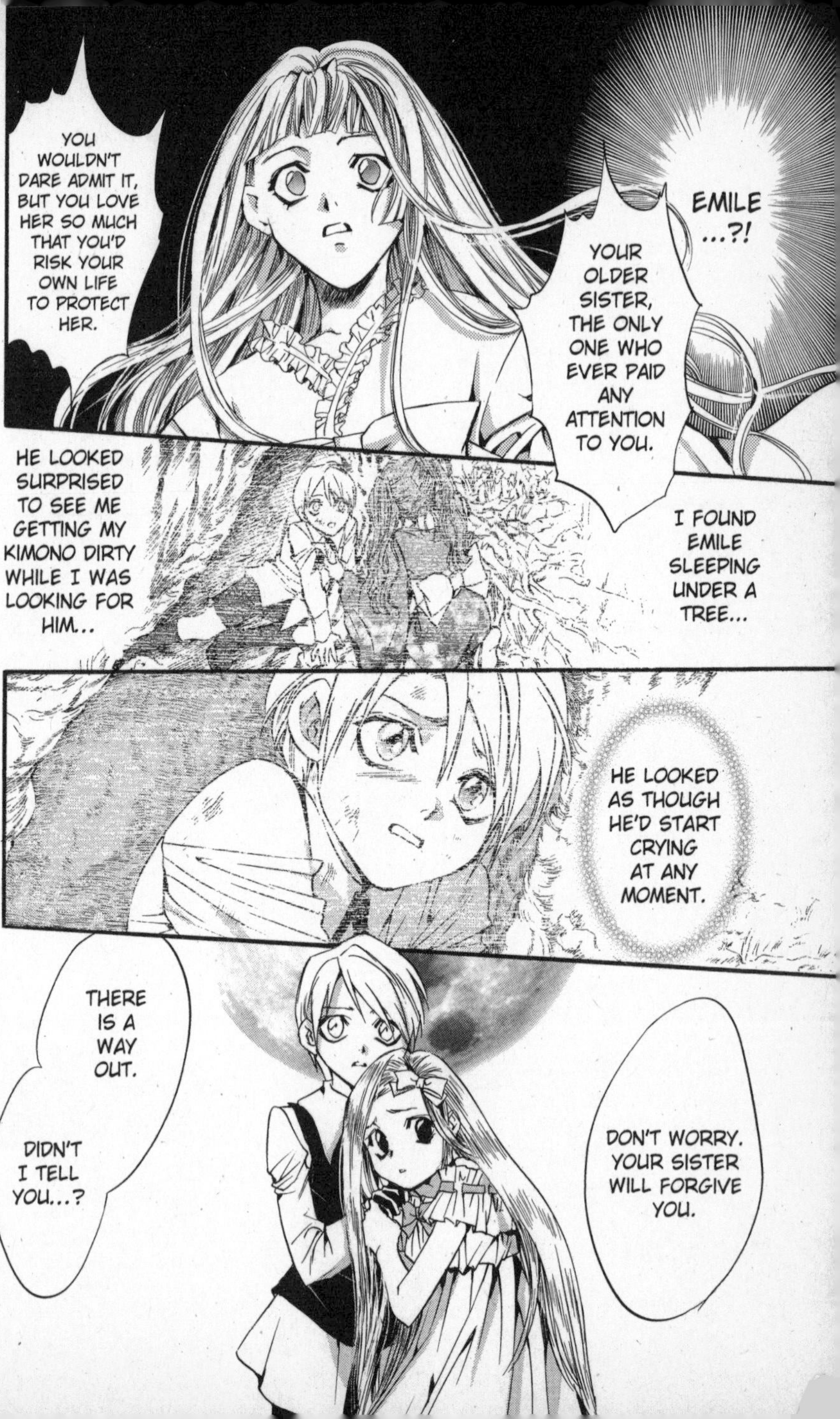
EMILE ...?!
YOUR OLDER SISTER, THE ONLY ONE WHO EVER PAID ANY ATTENTION TO YOU.
YOU WOULDN'T DARE ADMIT IT, BUT YOU LOVE HER SO MUCH THAT YOU'D RISK YOUR OWN LIFE TO PROTECT HER.
I FOUND EMILE SLEEPING UNDER A TREE...
HE LOOKED SURPRISED TO SEE ME GETTING MY KIMONO DIRTY WHILE I WAS LOOKING FOR HIM...
HE LOOKED AS THOUGH HE'D START CRYING AT ANY MOMENT.
DON'T WORRY. YOUR SISTER WILL FORGIVE YOU.
THERE IS A WAY OUT.
DIDN'T I TELL YOU...?

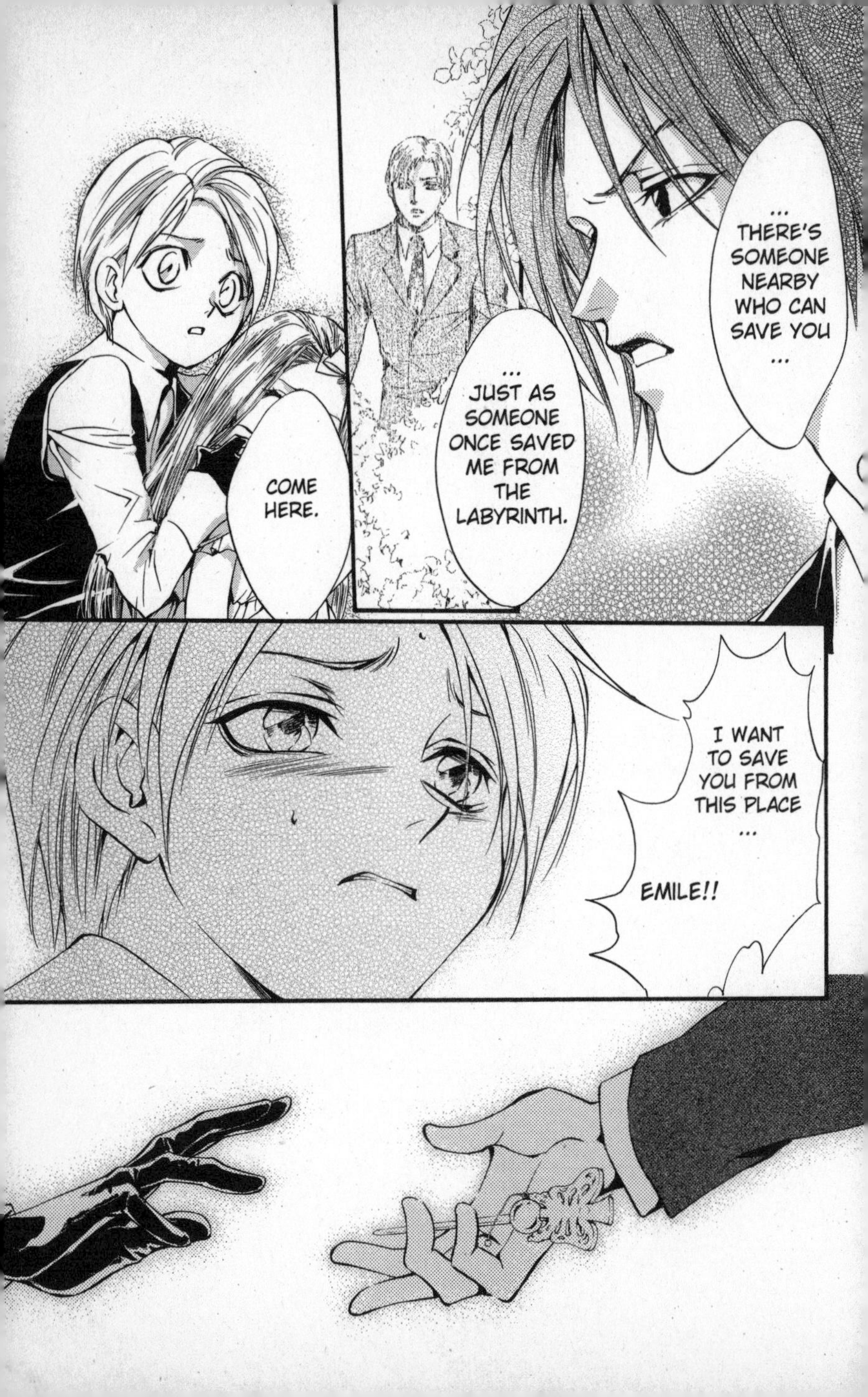
... THERE'S SOMEONE NEARBY WHO CAN SAVE YOU ...
... JUST AS SOMEONE ONCE SAVED ME FROM THE LABYRINTH.
COME HERE.
I WANT TO SAVE YOU FROM THIS PLACE ...
EMILE!!

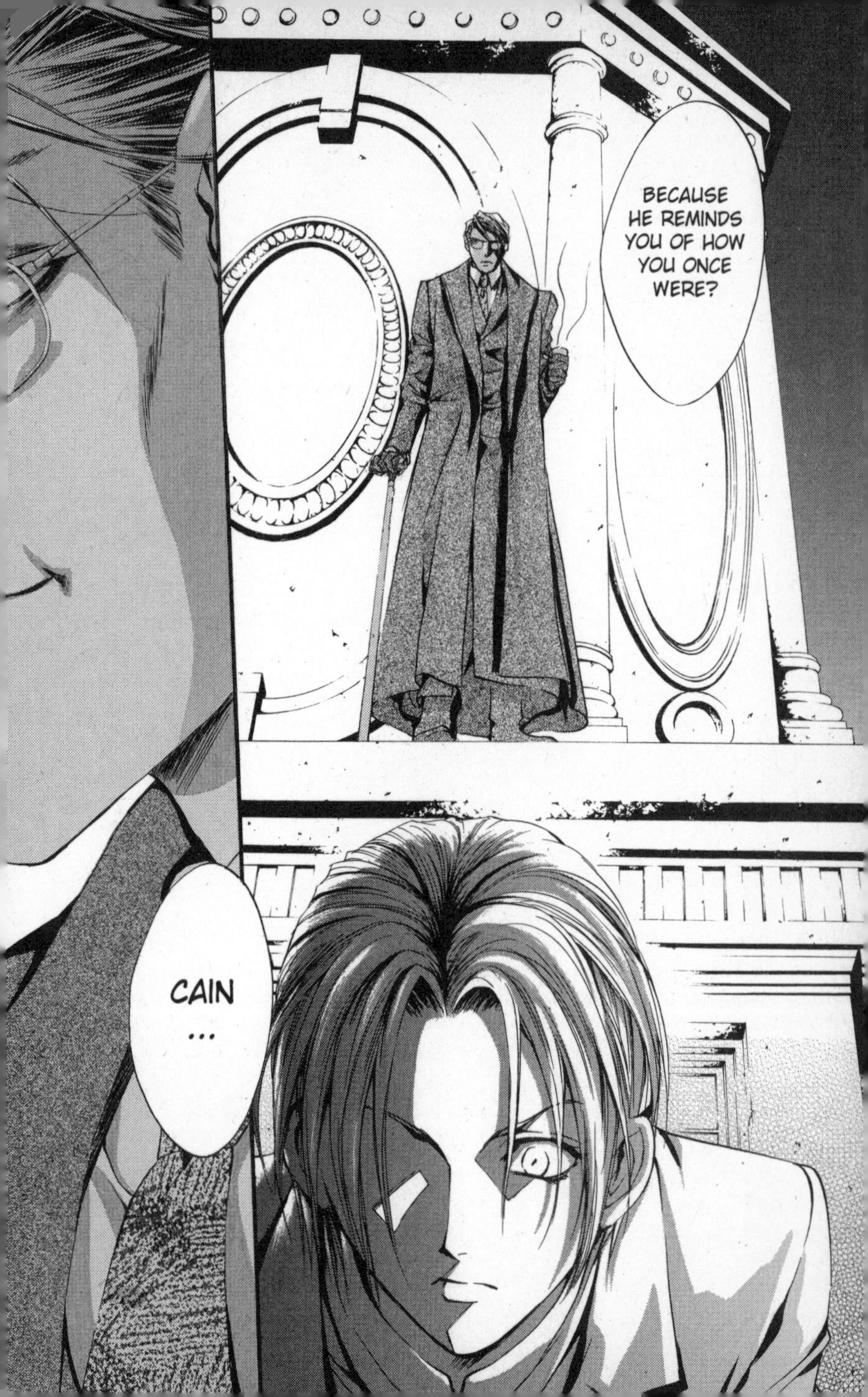
BECAUSE HE REMINDS YOU OF HOW YOU ONCE WERE?
CAIN ...

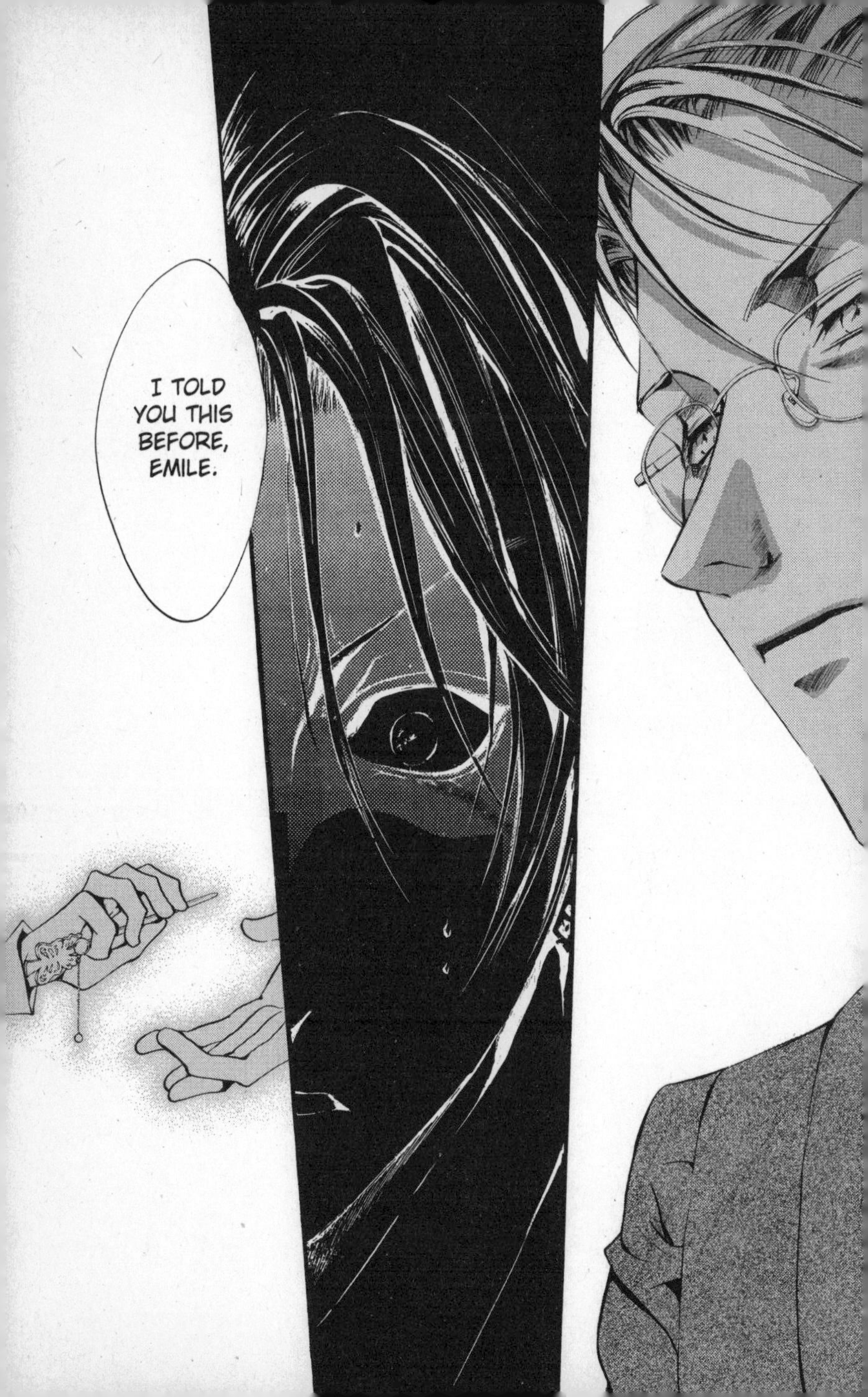
I TOLD YOU THIS BEFORE, EMILE.

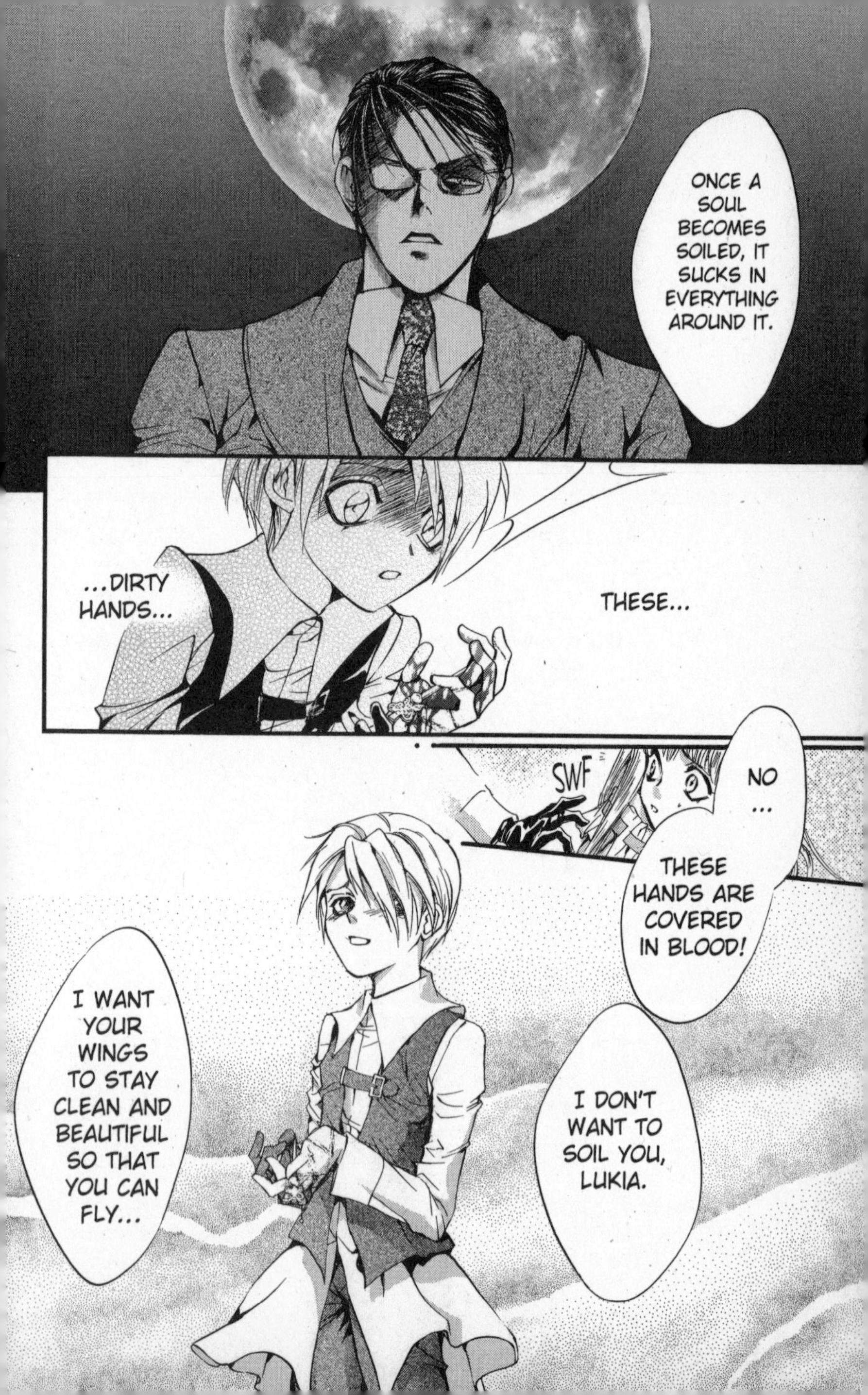
ONCE A SOUL BECOMES SOILED, IT SUCKS IN EVERYTHING AROUND IT.
THESE...
...DIRTY HANDS...
SWF
NO ...
THESE HANDS ARE COVERED IN BLOOD!
I DON'T WANT TO SOIL YOU, LUKIA.
I WANT YOUR WINGS TO STAY CLEAN AND BEAUTIFUL SO THAT YOU CAN FLY...

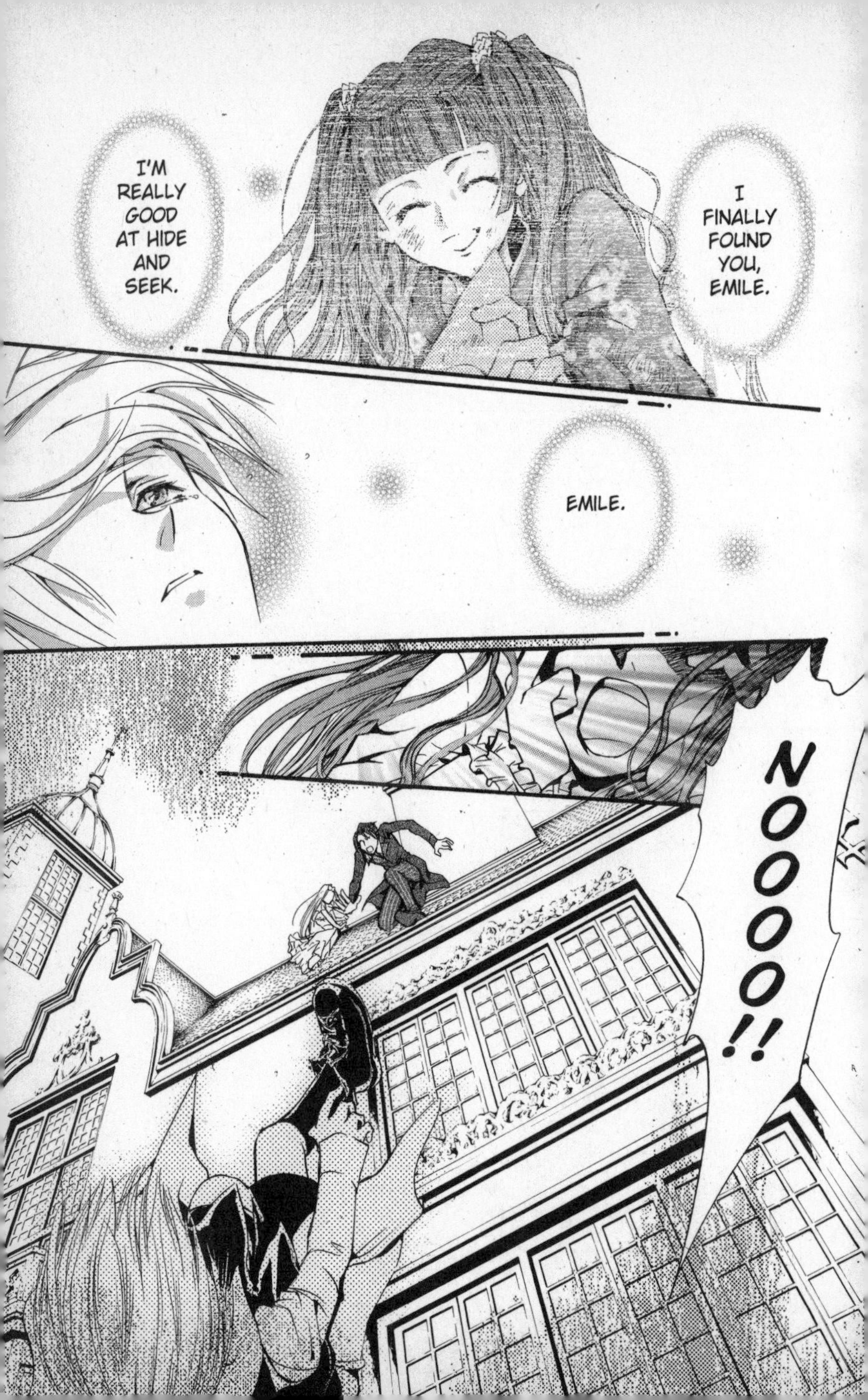
I FINALLY FOUND YOU, EMILE.
I'M REALLY GOOD AT HIDE AND SEEK.
EMILE.
NOOOOO!!

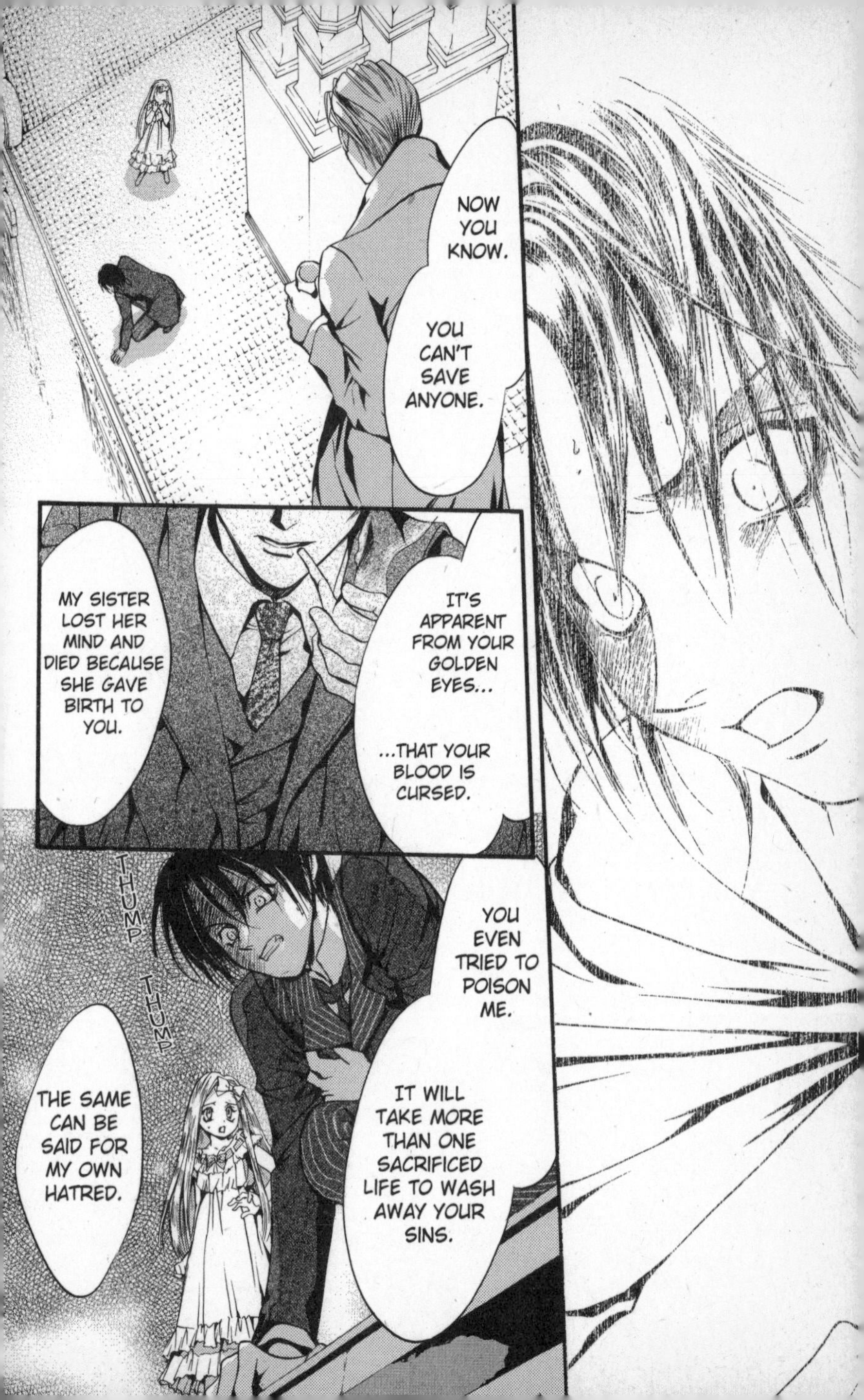
NOW YOU KNOW.
YOU CAN'T SAVE ANYONE.
IT'S APPARENT FROM YOUR GOLDEN EYES...
...THAT YOUR BLOOD IS CURSED.
MY SISTER LOST HER MIND AND DIED BECAUSE SHE GAVE BIRTH TO YOU.
YOU EVEN TRIED TO POISON ME.
IT WILL TAKE MORE THAN ONE SACRIFICED LIFE TO WASH AWAY YOUR SINS.
THUMP
THUMP
THE SAME CAN BE SAID FOR MY OWN HATRED.

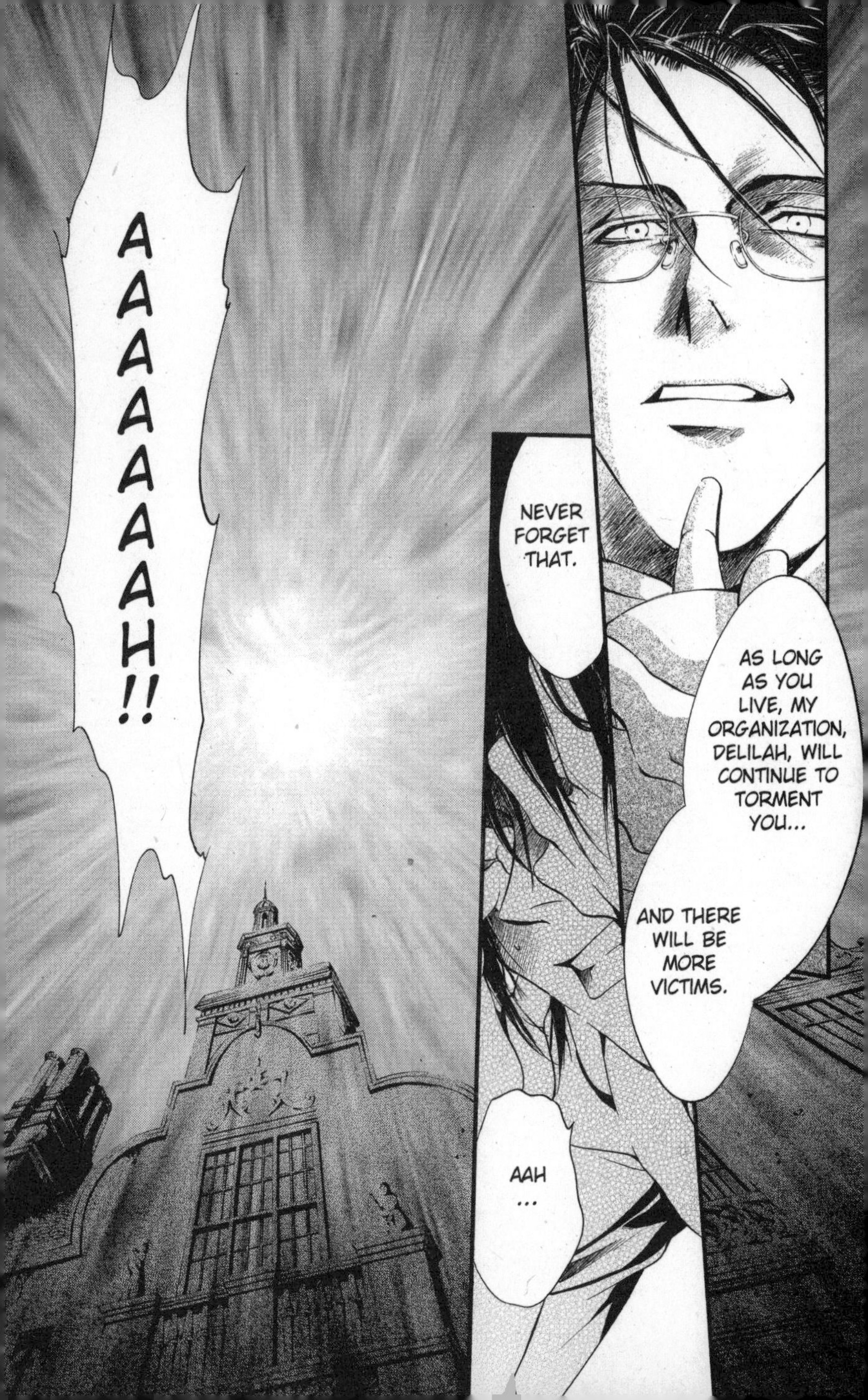

AS LONG AS YOU LIVE, MY ORGANIZATION, DELILAH, WILL CONTINUE TO TORMENT YOU...
AND THERE WILL BE MORE VICTIMS.
NEVER FORGET THAT.
AAH ...
AAAAAAAAH!!

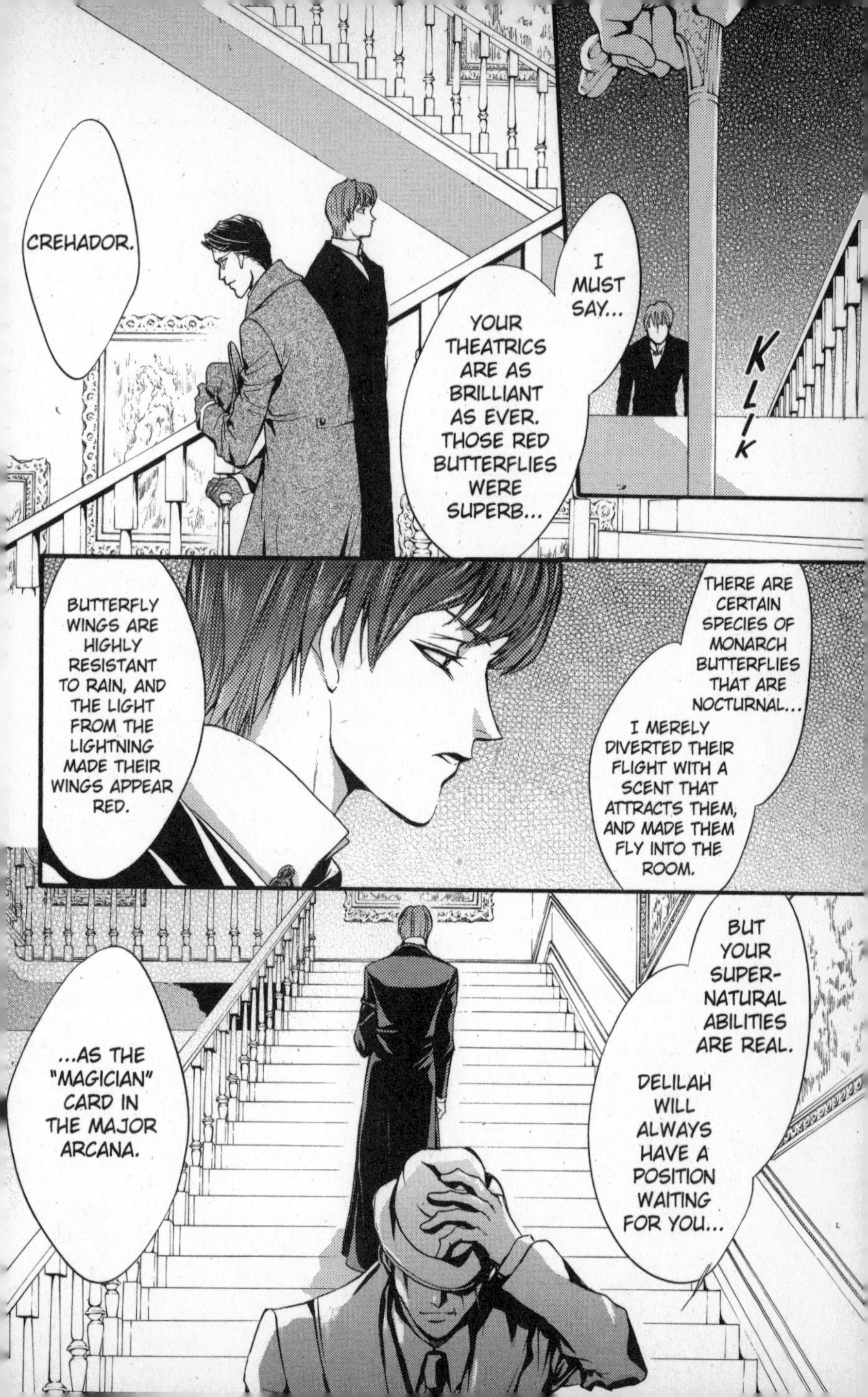
KLIK
I MUST SAY...
YOUR THEATRICS ARE AS BRILLIANT AS EVER. THOSE RED BUTTERFLIES WERE SUPERB...
CREHADOR.
THERE ARE CERTAIN SPECIES OF MONARCH BUTTERFLIES THAT ARE NOCTURNAL...
I MERELY DIVERTED THEIR FLIGHT WITH A SCENT THAT ATTRACTS THEM, AND MADE THEM FLY INTO THE ROOM.
BUTTERFLY WINGS ARE HIGHLY RESISTANT TO RAIN, AND THE LIGHT FROM THE LIGHTNING MADE THEIR WINGS APPEAR RED.
BUT YOUR SUPER-NATURAL ABILITIES ARE REAL.
DELILAH WILL ALWAYS HAVE A POSITION WAITING FOR YOU...
...AS THE "MAGICIAN" CARD IN THE MAJOR ARCANA.

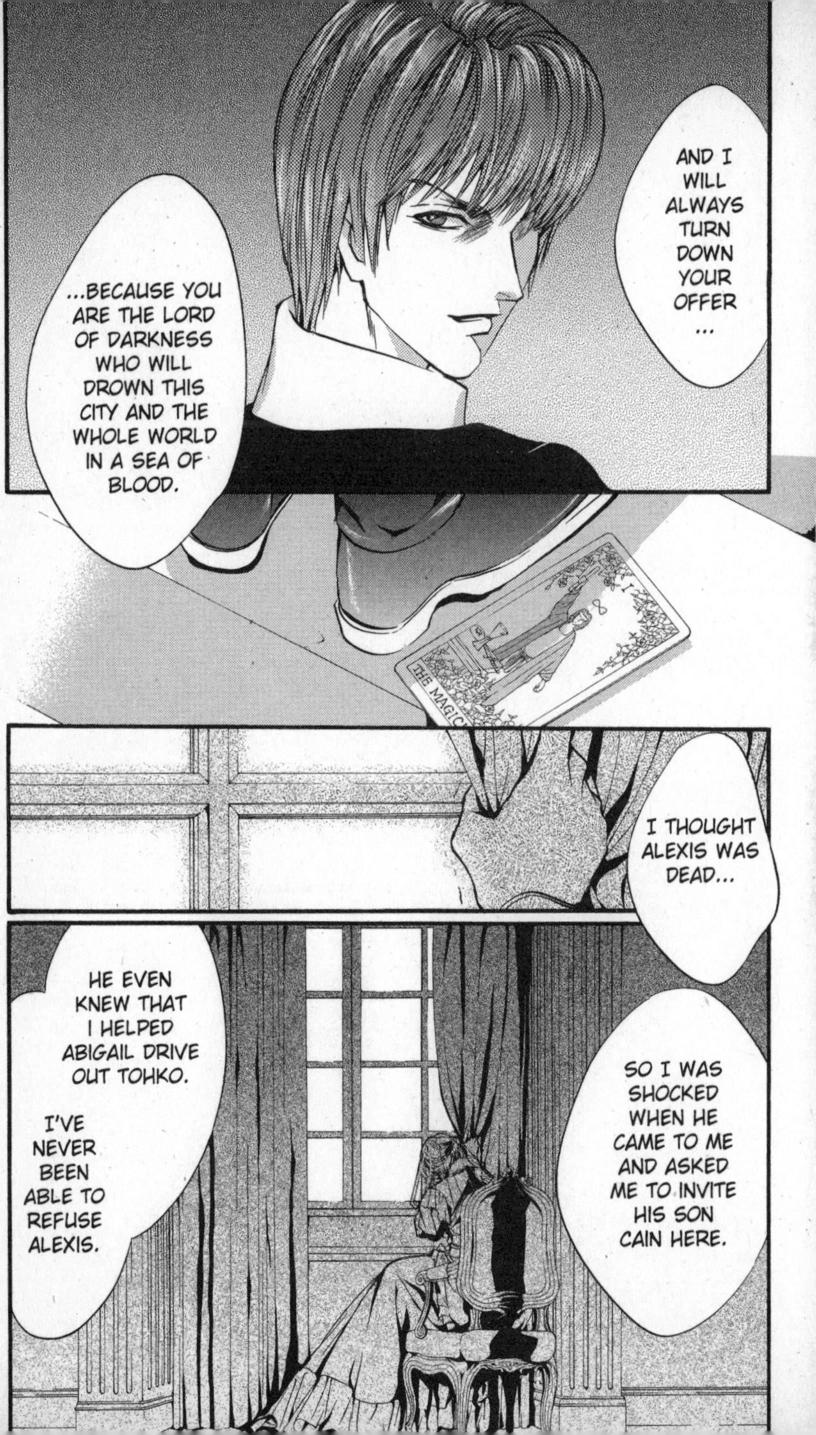

AND I WILL ALWAYS TURN DOWN YOUR OFFER ...
...BECAUSE YOU ARE THE LORD OF DARKNESS WHO WILL DROWN THIS CITY AND THE WHOLE WORLD IN A SEA OF BLOOD.
I THOUGHT ALEXIS WAS DEAD...
SO I WAS SHOCKED WHEN HE CAME TO ME AND ASKED ME TO INVITE HIS SON CAIN HERE.
HE EVEN KNEW THAT I HELPED ABIGAIL DRIVE OUT TOHKO.
I'VE NEVER BEEN ABLE TO REFUSE ALEXIS.

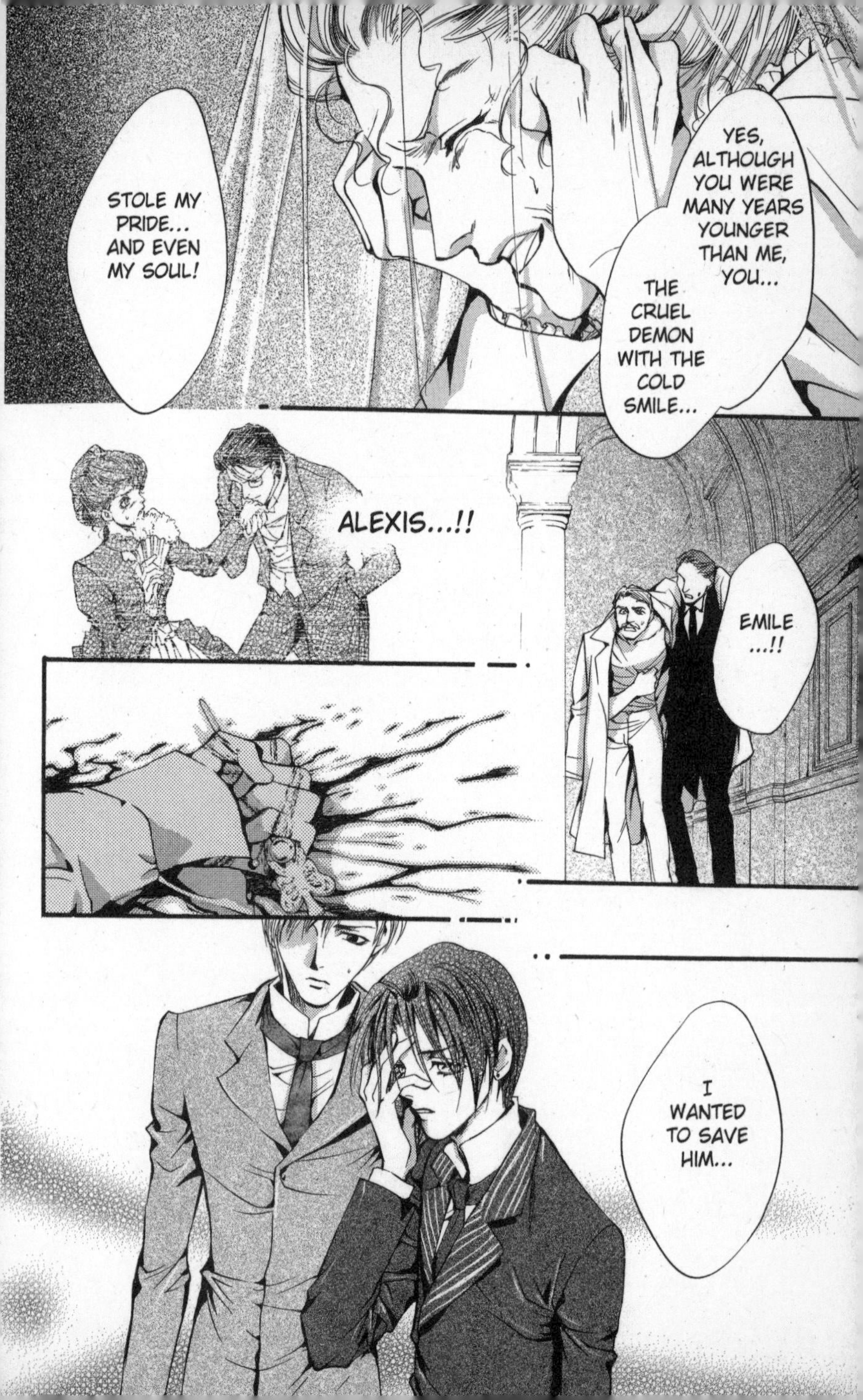
YES, ALTHOUGH YOU WERE MANY YEARS YOUNGER THAN ME, YOU...
THE CRUEL DEMON WITH THE COLD SMILE...
STOLE MY PRIDE... AND EVEN MY SOUL!
EMILE ...!!
ALEXIS...!!
I WANTED TO SAVE HIM...

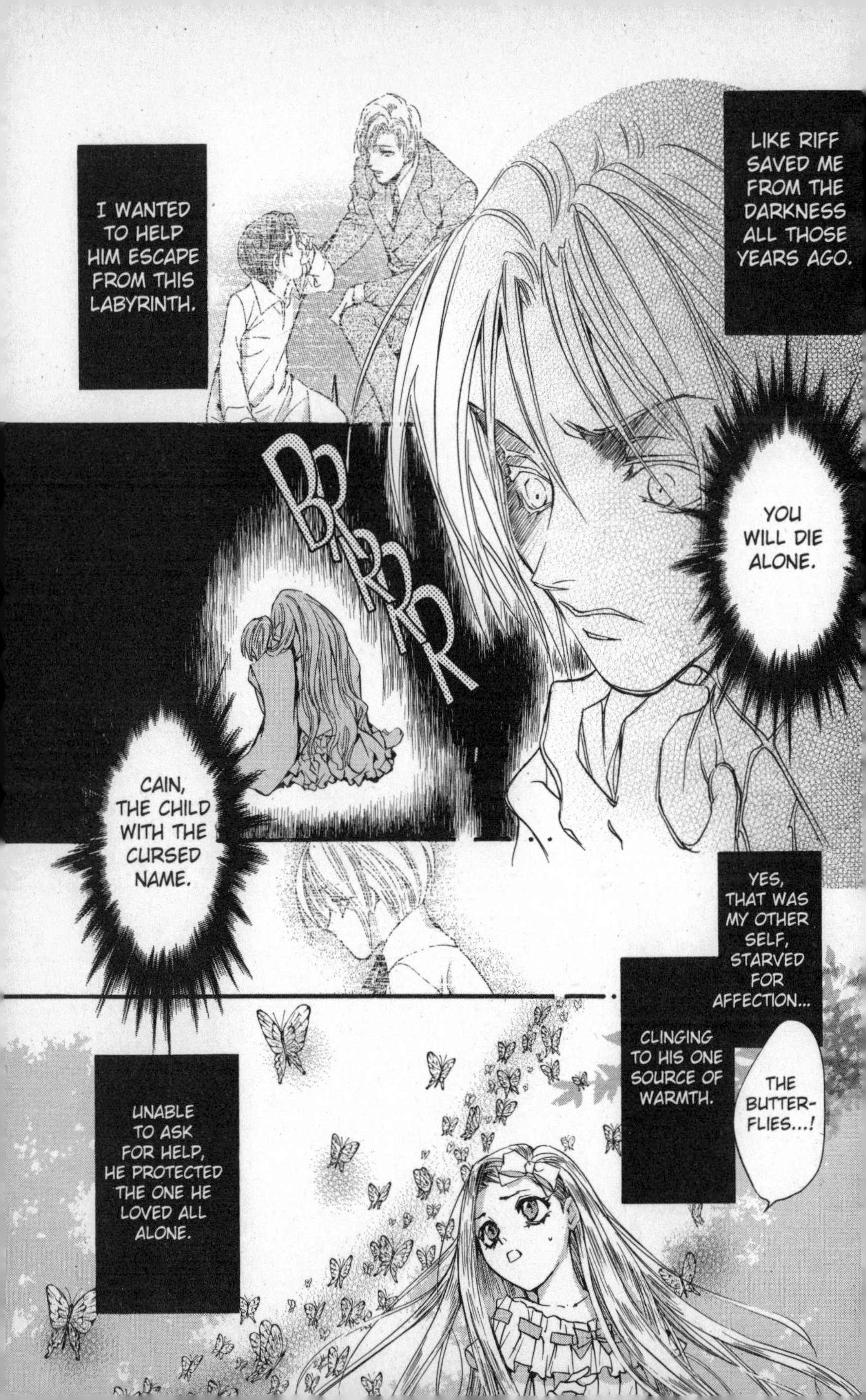
LIKE RIFF SAVED ME FROM THE DARKNESS ALL THOSE YEARS AGO.
I WANTED TO HELP HIM ESCAPE FROM THIS LABYRINTH.
YOU WILL DIE ALONE.
BRRRRR
CAIN, THE CHILD WITH THE CURSED NAME.
YES, THAT WAS MY OTHER SELF, STARVED FOR AFFECTION...
CLINGING TO HIS ONE SOURCE OF WARMTH.
THE BUTTER-FLIES...!
UNABLE TO ASK FOR HELP, HE PROTECTED THE ONE HE LOVED ALL ALONE.

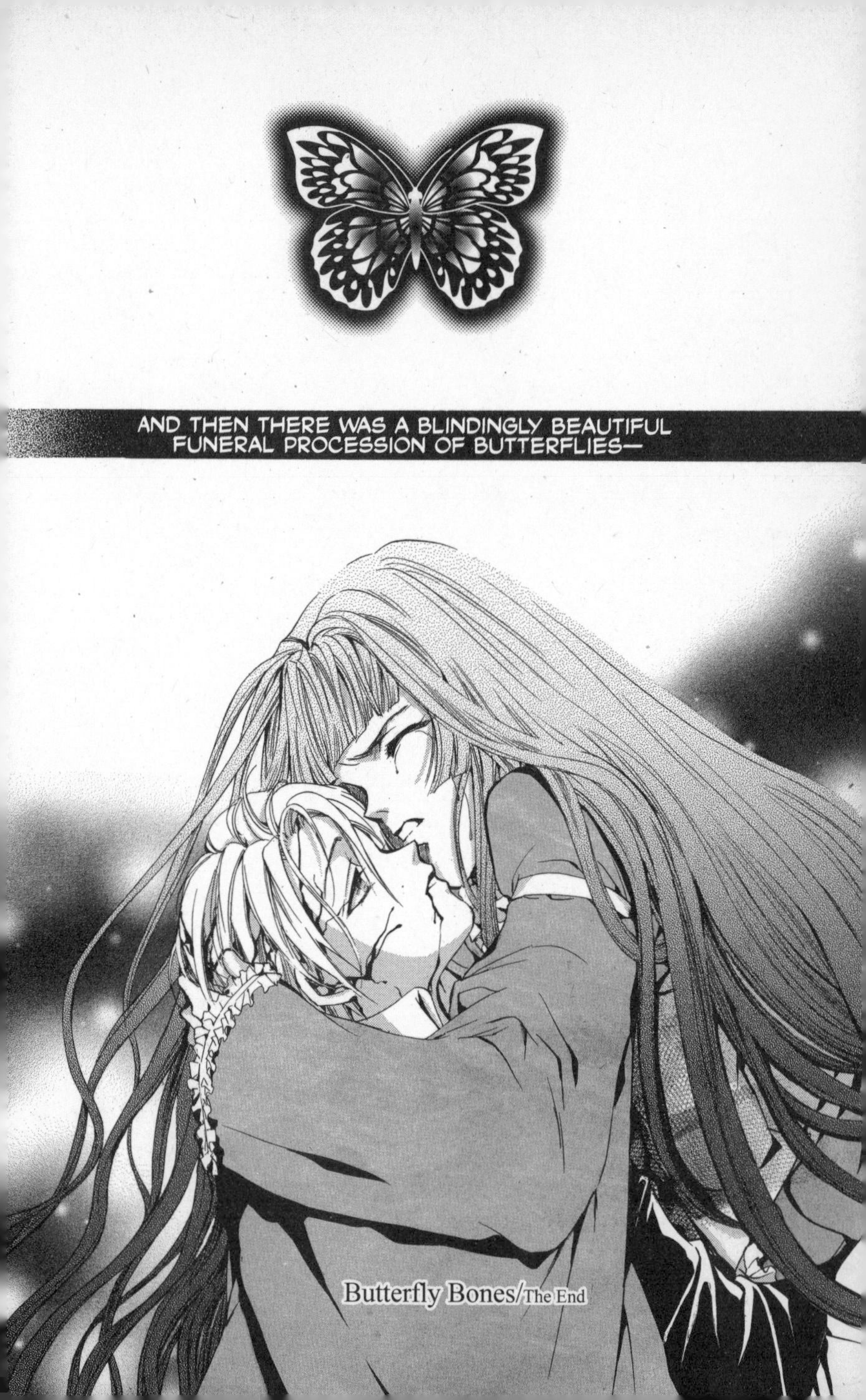
AND THEN THERE WAS A BLINDINGLY BEAUTIFUL FUNERAL PROCESSION OF BUTTERFLIES—
Butterfly Bones/The End

Bloodberry Jam

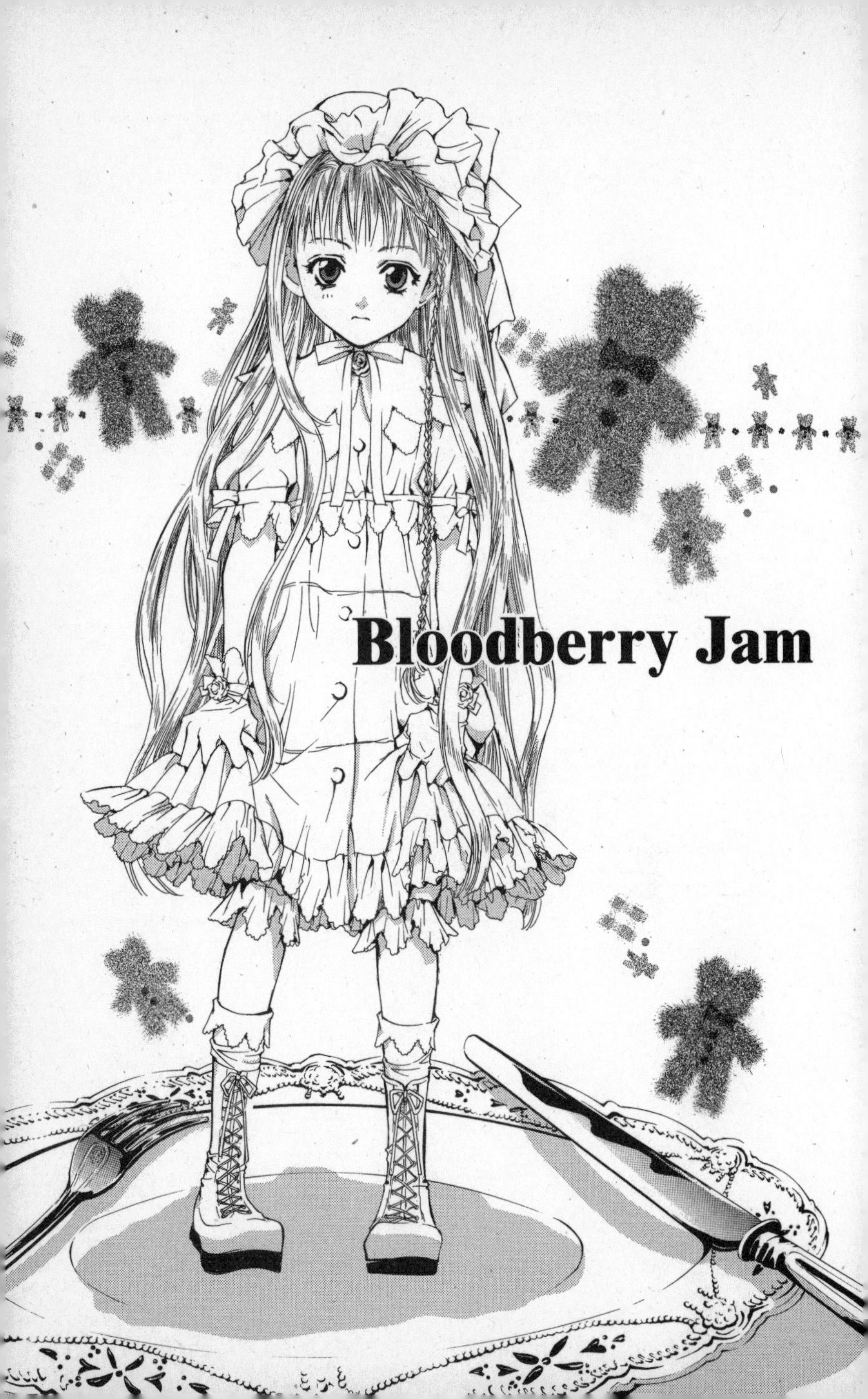

Bloodberry Jam

SING A SONG OF SIXPENCE,
A POCKET FULL OF RYE;
FOUR AND TWENTY BLACKBIRDS
BAKED IN A PIE.
WHEN THE PIE WAS OPENED
THE BIRDS BEGAN TO SING;
WAS NOT THAT A DAINTY DISH
TO SET BEFORE THE KING?

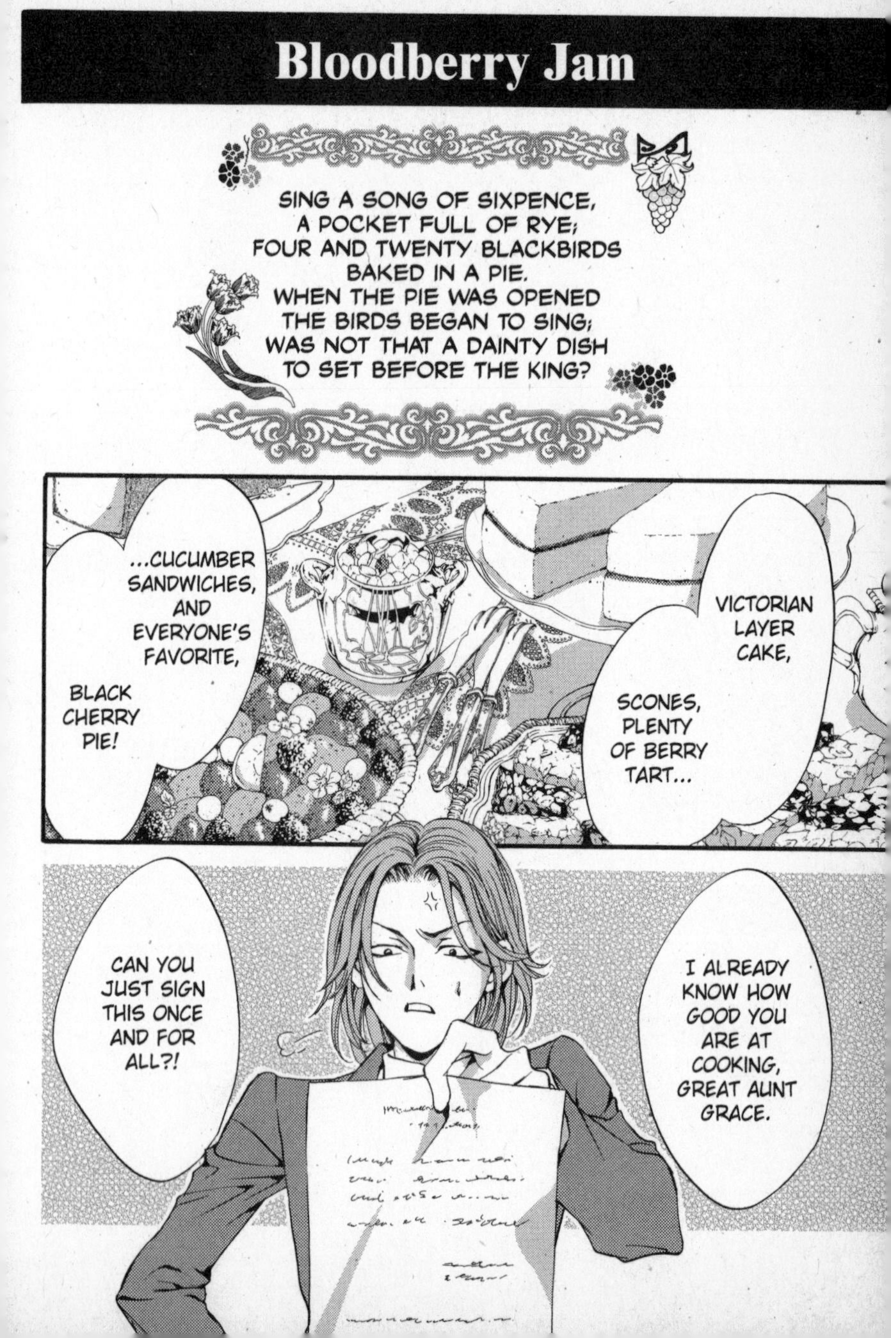
VICTORIAN LAYER CAKE,
SCONES, PLENTY OF BERRY TART...
...CUCUMBER SANDWICHES, AND EVERYONE'S FAVORITE,
BLACK CHERRY PIE!
I ALREADY KNOW HOW GOOD YOU ARE AT COOKING, GREAT AUNT GRACE.
CAN YOU JUST SIGN THIS ONCE AND FOR ALL?!

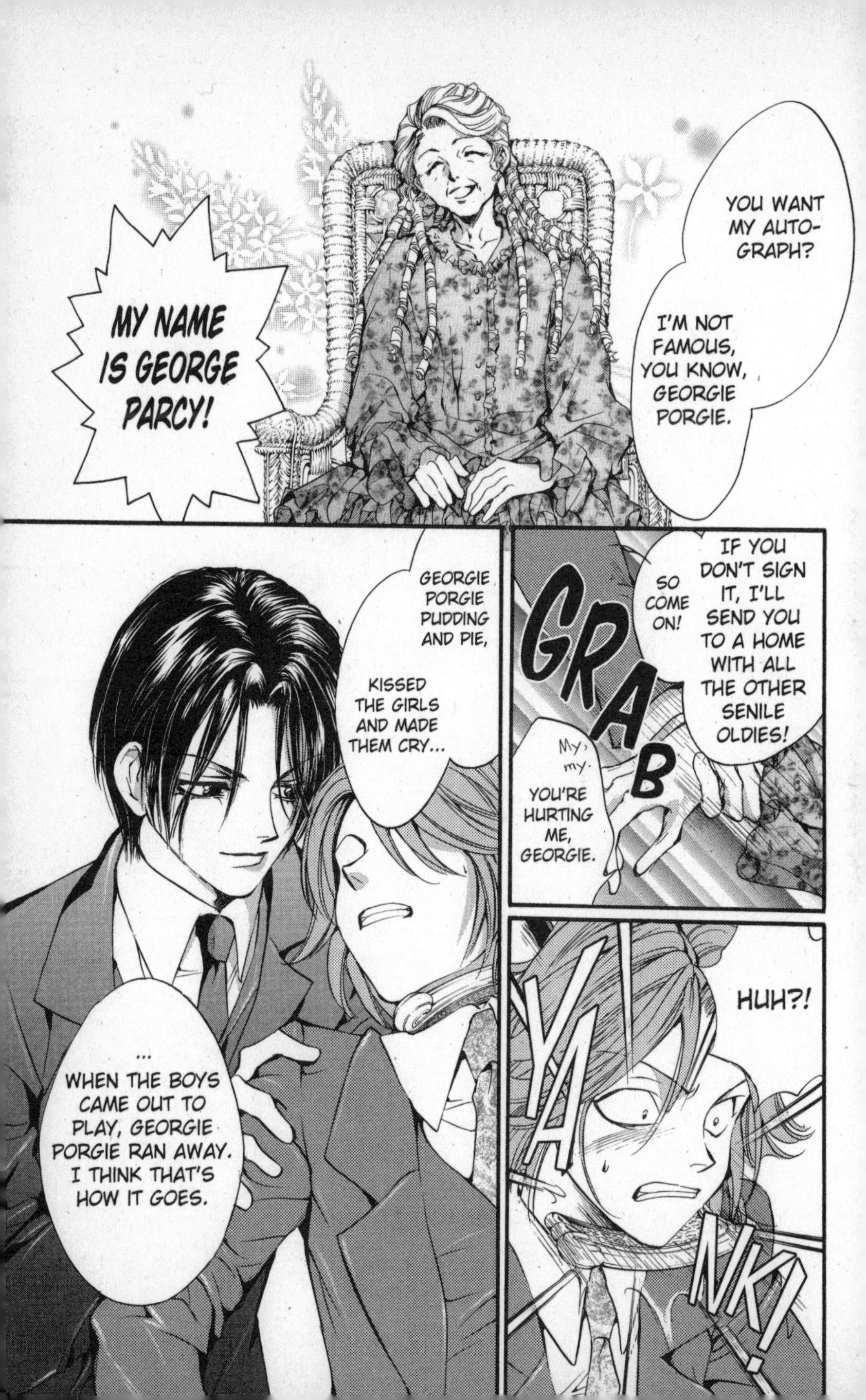

YOU WANT MY AUTO-GRAPH?
I'M NOT FAMOUS, YOU KNOW, GEORGIE PORGIE.
MY NAME IS GEORGE PARCY!
IF YOU DON'T SIGN IT, I'LL SEND YOU TO A HOME WITH ALL THE OTHER SENILE OLDIES!
SO COME ON!
GRAB
My, my.
YOU'RE HURTING ME, GEORGIE.
HUH?!
YANK!
GEORGIE PORGIE PUDDING AND PIE,
KISSED THE GIRLS AND MADE THEM CRY...
... WHEN THE BOYS CAME OUT TO PLAY, GEORGIE PORGIE RAN AWAY. I THINK THAT'S HOW IT GOES.

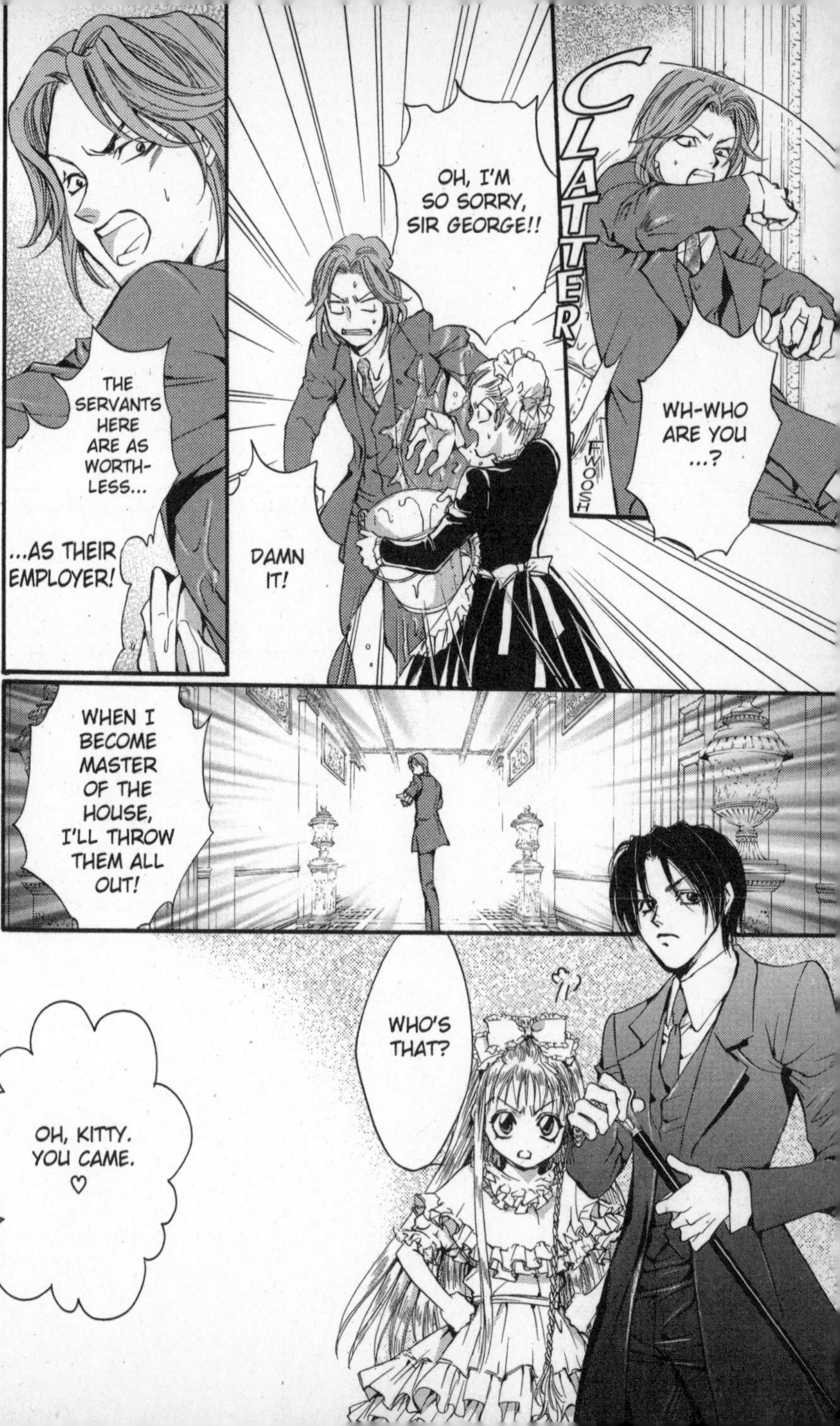
CLATTER
WH-WHO ARE YOU ...?
FWOOSH
OH, I'M SO SORRY, SIR GEORGE!!
DAMN IT!
THE SERVANTS HERE ARE AS WORTH-LESS...
...AS THEIR EMPLOYER!
WHEN I BECOME MASTER OF THE HOUSE, I'LL THROW THEM ALL OUT!
WHO'S THAT?
OH, KITTY. YOU CAME. ♡

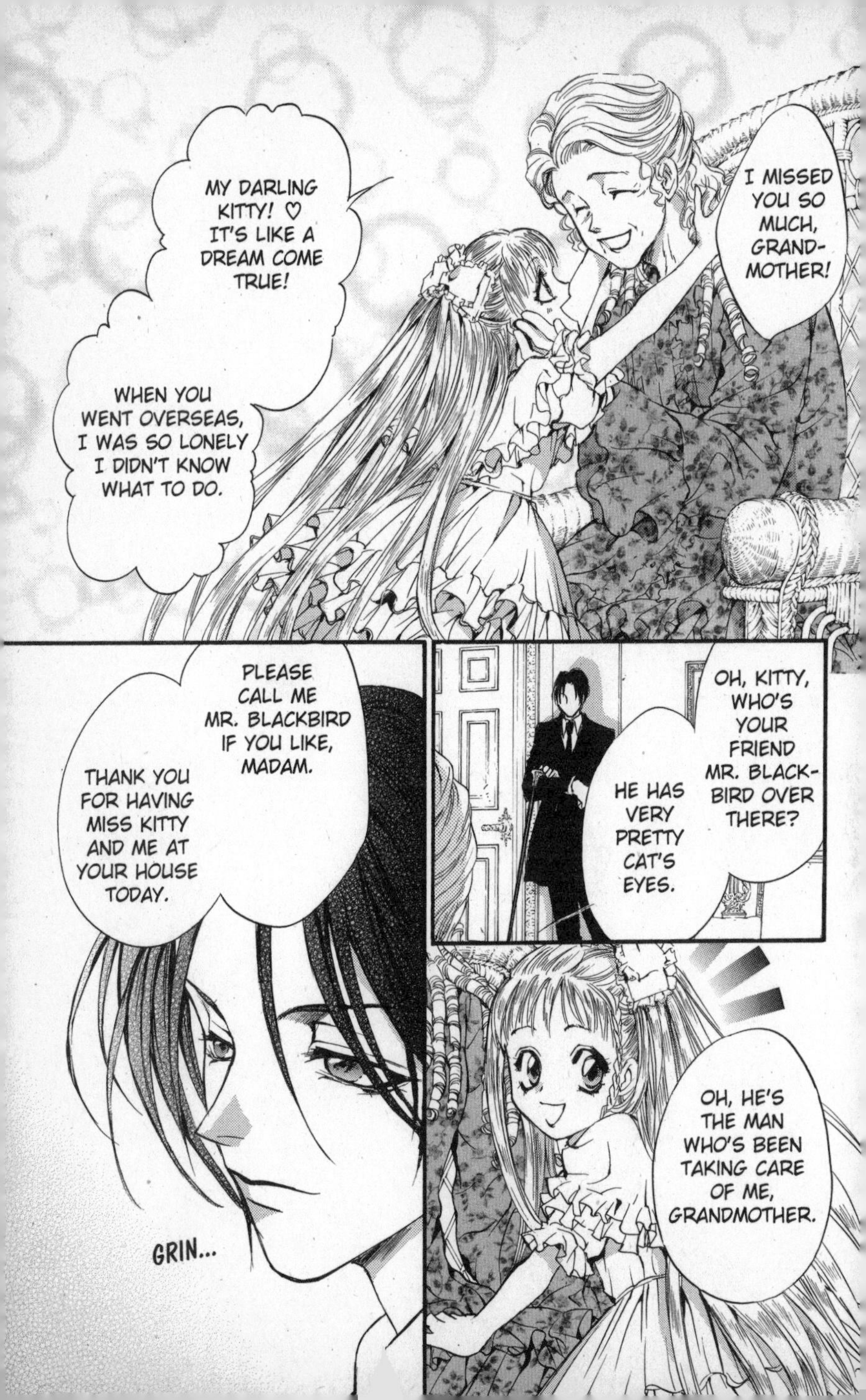
I MISSED YOU SO MUCH, GRANDMOTHER!
MY DARLING KITTY! ♡ IT'S LIKE A DREAM COME TRUE!
WHEN YOU WENT OVERSEAS, I WAS SO LONELY I DIDN'T KNOW WHAT TO DO.
OH, KITTY, WHO'S YOUR FRIEND MR. BLACKBIRD OVER THERE?
HE HAS VERY PRETTY CAT'S EYES.
OH, HE'S THE MAN WHO'S BEEN TAKING CARE OF ME, GRANDMOTHER.
PLEASE CALL ME MR. BLACKBIRD IF YOU LIKE, MADAM.
THANK YOU FOR HAVING MISS KITTY AND ME AT YOUR HOUSE TODAY.
GRIN...

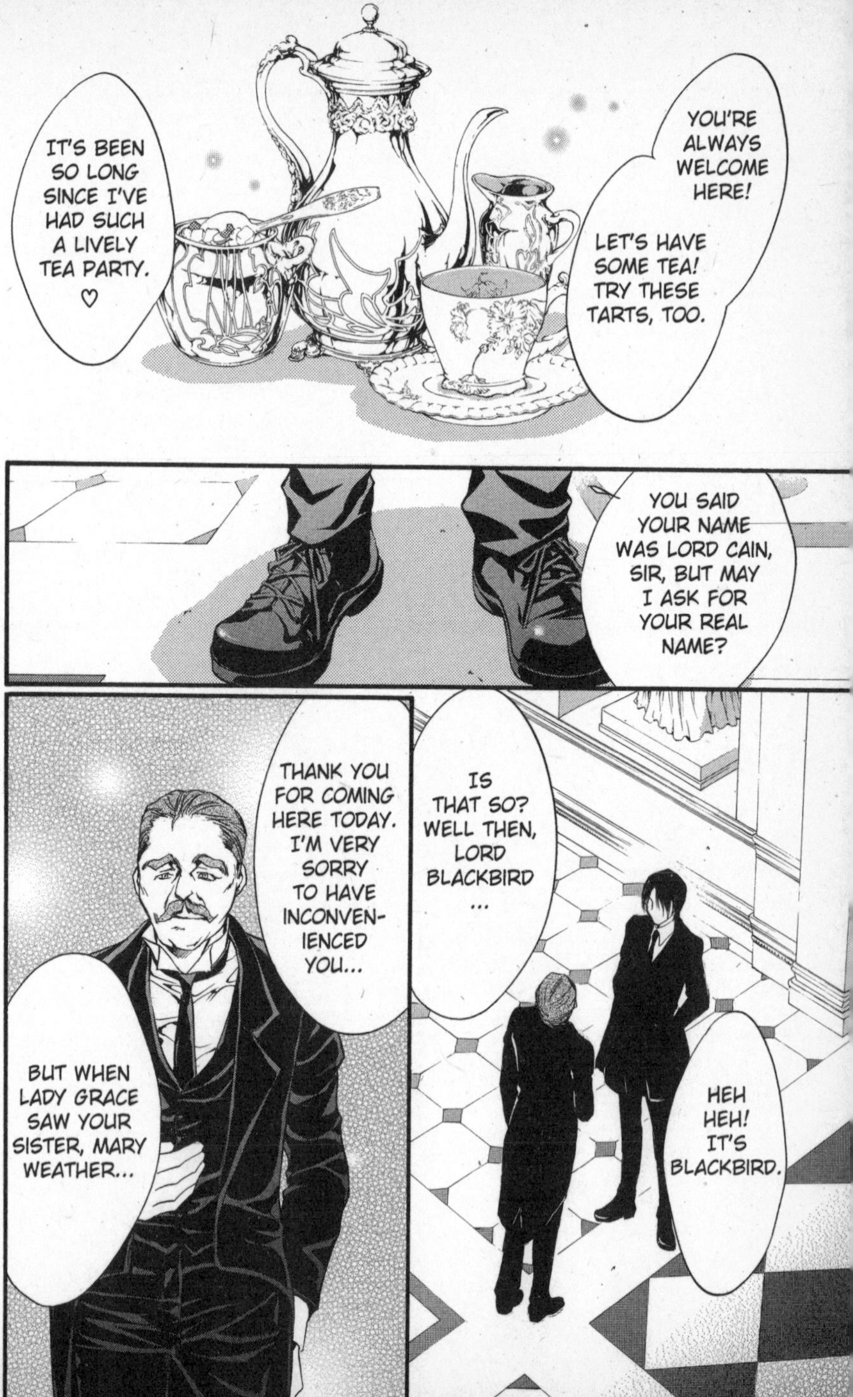
YOU'RE ALWAYS WELCOME HERE!
LET'S HAVE SOME TEA! TRY THESE TARTS, TOO.
IT'S BEEN SO LONG SINCE I'VE HAD SUCH A LIVELY TEA PARTY. ♡
YOU SAID YOUR NAME WAS LORD CAIN, SIR, BUT MAY I ASK FOR YOUR REAL NAME?
HEH HEH! IT'S BLACKBIRD.
IS THAT SO? WELL THEN, LORD BLACKBIRD...
THANK YOU FOR COMING HERE TODAY. I'M VERY SORRY TO HAVE INCONVENIENCED YOU...
BUT WHEN LADY GRACE SAW YOUR SISTER, MARY WEATHER...

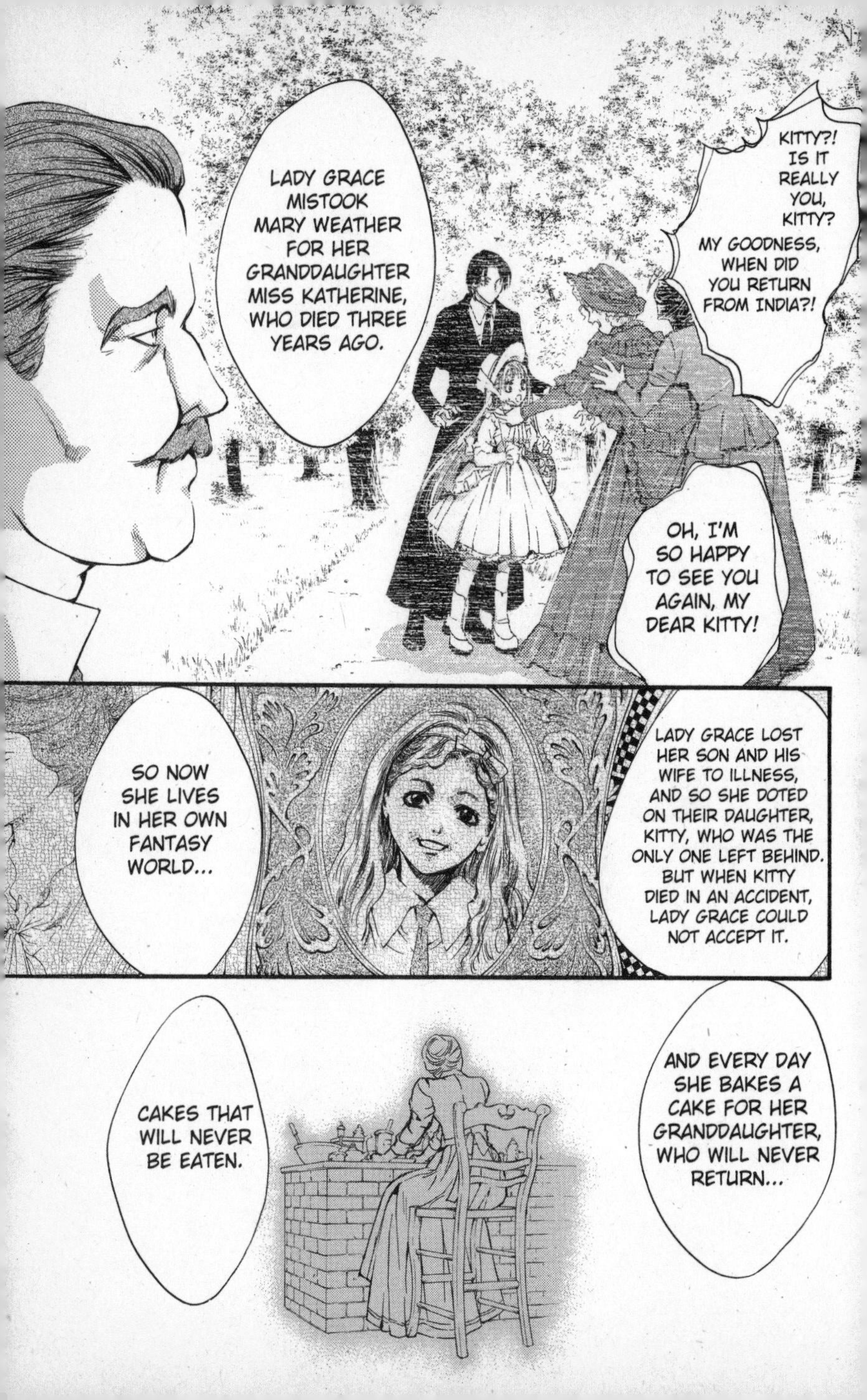
KITTY?! IS IT REALLY YOU, KITTY? MY GOODNESS, WHEN DID YOU RETURN FROM INDIA?!
OH, I'M SO HAPPY TO SEE YOU AGAIN, MY DEAR KITTY!
LADY GRACE MISTOOK MARY WEATHER FOR HER GRANDDAUGHTER MISS KATHERINE, WHO DIED THREE YEARS AGO.
LADY GRACE LOST HER SON AND HIS WIFE TO ILLNESS, AND SO SHE DOTED ON THEIR DAUGHTER, KITTY, WHO WAS THE ONLY ONE LEFT BEHIND. BUT WHEN KITTY DIED IN AN ACCIDENT, LADY GRACE COULD NOT ACCEPT IT.
SO NOW SHE LIVES IN HER OWN FANTASY WORLD...
AND EVERY DAY SHE BAKES A CAKE FOR HER GRANDDAUGHTER, WHO WILL NEVER RETURN...
CAKES THAT WILL NEVER BE EATEN.

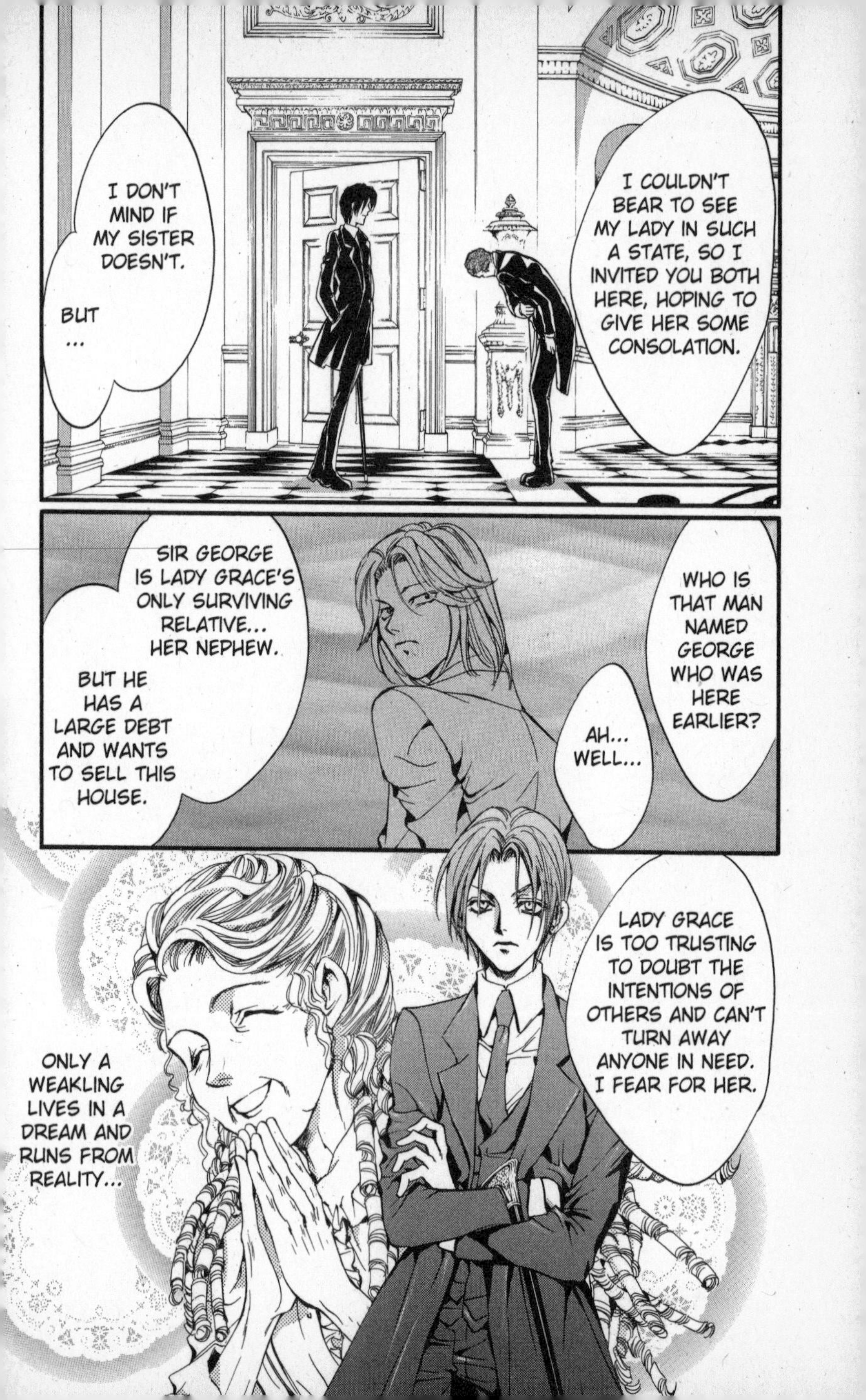
I COULDN'T BEAR TO SEE MY LADY IN SUCH A STATE, SO I INVITED YOU BOTH HERE, HOPING TO GIVE HER SOME CONSOLATION.
I DON'T MIND IF MY SISTER DOESN'T.
BUT ...
WHO IS THAT MAN NAMED GEORGE WHO WAS HERE EARLIER?
AH... WELL...
SIR GEORGE IS LADY GRACE'S ONLY SURVIVING RELATIVE... HER NEPHEW.
BUT HE HAS A LARGE DEBT AND WANTS TO SELL THIS HOUSE.
LADY GRACE IS TOO TRUSTING TO DOUBT THE INTENTIONS OF OTHERS AND CAN'T TURN AWAY ANYONE IN NEED. I FEAR FOR HER.
ONLY A WEAKLING LIVES IN A DREAM AND RUNS FROM REALITY...

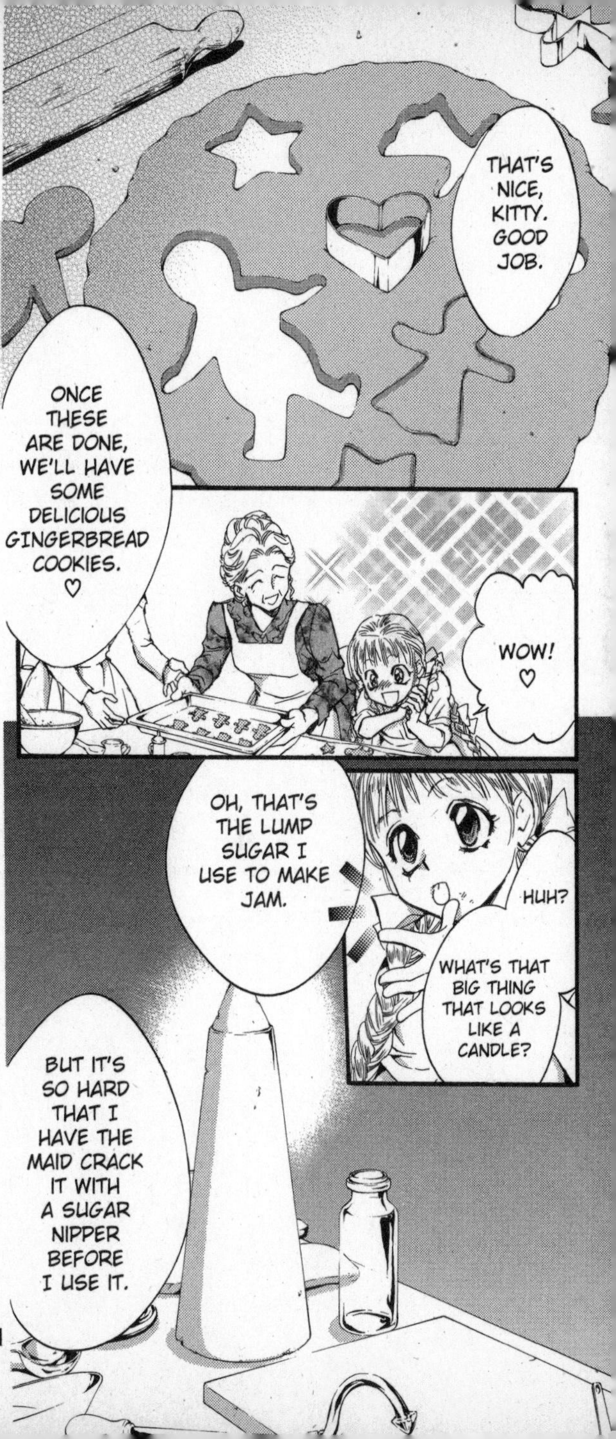
THAT'S NICE, KITTY. GOOD JOB.
ONCE THESE ARE DONE, WE'LL HAVE SOME DELICIOUS GINGERBREAD COOKIES. ♡
WOW! ♡
HUH?
WHAT'S THAT BIG THING THAT LOOKS LIKE A CANDLE?
OH, THAT'S THE LUMP SUGAR I USE TO MAKE JAM.
BUT IT'S SO HARD THAT I HAVE THE MAID CRACK IT WITH A SUGAR NIPPER BEFORE I USE IT.

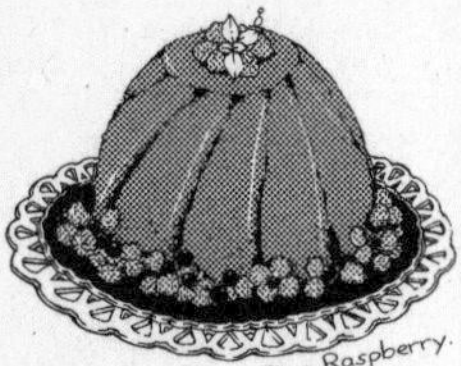

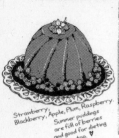

Strawberry, Blackberry, Apple, Plum, Raspberry. Summer puddings are full of berries and good for dieting too. ♡

The previous story was in four parts, so this one is just a single episode. It was really hard to do the dialogue on this one. (I'm going to reveal some of the plot here, so don't read this if you haven't finished the story yet.) The hardest thing to decide was the color of the jam. If it was red, then you wouldn't be able to see the color of the nail polish, and blue would be too dark. Orange would have been okay, but I really wanted to go with an English gardening theme!! I once read about a jam that was made with currant juice added to it. So I decided on a light-colored blueberry jam mixed with currant juice. And coincidentally, the fingernail (specifically the polished part) just happened to be near the glass part of the jar, so it was easier to find! Ginger cookies have a more American feel to them, though.

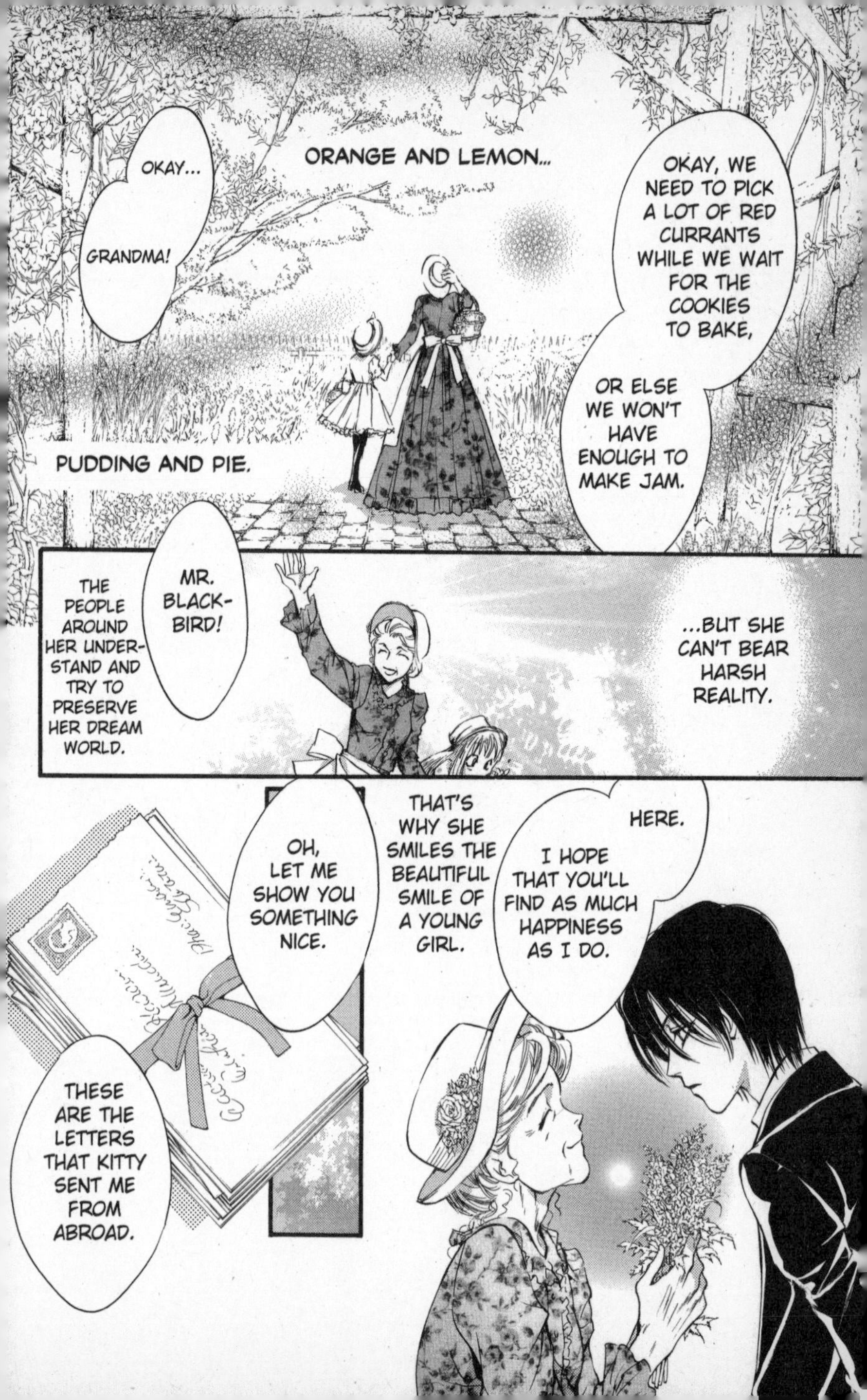
OKAY, WE NEED TO PICK A LOT OF RED CURRANTS WHILE WE WAIT FOR THE COOKIES TO BAKE,
OR ELSE WE WON'T HAVE ENOUGH TO MAKE JAM.
ORANGE AND LEMON...
OKAY... GRANDMA!
PUDDING AND PIE.
...BUT SHE CAN'T BEAR HARSH REALITY.
MR. BLACK-BIRD!
THE PEOPLE AROUND HER UNDER-STAND AND TRY TO PRESERVE HER DREAM WORLD.
HERE.
I HOPE THAT YOU'LL FIND AS MUCH HAPPINESS AS I DO.
THAT'S WHY SHE SMILES THE BEAUTIFUL SMILE OF A YOUNG GIRL.
OH, LET ME SHOW YOU SOMETHING NICE.
THESE ARE THE LETTERS THAT KITTY SENT ME FROM ABROAD.

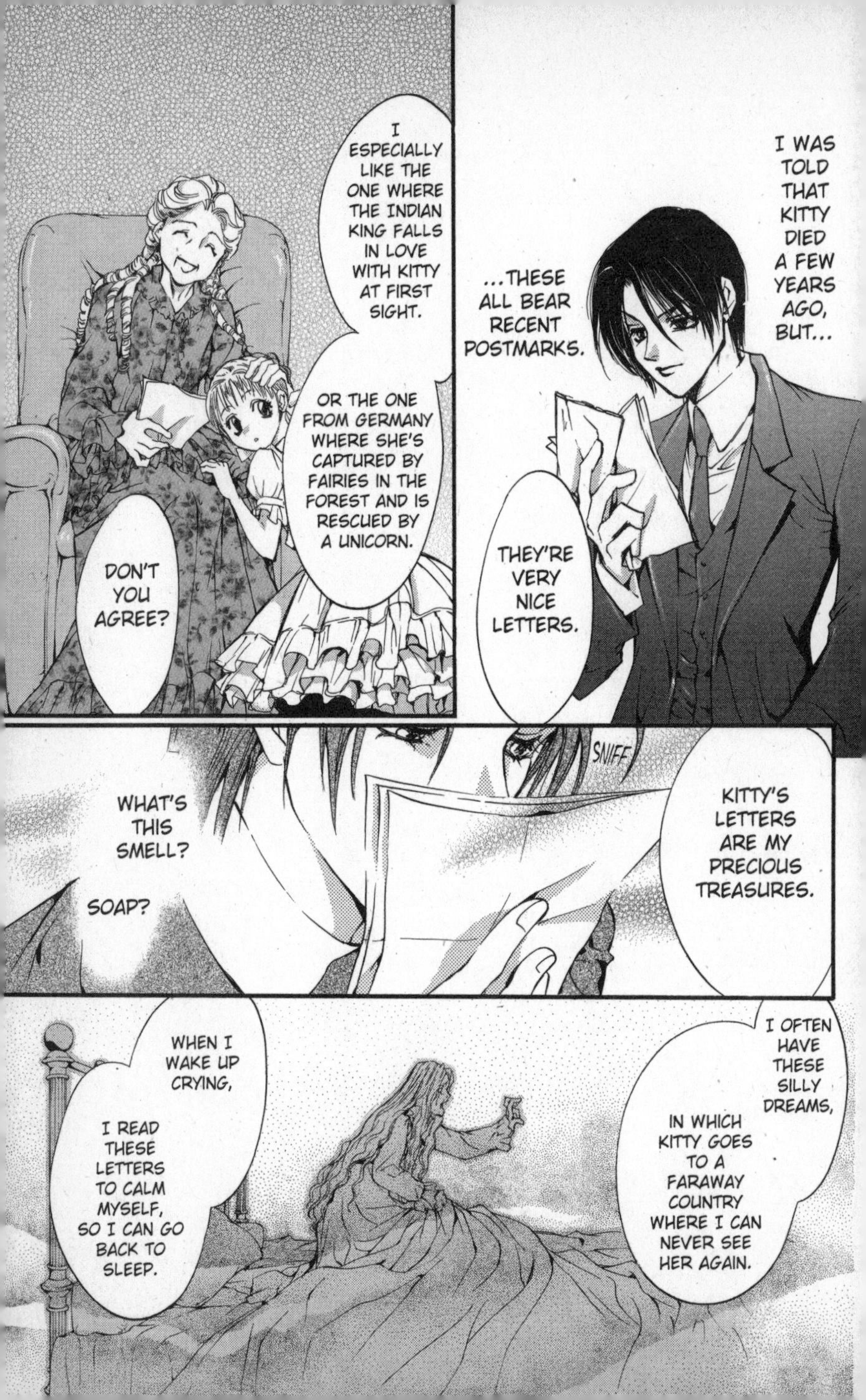
I WAS TOLD THAT KITTY DIED A FEW YEARS AGO, BUT...
...THESE ALL BEAR RECENT POSTMARKS.
THEY'RE VERY NICE LETTERS.
I ESPECIALLY LIKE THE ONE WHERE THE INDIAN KING FALLS IN LOVE WITH KITTY AT FIRST SIGHT.
OR THE ONE FROM GERMANY WHERE SHE'S CAPTURED BY FAIRIES IN THE FOREST AND IS RESCUED BY A UNICORN.
DON'T YOU AGREE?
SNIFF
KITTY'S LETTERS ARE MY PRECIOUS TREASURES.
WHAT'S THIS SMELL?
SOAP?
I OFTEN HAVE THESE SILLY DREAMS,
IN WHICH KITTY GOES TO A FARAWAY COUNTRY WHERE I CAN NEVER SEE HER AGAIN.
WHEN I WAKE UP CRYING,
I READ THESE LETTERS TO CALM MYSELF, SO I CAN GO BACK TO SLEEP.

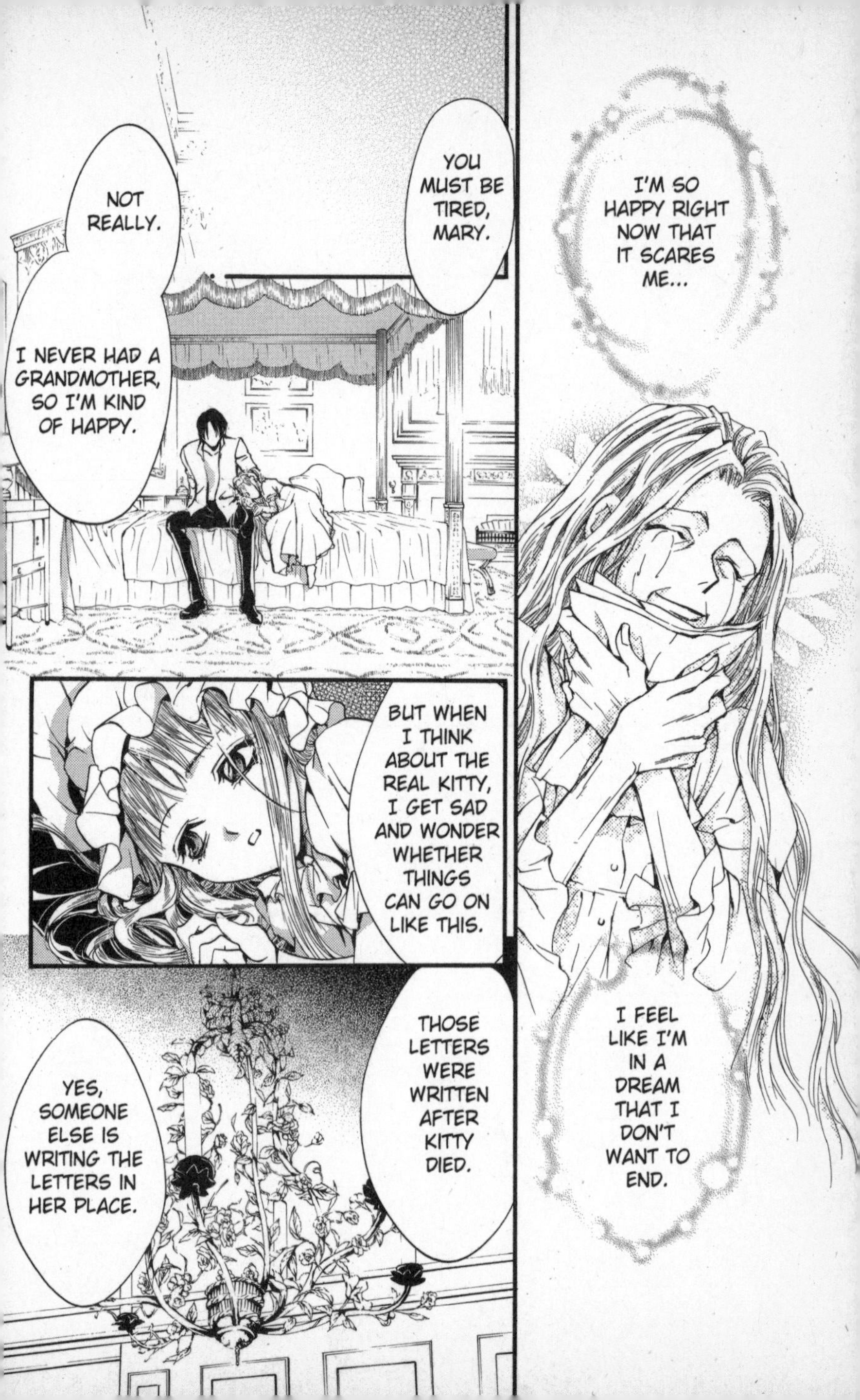
I'M SO HAPPY RIGHT NOW THAT IT SCARES ME...
I FEEL LIKE I'M IN A DREAM THAT I DON'T WANT TO END.
YOU MUST BE TIRED, MARY.
NOT REALLY.
I NEVER HAD A GRANDMOTHER, SO I'M KIND OF HAPPY.
BUT WHEN I THINK ABOUT THE REAL KITTY, I GET SAD AND WONDER WHETHER THINGS CAN GO ON LIKE THIS.
THOSE LETTERS WERE WRITTEN AFTER KITTY DIED.
YES, SOMEONE ELSE IS WRITING THE LETTERS IN HER PLACE.

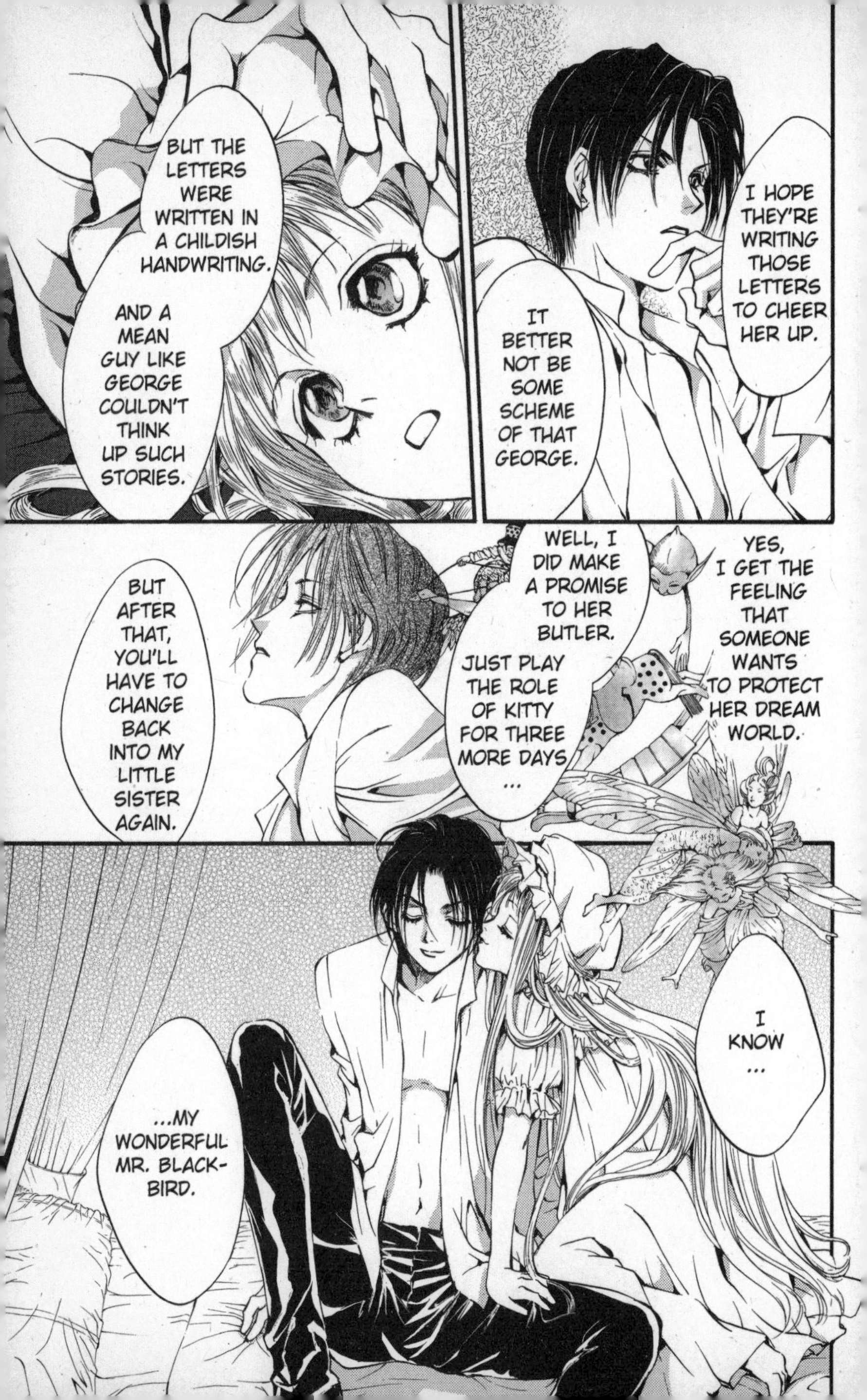
I HOPE THEY'RE WRITING THOSE LETTERS TO CHEER HER UP.
IT BETTER NOT BE SOME SCHEME OF THAT GEORGE.
BUT THE LETTERS WERE WRITTEN IN A CHILDISH HANDWRITING.
AND A MEAN GUY LIKE GEORGE COULDN'T THINK UP SUCH STORIES.
YES, I GET THE FEELING THAT SOMEONE WANTS TO PROTECT HER DREAM WORLD.
WELL, I DID MAKE A PROMISE TO HER BUTLER.
JUST PLAY THE ROLE OF KITTY FOR THREE MORE DAYS ...
BUT AFTER THAT, YOU'LL HAVE TO CHANGE BACK INTO MY LITTLE SISTER AGAIN.
I KNOW ...
...MY WONDERFUL MR. BLACK-BIRD.

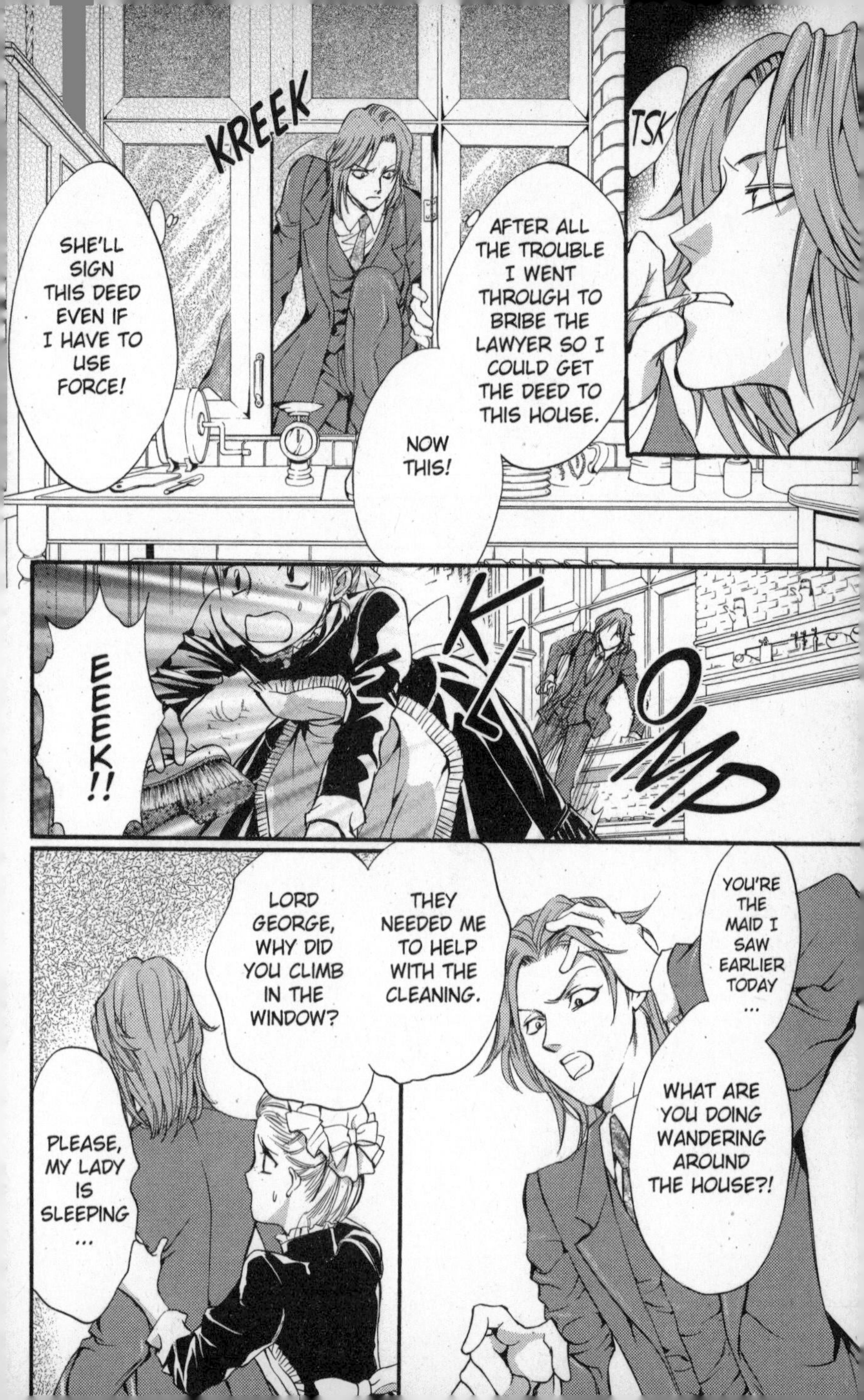
TSK
KREEK
AFTER ALL THE TROUBLE I WENT THROUGH TO BRIBE THE LAWYER SO I COULD GET THE DEED TO THIS HOUSE.
NOW THIS!
SHE'LL SIGN THIS DEED EVEN IF I HAVE TO USE FORCE!
KLOMP
EEEK!!
YOU'RE THE MAID I SAW EARLIER TODAY ...
WHAT ARE YOU DOING WANDERING AROUND THE HOUSE?!
THEY NEEDED ME TO HELP WITH THE CLEANING.
LORD GEORGE, WHY DID YOU CLIMB IN THE WINDOW?
PLEASE, MY LADY IS SLEEPING ...

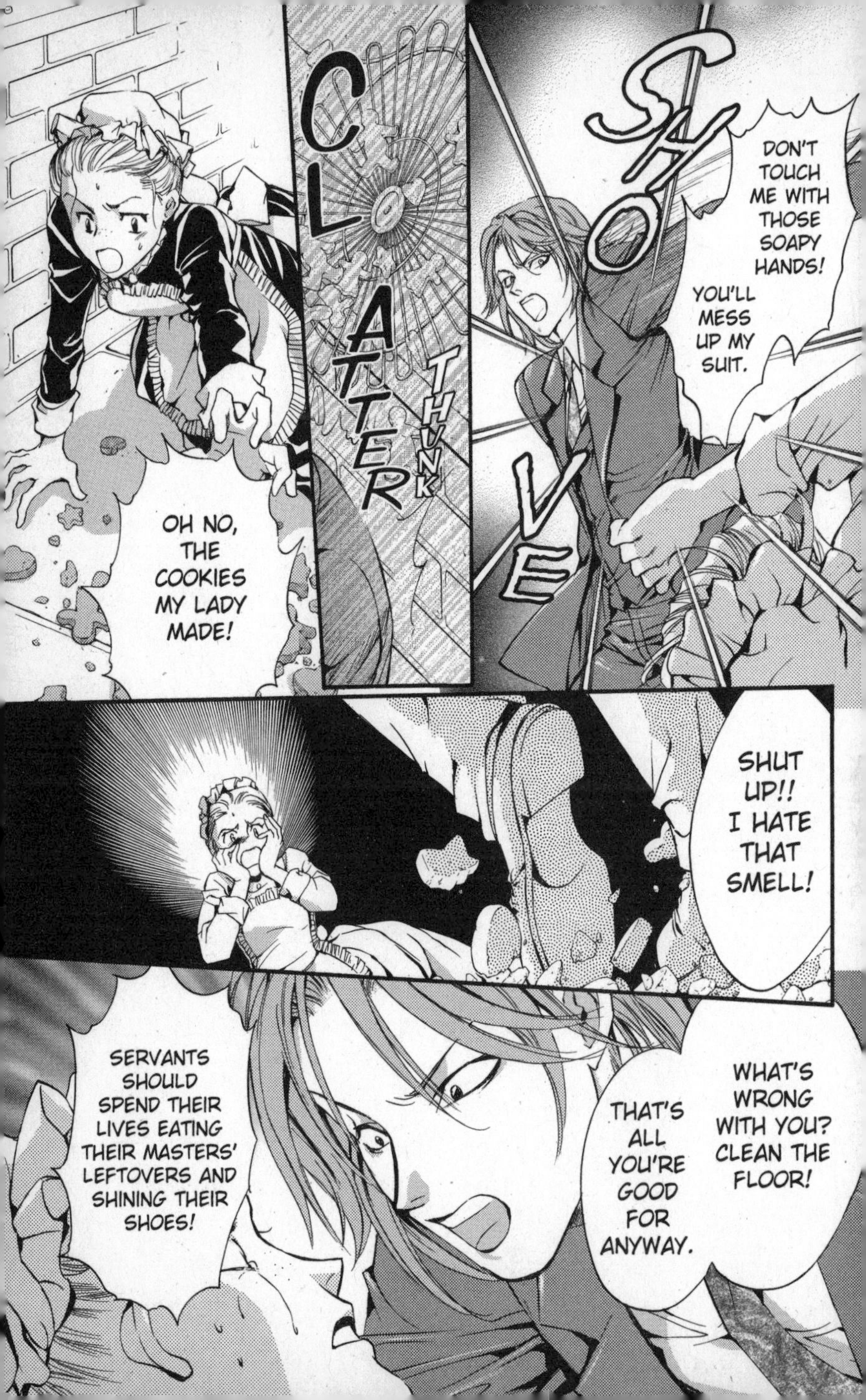
SHOVE
DON'T TOUCH ME WITH THOSE SOAPY HANDS!
YOU'LL MESS UP MY SUIT.
CLATTER
THUNK
OH NO, THE COOKIES MY LADY MADE!
SHUT UP!! I HATE THAT SMELL!
WHAT'S WRONG WITH YOU? CLEAN THE FLOOR!
THAT'S ALL YOU'RE GOOD FOR ANYWAY.
SERVANTS SHOULD SPEND THEIR LIVES EATING THEIR MASTERS' LEFTOVERS AND SHINING THEIR SHOES!

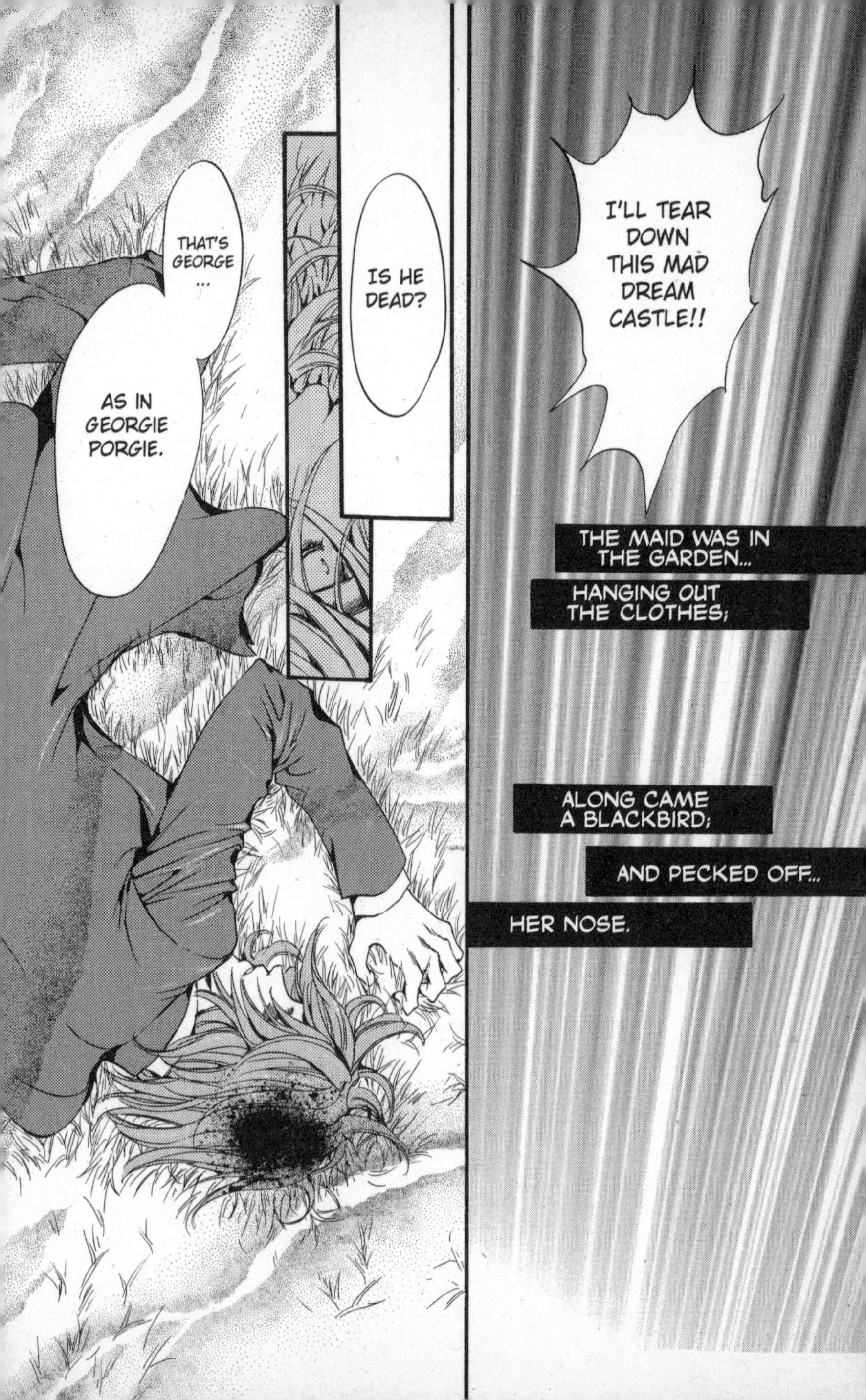
I'LL TEAR DOWN THIS MAD DREAM CASTLE!!
THE MAID WAS IN THE GARDEN...
HANGING OUT THE CLOTHES;
ALONG CAME A BLACKBIRD;
AND PECKED OFF...
HER NOSE.
IS HE DEAD?
THAT'S GEORGE ...
AS IN GEORGIE PORGIE.

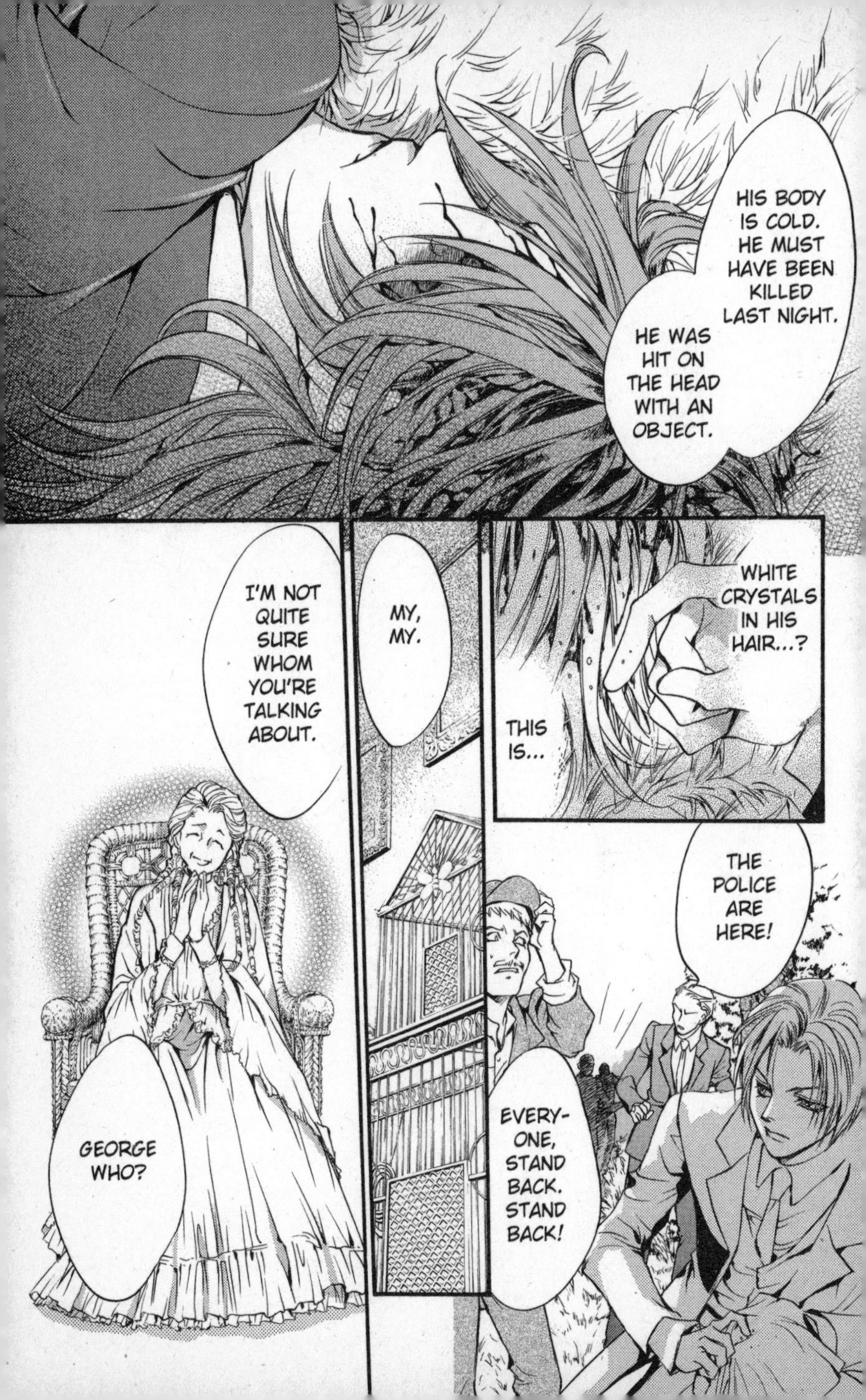
HIS BODY IS COLD. HE MUST HAVE BEEN KILLED LAST NIGHT.
HE WAS HIT ON THE HEAD WITH AN OBJECT.
WHITE CRYSTALS IN HIS HAIR...?
THIS IS...
THE POLICE ARE HERE!
EVERY-ONE, STAND BACK. STAND BACK!
MY, MY.
I'M NOT QUITE SURE WHOM YOU'RE TALKING ABOUT.
GEORGE WHO?

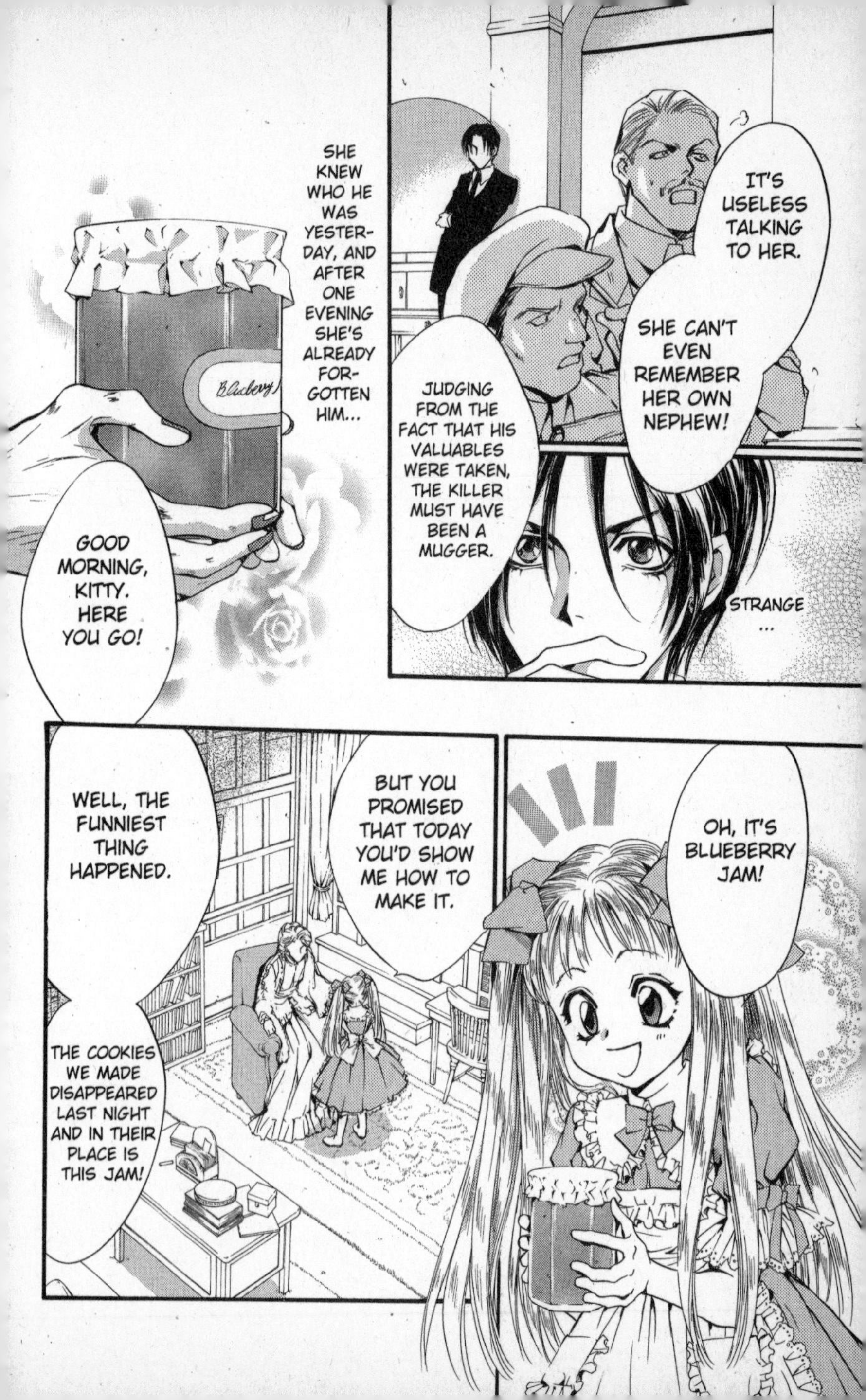

IT'S USELESS TALKING TO HER.
SHE CAN'T EVEN REMEMBER HER OWN NEPHEW!
JUDGING FROM THE FACT THAT HIS VALUABLES WERE TAKEN, THE KILLER MUST HAVE BEEN A MUGGER.
STRANGE ...
SHE KNEW WHO HE WAS YESTER-DAY, AND AFTER ONE EVENING SHE'S ALREADY FOR-GOTTEN HIM...
GOOD MORNING, KITTY. HERE YOU GO!
OH, IT'S BLUEBERRY JAM!
BUT YOU PROMISED THAT TODAY YOU'D SHOW ME HOW TO MAKE IT.
WELL, THE FUNNIEST THING HAPPENED.
THE COOKIES WE MADE DISAPPEARED LAST NIGHT AND IN THEIR PLACE IS THIS JAM!

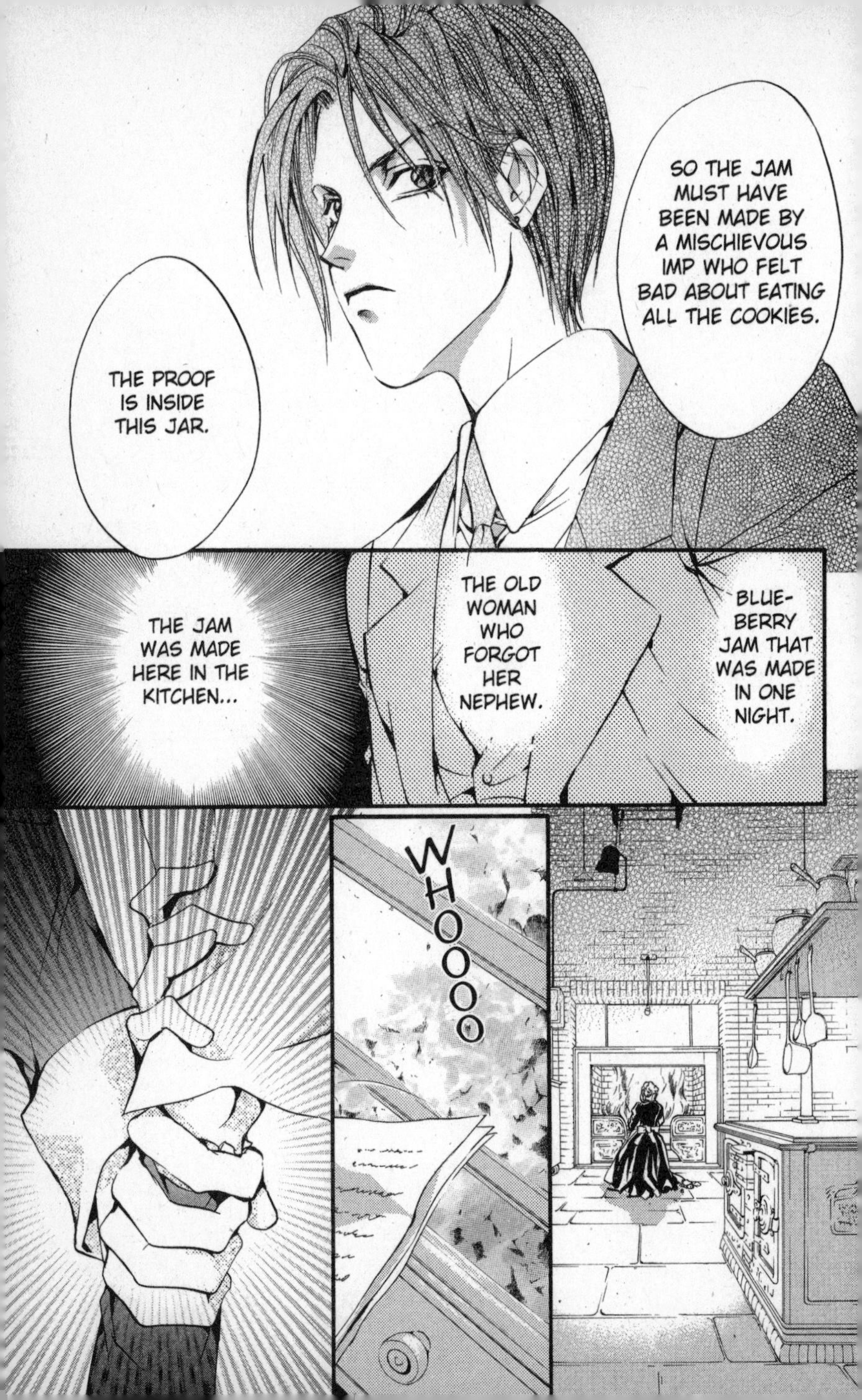
SO THE JAM MUST HAVE BEEN MADE BY A MISCHIEVOUS IMP WHO FELT BAD ABOUT EATING ALL THE COOKIES.
THE PROOF IS INSIDE THIS JAR.
BLUE-BERRY JAM THAT WAS MADE IN ONE NIGHT.
THE OLD WOMAN WHO FORGOT HER NEPHEW.
THE JAM WAS MADE HERE IN THE KITCHEN...
WHOOOO

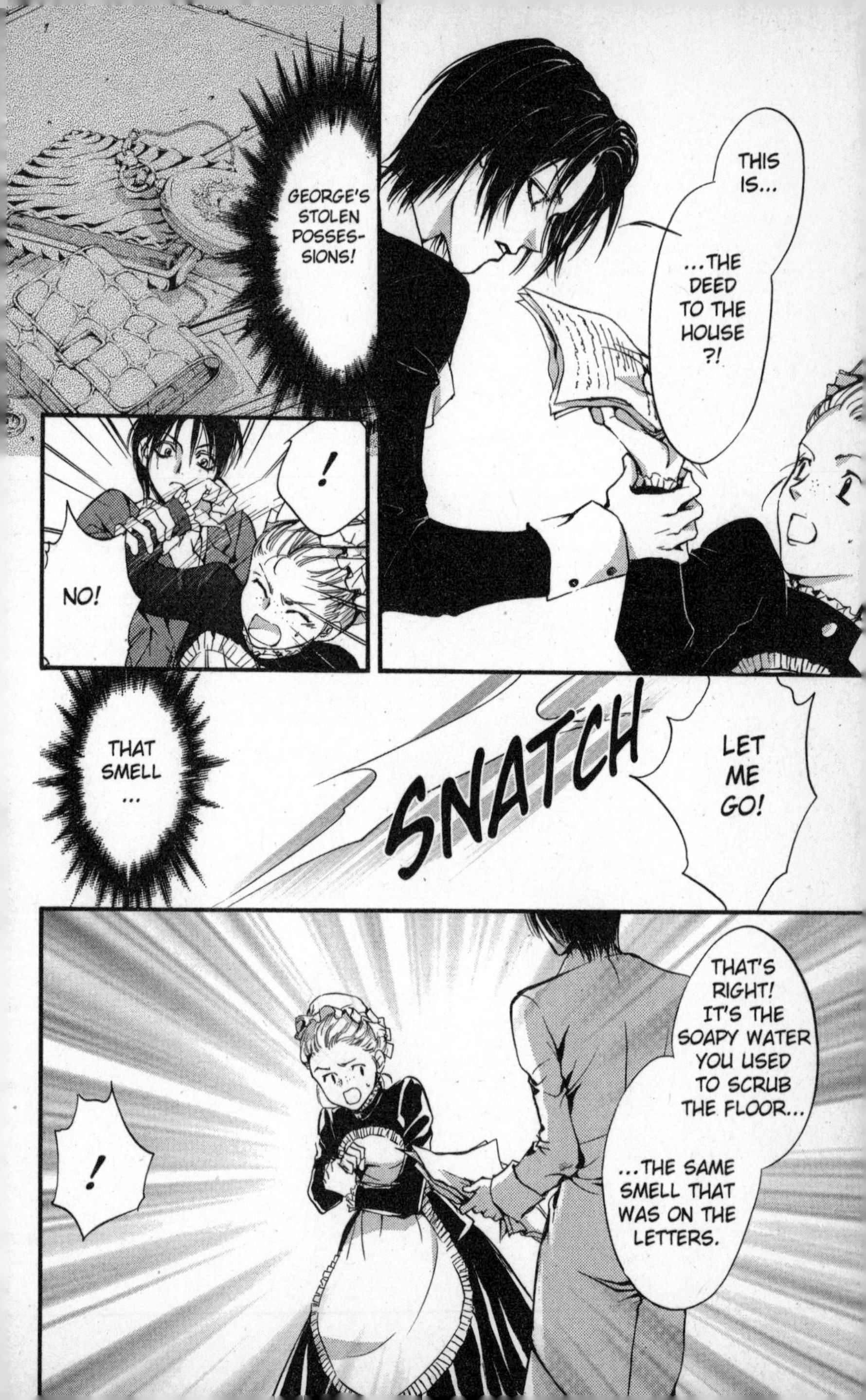
THIS IS...
...THE DEED TO THE HOUSE ?!
GEORGE'S STOLEN POSSES-SIONS!
!
NO!
LET ME GO!
SNATCH
THAT SMELL ...
THAT'S RIGHT! IT'S THE SOAPY WATER YOU USED TO SCRUB THE FLOOR...
...THE SAME SMELL THAT WAS ON THE LETTERS.
!

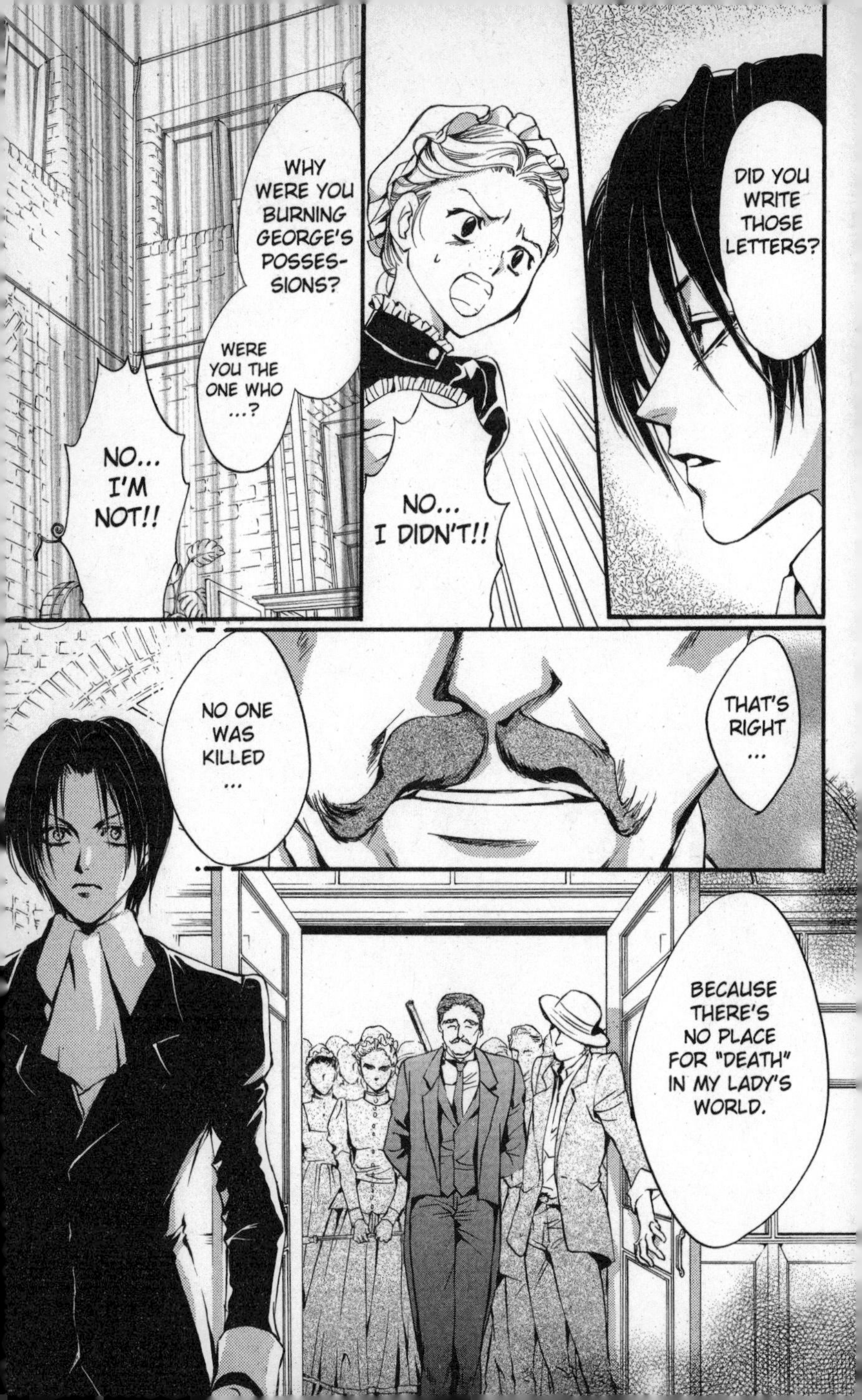
DID YOU WRITE THOSE LETTERS?
NO... I DIDN'T!!
WHY WERE YOU BURNING GEORGE'S POSSES-SIONS?
WERE YOU THE ONE WHO ...?
NO... I'M NOT!!
THAT'S RIGHT ...
NO ONE WAS KILLED ...
BECAUSE THERE'S NO PLACE FOR "DEATH" IN MY LADY'S WORLD.

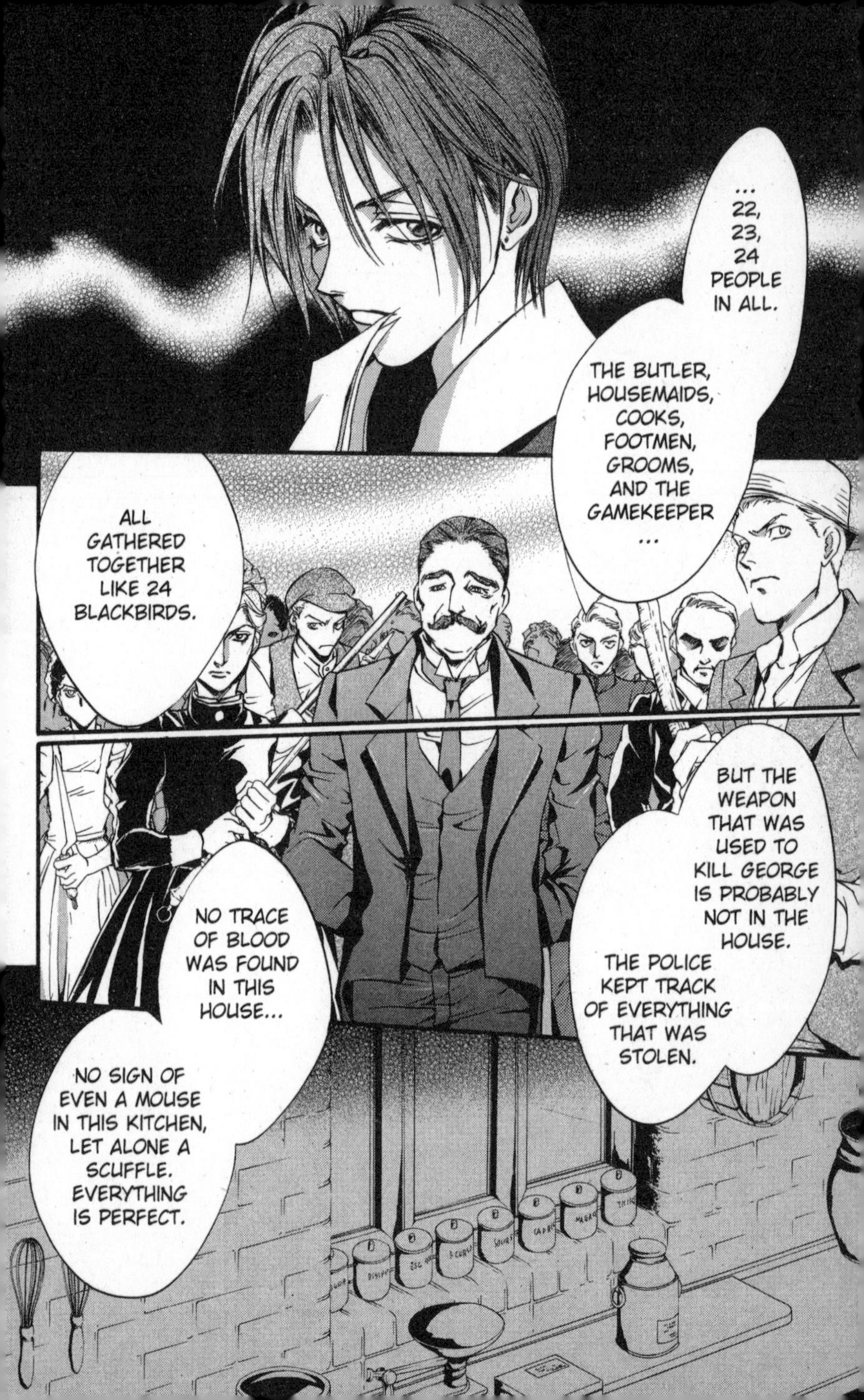
... 22, 23, 24 PEOPLE IN ALL.
THE BUTLER, HOUSEMAIDS, COOKS, FOOTMEN, GROOMS, AND THE GAMEKEEPER ...
ALL GATHERED TOGETHER LIKE 24 BLACKBIRDS.
BUT THE WEAPON THAT WAS USED TO KILL GEORGE IS PROBABLY NOT IN THE HOUSE.
THE POLICE KEPT TRACK OF EVERYTHING THAT WAS STOLEN.
NO TRACE OF BLOOD WAS FOUND IN THIS HOUSE...
NO SIGN OF EVEN A MOUSE IN THIS KITCHEN, LET ALONE A SCUFFLE. EVERYTHING IS PERFECT.

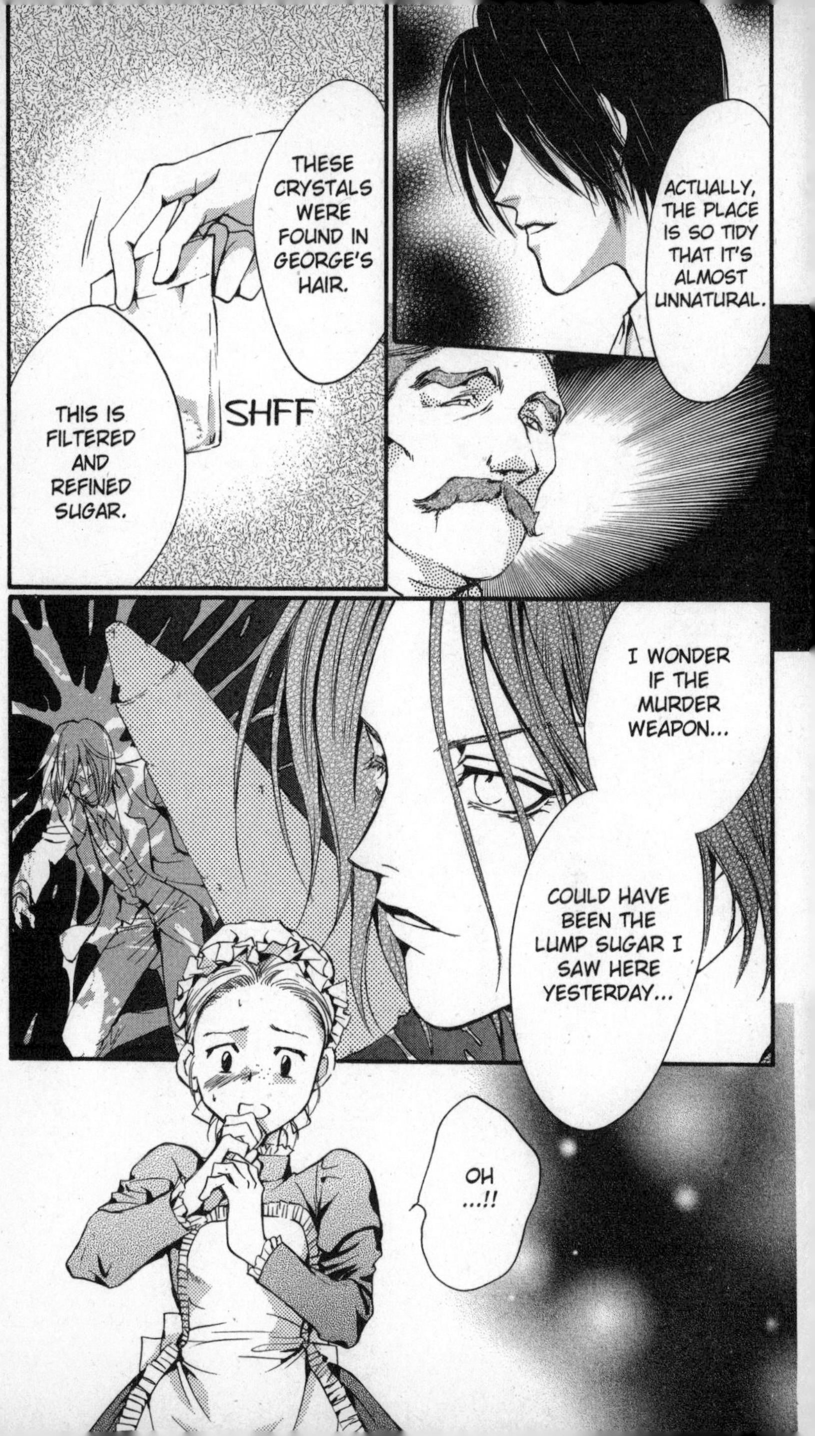
ACTUALLY, THE PLACE IS SO TIDY THAT IT'S ALMOST UNNATURAL.
THESE CRYSTALS WERE FOUND IN GEORGE'S HAIR.
SHFF
THIS IS FILTERED AND REFINED SUGAR.
I WONDER IF THE MURDER WEAPON...
COULD HAVE BEEN THE LUMP SUGAR I SAW HERE YESTERDAY...
OH ...!!

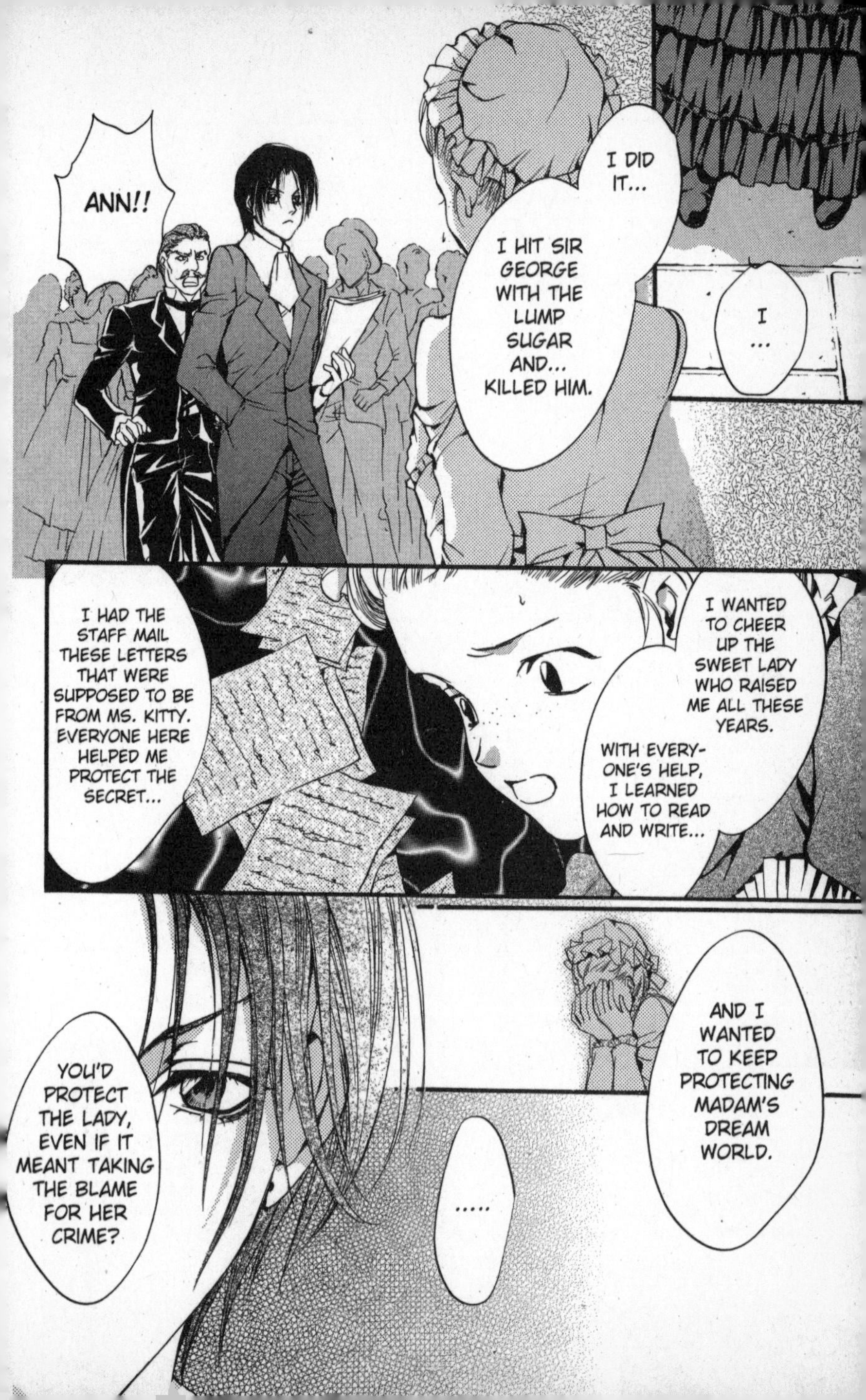
I ...
I DID IT...
I HIT SIR GEORGE WITH THE LUMP SUGAR AND... KILLED HIM.
ANN!!
I WANTED TO CHEER UP THE SWEET LADY WHO RAISED ME ALL THESE YEARS.
WITH EVERY-ONE'S HELP, I LEARNED HOW TO READ AND WRITE...
I HAD THE STAFF MAIL THESE LETTERS THAT WERE SUPPOSED TO BE FROM MS. KITTY. EVERYONE HERE HELPED ME PROTECT THE SECRET...
AND I WANTED TO KEEP PROTECTING MADAM'S DREAM WORLD.
.....
YOU'D PROTECT THE LADY, EVEN IF IT MEANT TAKING THE BLAME FOR HER CRIME?

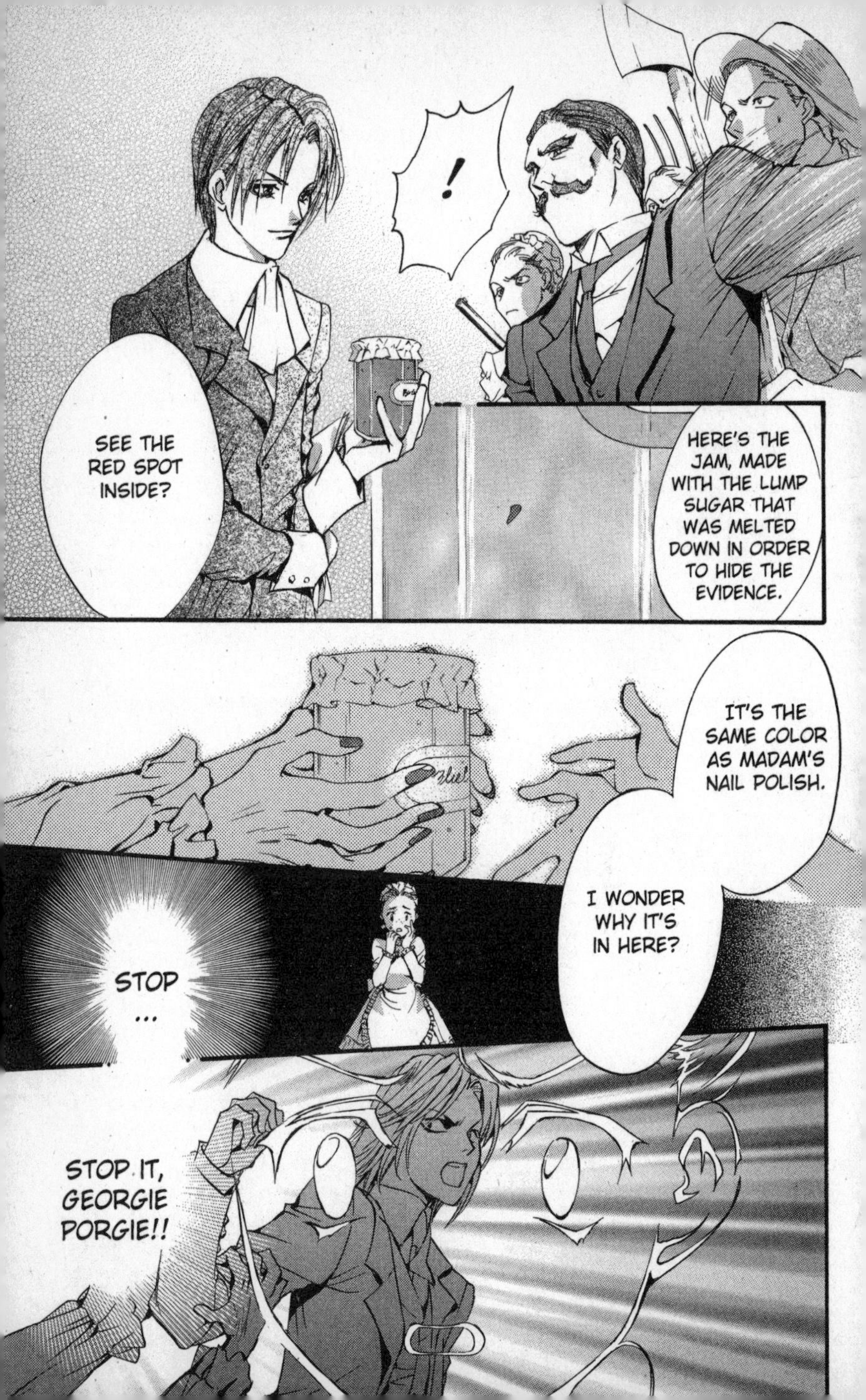
!
HERE'S THE JAM, MADE WITH THE LUMP SUGAR THAT WAS MELTED DOWN IN ORDER TO HIDE THE EVIDENCE.
SEE THE RED SPOT INSIDE?
IT'S THE SAME COLOR AS MADAM'S NAIL POLISH.
I WONDER WHY IT'S IN HERE?
STOP ...
STOP IT, GEORGIE PORGIE!!

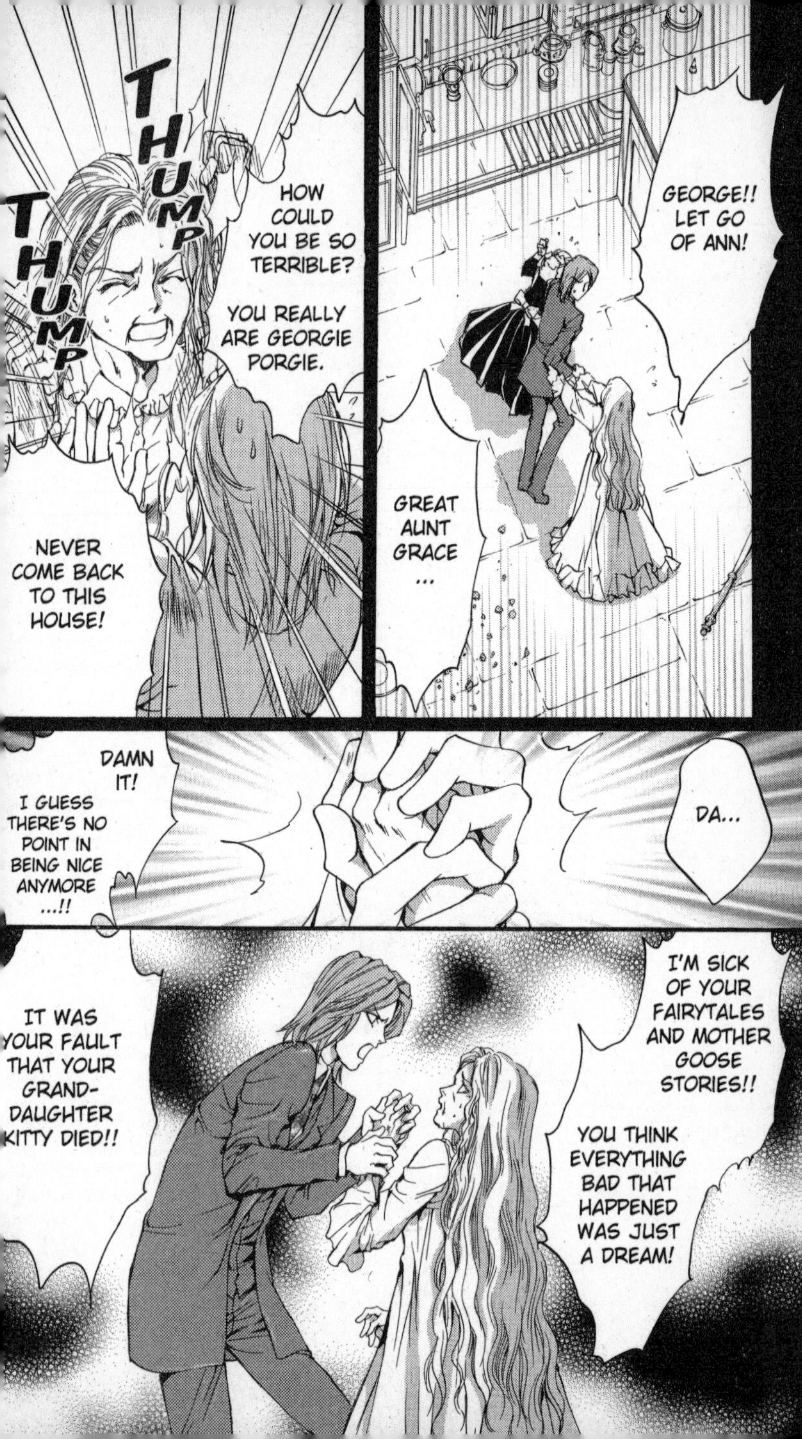
GEORGE!! LET GO OF ANN!
GREAT AUNT GRACE ...
THUMP
THUMP
HOW COULD YOU BE SO TERRIBLE?
YOU REALLY ARE GEORGIE PORGIE.
NEVER COME BACK TO THIS HOUSE!
DA...
DAMN IT!
I GUESS THERE'S NO POINT IN BEING NICE ANYMORE ...!!
I'M SICK OF YOUR FAIRYTALES AND MOTHER GOOSE STORIES!!
YOU THINK EVERYTHING BAD THAT HAPPENED WAS JUST A DREAM!
IT WAS YOUR FAULT THAT YOUR GRAND-DAUGHTER KITTY DIED!!

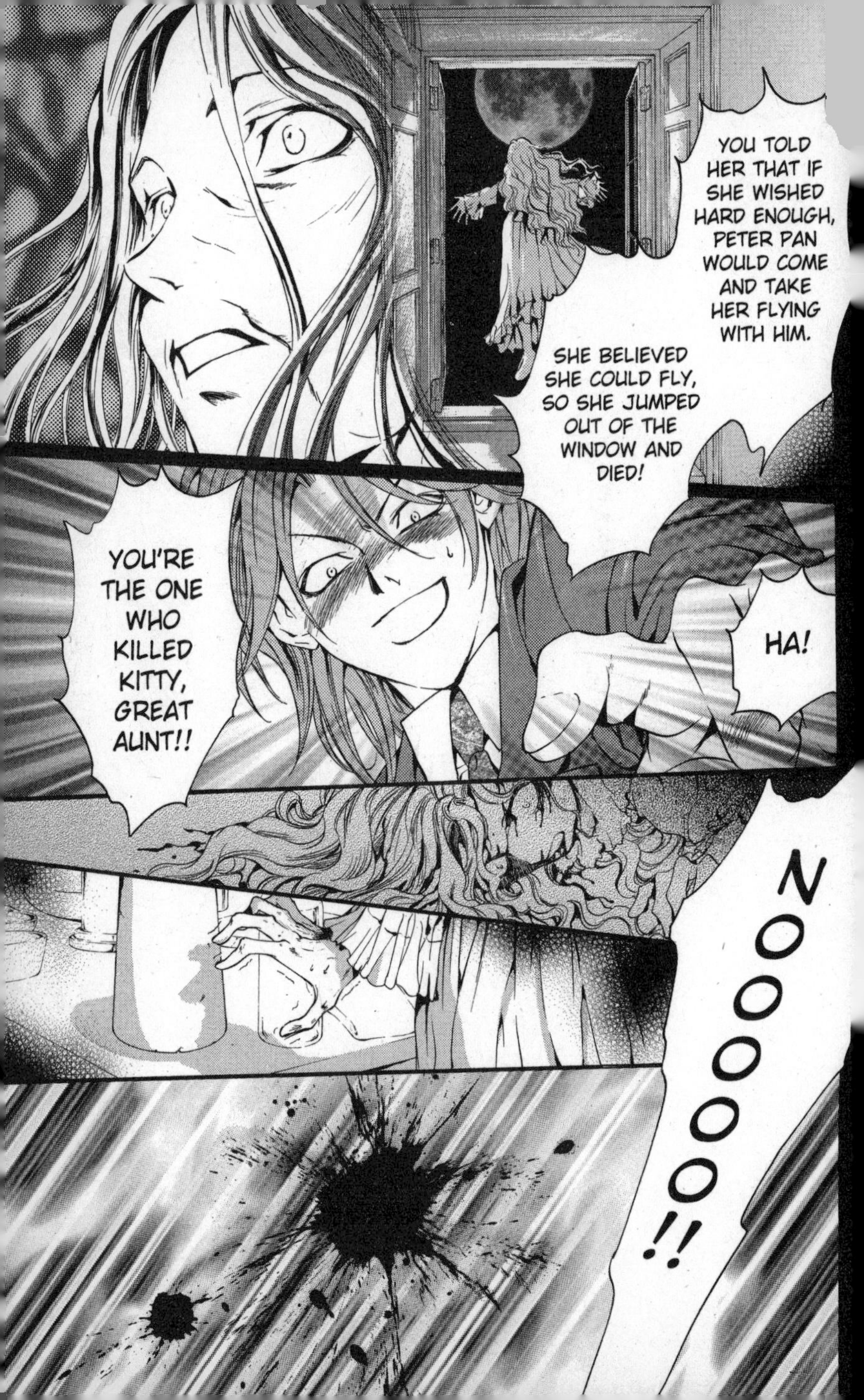
YOU TOLD HER THAT IF SHE WISHED HARD ENOUGH, PETER PAN WOULD COME AND TAKE HER FLYING WITH HIM.
SHE BELIEVED SHE COULD FLY, SO SHE JUMPED OUT OF THE WINDOW AND DIED!
HA!
YOU'RE THE ONE WHO KILLED KITTY, GREAT AUNT!!
NOOOOOO!!

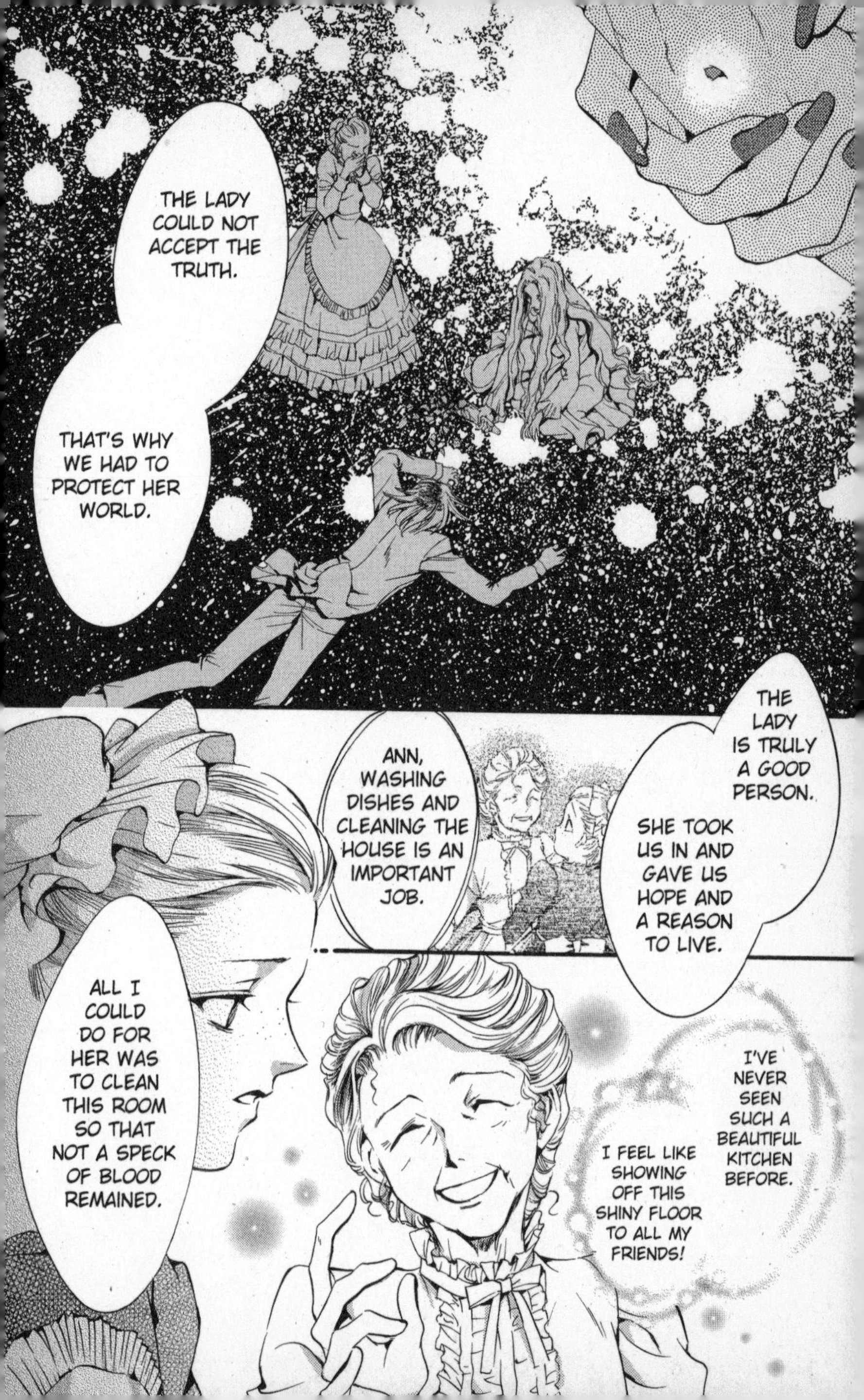
THE LADY COULD NOT ACCEPT THE TRUTH.
THAT'S WHY WE HAD TO PROTECT HER WORLD.
THE LADY IS TRULY A GOOD PERSON.
SHE TOOK US IN AND GAVE US HOPE AND A REASON TO LIVE.
ANN, WASHING DISHES AND CLEANING THE HOUSE IS AN IMPORTANT JOB.
I'VE NEVER SEEN SUCH A BEAUTIFUL KITCHEN BEFORE.
I FEEL LIKE SHOWING OFF THIS SHINY FLOOR TO ALL MY FRIENDS!
ALL I COULD DO FOR HER WAS TO CLEAN THIS ROOM SO THAT NOT A SPECK OF BLOOD REMAINED.

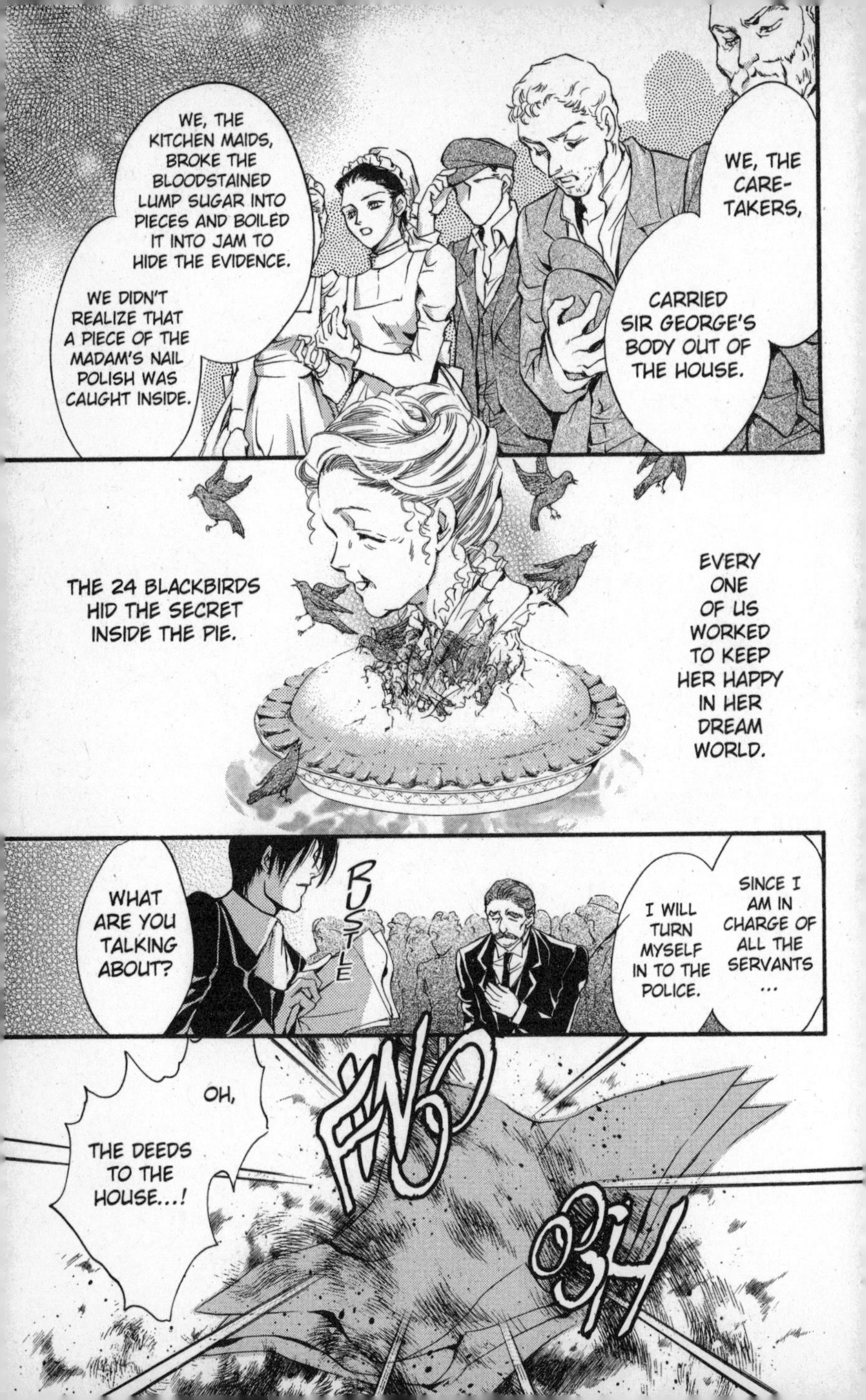
WE, THE CARE-TAKERS,
CARRIED SIR GEORGE'S BODY OUT OF THE HOUSE.
WE, THE KITCHEN MAIDS, BROKE THE BLOODSTAINED LUMP SUGAR INTO PIECES AND BOILED IT INTO JAM TO HIDE THE EVIDENCE.
WE DIDN'T REALIZE THAT A PIECE OF THE MADAM'S NAIL POLISH WAS CAUGHT INSIDE.
EVERY ONE OF US WORKED TO KEEP HER HAPPY IN HER DREAM WORLD.
THE 24 BLACKBIRDS HID THE SECRET INSIDE THE PIE.
SINCE I AM IN CHARGE OF ALL THE SERVANTS ...
I WILL TURN MYSELF IN TO THE POLICE.
RUSTLE
WHAT ARE YOU TALKING ABOUT?
FWO
OSH
OH,
THE DEEDS TO THE HOUSE...!

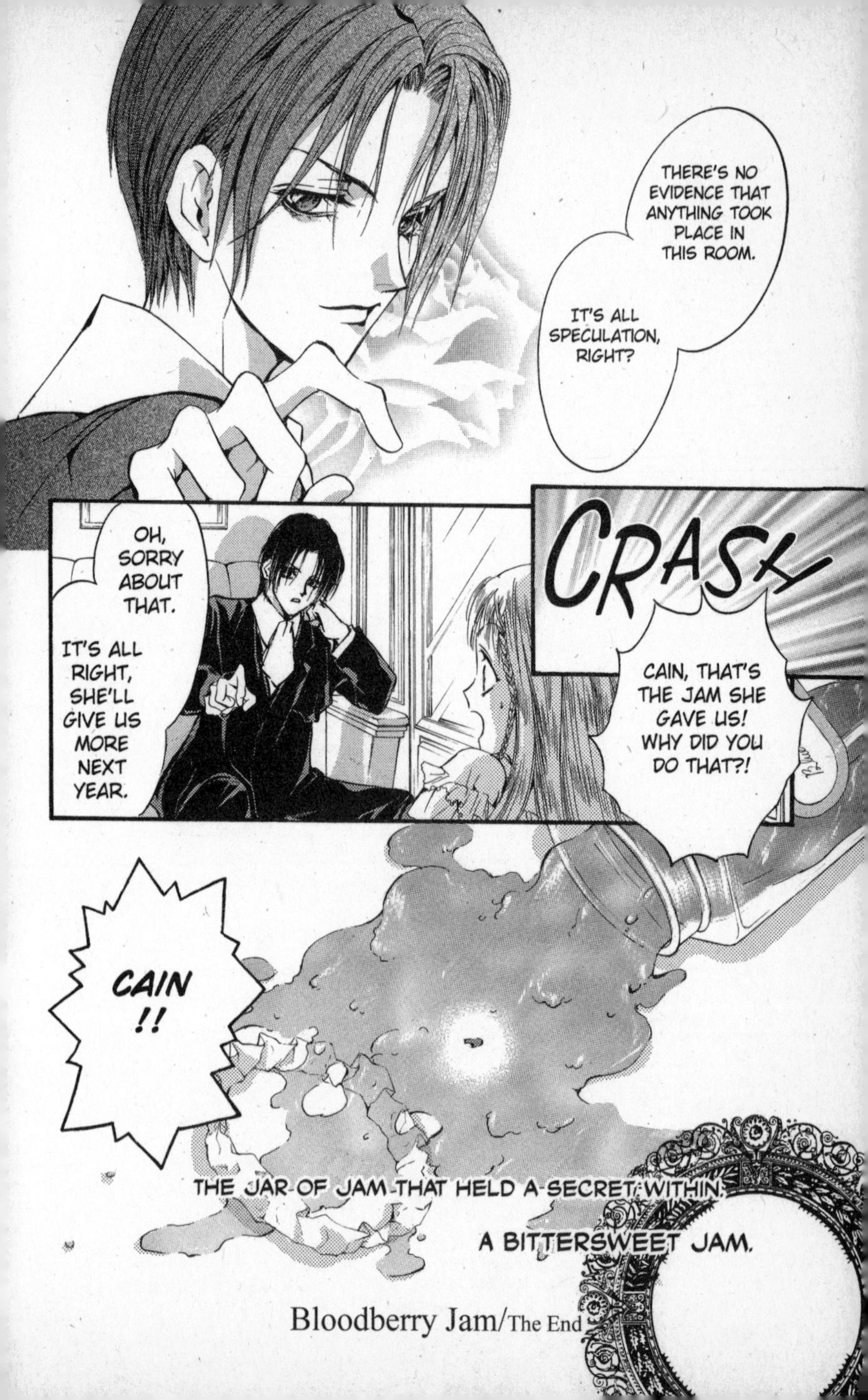
THERE'S NO EVIDENCE THAT ANYTHING TOOK PLACE IN THIS ROOM.
IT'S ALL SPECULATION, RIGHT?
CRASH
CAIN, THAT'S THE JAM SHE GAVE US! WHY DID YOU DO THAT?!
OH, SORRY ABOUT THAT.
IT'S ALL RIGHT, SHE'LL GIVE US MORE NEXT YEAR.
CAIN !!
THE JAR OF JAM THAT HELD A SECRET WITHIN.
A BITTERSWEET JAM.

Bloodberry Jam/The End

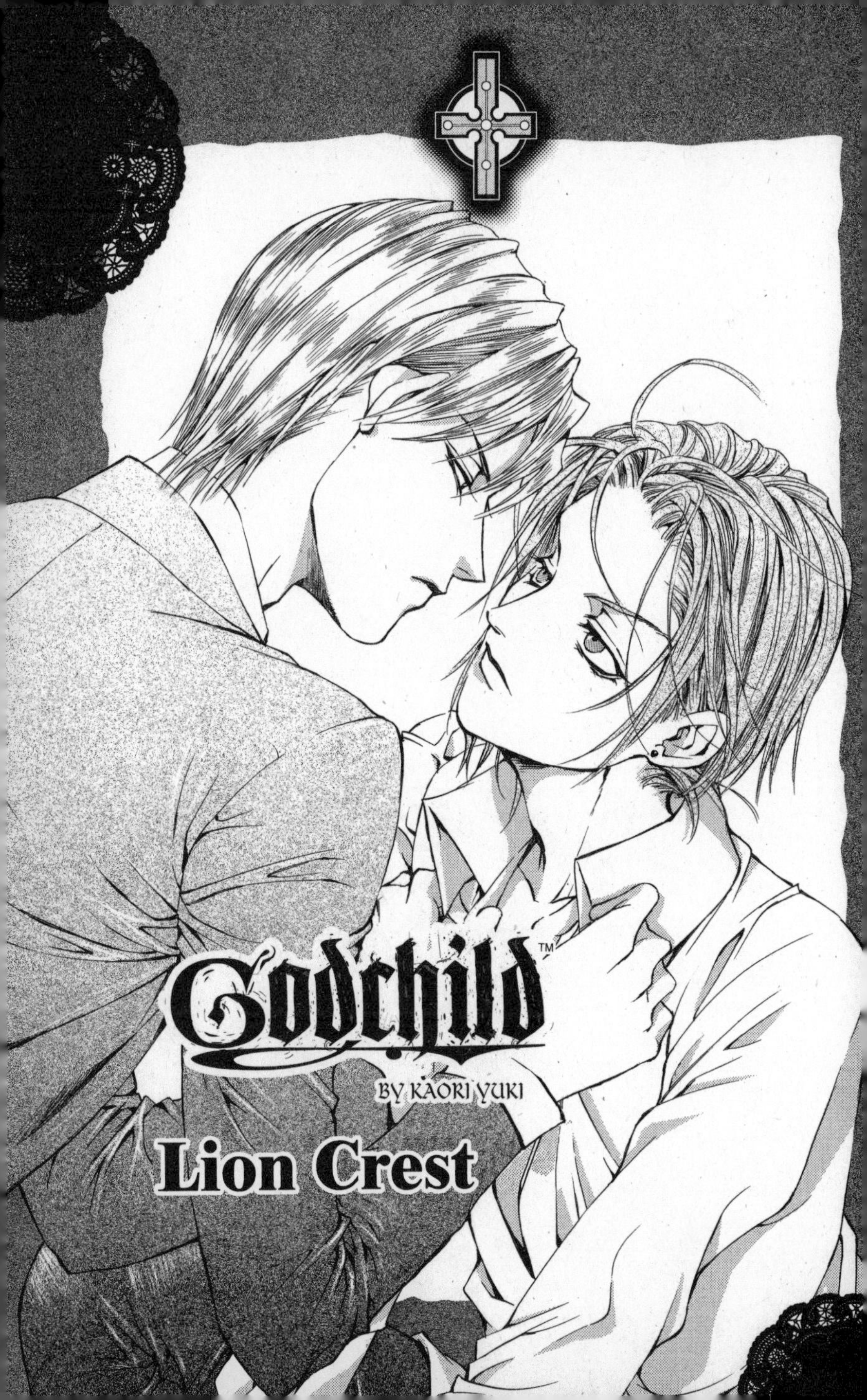
Godchild™
BY KAORI YUKI
Lion Crest

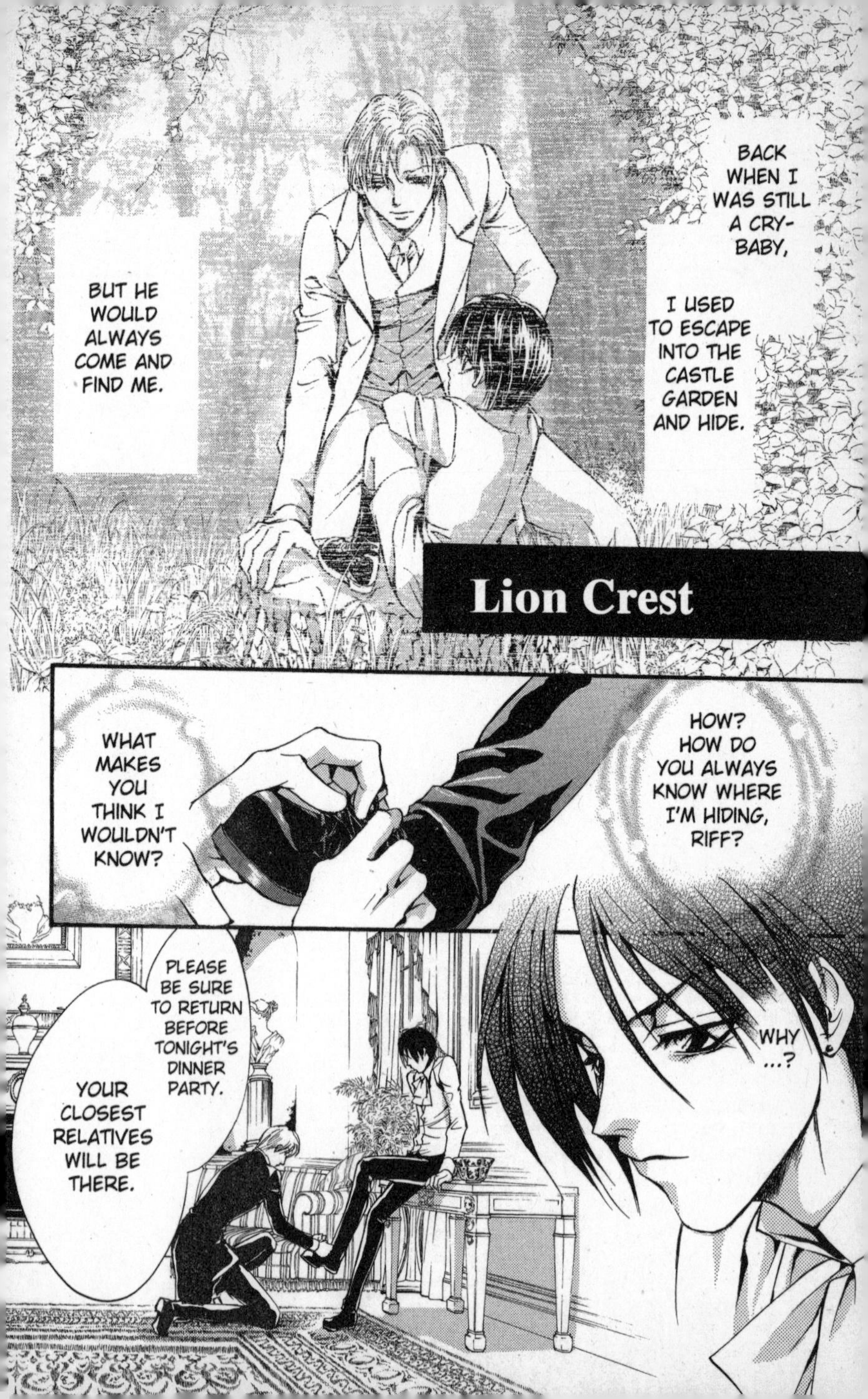
BACK WHEN I WAS STILL A CRY-BABY,
I USED TO ESCAPE INTO THE CASTLE GARDEN AND HIDE.
BUT HE WOULD ALWAYS COME AND FIND ME.
Lion Crest
HOW? HOW DO YOU ALWAYS KNOW WHERE I'M HIDING, RIFF?
WHAT MAKES YOU THINK I WOULDN'T KNOW?
WHY...?
PLEASE BE SURE TO RETURN BEFORE TONIGHT'S DINNER PARTY.
YOUR CLOSEST RELATIVES WILL BE THERE.

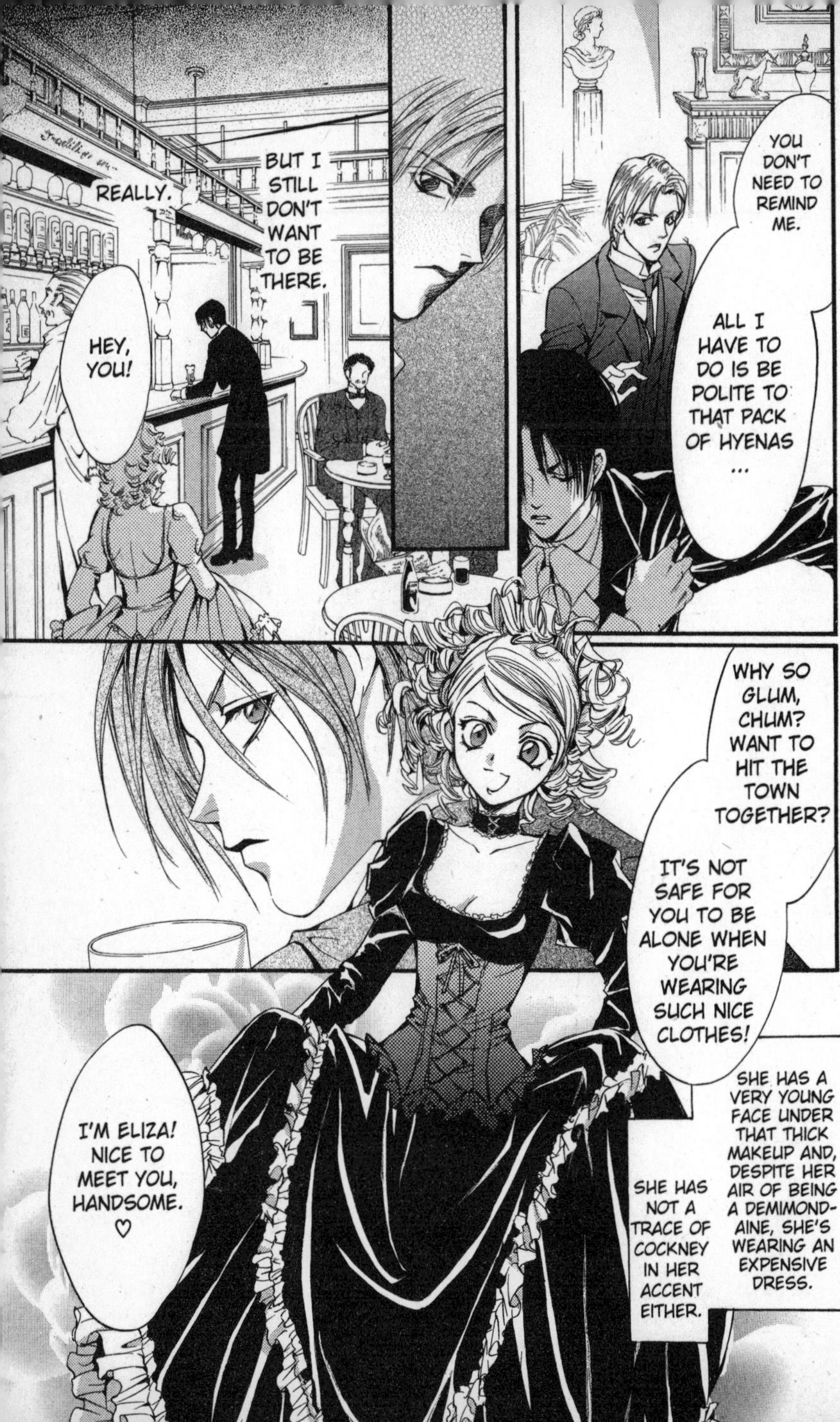
YOU DON'T NEED TO REMIND ME.
ALL I HAVE TO DO IS BE POLITE TO THAT PACK OF HYENAS ...
BUT I STILL DON'T WANT TO BE THERE.
REALLY.
HEY, YOU!
WHY SO GLUM, CHUM? WANT TO HIT THE TOWN TOGETHER?
IT'S NOT SAFE FOR YOU TO BE ALONE WHEN YOU'RE WEARING SUCH NICE CLOTHES!
SHE HAS A VERY YOUNG FACE UNDER THAT THICK MAKEUP AND, DESPITE HER AIR OF BEING A DEMIMOND-AINE, SHE'S WEARING AN EXPENSIVE DRESS.
SHE HAS NOT A TRACE OF COCKNEY IN HER ACCENT EITHER.
I'M ELIZA! NICE TO MEET YOU, HANDSOME. ♡

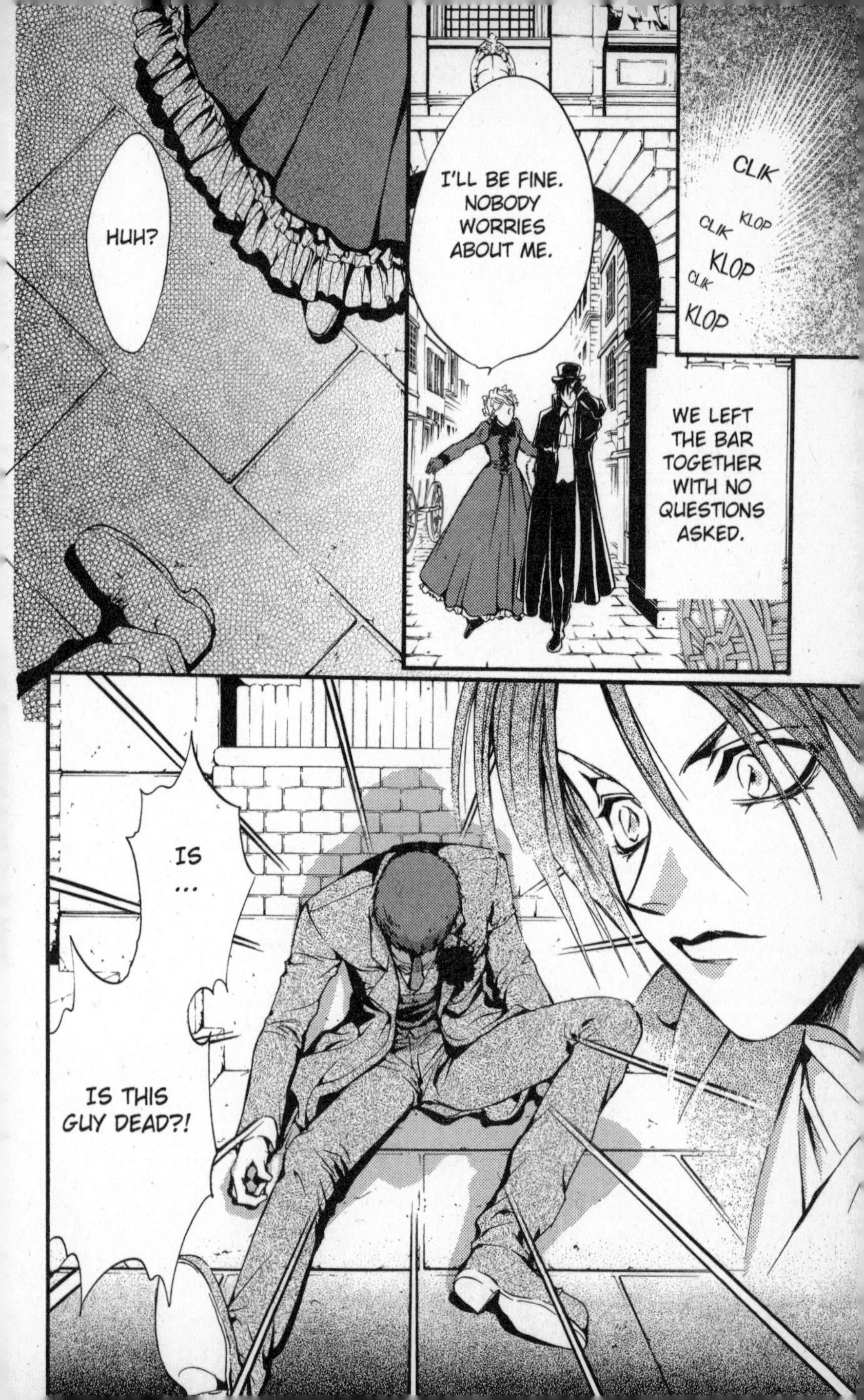
CLIK
CLIK KLOP
KLOP
CLIK
KLOP
I'LL BE FINE. NOBODY WORRIES ABOUT ME.
WE LEFT THE BAR TOGETHER WITH NO QUESTIONS ASKED.
HUH?
IS ...
IS THIS GUY DEAD?!

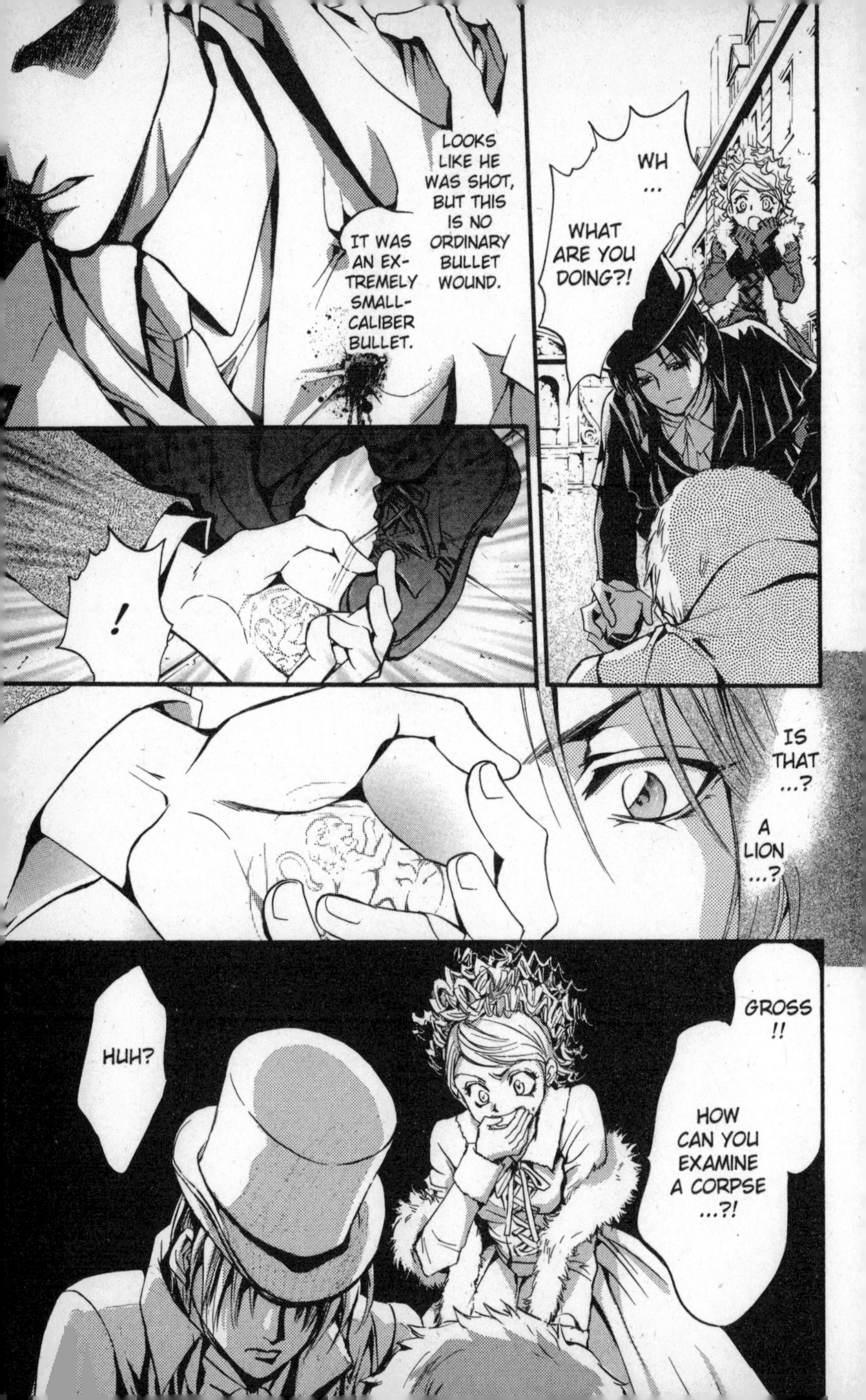
WH ...
WHAT ARE YOU DOING?!
LOOKS LIKE HE WAS SHOT, BUT THIS IS NO ORDINARY BULLET WOUND.
IT WAS AN EX-TREMELY SMALL-CALIBER BULLET.
!
IS THAT ...?
A LION ...?
GROSS !!
HOW CAN YOU EXAMINE A CORPSE ...?!
HUH?

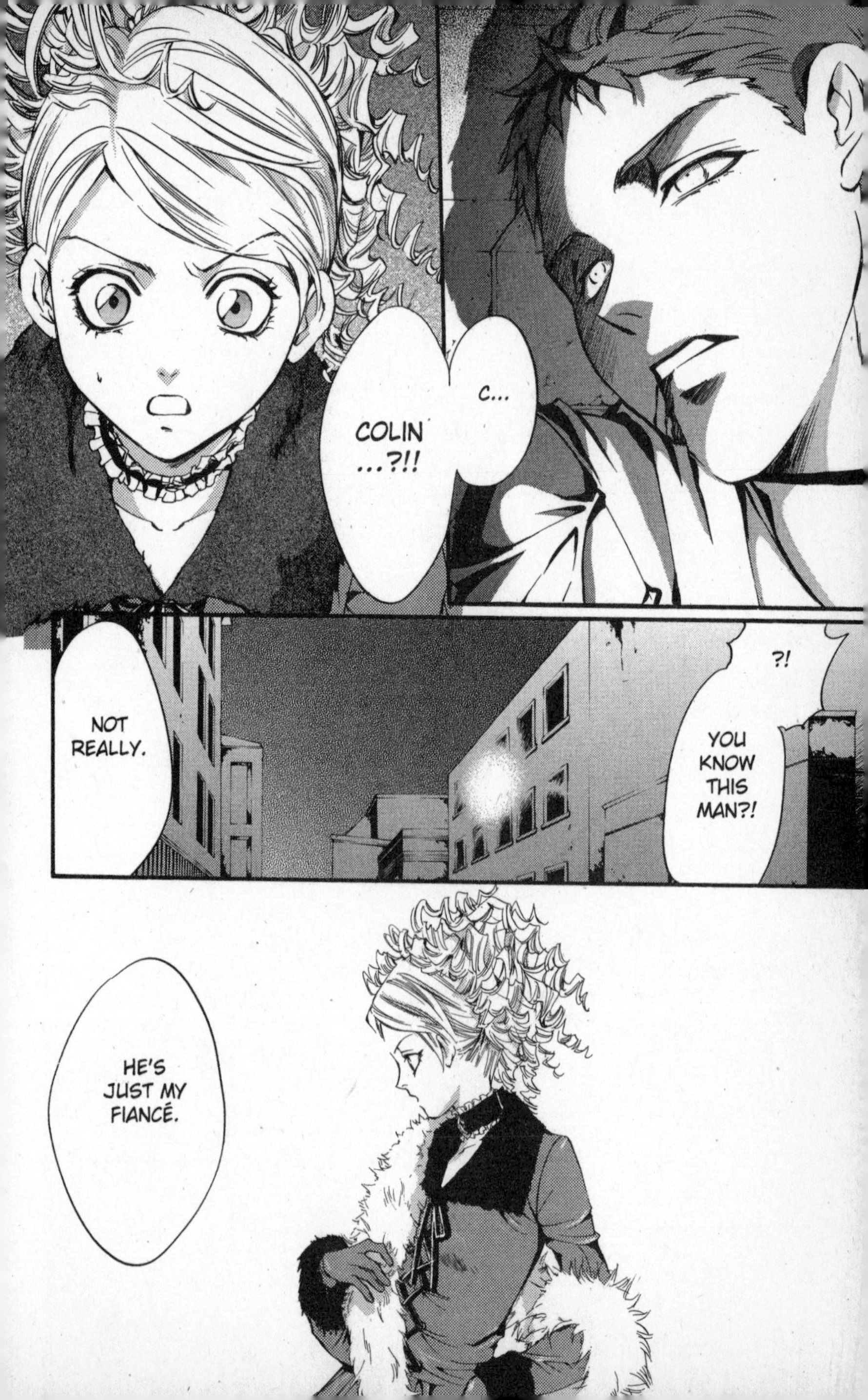
C...
COLIN ...?!!
?! YOU KNOW THIS MAN?!
NOT REALLY.
HE'S JUST MY FIANCÉ.

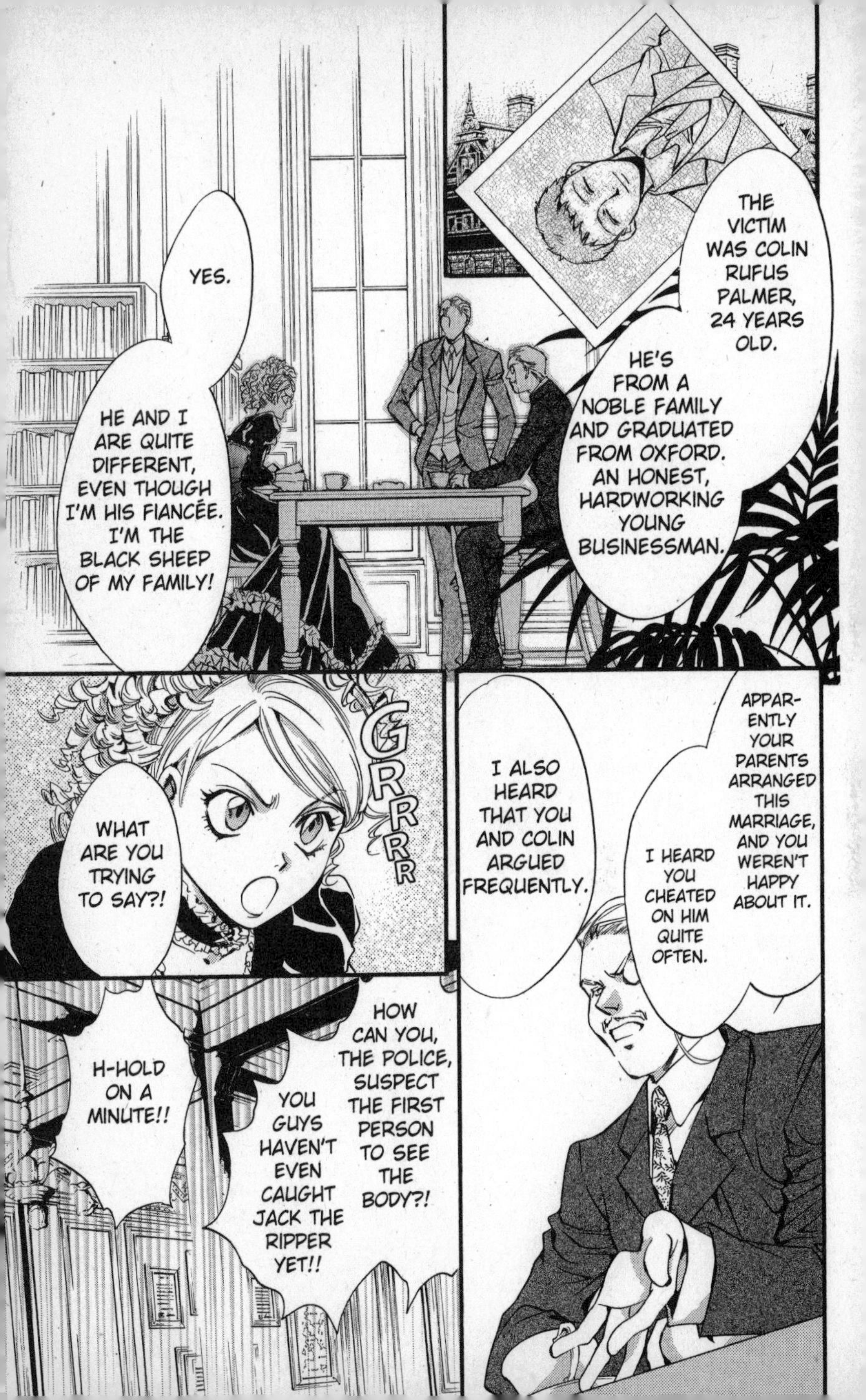
THE VICTIM WAS COLIN RUFUS PALMER, 24 YEARS OLD.
HE'S FROM A NOBLE FAMILY AND GRADUATED FROM OXFORD. AN HONEST, HARDWORKING YOUNG BUSINESSMAN.
YES.
HE AND I ARE QUITE DIFFERENT, EVEN THOUGH I'M HIS FIANCÉE. I'M THE BLACK SHEEP OF MY FAMILY!
APPARENTLY YOUR PARENTS ARRANGED THIS MARRIAGE, AND YOU WEREN'T HAPPY ABOUT IT.
I HEARD YOU CHEATED ON HIM QUITE OFTEN.
I ALSO HEARD THAT YOU AND COLIN ARGUED FREQUENTLY.
GRRRR
WHAT ARE YOU TRYING TO SAY?!
HOW CAN YOU, THE POLICE, SUSPECT THE FIRST PERSON TO SEE THE BODY?!
YOU GUYS HAVEN'T EVEN CAUGHT JACK THE RIPPER YET!!
H-HOLD ON A MINUTE!!

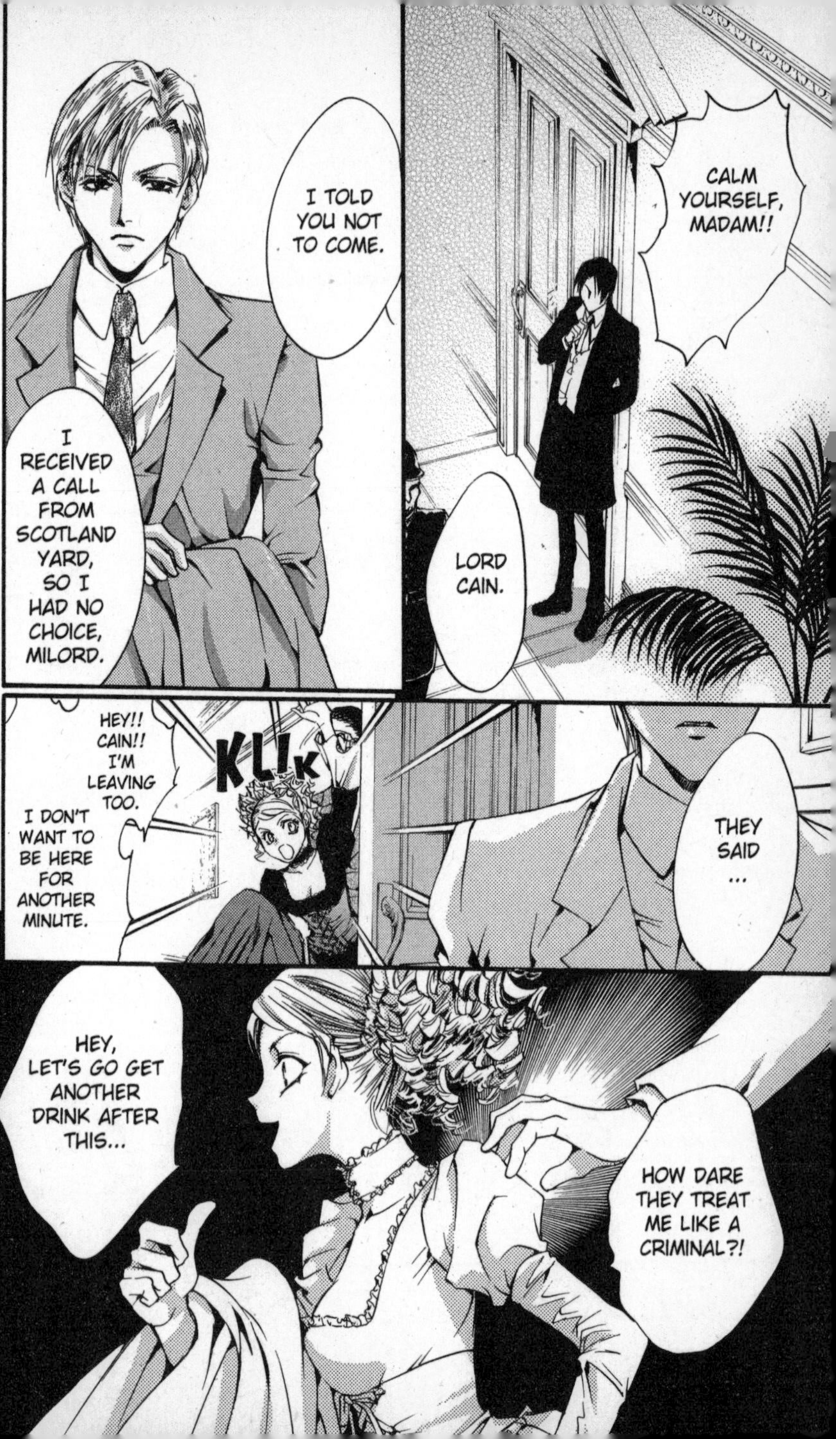
CALM YOURSELF, MADAM!!
LORD CAIN.
I TOLD YOU NOT TO COME.
I RECEIVED A CALL FROM SCOTLAND YARD, SO I HAD NO CHOICE, MILORD.
THEY SAID ...
HEY!! CAIN!! I'M LEAVING TOO.
KLIK
I DON'T WANT TO BE HERE FOR ANOTHER MINUTE.
HOW DARE THEY TREAT ME LIKE A CRIMINAL?!
HEY, LET'S GO GET ANOTHER DRINK AFTER THIS...

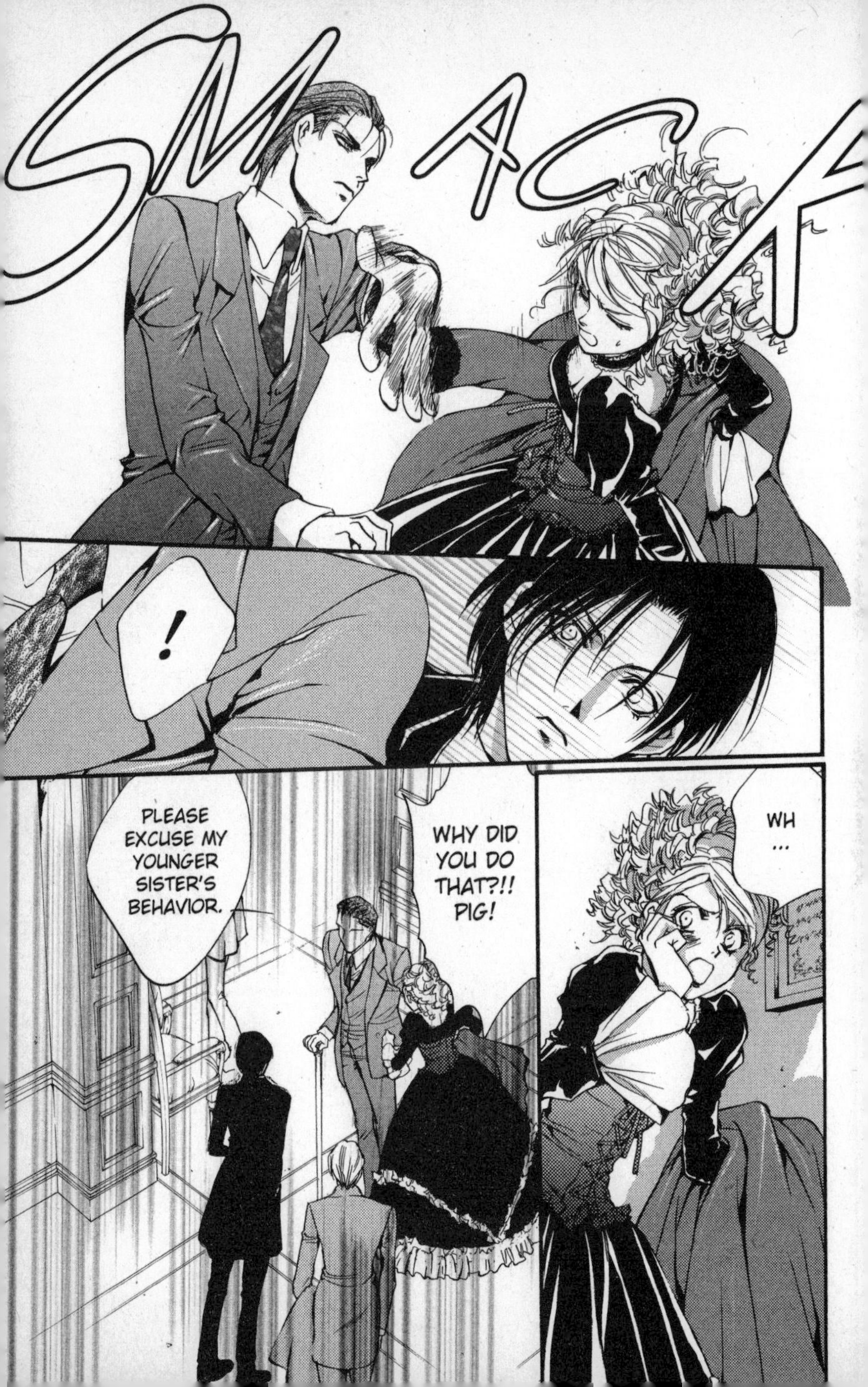
SMACK
!
WH ...
WHY DID YOU DO THAT?!! PIG!
PLEASE EXCUSE MY YOUNGER SISTER'S BEHAVIOR.

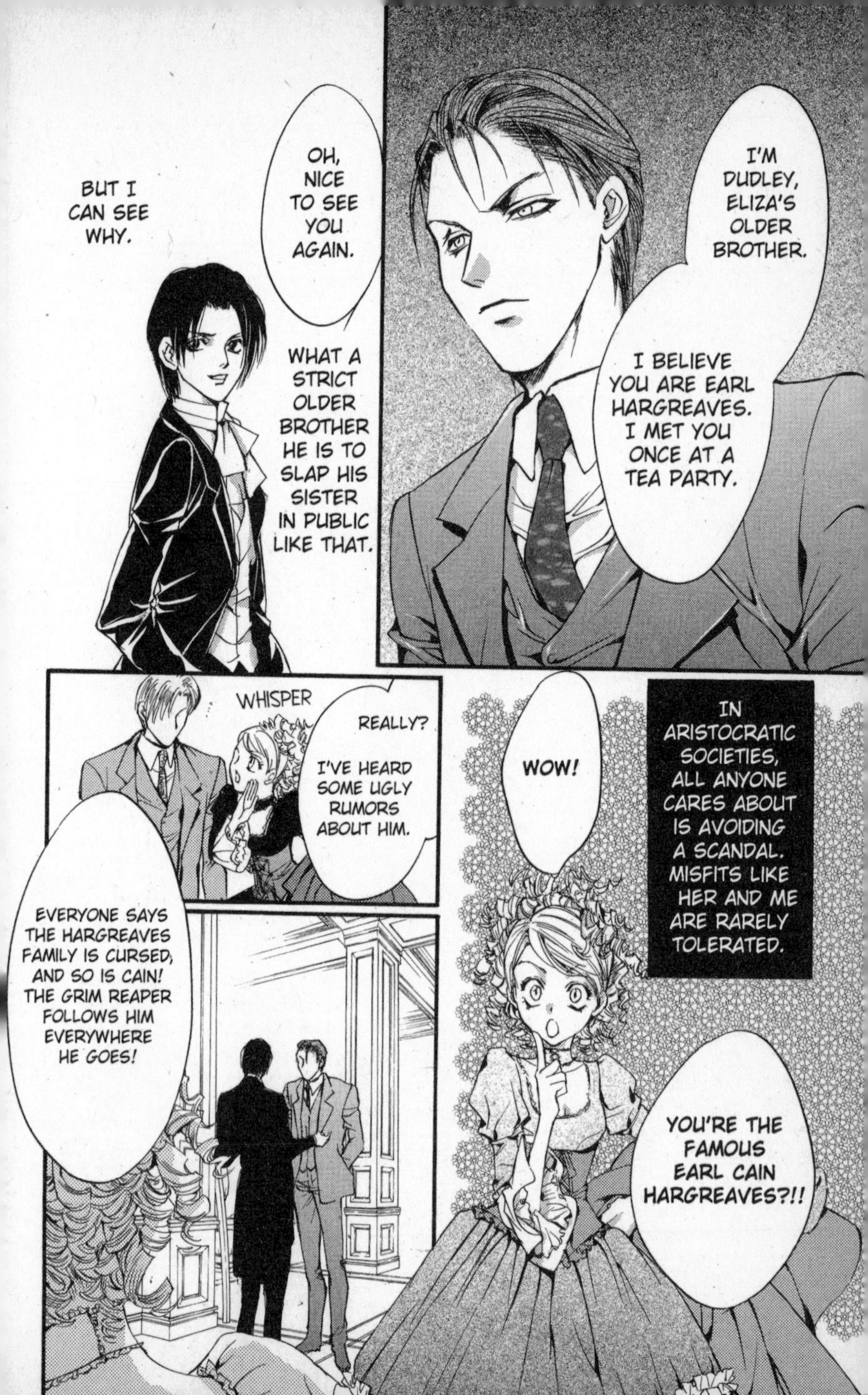
I'M DUDLEY, ELIZA'S OLDER BROTHER.
I BELIEVE YOU ARE EARL HARGREAVES. I MET YOU ONCE AT A TEA PARTY.
OH, NICE TO SEE YOU AGAIN.
BUT I CAN SEE WHY.
WHAT A STRICT OLDER BROTHER HE IS TO SLAP HIS SISTER IN PUBLIC LIKE THAT.
IN ARISTOCRATIC SOCIETIES, ALL ANYONE CARES ABOUT IS AVOIDING A SCANDAL. MISFITS LIKE HER AND ME ARE RARELY TOLERATED.
WOW!
YOU'RE THE FAMOUS EARL CAIN HARGREAVES?!!
WHISPER
REALLY?
I'VE HEARD SOME UGLY RUMORS ABOUT HIM.
EVERYONE SAYS THE HARGREAVES FAMILY IS CURSED, AND SO IS CAIN! THE GRIM REAPER FOLLOWS HIM EVERYWHERE HE GOES!

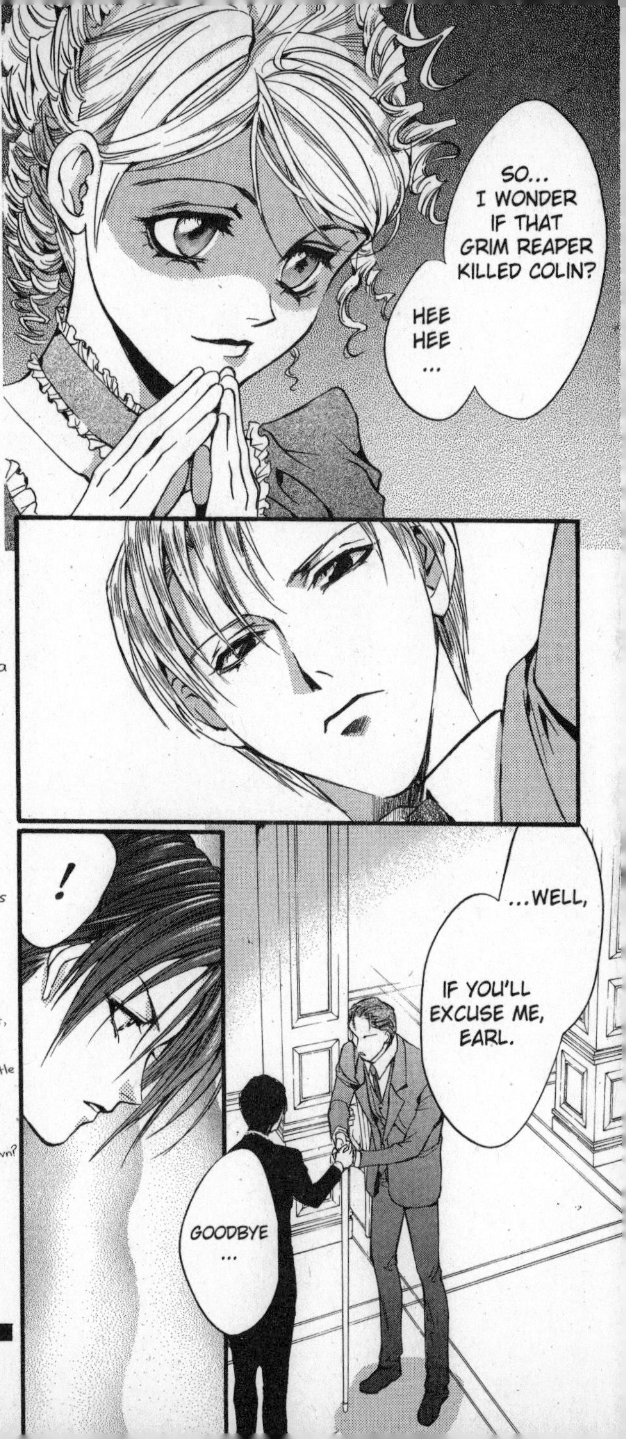
SO... I WONDER IF THAT GRIM REAPER KILLED COLIN?
HEE HEE ...
...WELL,
IF YOU'LL EXCUSE ME, EARL.
GOODBYE ...
!

"Mary, the oasis of my heart, isn't in the story this time" is what a lot of guys must be thinking. Things went really smoothly for me on this story. With no tricks (not that there ever are any but...) or anything else used... Maybe that's why there are so many large panels. And there aren't any female characters other than Eliza. Society women of her age back then always wore their hair up and wore gloves. I wanted to be creative about the dress too, and not make it look too stylized in a shojo manga way, so I took liberties with the designs. I was fairly free with the hairstyles, too. I think all girls tend to look older when they wear their hair up. This is a shojo manga, so the images are important... I even changed the men's fashion back to a style that I used before the last series. It looked so elegant and wonderful...

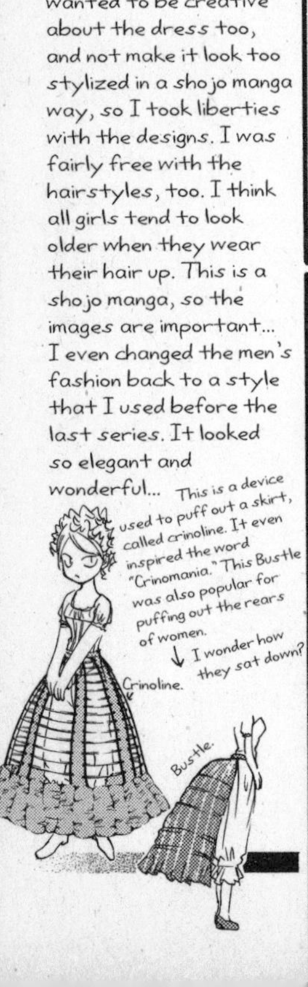
This is a device used to puff out a skirt, called crinoline. It even inspired the word "Crinomania." This Bustle was also popular for puffing out the rears of women.
I wonder how they sat down?
Crinoline.
Bustle.

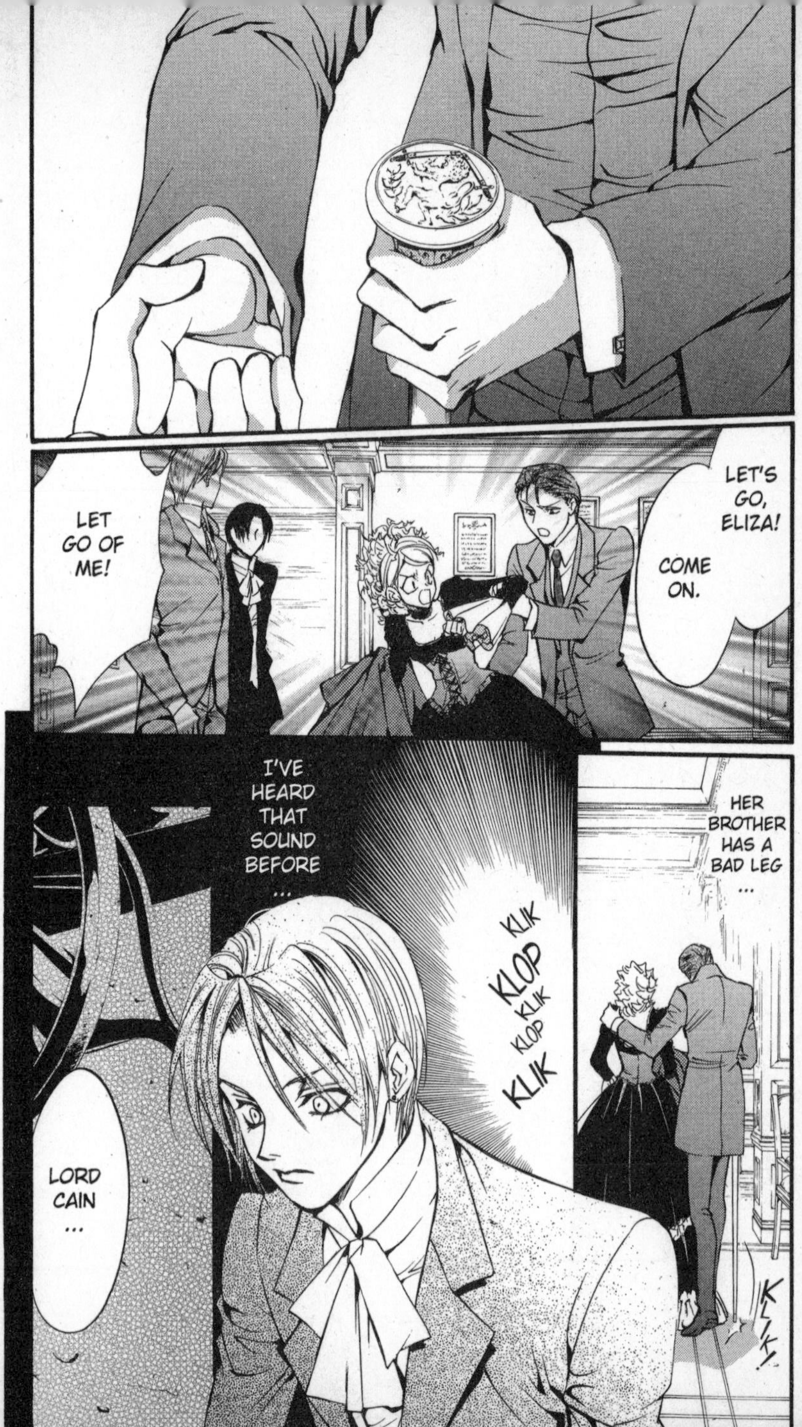
LET'S GO, ELIZA!
COME ON.
LET GO OF ME!
HER BROTHER HAS A BAD LEG ...
KLIK!
I'VE HEARD THAT SOUND BEFORE ...
KLIK KLOP KLIK KLOP KLIK
LORD CAIN ...

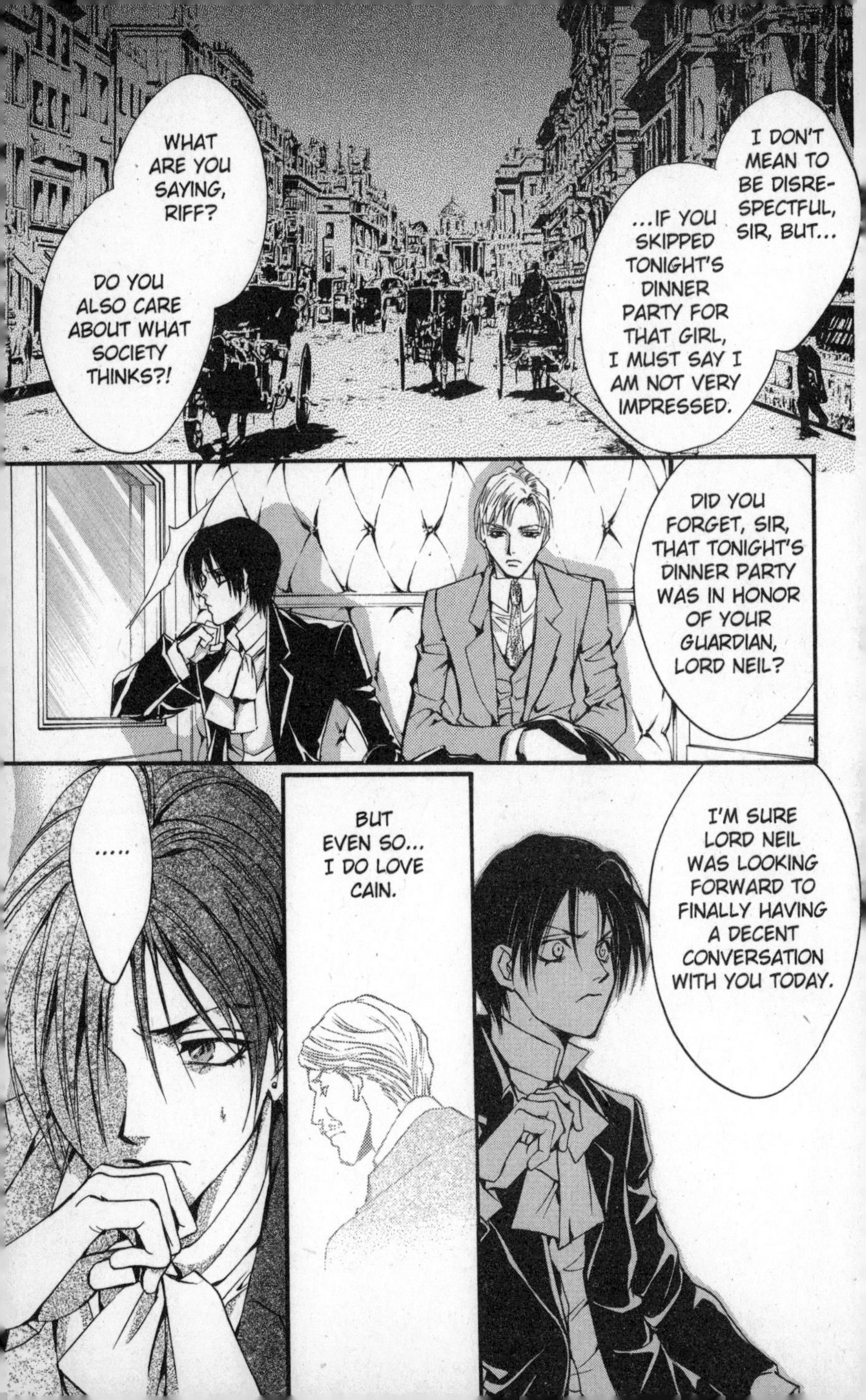
I DON'T MEAN TO BE DISRE-SPECTFUL, SIR, BUT...
...IF YOU SKIPPED TONIGHT'S DINNER PARTY FOR THAT GIRL, I MUST SAY I AM NOT VERY IMPRESSED.
WHAT ARE YOU SAYING, RIFF?
DO YOU ALSO CARE ABOUT WHAT SOCIETY THINKS?!
DID YOU FORGET, SIR, THAT TONIGHT'S DINNER PARTY WAS IN HONOR OF YOUR GUARDIAN, LORD NEIL?
I'M SURE LORD NEIL WAS LOOKING FORWARD TO FINALLY HAVING A DECENT CONVERSATION WITH YOU TODAY.
BUT EVEN SO... I DO LOVE CAIN.
.....

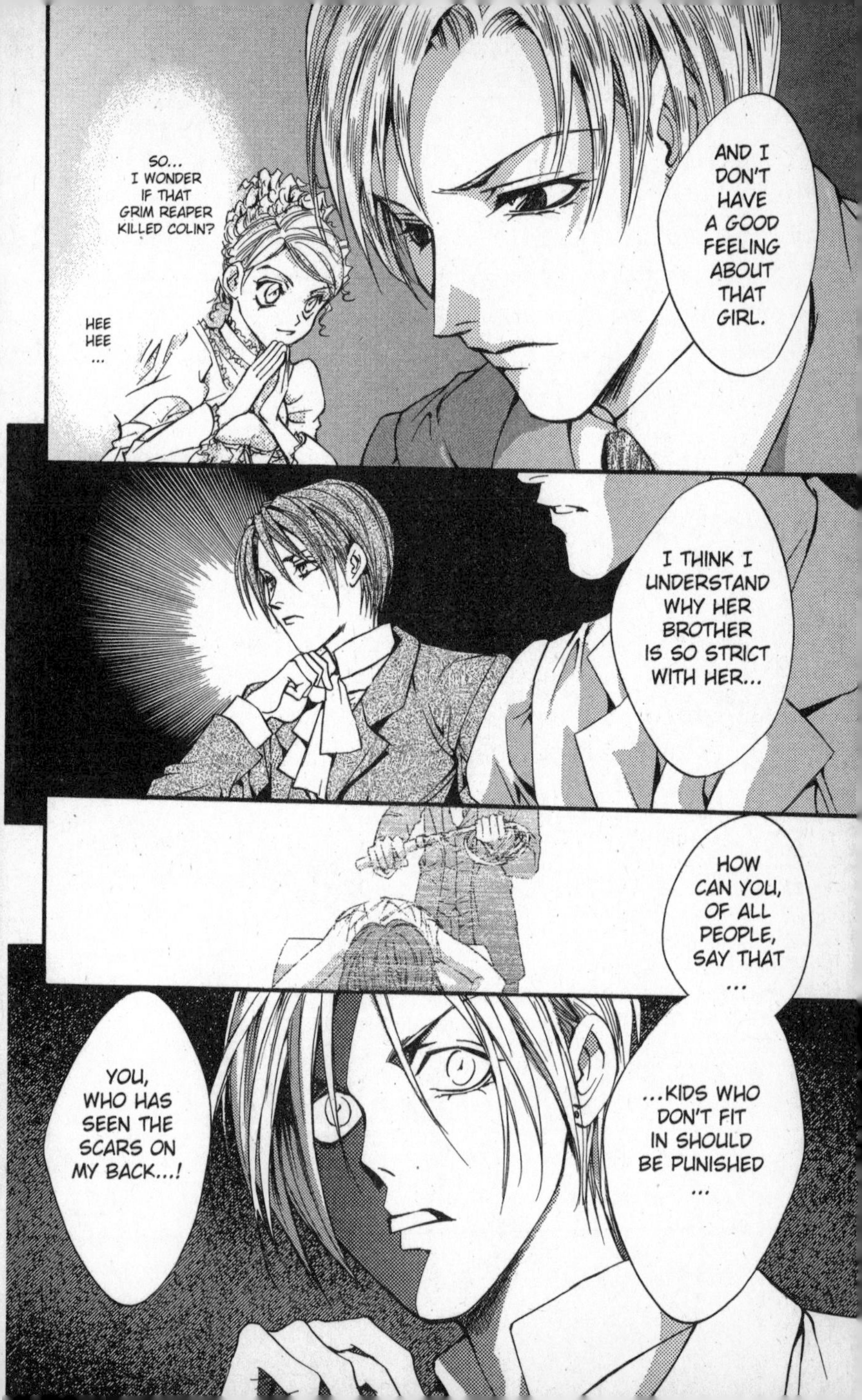
AND I DON'T HAVE A GOOD FEELING ABOUT THAT GIRL.
SO... I WONDER IF THAT GRIM REAPER KILLED COLIN?
HEE HEE ...
I THINK I UNDERSTAND WHY HER BROTHER IS SO STRICT WITH HER...
HOW CAN YOU, OF ALL PEOPLE, SAY THAT ...
...KIDS WHO DON'T FIT IN SHOULD BE PUNISHED ...
YOU, WHO HAS SEEN THE SCARS ON MY BACK...!

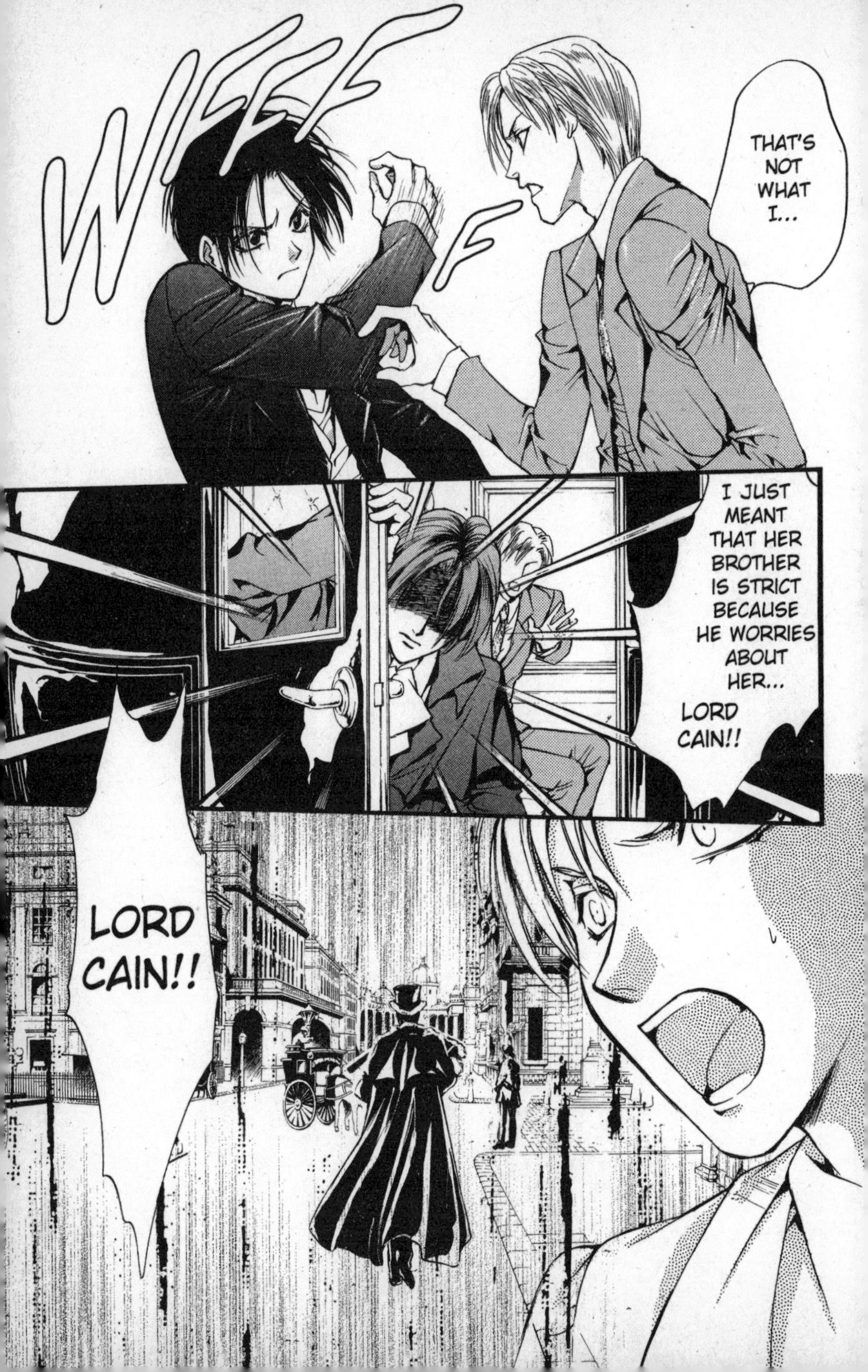
WIFFF
THAT'S NOT WHAT I...
I JUST MEANT THAT HER BROTHER IS STRICT BECAUSE HE WORRIES ABOUT HER...
LORD CAIN!!
LORD CAIN!!

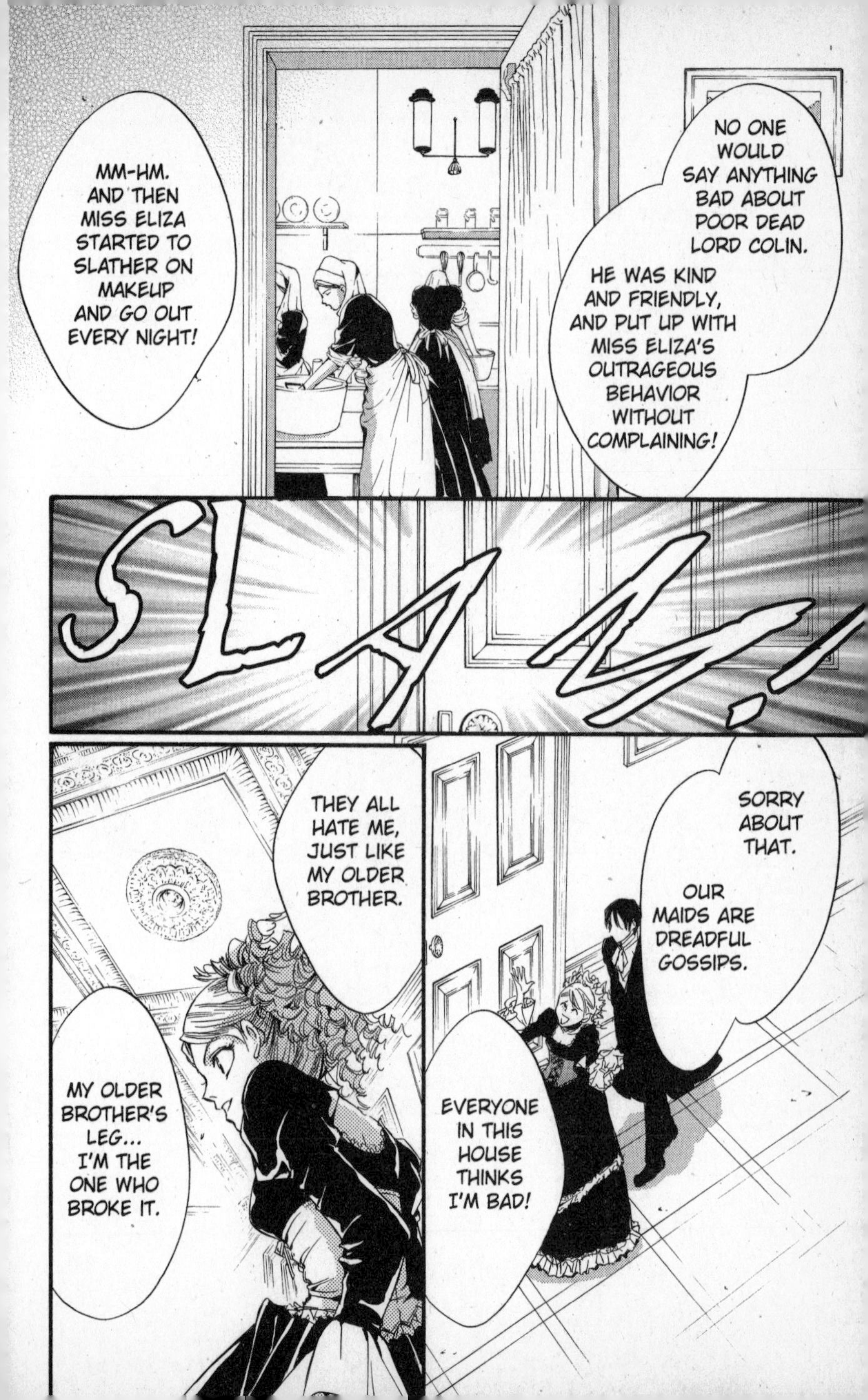
NO ONE WOULD SAY ANYTHING BAD ABOUT POOR DEAD LORD COLIN.
HE WAS KIND AND FRIENDLY, AND PUT UP WITH MISS ELIZA'S OUTRAGEOUS BEHAVIOR WITHOUT COMPLAINING!
MM-HM. AND THEN MISS ELIZA STARTED TO SLATHER ON MAKEUP AND GO OUT EVERY NIGHT!
SLAM!!
SORRY ABOUT THAT.
OUR MAIDS ARE DREADFUL GOSSIPS.
EVERYONE IN THIS HOUSE THINKS I'M BAD!
THEY ALL HATE ME, JUST LIKE MY OLDER BROTHER.
MY OLDER BROTHER'S LEG... I'M THE ONE WHO BROKE IT.

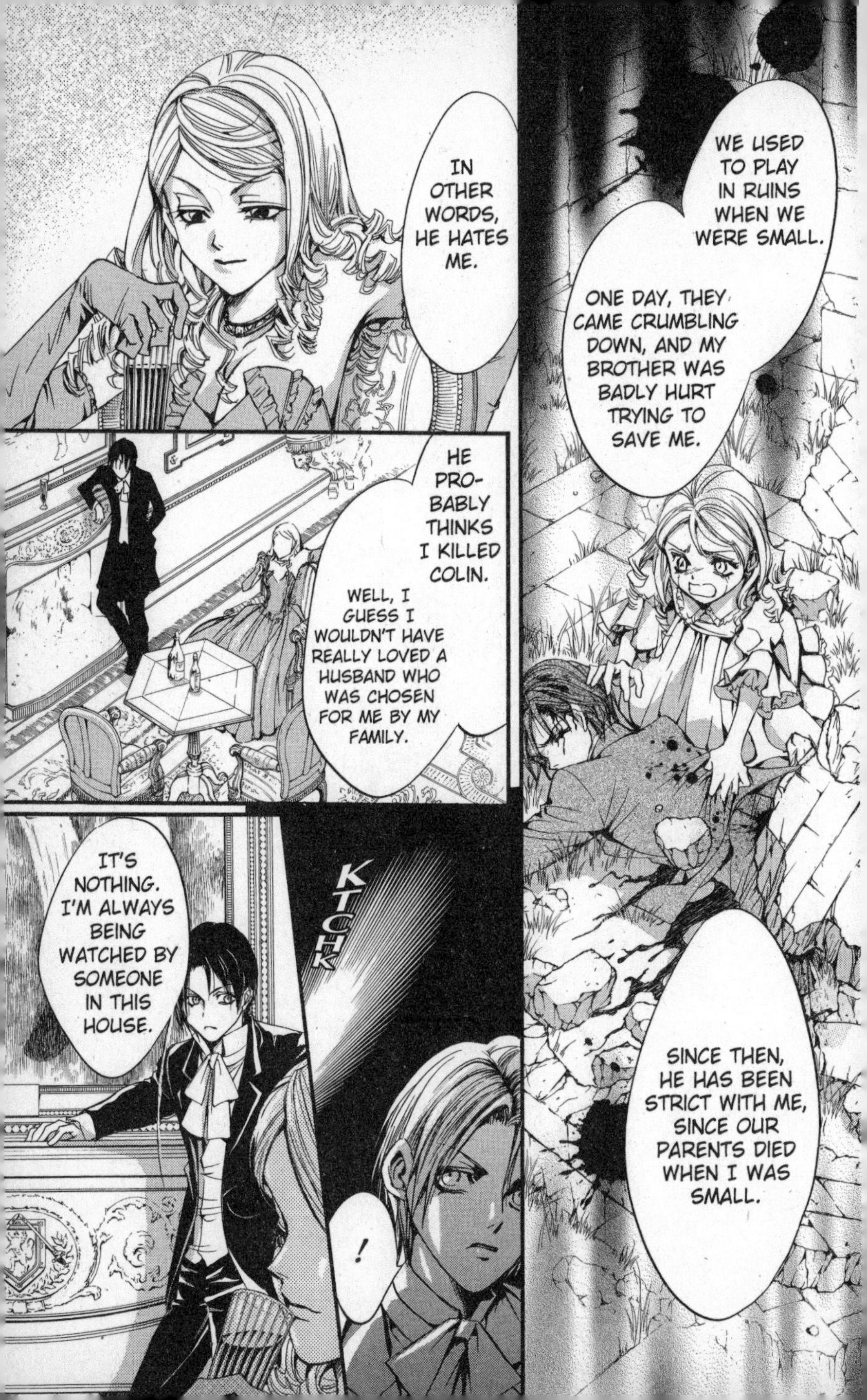
WE USED TO PLAY IN RUINS WHEN WE WERE SMALL.
ONE DAY, THEY CAME CRUMBLING DOWN, AND MY BROTHER WAS BADLY HURT TRYING TO SAVE ME.
SINCE THEN, HE HAS BEEN STRICT WITH ME, SINCE OUR PARENTS DIED WHEN I WAS SMALL.
IN OTHER WORDS, HE HATES ME.
HE PROBABLY THINKS I KILLED COLIN.
WELL, I GUESS I WOULDN'T HAVE REALLY LOVED A HUSBAND WHO WAS CHOSEN FOR ME BY MY FAMILY.
KTCHK
!
IT'S NOTHING. I'M ALWAYS BEING WATCHED BY SOMEONE IN THIS HOUSE.

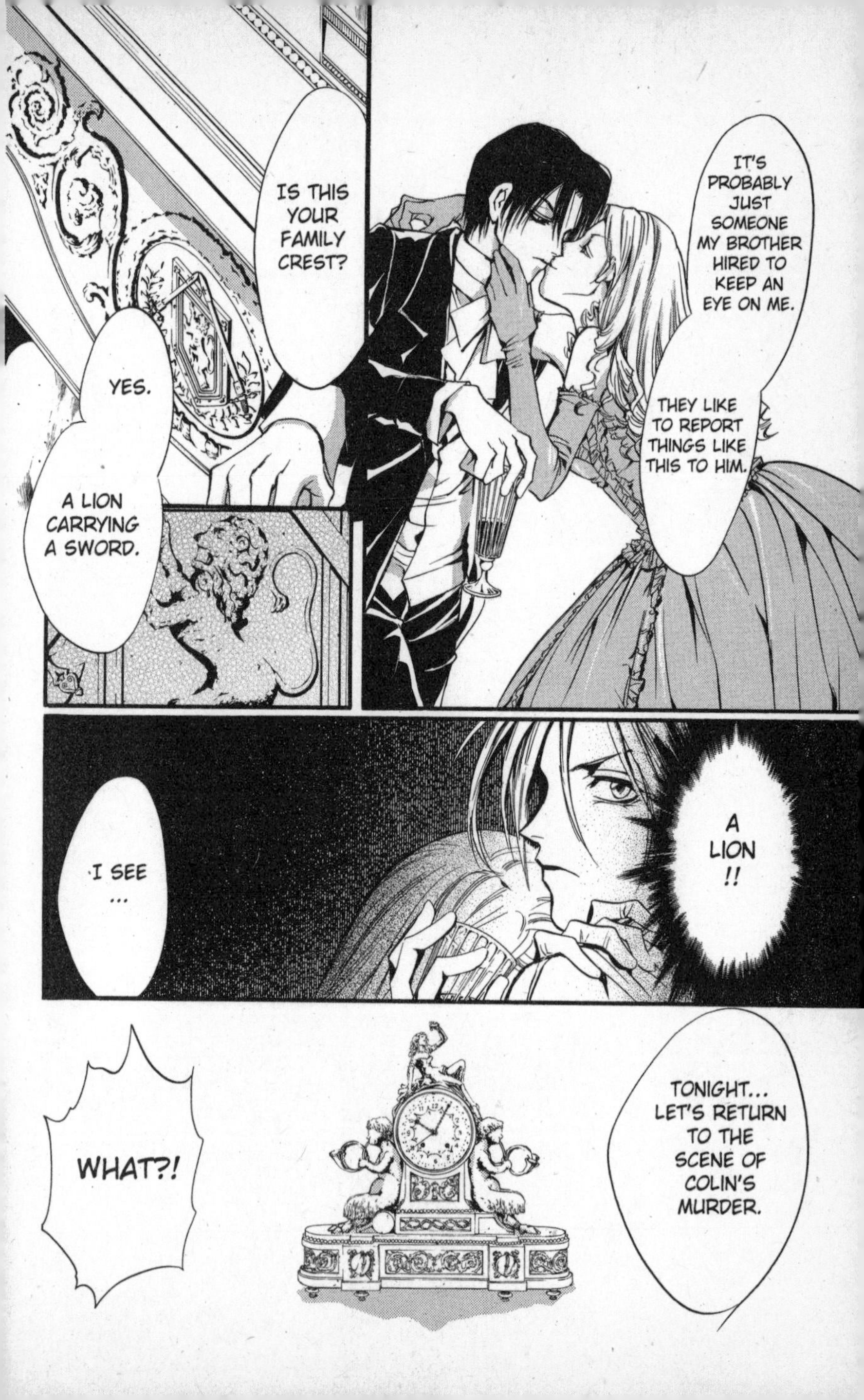
IT'S PROBABLY JUST SOMEONE MY BROTHER HIRED TO KEEP AN EYE ON ME.
THEY LIKE TO REPORT THINGS LIKE THIS TO HIM.
IS THIS YOUR FAMILY CREST?
YES.
A LION CARRYING A SWORD.
A LION !!
I SEE ...
TONIGHT... LET'S RETURN TO THE SCENE OF COLIN'S MURDER.
WHAT?!

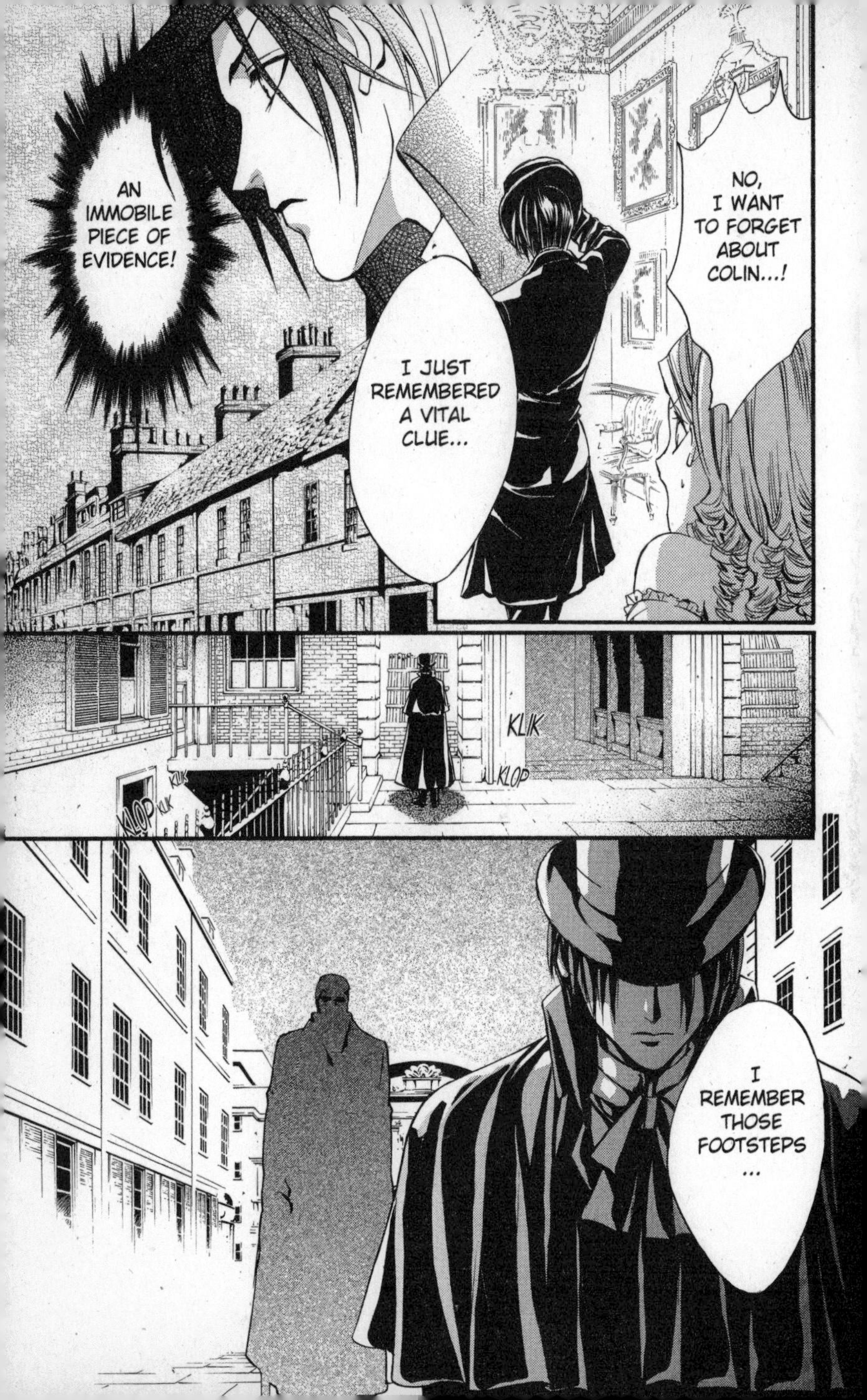
NO, I WANT TO FORGET ABOUT COLIN...!
I JUST REMEMBERED A VITAL CLUE...
AN IMMOBILE PIECE OF EVIDENCE!
KLIK
KLOP
KLIK
KLOP KLIK
I REMEMBER THOSE FOOTSTEPS ...

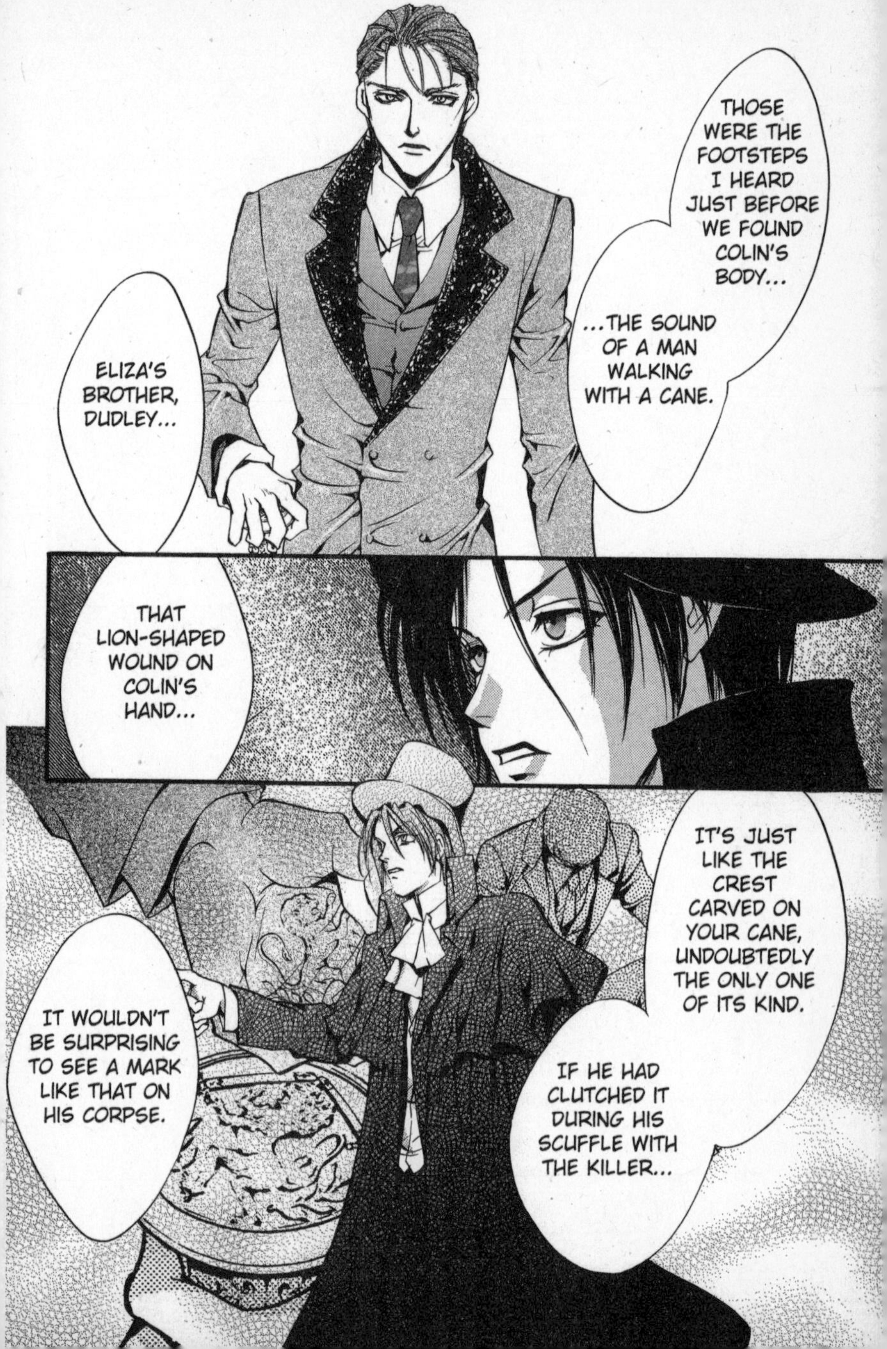
THOSE WERE THE FOOTSTEPS I HEARD JUST BEFORE WE FOUND COLIN'S BODY...
...THE SOUND OF A MAN WALKING WITH A CANE.
ELIZA'S BROTHER, DUDLEY...
THAT LION-SHAPED WOUND ON COLIN'S HAND...
IT'S JUST LIKE THE CREST CARVED ON YOUR CANE, UNDOUBTEDLY THE ONLY ONE OF ITS KIND.
IF HE HAD CLUTCHED IT DURING HIS SCUFFLE WITH THE KILLER...
IT WOULDN'T BE SURPRISING TO SEE A MARK LIKE THAT ON HIS CORPSE.

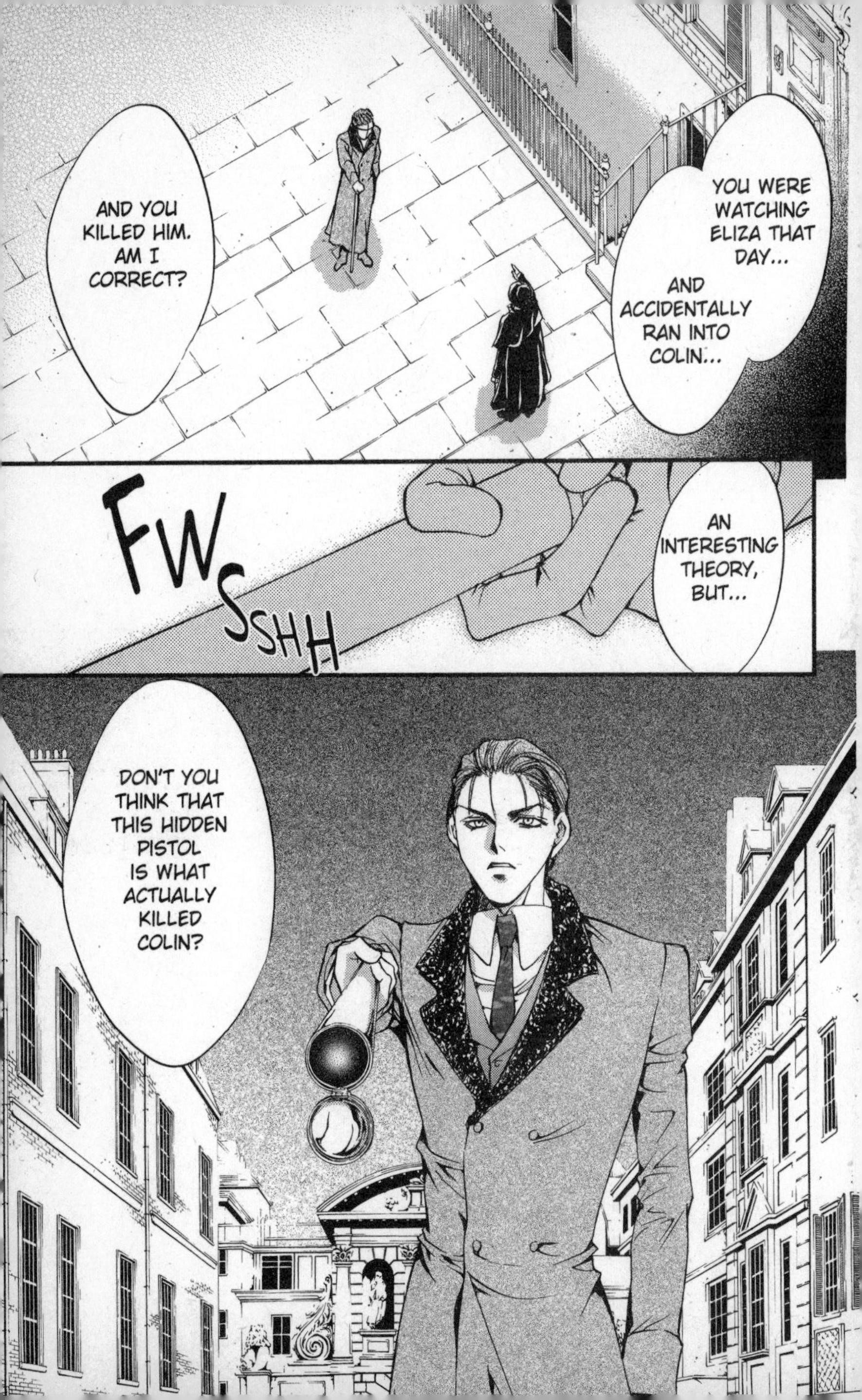
YOU WERE WATCHING ELIZA THAT DAY...
AND ACCIDENTALLY RAN INTO COLIN...
AND YOU KILLED HIM. AM I CORRECT?
AN INTERESTING THEORY, BUT...
FWSSHH
DON'T YOU THINK THAT THIS HIDDEN PISTOL IS WHAT ACTUALLY KILLED COLIN?

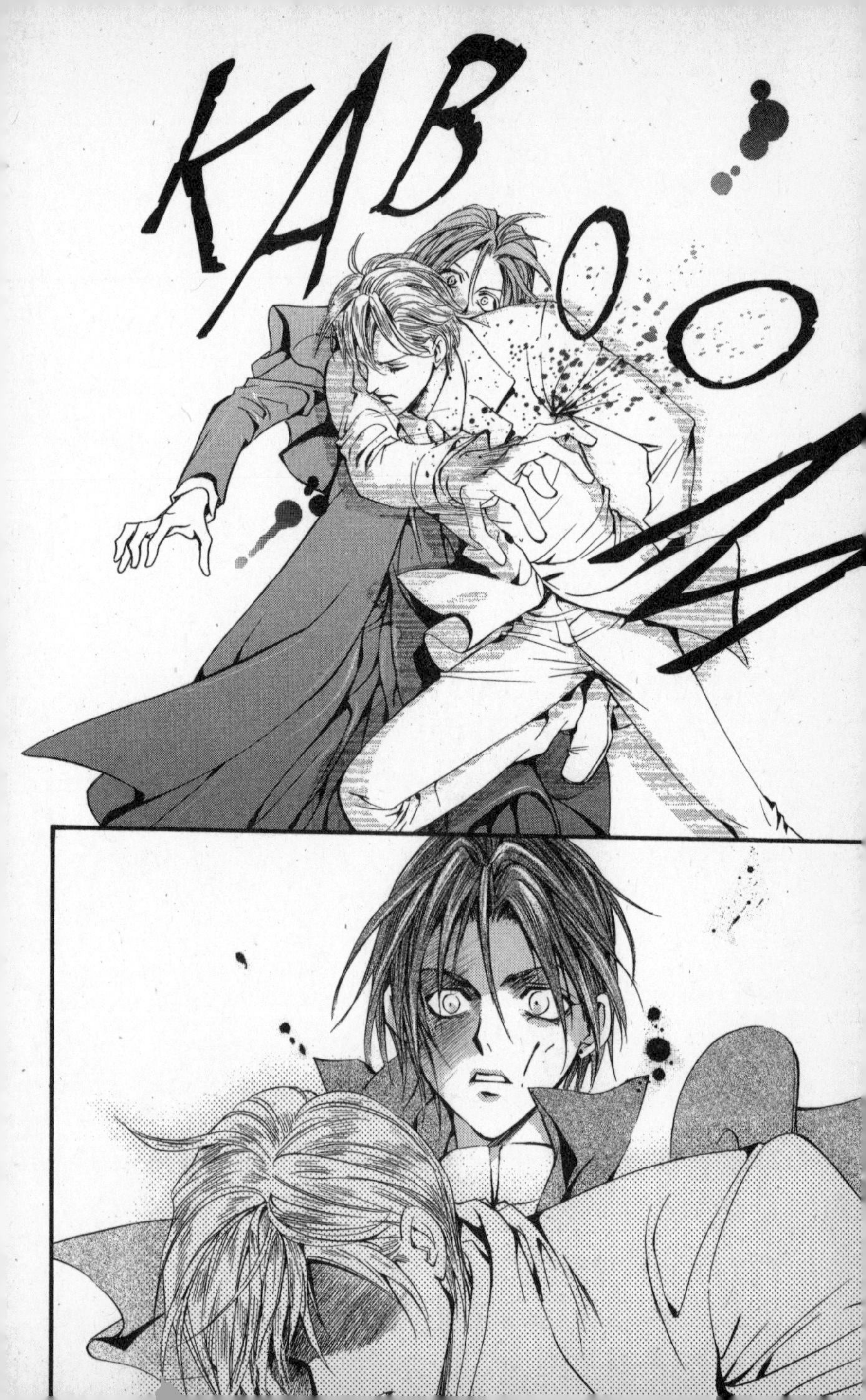
KABOOOM

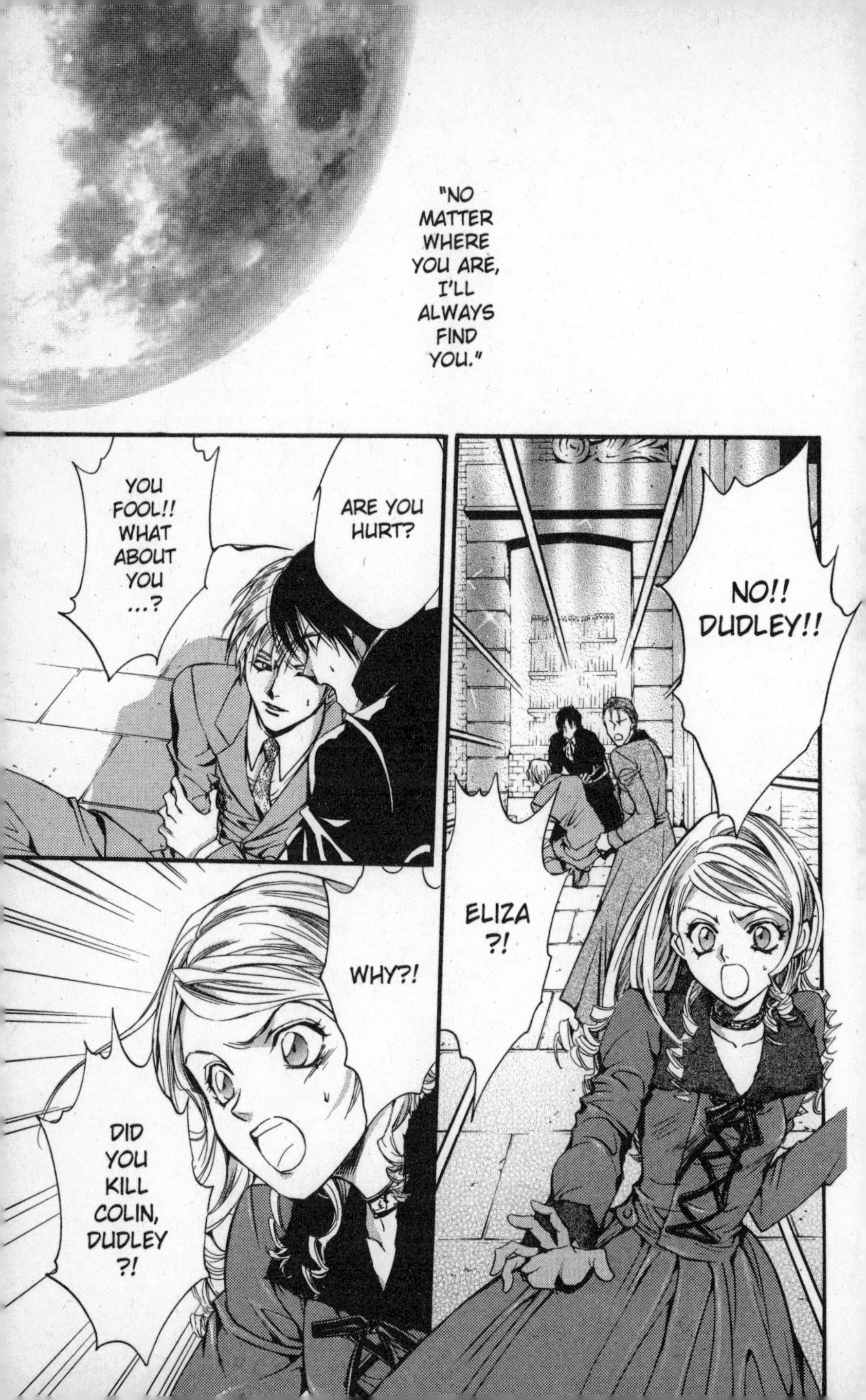
"NO MATTER WHERE YOU ARE, I'LL ALWAYS FIND YOU."
NO!! DUDLEY!!
ELIZA ?!
ARE YOU HURT?
YOU FOOL!! WHAT ABOUT YOU ...?
WHY?!
DID YOU KILL COLIN, DUDLEY ?!

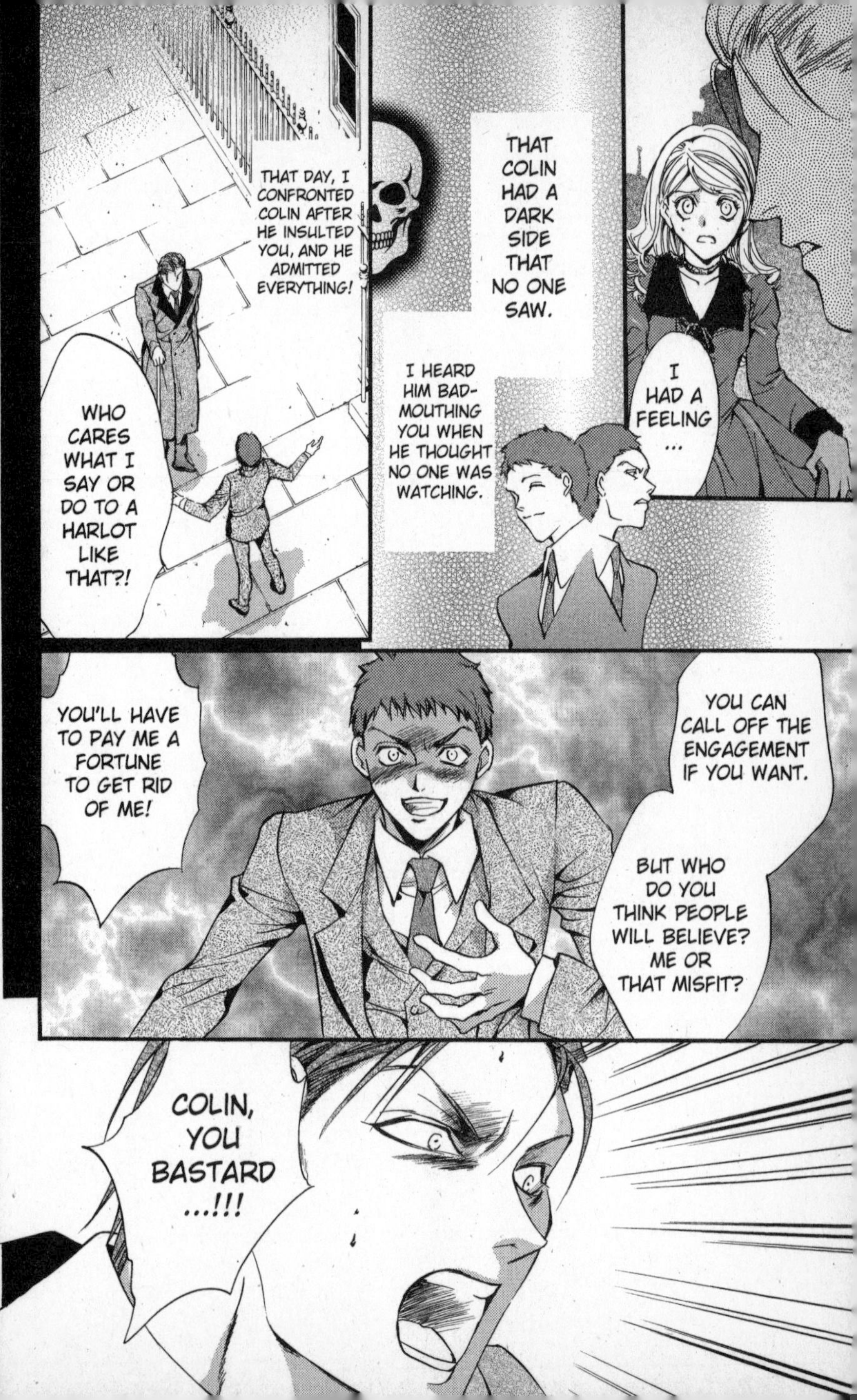
I HAD A FEELING ...
THAT COLIN HAD A DARK SIDE THAT NO ONE SAW.
I HEARD HIM BAD-MOUTHING YOU WHEN HE THOUGHT NO ONE WAS WATCHING.
THAT DAY, I CONFRONTED COLIN AFTER HE INSULTED YOU, AND HE ADMITTED EVERYTHING!
WHO CARES WHAT I SAY OR DO TO A HARLOT LIKE THAT?!
YOU CAN CALL OFF THE ENGAGEMENT IF YOU WANT.
BUT WHO DO YOU THINK PEOPLE WILL BELIEVE? ME OR THAT MISFIT?
YOU'LL HAVE TO PAY ME A FORTUNE TO GET RID OF ME!
COLIN, YOU BASTARD ...!!!

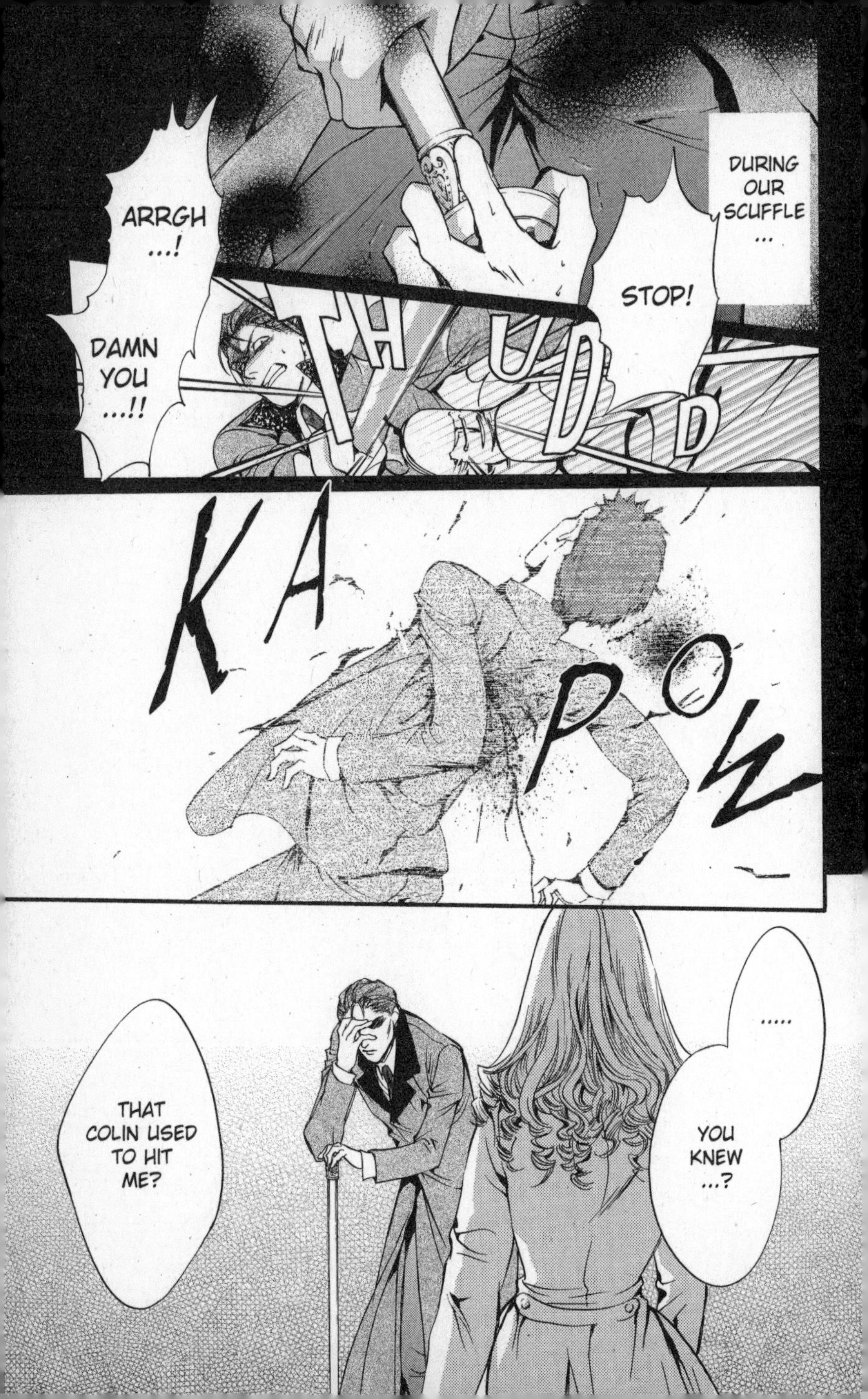
DURING OUR SCUFFLE ...
ARRGH ...!
STOP!
THUD
DAMN YOU ...!!
KAPOW
.....
YOU KNEW ...?
THAT COLIN USED TO HIT ME?

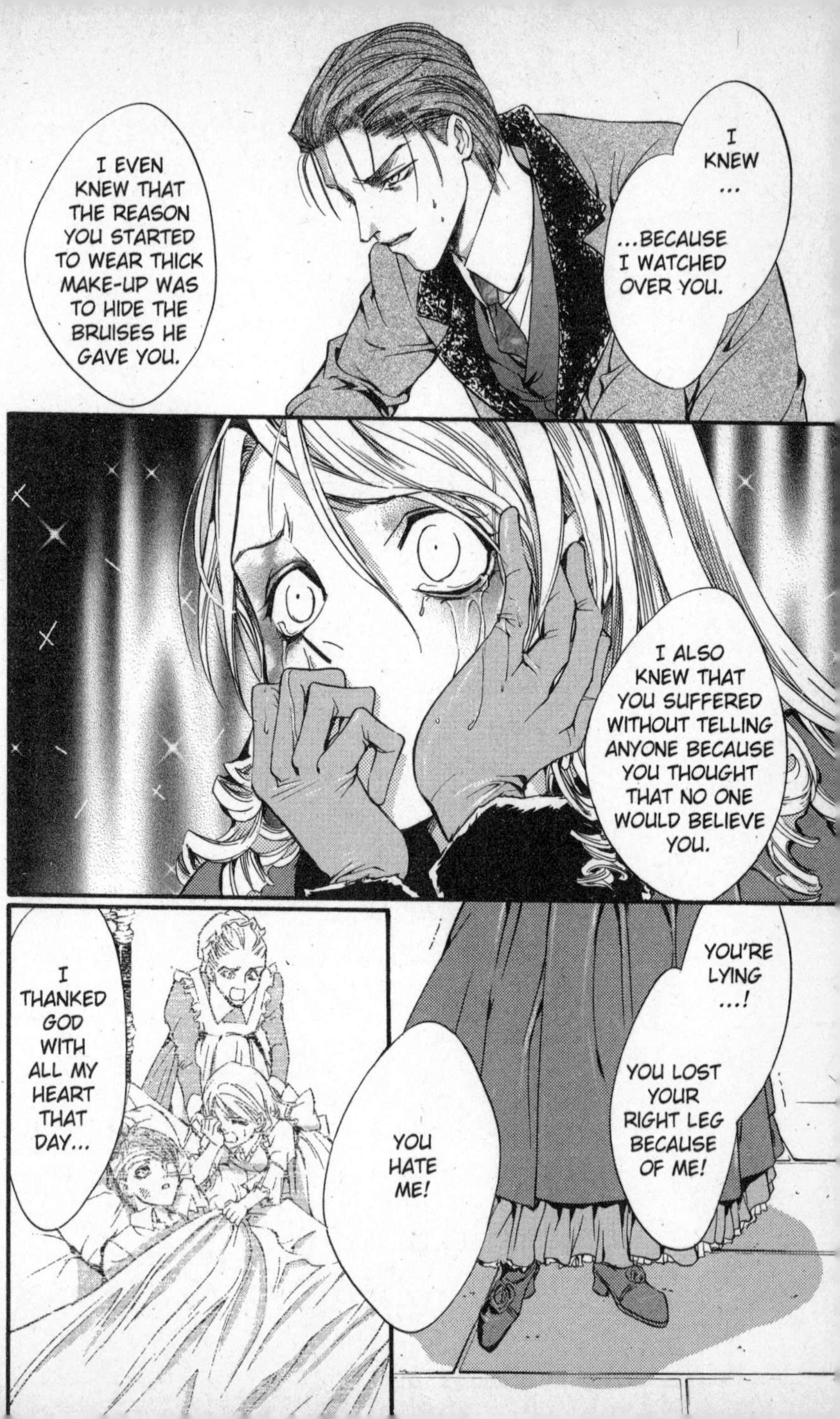
I KNEW ...
...BECAUSE I WATCHED OVER YOU.
I EVEN KNEW THAT THE REASON YOU STARTED TO WEAR THICK MAKE-UP WAS TO HIDE THE BRUISES HE GAVE YOU.
I ALSO KNEW THAT YOU SUFFERED WITHOUT TELLING ANYONE BECAUSE YOU THOUGHT THAT NO ONE WOULD BELIEVE YOU.
YOU'RE LYING ...!
YOU LOST YOUR RIGHT LEG BECAUSE OF ME!
YOU HATE ME!
I THANKED GOD WITH ALL MY HEART THAT DAY...

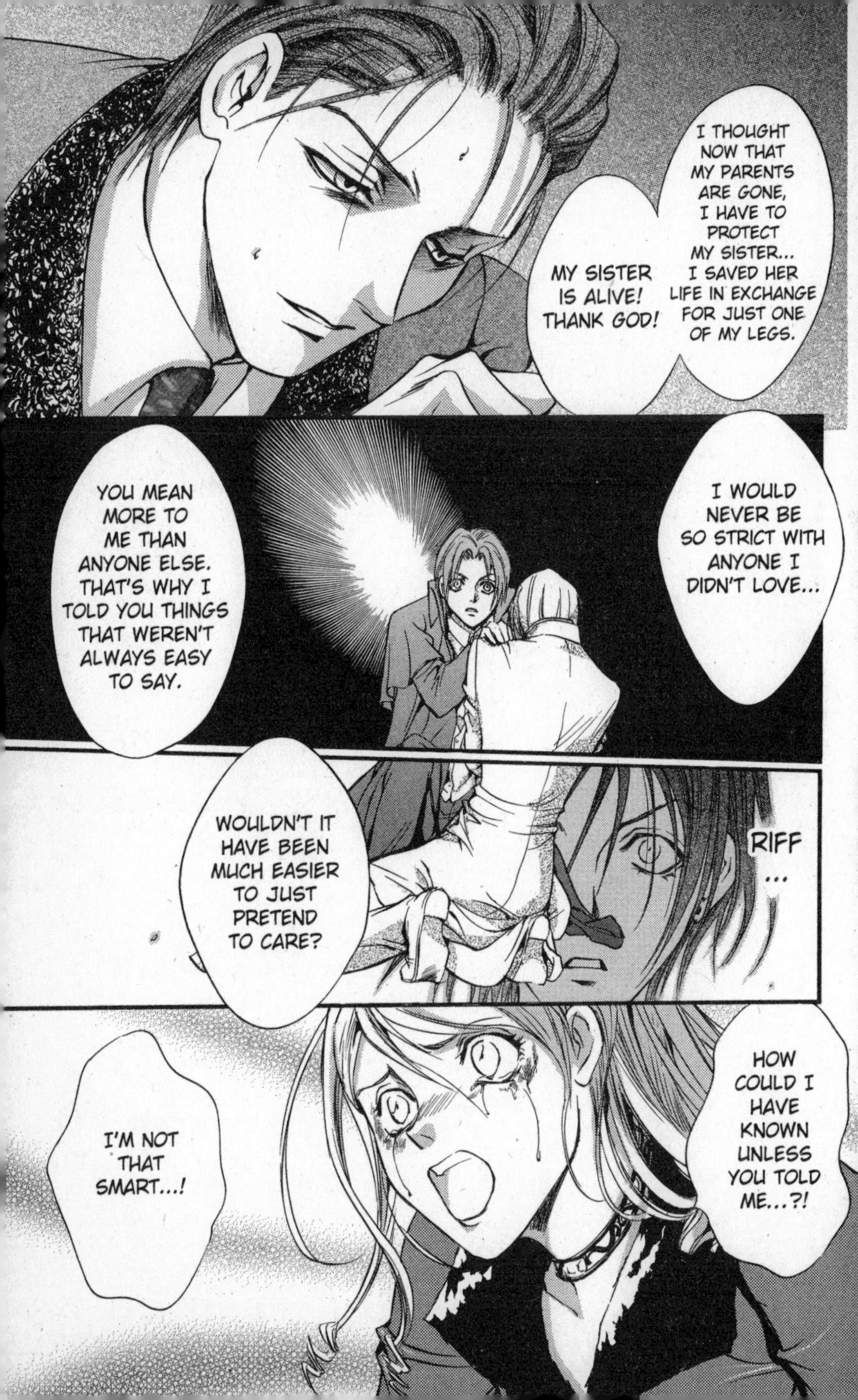
I THOUGHT NOW THAT MY PARENTS ARE GONE, I HAVE TO PROTECT MY SISTER... I SAVED HER LIFE IN EXCHANGE FOR JUST ONE OF MY LEGS.
MY SISTER IS ALIVE! THANK GOD!
I WOULD NEVER BE SO STRICT WITH ANYONE I DIDN'T LOVE...
YOU MEAN MORE TO ME THAN ANYONE ELSE. THAT'S WHY I TOLD YOU THINGS THAT WEREN'T ALWAYS EASY TO SAY.
WOULDN'T IT HAVE BEEN MUCH EASIER TO JUST PRETEND TO CARE?
RIFF ...
HOW COULD I HAVE KNOWN UNLESS YOU TOLD ME...?!
I'M NOT THAT SMART...!

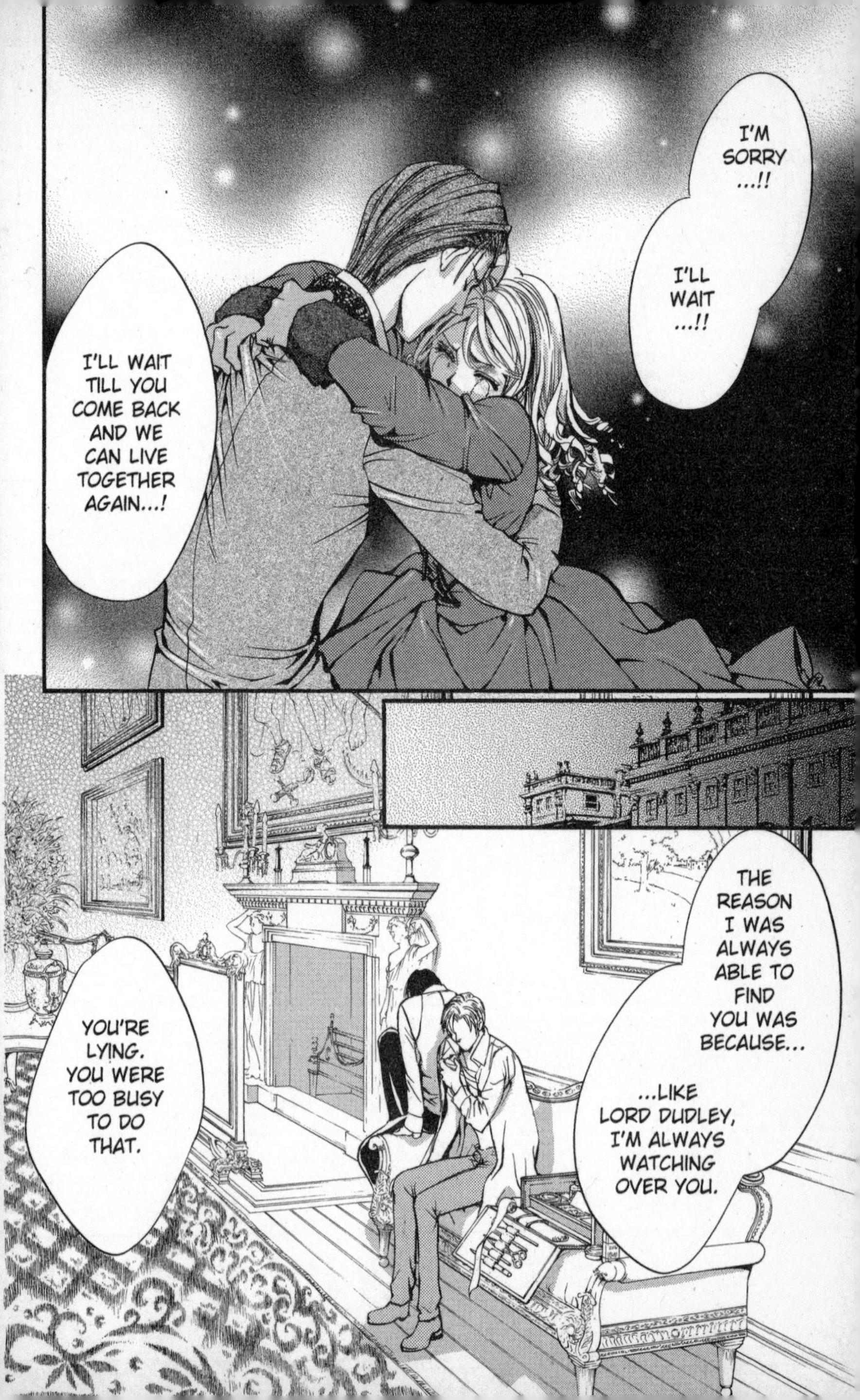
I'M SORRY ...!!
I'LL WAIT ...!!
I'LL WAIT TILL YOU COME BACK AND WE CAN LIVE TOGETHER AGAIN...!
THE REASON I WAS ALWAYS ABLE TO FIND YOU WAS BECAUSE...
...LIKE LORD DUDLEY, I'M ALWAYS WATCHING OVER YOU.
YOU'RE LYING. YOU WERE TOO BUSY TO DO THAT.

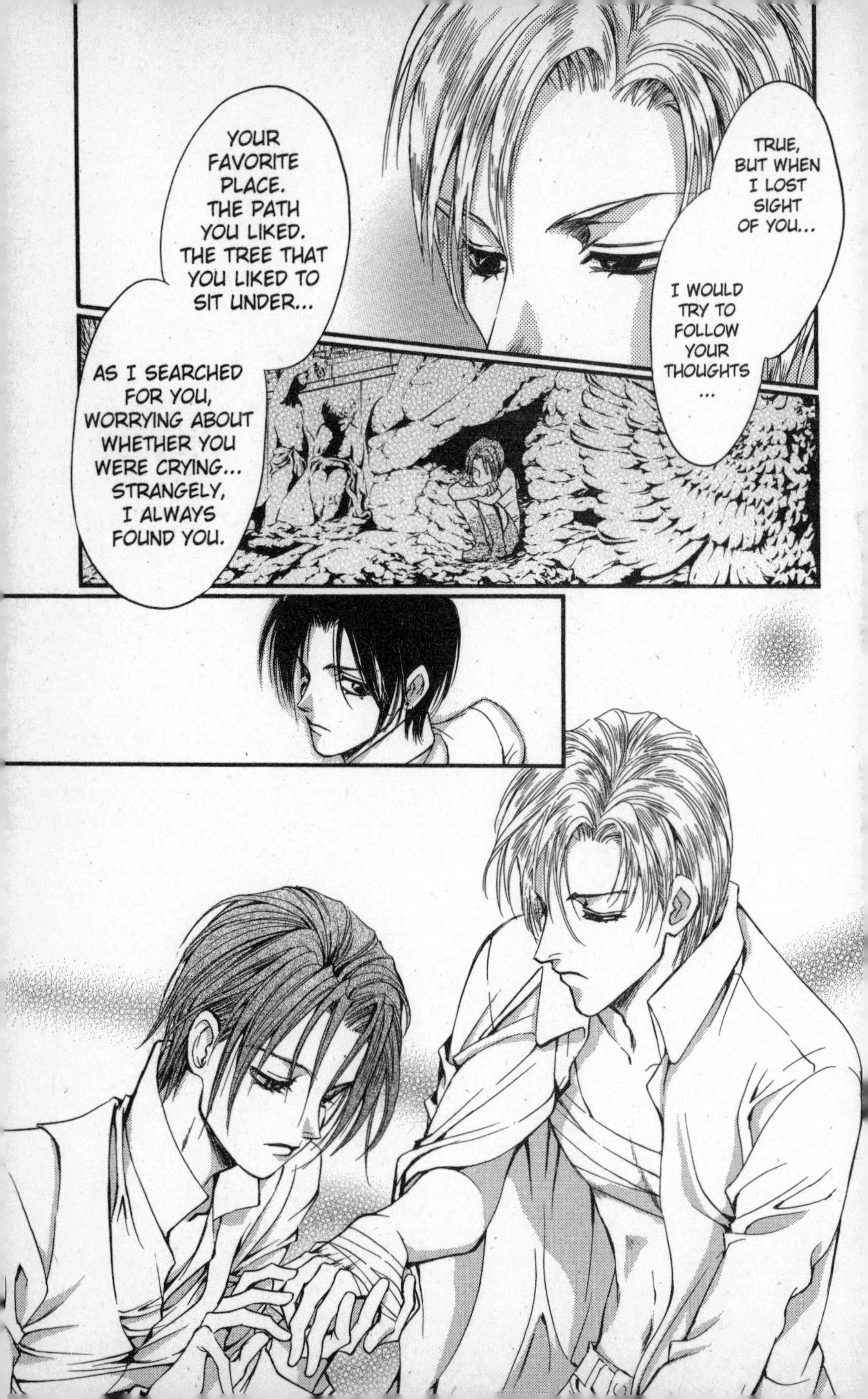
TRUE, BUT WHEN I LOST SIGHT OF YOU...
I WOULD TRY TO FOLLOW YOUR THOUGHTS...
YOUR FAVORITE PLACE. THE PATH YOU LIKED. THE TREE THAT YOU LIKED TO SIT UNDER...
AS I SEARCHED FOR YOU, WORRYING ABOUT WHETHER YOU WERE CRYING... STRANGELY, I ALWAYS FOUND YOU.

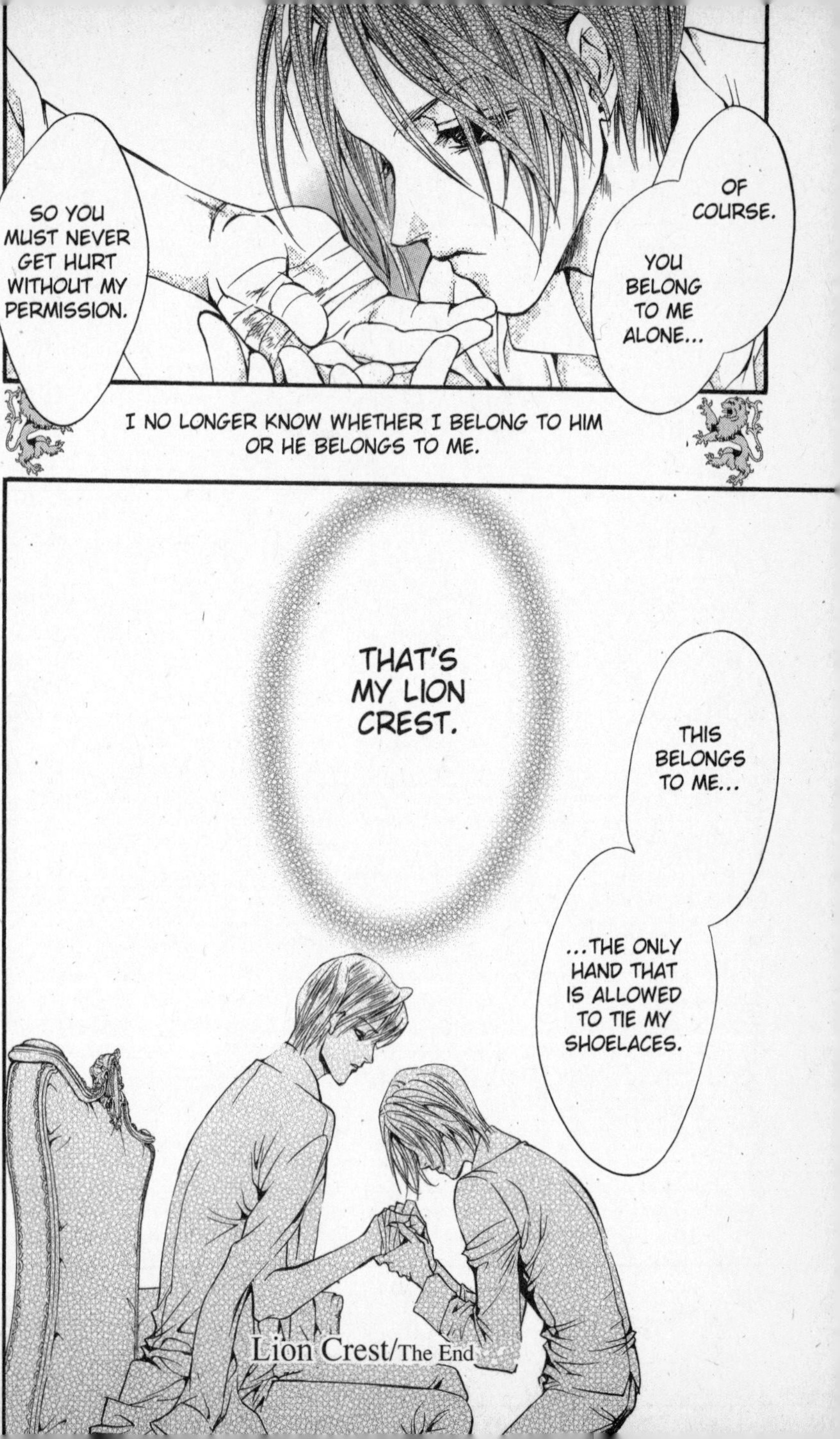
OF COURSE. YOU BELONG TO ME ALONE...
SO YOU MUST NEVER GET HURT WITHOUT MY PERMISSION.
I NO LONGER KNOW WHETHER I BELONG TO HIM OR HE BELONGS TO ME.
THIS BELONGS TO ME...
...THE ONLY HAND THAT IS ALLOWED TO TIE MY SHOELACES.
THAT'S MY LION CREST.
Lion Crest/The End

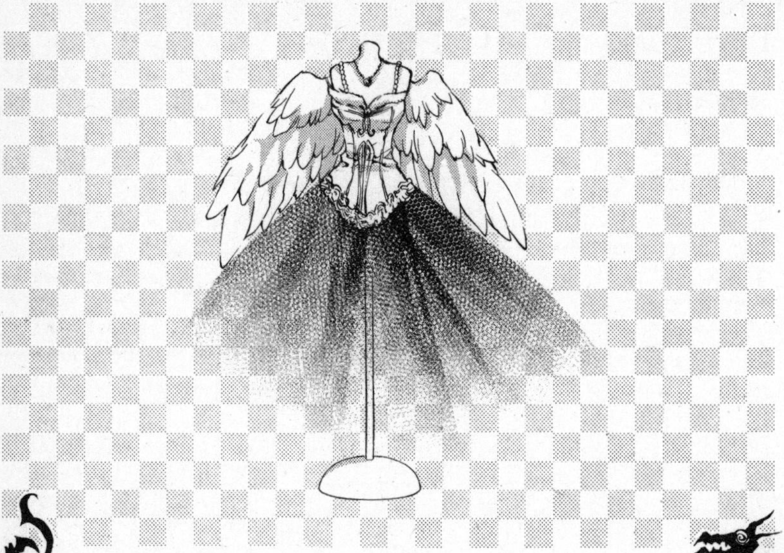

Thank you for reading this book. In Volume 1, I asked the readers to send me letters, and I have received tons of letters from all of you. I really appreciate it. I've heard from some of my new fans that you're having a hard time finding some of the earlier volumes of this series. We're still publishing it, so please have your favorite bookstore order it for you. Cain is as popular as ever, but Mary is getting more popular too, which makes me really happy. She's truly the heroine (mascot?) of this series. (Maybe not quite.) Some readers are worried that Cain and Mary might become involved in a dangerous sort of incestuous relationship, but there's nothing to worry about. It won't happen! Cain's love for Mary is strictly the love of a brother for his sister. (Mary too.) The above illustration was based on a Christmas present that I received. I bought the wings on my own and stuck them on myself. The bodice is made of real lace. I can go on a little mind trip just looking at it. For some reason at my house, there is an Excalibur, black wings, and a top hat. I just love collecting strange things, and the next thing I want to get is a cane with a hidden knife in it. My life is starting to get cluttered with things that have no use in my daily life, like my Amethyst Knife and my cluster of crystals, but I love beautiful things and can't help it. But my room is a mess! These things are so out of place in a space full of books and screen tones. Last year I received so many presents from readers, like an hourglass, an "Alice In Wonderland" book, fanzines, accessories, thank you letters, and all kinds of other things! I'm sorry I can't remember everything. Some pop-up Christmas cards, too! I'll be so happy if we could meet again in Volume 3.

Creator: Kaori Yuki

Date of Birth: December 18

Blood Type: B

Major Works: *Angel Sanctuary*
and *The Cain Saga*

Kaori Yuki was born in Tokyo and started drawing at a very early age. Following her debut work *Natsufuku no Erie* (Erie in Summer Uniform) in the Japanese magazine *Bessatsu Hana to Yume* (1987), she wrote a compelling series of short stories: *Zankoku na Douwatachi* (Cruel Fairy Tales), *Neji* (Screw), and *Sareki Ôkoku* (Gravel Kingdom).

As proven by her best-selling series *Angel Sanctuary* and *The Cain Saga*, her celebrated body of work has etched an indelible mark on the gothic comics genre. She likes mysteries and British films, and is a fan of the movie *Dead Poets Society* and the show *Twin Peaks*.

GODCHILD, vol. 2

The Shojo Beat Manga Edition

This manga volume contains material that was originally published in English
in *Shojo Beat* magazine, January-June 2006 issues.

STORY & ART BY **KAORI YUKI**

English Adaptation/Trina Robbins
Translation/Akira Watanabe
Touch-up Art & Lettering/James Gaubatz
Design/Courtney Utt
Editors/Michelle Pangilinan & Pancha Diaz

Managing Editor/Megan Bates
Director of Production/Noboru Watanabe
Vice President of Publishing/Alvin Lu
Vice President & Editor in Chief/Yumi Hoashi
Sr. Director of Acquisitions/Rika Inouye
Vice President of Sales & Marketing/Liza Coppola
Publisher/Hyoe Narita

Printed in Canada

Published by VIZ Media, LLC
P.O. Box 77010
San Francisco, CA 94107

Shojo Beat Manga Edition
10 9 8 7 6 5 4 3 2 1
First printing, August 2006

PARENTAL ADVISORY
GODCHILD is rated T+ for Older Teen and is
recommended for ages 16 and up. This volume
contains graphic violence and adult themes.

store.viz.com

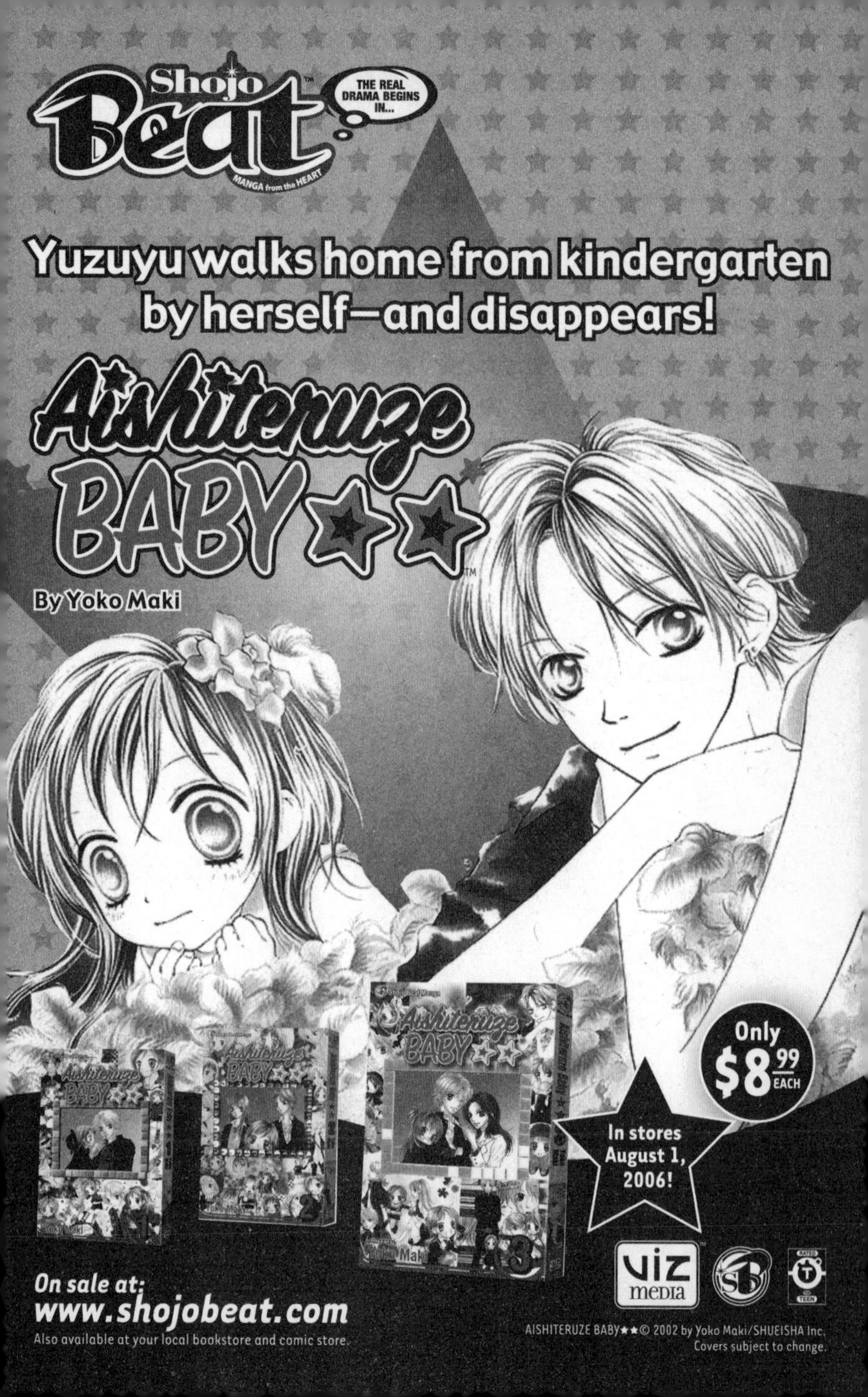
Shojo Beat™
MANGA from the HEART
THE REAL DRAMA BEGINS IN...
Yuzuyu walks home from kindergarten by herself—and disappears!
Aishiteruze BABY★★™
By Yoko Maki
Only $8.99 EACH
In stores August 1, 2006!
On sale at:
www.shojobeat.com
Also available at your local bookstore and comic store.
viz media
AISHITERUZE BABY★★ © 2002 by Yoko Maki/SHUEISHA Inc.
Covers subject to change.

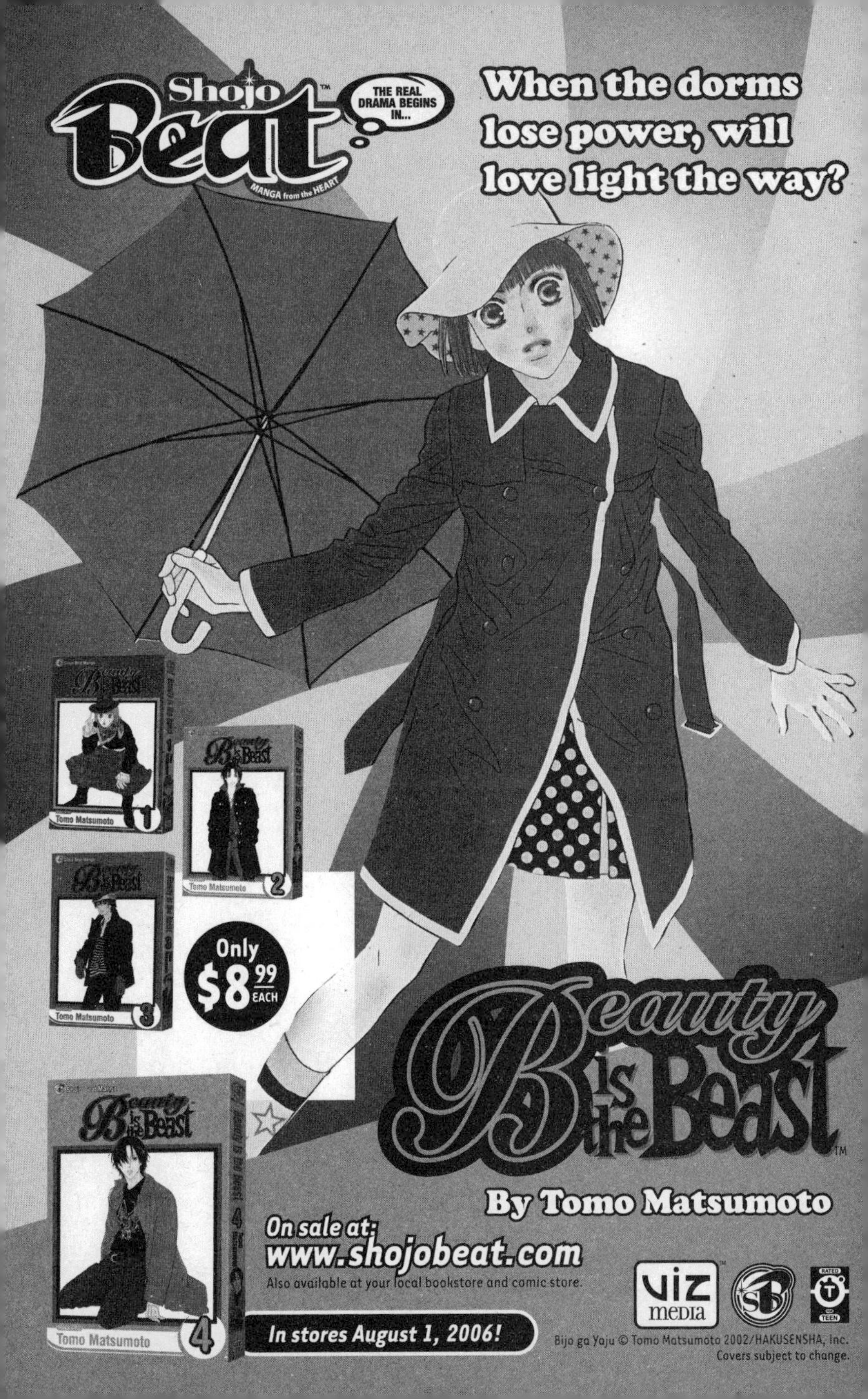

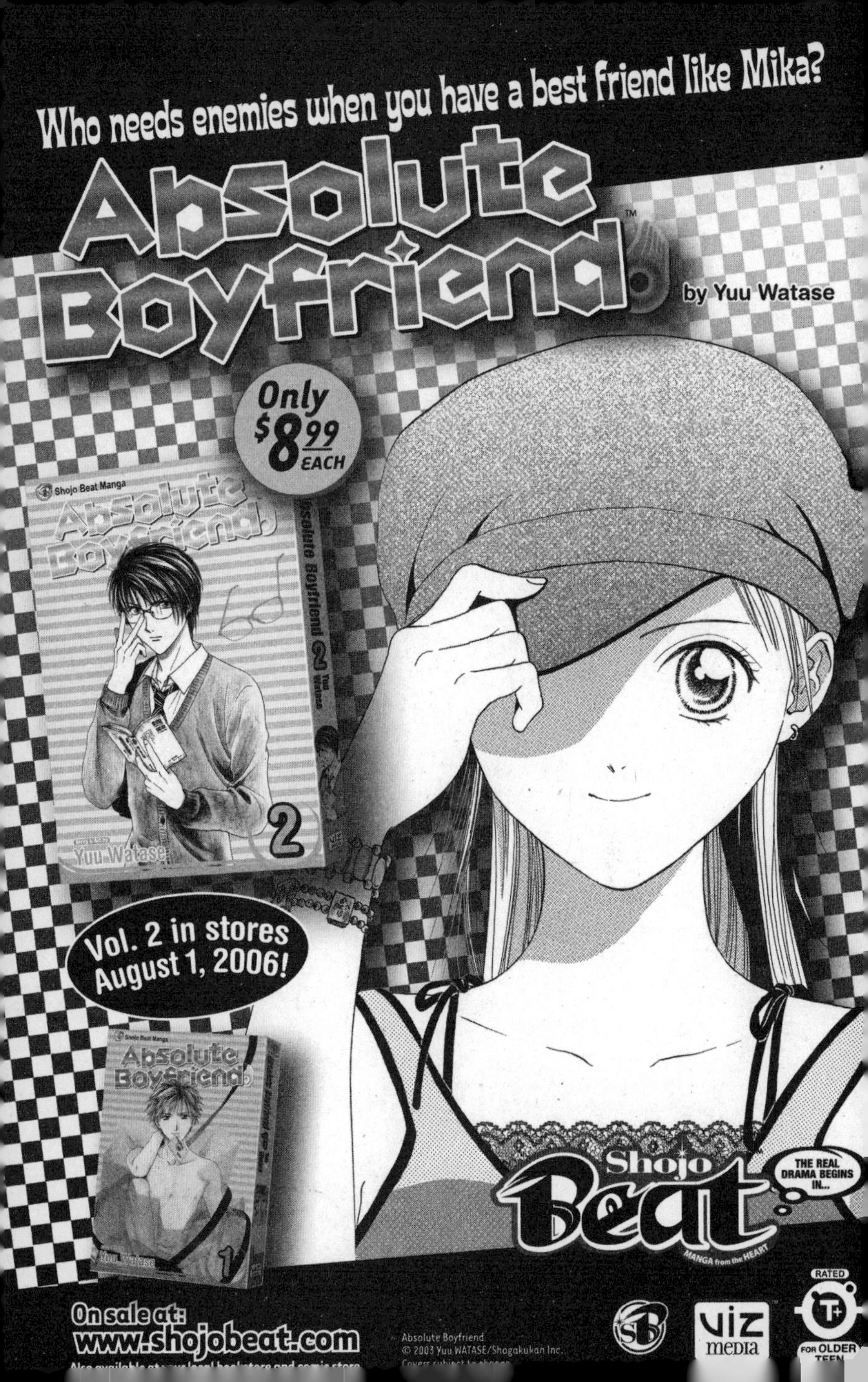

Who needs enemies when you have a best friend like Mika?
Absolute Boyfriend™
by Yuu Watase
Only $8.99 EACH
Shojo Beat Manga
Absolute Boyfriend
Absolute Boyfriend 2 Yuu Watase
2
Yuu Watase
Vol. 2 in stores August 1, 2006!
Shojo Beat Manga
Absolute Boyfriend
Yuu Watase
1
Shojo Beat
MANGA from the HEART
THE REAL DRAMA BEGINS IN...
On sale at:
www.shojobeat.com
Absolute Boyfriend
© 2003 Yuu WATASE/Shogakukan Inc.
VIZ media
RATED
T+
FOR OLDER TEEN